AF595364

NEW FRONTIER ESSAYS
THEORY AND PRACTICE OF SOCIALISM IN DEVELOPMENT

co-edited by Zhang Leisheng and Wu Jingmin

translated by Ge Weihong and Dennis Etler

translation edited by Cem Kızılçeç

CANUT INTERNATIONAL PUBLISHERS

Istanbul - Berlin - London - Santiago

New Frontier Essays: Theory and Practice of Socialism in Development
Co-edited by Zhang Leisheng and Wu Jingmin
Translated by Ge Weihong and Dennis Etler
English translation edited by Cem Kızılçeç

The English version is published in cooperation with China Renmin University Press

This publication is realized by the support of“中华社会科学基金 (Chinese Fund for Humanities and Social Sciences)资助”
Chinese Title: 发展中的社会主义理论与实践

Canut International Publishers
Canut Intl. Turkey, Batı Mh Karanfil Sk. 10/5. Pendik, Istanbul, Turkey
Canut Intl. Germany, Heerstr. 266, D-47053, Duisburg, Germany
Canut Intl. United Kingdom, 12a Guernsay Road, London E11 4BJ, England

ISBN: 978-605-7693-24-2

About the Editors-in-Chief

Zhang Leisheng, born in 1954, famous Marxist theorist, Professor of Marxism College of Renmin University of China and Doctoral Supervisor. She was Secretary of the Party committee and vice president of the Institute of Marxism of Renmin University of China. From 1988 to 2005, she served as the director of the Marxist theory teaching and research section of the Marxist Theory Education Institute. Her research directions are basic principles of Marxism, Marxist economic thought and theories of economic development of developing countries. Her respresentative works are *Economic Construction and Overall Well-off Society* (2009), *On the Economic Development of Developing Countries* (2002), *American Economy* (1994).

Wu Jingmin, editor, master of economics. Graduated from the Department of Political Economy, Renmin University of China in 1986, and then stayed at the university to work. He has been engaged in the editing and publishing of academic journals since 1996, and is currently the deputy editor of the *Journal of Renmin University of China*. The main social part-time jobs include: Vice President and Secretary-General of the National Society for the History of Marxist-Leninist Economics, Standing Director of the China Periodical Association, and Consultant of the National College of Liberal Arts Journal Research. The main writings he participated in include *European Market Organization, State-owned Economy, The Way of University and The Path of Journals, The Way to Improve the International Influence of Academic Journals*, etc.

Contents

PART THREE

PART FOUR

Publisher's Note

Marxism is the fundamental guiding ideology of our party building. It is a powerful theoretical weapon for us both to know the world and transform the world. Thus, it is very significant to strengthen and promote the study and construction of Marxist theory.

At present, with the deepening of the grand practice of socialism with Chinese characteristics, new situations and new problems emerge in an endless stream.

There is an urgent need for us to closely combine China's national conditions and characteristics of the times to vigorously promote theoretical innovation, to test the truth and develop the truth in practice, to study new situations, analyze new contradictions and solve new problems, and to guide the new practice with the development of Marxism.

The Change of the Times Calls for Theoretical Innovation and Practical Development to Promote Theoretical Innovation

In order to adapt to the requirements of the times and even lead the thought trends, contemporary Chinese scholars, especially Marxist scholars, must always possess a high degree of theoretical consciousness and theoretical self-confidence, and constantly promote the Marxism in China.

If Marxism can contribute to the development of the time and the people, it can glow with a strong vitality, creativity, attractivity, emitting a more brilliant light of truth. In order to further promote the study of Marxist theory, China Renmin University Press organized the "Marxist research library" series.

As an open library, this series of books focus on the introduction of a number of influential domestic and international research of high-end Marxist works.

Through the publication of a large number of Marxist research works, it aims to response to the new challenges posed by changes in the times and to seize the new issues raised by practical development, promote domestic Marxist research, and promote the prosperity and development of domestic philosophy and social sciences.

We hope that the publication of the "Marxist Research Series" can be welcomed by the majority of readers, and can contribute to the domestic Marxist research and teaching thus promote greater contributions.

PART ONE

The Practice of Scientific Socialism Theory

In the mid-19th century, the creation of scientific socialism by Marx and Engels transformed the socialism thoughts from an utopic character to a scientific character. Since the beginning of the 20th century, the establishment and development of socialism in underdeveloped countries turned socialism from theory into practice. The basic principles of scientific socialism are to be based on historical materialism, to take the realization of communism as the highest ideal, to advocate proletarian party as the core leadership, to stick to the fundamental task of liberating and developing productive forces, to relate with socialized mass production, to keep public ownership and distribution according to work as the basis for the socialist economic system, to uphold people being the master of the country as the essential feature of socialist democracy, and to keep reforming and improving the socialist system and institutional mechanisms. These basic principles are fully embodied in socialist practice, which means that scientific socialism is open science and develops in practice. This is also the source of the great vitality of the everlasting scientific socialism.

Since the 20th century, socialism has experienced ups and downs in its establishment and development. There was experience of the success such as the October Revolution of the Soviet Union, Chinese revolution and the great achievements in the development socialism with Chinese characteristics, and also lessons learned such as the drastic change in Soviet Union and East Europe and the off-tracks of socialism development in China. It can be argued that these are extremely valuable wealth in the development of socialism. It shows not only that the establishment, consolidation and perfection of the socialist system are a long-term and difficult task, but also that the development of socialism is a process of constant understanding and continuous practice. It can be seen that the subject of scientific socialism has been changing in the course of more than 160 years of development, from socialism necessarily replacing capitalism to how to replace capitalism with socialism, to how socialism could coexist, communicate, conflict and compete with capitalism while developing itself. These major changes mean that the development of scientific socialism pays more attention to innovation and exploring new situations thus laying a solid foundation for the belief that socialism will necessarily replace capitalism as a historical trend of the development of human society.

The Changes in the Subject of Scientific Socialism

Since the publication of the Communist Manifesto in early 1848, scientific socialism has undergone 160 years of development. This is a history that highlights the basic principles of the thought essence of science and socialism, closely relates to the development of the times and the specific circumstances of each country, and keeps developing and innovating scientific socialism theories. It is also a history that scientific socialism developed from theoretical demonstration to social practice and keeps advancing forward in social practice. From the perspective of history, theory and reality, and through the historical study of the development stages of scientific socialism and its subject changes, we try to understand the modern value of the basic principles of scientific socialism, clarify scientific socialism theme of the times, explore new spaces for scientific socialism, and find new answer to the historical destiny of scientific socialism. For a century and a half, the development of scientific socialism has been divided into three stages in a period of 50 years. Accordingly, the subject of scientific socialism has gone through major changes from socialism necessarily replacing capitalism to how to replace capitalism with socialism, to how socialism could coexist, communicate, conflict and compete with capitalism while developing itself.

1. The subject of scientific socialism from the latter half of the 1840s to the mid-1890s

In the 14th and 15th centuries, the earliest capitalism sparsely emerged in cities along the Mediterranean coast, such as Florence of Italy. In the 16th century, some countries in Western Europe had the basic conditions for the development of capitalism. The outbreak of the British bourgeois revolution in the 1640s really opened a new era of capitalism development. Till the middle of the 18th century when the British bourgeoisie stabilized its regime, they had the ability to prioritize developing the advanced productive forces that were compatible with the capitalist economic relations, ambitiously discover the huge productive forces hidden in the nature, science, industry and agriculture, and revolutionarily and timely seized the opportunity of the first industrial revolution which led to a rapid establishment of the capitalism social productive forces system. At this time, the bourgeoisie, holding the banner of "freedom", continuously consolidated their economic dominance. French scholar Michel Beaud pointed out, "In England, where [the bourgeoisie] was involved with affairs of the state, the freedom in question was above all economic freedom: freedom of trade and of production, as well as freedom to pay for labor power at the lowest possible price, and so to defend itself against workers' alliances and revolts".[1] Following the British bourgeois revolution, in the second half of the 18th century, the United States and France also succeeded in the bourgeois revolution; in the mid-19th century, Germany, Russia and Japan also experienced different forms of bourgeois revolution. After the victory of revolution, these countries also finished the industrial revolution.

The industrial revolution brought about rapid development of social material civilization and profound changes in the social and economic relations of capitalist society. While creating an industrial capitalist class, the industrial revolution also created an industrial worker class that is far more than the former; while constantly stimulating the accumulation of capital wealth and strengthening the power of capital, the industrial revolution also kept worsening workers' poverty and polymerizing the rebellion forces of the work class. The basic contradiction between the socialization of production and private ownership of means of production by capitalists is increasingly acute. With the outbreak of the first capitalist economic crisis in 1825 and the rise of a series of workers' movement in the 1830s and 1840s in Europe, capitalism struggled to seek social change and adjustment in the process of periodically destroying its own social productive forces. In the first half of the nineteenth century, this drastic change in the capitalist era forced people to reflect on some deep-seated problems, the most important of which was where capitalism plagued by economic, political and social difficulty should go. At that time some of the most outstanding Western European thinkers and theorists did not avoid this problem involving history and development of times. However, neither these most outstanding thinkers and theorists themselves, nor their most faithful successors, were able to answer the question successfully.[2]

At that time, Hegel, the most renowned philosopher in Germany, in his grand and profound philosophical system, for the first time tried to describe the whole world of nature, history and spirit as a process, and considered the contradiction within things as the internal impetus for movement and development.

However, Hegel did not make any contribution to the question of the destiny of capitalism.

He affirmed that all things in the world are developing and changing, and also asserted that Prussian autocratic system is in harmony and it is the "peak" of the whole German history.

1 Michel Beaud, A History of Capitalism (1500-1980), New York, Palgrave MacMillan,1981, p. 73.

2 See Gu Hailiang, The Historical Destiny of Marxism, Changchun, Jilin People's Publishing House, 1997, pp. 5-10.

The dialectics of the development of history and times were stifled by his idealist view of history. When the European intellectuals were confined to the Hegelian philosophical system, another German philosopher Ludwig Feuerbach boldly criticized Hegel's philosophical system and proposed some basic materialist propositions such as the world being material and the nature being independent from human will. However, Feuerbach's materialism was half done, because he would retreat to the idealist position when answering the question of the destiny of capitalism. He argued that the stages of human social development are only the result of religious change and the development of world history is driven by religion and the abstract human "love", detached from material and economic basis. With his view of history, Feuerbach's idealism had indicated that bourgeois master philosophers were no longer able to create anything new on the major issues related to the development of history and times.

Back then, there were also classical economists from the Great Britain and France trying to explain the destiny of capitalism. At the beginning of the 19th century, all the theoretical and policy propositions of Ricardo in England were aimed at opposing and eliminating all factors that impeded the improvement of capital profit and the development of productive forces.

He emphasized that labor was the only source of value creation and that there was an antagonistic relationship (contradiction) between the three classes of the capitalist society (the working class, the capitalist class and the landowner class). But he tried very hard to cover sharp conflicts between the capitalist productive forces and the relations that had emerged in the process of industrial revolution, and categorically denied the possibility of a widespread overproduction crisis in capitalism. His bourgeoisie position on the development of history and times and the non-social and anti-historical method she used could only lead to theories and views inconsistent with social and economic development. As a final supplement to Ricardo's theory of economics, Sismondi from France severely rebuked the disasters brought to people by the capitalist system and confirmed that the development of capitalist society would inevitably lead to widespread crisis of overproduction. But he regarded the various drawbacks of the capitalist system as the result of the rapid development of social productive forces. Therefore, he strongly advocated the restoration of patriarchal and guild principles, trying to add their principles and norms into the capitalist production relations. On the issue of historical trend of capitalism development, Sismondi was also in the dark.

When the philosopher and economists could do nothing to solve the problems of capitalism development, the utopian socialists stand out from the bourgeois camp. Saint-Simon and Fourier from France or Robert Owen from Britain all had the theoretical courage to break with the old system of capitalism and the good will to work for the coming of the new world. They elaborated on the inevitability of the new social system, expressed their desire to establish a new social system, and proposed some genius ideas regarding the specific details of this kind of society. However, they were still hesitant to understand the major issues such as the driving force for world history development and the social destiny of capitalism. They exposed all kinds of contradictions in the capitalist system, but couldn't scientifically clarify the historical inevitability of these contradictions from the perspective of world historical development; they forsaw that the capitalist system must be replaced by a new social system, but could not understand the realistic basis for the transition and the material force for carrying out this change. After the 1830s, utopian socialists gradually divorced from the reality of capitalist society and just hid in their fantasy mirage for a trace of comfort. The sporadic thoughts they left could no longer form any ground-breaking theories.

In the 1830s and 1840s, the development of the capitalist economy and society urgently required a new theory to make a scientific explanation of the laws of the development of human society and provide a scientific explanation of the historical trend of the capitalism development. In the 1840s and 1860s, the new proletarian worldview founded by Marx and Engels, which was later named after one of its founders as Marxism, made a scientific exposition of the theoretical issues raised in the development of the capitalist era. On the basis of the two discoveries of the materialist philosophy and the surplus value theory of political economy, the scientific socialism revealed the fundamental nature and historical mission of the proletarian revolution and liberation in the capitalist era. Marx and Engels's scientific exposition of the historical trend of capitalist development opened a new chapter in the history of human thought.

At the beginning of 1848, Marx and Engels cooperated to complete *The Communist Manifesto*, which is an important symbol of the formation of the basic principles of scientific socialism, and also the first comprehensive elaboration of scientific socialism development subject for the next 50 years. The Communist Manifesto focused on why capitalism is necessarily replaced by future society, that is, why socialism is bound to replace capitalism. For the purposes of this article, it is worth noting that the following three basic topics:

Firstly, *The Communist Manifesto*, guided by the basic principles of historical materialism, scientifically expounded the generation and development of capitalist economic relations and the inevitability of its transition into new socio-economic relations from the perspective of the general law of human social development. *The Communist Manifesto* profoundly stated that the bourgeoisie has historically played a very revolutionary role in relentlessly destroying the feudal mode of production and creating enormous productivity beyond the sum of productive forces in any given age. However, the development of the contradictions of capitalist production itself relentlessly in the same way generated the power the destroy themselves. This is because the outbreak of the cyclical crisis of the capitalist economy means "The productive forces at the disposal of society no longer tend to further the development of the conditions of bourgeois property; on the contrary, they have become too powerful for these conditions, by which they are fettered, and so soon as they overcome these fetters, they bring disorder into the whole of bourgeois society, endanger the existence of bourgeois property. Productivity no longer promotes the relations between bourgeois civilization and bourgeois ownership"[3].

Marx's and Engels' conclusion was that: "The weapons with which the bourgeoisie felled feudalism to the ground are now turned against the bourgeoisie itself."[4]

These expositions laid the foundation for the subject of scientific socialism development at this stage.

Secondly, the scientific principles set forth in the Communist Manifestoare not intended to solve the partial problems of capitalist social development, but to reveal the general issue of the social development of human being. It is not to answer the questions in a certain stage of capitalism development, but to reveal the law of development of the entire capitalism history. Scientific socialism reveals a series of basic principles of human social development which will always maintain its vitality in the history of human social development. The general law of thecapitalist development revealed by scientific socialism will not be out of date at all development stages in this era. These arguments are the mordern value contained in the subject of scientific socialism development at this stage.

Thirdly, the scientific principle that why capitalism will necessarily change into socialism or why socialism is bound to replace capitalism has opened up a vast space for socialist development. However, Marx and Engels had never intended to design a comprehensive program of implementation and specific institutional arrangements for future society. As Engels repeated in his later years, we had never described socialism as the "millenium kingdom". In their view, the question of what the socialism will be like in the future shall be answered creatively by the people in that era, using Marxist scientific principles and spirit and through the continuous practice. These are the essence of the subject of socialism development at this stage.

3 Marx-Engels Collected Works.

4 Marx-Engels Collected Works, Vol. 2, Beijing, People's Publishing House, 2009, p. 37.

In the following 50 years, Marx and Engels made a number of discussion on the basic principles of scientific socialism which enriched and developed the connotation of scientific socialism at this stage, especially in the Preface to Critique of Political Economy in the end of the 1850s, the Capital, Volume 1, the 1st German Edition in the second half of the 1860s and Critique of the Gotha Programme and Anti-Duhring in the 1870s.

2. The subject of scientific socialism from the end of the 19th century to the mid-1950s

In the 1870s and 1880s, the social and economic relations of capitalism had undergone profound changes. On the one hand, during those decades, the science and technology in the US and the major capitalist countries in Europe once again changed dramatically. The second industrial revolution featuring the discovery of electricity and itsextensive application in industry once again promoted the great development of social productive forces. On the other hand, with the rapid development of social productive forces, the accumulation of capital and the rapid expansion of capital concentration led to the transition from capitalism characterized by free competition to capitalism characterized by monopoly.

Lenin profoundly grasped the historical process of capitalism development, made a a scientific analysis on the stage development and subject change of socialism at the turn of the 19th century, and reached a new theoretical conclusion suitable for the development of times. Lenin put forward the theory of imperialism which analyzes the historical changes of capitalism on the basis of the universal law of world development. Based on Marx's and Engels' conclusion is that The bourgeoisie used to overthrow the feudal system of arms, It is now aimed at the bourgeoisie itself.

On this basis, the two major conclusions of Lenin laid the theoretical foundation for the establishment of the new subject of scientific socialism.

These two important conclusions are: firstly, Lenin believed that the new changes in the mode of capitalist production had not changed the historical inevitability of the transition from capitalism to socialism, and that "this in itself determines its place in history, for monopoly that grows out of the soil of free competition, and precisely out of free competition, is the transition from the capitalist system to a higher socio-economic order."[5]

That is to say the conclusion of the inevitable transition from capitalism to socialism put forward by Marx and Engels in the first phase of scientific socialism development is still the connotation of the development of the times. Secondly, Lenin argued that the new changes in the mode of

5 Ibid., p. 208.

capitalist production advanced the issue of the inevitable transition from capitalism to socialism into how capitalism could change into socialism. It should be concluded that: "Hence, the victory of socialism is possible first in several or even in one capitalist country alone."[6] The issue of how capitalism could change into socialism has become a new subject of the scientific socialism development.

The victory of the Russian October Revolution started the historical process of how socialism would replace capitalism. Lenin developed his theories according to the new features of times and profoundly analyzed Russia's concrete economic and political development, and discussed in depth the question of transition from capitalism to socialism in an economically backward country like that of Russia According to the new characteristics of the development of the times, Lenin profoundly analyzed the reality of Russia's economic and political development and explored how to achieve the transition from capitalism to socialism in economically and culurally backward Russia[7], which significantly enriched the new subject of scientific socialism development. Related to the topic of this article, the following three aspects proposed by Lenin are of great importance:

Firstly, the issue of the replacement of capitalism by socialism. On the question of how socialism would replace capitalism, Lenin envisioned the direct transition and indirect transition. In practice, he gradually leaned toward the indirect transition. In the *Critique of the Gotha Programme*, Marx had pointed out that the communist social system was born out of the capitalist society, and "Between capitalist and communist society lies the period of the revolutionary transformation of the one into the other."[8] Lenin attached great importance to Marx's theoretical view. Before the October Revolution, in *The State and Revolution*, Lenin elaborated the thought of two stages of communism expressed in the Critique of the Gotha Program and restated Marx's transition theory which he considered as "The first fact that has been established with complete exactness by the whole theory of evolution, by science as a whole-a fact which the Utopians forgot, and which is forgotten by the present day opportunists who are afraid of the Socialist revolution-is that, historically, there must undoubtedly be a special state or epoch of transition from capitalism to Communism."[9] During this period, Lenin's understanding of how socialism would replace capitalism showed a clear tendency to "direct transition". But, after the initial practice of transition to socialism Lenin has changed his thought of "direct

6 Lenin's Monographs on Socialism, Beijing, People's Publishing House, 2009, p. 4.

7 See in Wu Yifeng et al., The Formation and Development of Marxist Economic Theory, Beijing, China Renmin University Press, 1998, Chapter 12.

8 Marx-Engels Collected Works, Vol. 3, Beijing, People's Publishing House, 2009, p. 445.

9 Lenin's Monographs on Socialism, Beijing, People's Publishing House, 2009, p. 26.

transition" to "indirect transition". Lenin argued that, in Russia, an economically and culturally backward country, a "direct transition" from capitalism to socialism was very difficult and complicated. Because "We have only just taken the first steps towards shaking off capitalism altogether and beginning the transition to socialism. We have not gone farther than the first steps in the transition from capitalism to socialism, and our transition is made more intricate by features that are specific to Russia and do not exist in most civilised countries" "it is not only possible but inevitable that the stages of transition will be different in Europe; it would be theoretically incorrect to turn all attention to specific national stages of transition that are essential to us but may not be essential in Europe". He was clearly aware that Russia is experiencing a transitional stage which was different from that of the developed countries in Western Europe, "a transition period imbued with national characteristics."[10]

In fact, Marx's transitional theory proposed in the Critique of the Gotha Program was based on the situation of the developed capitalist countries. He does not specifically predict the complex situations and specific ways of replacing capitalism with socialism in countries with backward economy and culture. Lenin thought that, for Russia, "We do not know and we cannot know how many stages of transition to socialism there will be"[11], and during that process "it will be impossible to know the forms of transformation and the speed and concrete forms of this transformation".[12]

Obviously, Lenin had changed his original idea of "direct transition". However, at that time, in the institutional design for the indirect transition, commodity and money relationship and the role market mechanism were excluded and a product economy mode with means of production fully state ownership was put forward.

The practices of replacing capitalism with socialism in Russia further deepened Lenin's thought. At the beginning of 1919, Lenin made a major revision of his idea of an indirect transition and clearly recognized that countries with backward economy and culture like Russia needed to go through a long-term process to eliminate the use of money. "It has become evident that we had suffered defeat in our attempt to introduce the socialist principles of production and distribution by "direct assault", i.e., in the shortest, quickest and most direct way"[13]. Therefore, in the process of replacing capitalism with socialism, the first thing was to find the key for the "transition" "which will need to go through a gradual course of development, and in this course we can make use of capitalism before various old

10 Ibid., p. 69.

11 Lenin's Monographs on Socialism, Beijing, People's Publishing House, 2009, p. 68.

12 Lenin Selected Works, 3rd edition, Vol. 3, Beijing, People's Publishing House, 1995, p. 545.

13 Lenin's Monographs on Socialism, Beijing, People's Publishing House, 2009, p. 279-280

relations are transformed to socialism. This is the key point we should bear in mind."[14]

Then the methods, forms and ways of "indirect transition" suitable for Russia's economic and social development could be found. The change of idea from direct transition to indirect transition shows that during the early years after the Russian October Revolution Lenin had enriched and developed Marx's and Engels' theory of the inevitable transition from capitalism to socialism based on Russia's economic and social development and started the scientific socialism's new subject of how socialism would replace capitalism.

Secondly, the basic features and tasks of economic system in the process of socialism replacing capitalism. Lenin argued at the beginning of the transitional period, the socialist reform of the ownership of the means of production m must be completed by leading small-scale peasant economy into cooperative system and achieving the transition from the individual small commodity economy to the large public economy. With the low level of productive forces and unbalanced development in Russia, the "intermediate links" must be found to achieve the initial transition, which is the "key" of the transition to socialism. The social development stage made up of these "intermediate links" would show different economic characteristics due to different level of economic and social development of each country. But they would also have some common economic characteristics, among which one of the most significant is the coexistence of a variety of economic sectors. As Lenin had pointed out: there can be no doubt that between capitalism and communism there lies a definite tranition period which must combine the features and properties of both these forms of social economy. This transition period has to be a period of struggle between dying capitalism and nascent communism.[15] The economic system of Russia in the transitional period would be a "specific system" which includes both capitalism and socialism, as well as mixed sectors and elements of capitalism and socialism.

On the occasion of the victory of the socialist October Revolution, Lenin made it clear that the realization of the socialist public ownership would be a major task for Russia to complete the transition to socialism. From November, 1917 to the spring of 1918, Lenin proposed to confiscate the large enterprises under the state supervision, nationalize the banks and capital syndicate by redemption, coercively syndicate the middle and small-sized enterprises, and try to reorganize the confiscated local estates into larges model farms, in order to achieve the transition to socialism. At the end of spring and the beginning of summer in 1918, Lenin also suggested

14 Ibid., p. 224.

15 Lenin's Monographs on Socialism, Beijing, People's Publishing House, 2009, p. 154.

that Russia should "That is why a new and higher form of struggle against the bourgeoisie is on the order of the day, the transition from the very simple task of further expropriating the capitalists to the much more complicated and difficult task of creating conditions in which it will be impossible for the bourgeoisie to exist, or for a new bourgeoisie to arise. Clearly, this task is immeasurably more significant than the previous one; and until it is fulfilled there will be no Socialism."[16]

At this stage, it was necessary to adopt a "reformist", gradual, prudent and round-about way to transform the private capitalist and commodity economy, which should be the "state capitalism". State capitalism is a centralized, statistically supervised and socialized system which is " economically immeasurably superior to our present economic system." "There is nothing terrible in it for the Soviet power". It is the "most guaranteed passage"[17] to socialism. Lenin's state capitalism is a "specific form of state capitalism"[18] that could be restricted by the proletarian state and set its sphere of activity. This kind of special state capitalism has its dual nature. On the one hand, it is a kind of organized, planned and counted way of production and circulation that could be supervised by the state, which is conducive to the development of the Russian economy. On the other hand, it is a form of production and circulation operated in a capitalist way in order to obtain profits. The capitalist is to be paid a lot at the expense of certain sacrifices. Therefore, its sphere of activities must be limited.

Third, the choice of the economic model in the process of socialism replacing capitalism. Lenin's discussion on the theory of new economic policy was based on the transitional period of socialism replacing capitalism and the specific historical conditions of the Russian indirect transition and was to be gradually realized in practice. It had actually solved a series of major issues such as the path, the way, the steps and the policies of the transition from capitalism to socialism in Russia, which was an economically and economically backward country. The use of commodity currency relations and market mechanism in the new economic policy was based on the fact that Lenin was constantly summing up the practical experience of Russia's economic and social development. This theory had gone through quite a exploring process, from product exchange system under state monopoly to the state capitalist commodity exchange system, to the state regulation of business and currency circulation, which was also the result of continuous policy adjustment and improvement during the indirect transition. Based on Lenin's summary of the experience of the wartime

16 Ibid., p. 85.

17 Ibid., p. 122.

18 Lenin Complete Works, Chinese 2nd edition, Vol. 43, Beijing, People's Publishing House, 1987, p.283.

communist policy in Russia, the new economic policy was Lenin's design and choice for the economic model of socialism replacing capitalism. At the end of 1920, Lenin, on the basis of summing up the experiences and lessons of the implementation of the wartime communist policy analyzed and demonstrated the necessity of the transition from wartime communist economic policy to new economic policy. The main task of the NEP was to retreat to the form of state capitalism and commodity exchange. "In the spring we said that we would not be afraid to revert to state capitalism, and that our task was to organise commodity exchange".[19] After October 1921, on the basis of summing up the initial experience of the implementation of the new economic policy, Lenin argued that returning from "wartime communism" to state capitalism was not enough and that it must go back further to allow farmers' free trade and private business which would be regulated by the state. Lenin's above discussion was the most important theoretical innovation in the change of the subject of scientific socialism at this stage. These theoretical innovations were most manifested in the discussion on how to realize the transition to socialism in economically and culturally backward countries. Meanwhile, Lenin's view that under the new era background it is no longer possible for economically and culturally backward countries to take the capitalist path to drive their economic and social development has been verified by the historical facts of the economic and social development in the twentieth century. Throughout the twentieth century, there was no rising country that has entered the ranks of developed capitalism by taking the capitalist path.

Under the influence of the October Revolution in Russia, the Chinese Communists represented by Mao Zedong, guided by Marxism-Leninism, combining the reality of China's social development and the new changes in the political and economic pattern of the world, have also made a series of theoretical innovations on the new subject of scientific socialism during China's practice of new-democratic revolution and socialist revolution. These theoretical innovations are embodied in the new democracy theory and the theory of transition from new democracy to socialism contained in Mao Zedong Thought. The first generation of CPC leadership with Mao Zedong as its core has made a wide range of exploration on how to transform into socialism an economically and culturally backward country like China. Mao Zedong's theoretical innovation on the subject of scientific socialism development focused on three basic issues: firstly, how the proletariat would seize power; secondly, how to realize the transition to socialism; thirdly, how to build socialism.

19 Lenin's Monographs on Socialism, Beijing, People's Publishing House, 2009, p. 282.

3. The development course of the study subjects of scientific socialism since the mid-1950s

During the decade after the end of the Second World War, the greatest change in the world economic and political pattern was the formation of the two camps of capitalism and socialism, as well as the confrontation between the two camps. In the mid-1950s, there were subtle changes in this confrontation model. Successively the debate within the socialist camp and the thawing between the socialist and capitalist camps became vital nodes of changes in capitalism and socialism and the turning point of the new changes in the relationship between these two social systems.

Since the mid-1950s, the adjustment and development of capitalist social and economic relations have been pushed forward along the path with monopoly as the main line. From the 1880s to the 1940s, capitalist private monopolies developed for 60 years. During the Second World War, the war brought great development to the state's adjustment of the military and the state's impact and intervention on economy was significantly enhanced. To meet the needs of the war, the state monopoly capital saw rapid development. In the mid-1950s, with the results of the third scientific and technological revolution and the successful experience of the development of socialist economic relations, including the planned economy, social welfare and social security system, the capitalist economic relations made some significant self-adjustments. During this period, the capitalist states' regulation and intervention on the economy had transformed from a temporary measure to serve the wartime requirements or to curb the effects of the serious economic crisis into a necessary mechanism for the normal regular economic operation, which was the symbol that the state monopoly capital developed into a higher level.

The adjustment of the capitalist economic relations by the state monopoly is highlighted in the "change of socialized form". The British scholar Ben Fine listed three main manifestations of this "change of socialized form". The first was that the state monopoly capitalism means a "higher level of socialization of productive relations", and it is characterized with the new and higher level of socializing mechanism that controls the production process. At that time, the dominant social mechanism controlling the production process was the state intervention rather than the force of market exchange and credit system. In socialization process of economic reproduction, the role of the state (by combining with the market) developed unprecedentedly. The second was the change in the way of possessing and controlling the surplus value. "The surplus value was largely appropriated by state's taxation." The distribution and exchange mode of surplus value had changed, leading to the gradual socialization of the struggle between different parts of the capital for interest or corporate profits because of the role of the state. The third is the "political transformation", that is "the state, the original embodiment of the political relations, is now inevitably and directly involved in all forms of economic struggle". Contemporary capitalist states inevitably became "the specific embodiment of ideological, economic and political relations". It was the opposite of the early stages of capitalism when the bourgeois state was based on the separation of three arms (executive, judicial and legislation).[20] These changes in the "socialized form" had not altered the historical destiny of capitalism but the development status of capitalism at a certain stage.

In the early 1970s, the state monopoly capitalism further developed and the so-called "contemporary capitalist model" emerged. In this model, technological progress required substantial investment in scientific research which could only be carried out by large enterprises and with substantial funding coming from the capitalist state budgets. The highly internationalized productive forces and relations of the enterprises and their complex have such a great effect that this kind of internationalization has become an indispensable and extremely important feature of contemporary capitalism. The internationalization of capital is no longer an "additional" factor in the internal development of the capitalist economy, but a "primary" factor. As the Polish scholar Minc pointed out, in the contemporary capitalist model, internationalization trend of capital is mainly manifested in the following aspects: the development of international cartels and multinational corporations; the establishment and expansion of the European Economic Community (European Common Market); gradual and partial realization of capital fusion among Western European countries, as well as the merge of capital between the United States and Western Europe; the further development of international economic relations and enhanced interdependence among countries, the export and import of capital and the international network of capital; labor migration, especially from economically underdeveloped countries to economically developed countries; the establishment of a new and fairer global economic order demanded by the third world countries.[21]

Since the 1990s, with the development of economic globalization, the trend of the state monopoly capitalism growing into international monopoly capitalism has obviously strengthened. The new development of capitalism led to a series of new issues, mainly including: the trend and characteristics of capitalism changing from private monopoly to state monopoly, and then to the contemporary international monopoly; the process of financial capital globalization and the role and characteristics of financial derivatives and

20 See Ben Fine et al., Rereading Capital, Macmillan, 1979.
21 See Minc B., Modern Capitalism, Beijing, the Eastern Publishing Co., Ltd., 1987, pp. 83-84.

international financial markets. In the context of information economy, the changes and characteristics of the integration between capital output form and allocation of resources such as technology, information and talents; the new roles of international economic organizations, especially the World Bank, the International Monetary Fund and the World Trade Organization; trends and characteristics of the polarization between developed and underdeveloped countries (regions) around the world; volatile tendency of international political situation in the process of economic globalization, especially the conflict and trend in the multi-polarization and unipolarity of the world's political pattern; in the context of the severe setbacks of the world socialist movement, the contradictions and changes of contemporary capitalism.

With the development of monopoly, the contradiction of capitalist economic relations, the basic contradiction of the society, has been to a large extent eased but not eliminated. On the contrary, it has been exacerbated in new forms. In the 21st century, the international monopoly capitalism will be developing for a long period of time, so the capitalist economic relations may see new adjustments. As Marx had pointed out: "No social order ever perishes before all the productive forces for which there is room in it have developed; and new, higher relations of production never appear before the material conditions of their existence have matured in the womb of the old society itself. Therefore mankind always sets itself only such tasks as it can solve; since looking at the matter more closely, it will always be found that the task itself arises only when the material conditions for its solution already exist or are at least in the process of formation. (Marx, Selected Works, Vol. I, pp. 269-70.)"[22] Therefore, the capitalist economic relations will maintain its vitality in a very long historical period, and its coexistence with the socialist system and their cooperation, communication, contradictions and conflicts will also last for a long time.

Correspondingly, in this period the socialist system also changed profoundly. In the mid-1950s, the completion of the socialist transformation of China's agriculture, handicraft industry and capitalist industry and commerce laid the economic foundation for China's socialism and opened up a new path of socialism with Chinese characteristics. At the same time, cracks between China and the Soviet Union emerged. In the 1960s, the "big debate" in the international communist movement broke out, which caused the exposure and reflection of the drawbacks of the Soviet model and the need for the reformation of the socialist economic system. The core issue of the socialist economic system reform is the relationship between planning and the market; the relationship between the socialist planned economy and the market economy, and the relationship between the socialist economic

22 Marx-Engels Collected Works, Vol. 2, Beijing, People's Publishing House, 2009, p. 592.

system and the market economic system; then the reflections on the marketization in the reform of socialist economic system, the use of the rational factors of capitalist economic system and capitalist mechanisms in the socialist economic reform, and theoretical and practical issues in learning and introducing the technology, capital and management experience from capitalist countries. Thus the space for communication and cooperation between socialism and capitalism has been greatly expanded.

In fact, since the mid-1950s, the historical trend of socialism replacing capitalism has not seen fundamental changes, but the stage characteristics of the development of scientific socialism was revealed, especially the new changes since the formation the theme of time as peace and development in the late 1970s. Although the two major issues of peace and development have not been resolved until now, these two themes of the times are reflected not only in the exchange and even cooperation between socialism and capitalism, but also in their competition, confrontation and conflict. Even in the context of deepening economic globalization, the dual character of the theme of time still exists.

The development subject of scientific socialism at this stage is how socialism can develop and perfect itself in cooperation, communication, contradiction and confrontation with capitalism. As Marx put it in the circuit of capital in the Volume 2 of *Capital*, the development subject of scientific socialism in the first and second stage which we have discussed above could be considered as an issue of time succession which mainly explores and discusses the issues of transition from an old social system to a new one; and that in the third stage could be seen as an issue of coexistence, i.e., the subject or the issue to be solved is to have an exact understanding on how socialism could develop and perfect itself while coexisting with the capitalism. This subject of exploration and study came fore in the process of economic globalization and became obvious in the last two decades of the 20th century.

Now, the study on the development stages of scientific socialism and subject of scientific socialism not only covers the issue of time succession but also the issue of spatial coexistence. Time succession is the premise of spatial coexistence. Only by scientifically and comprehensively understanding that socialism will inevitably replace capitalism can we correctly understand and deal with the coexistence of socialism and capitalism. The spatial coexistence is the process of time succession, because the coexistence of socialism and capitalism does not and cannot change the historical destiny of capitalism and the historical orientation of capitalism's inevitable transition to socialism. Only by combining the two together can we have a scientific understanding of the development of the socialist theory and practice in the context of economic globalization.

From the perspective of the relationship between time succession and spatial coexistence, the connotation of the subject of the contemporary scientific socialism is richer and more extensible. If we only focus on the succession of time, it is impossible to understand the inevitability of the current cooperation and exchange between socialism and capitalism. If we ignore the long-term coexistence of the two systems, it is impossible to effectively promote the development of socialism. If we only emphasize the spatial coexistence and ignore the succession of time, on the one hand, we may deny the historical trend that socialism will surely replace capitalism, and abandon the basic principles of scientific socialism founded by Marx and Engels; on the other hand, we may only see cooperation and exchanges during the coexistence and abandon the socialist basic system and development path, leading to the "convergence" with the capitalist system.

The change of exploration and study focus determined by the change of inner and surrounding context and corresponding theoretical innovations in developing scientific socialism embody the theoretical quality of Marxism, i.e., advancing with the times. Since the mid-1950s, the Communist Party of China, represented by Mao Zedong, Deng Xiaoping, Jiang Zemin and Hu Jintao, has focused on the discussion of this new subject of the development of scientific socialism in their theoretical innovation of Marxism. In the spring of 1992 when Deng Xiaoping visited the southern China, his words, as his political treasure, contained an extremely profound exposition of this change of subject. He made a comprehensive exposition on the inevitability of socialism replacing capitalism, the development and self-improvement of socialism in the coexistence and contradiction with capitalism, and the ultimate achievement of the historical mission of scientific socialism. Since the early 1990s, Comrade Jiang Zemin's series of important theoretical discourses, especially the important thought of "Three Represents", have included new expositions and judgments on the subject of scientific socialism development. Since the 16th CPC National Congress, the Party Central Committee with Comrade Hu Jintao as the general secretary has expressed new ideas and vision on the subject of scientific socialism development in a series of important theoretical exploration, especially in the elaboration of Scientific Outlook on Development.

(Gu Hailiang, Professor of Institute of Marxism, Wuhan University)

Building Socialism in Economically and Culturally Backward Countries

More than 160 years ago, in *The Communist Manifesto*, Marx and Engels revealed the objective law of the entire human society, especially that of the capitalist society: due to social development dialectics the emergence and demise of any social form has its historical inevitability. The capitalist society is only a specific stage in the process of historical development. With the development of socialized production, capitalist private ownership could not accommodate the massive productive forces and will surely be replaced by a higher social form. On the basis of a lot of scientific researches on the realistic development of the mature capitalist production mode, Marx and Engels made a general prediction of the basic rules of the future society in the most abstract and general theoretical aspect. In their view, despite the coexistence of the developed and underdeveloped countries in the world, "the country that is more developed industrially only shows, to the less developed the image of its own future"[23], and the general trend of human society finally developing into communism could not be altered. After the proletariat gains power, "they know that "In order to work out their own liberation, along with it that higher form to which the present society is irresistibly tending by its own economic agencies, they will have to pass through long struggles, through a series of historical processes, transforming circumstances of men."[24]

1. The law of human society development and historical development paths of all countries

The history of human society is essentially the history of the evolution of material wealth production. The development of human society is a natural historical process. The social form has been driven to evolve from low level to high level by social contradictions, especially the movement of the basic social contradictions.

In 1859, Marx made a classic expression on the evolution of human social form in the *Preface to Critique of Political Economy*: "In broad outlines we can designate the Asiatic, the ancient, the feudal, and the modern bourgeois modes of production as so many progressive epochs in the economic formation of society. The bourgeois relations of production are the last antagonistic form of the social process of production—antagonistic not in the sense of individual antagonism, but of one arising from the social conditions of life of the individuals; at the same time the productive forces

23 Marx-Engels Collected Works, Vol. 5, Beijing, People's Publishing House, 2009, p. 8.
24 Marx-Engels Collected Works, Vol. 3, Beijing, People's Publishing House, 2009, p. 159.

developing in the womb of bourgeois society create the material conditions for the solution of that antagonism. This social formation constitutes, therefore, the closing chapter of the prehistoric stage of human society."[25]

In 1867, in *Capital*, Marx further pointed out that at the stage when natural economy dominates, whether it is the primitive commune, slavery or feudal system, "Those ancient social organisms of production are, as compared with bourgeois society, is extremely simple and transparent. But they are founded either on the immature development of man individually, who has not yet severed the umbilical cord that unites him with his fellow men in a primitive tribal community, or upon direct relations of subjection. They can arise and exist only when the development of the productive power of labor has not risen beyond a low stage, and when, therefore, the social relations within the sphere of material life, between man and man, and between man and nature, are correspondingly narrow."[26]

At the stage when commodity economy dominates, social production relations of labor exchange between the laborers "the relations connecting the labor of one individual with that of the rest appear, not as social relations between people at work, but as… material relations between persons and social relations between things"[27], "producers in general enter into social relations with one another by treating their products as commodities and values, whereby they reduce their individual private labour to the standard of homogeneous human labour".[28]

Commodity economy not only contributed to the free development of social productive forces and the concentration of means of production, but also facilitated the formation and development of the world market. "People of all countries are increasingly being involved in the world market network, thus the capitalist system is increasingly attaining an international nature".[29]

At the stage of product economy, the social use of public means of production determined labor subject's direct social ownership of the labor object, with the material production process in a conscious and planned control and the material appearance of the social nature of labor eliminated, thus "guarantees to them the completely unrestricted development of their physical and mental faculties".[30] "By means of socialized production, an existence not only fully sufficient materially, and becoming day-by-day more full, but an existence guaranteeing to all the free development and

25 Marx-Engels Collected Works, Vol. 2, Beijing, People's Publishing House, 2009, p. 592.
26 Marx-Engels Collected Works, Vol. 5, Beijing, People's Publishing House, 2009, p. 97.
27 Ibid., p. 90.
28 Ibid., p. 97.
29 Ibid., p. 874.
30 Marx-Engels Collected Works, Vol. 3, Beijing, People's Publishing House, 2009, p. 466.

exercise of their physical and mental faculties—this possibility is now, for the first time, here, but *it is here*."

In Marx's and Engels' view, the development of human society has its own objective law and is not controlled by human will. In general, the form of human society that will only evolve from low level to high level could neither be artificially surpassed nor eliminated. "Even when a society has got upon the right track for the discovery of the natural laws of its movement... it can neither clear by bold leaps, nor remove by legal enactments, the obstacles offered by the successive stages of its natural evolution."[31]

Because "natural laws cannot be abolished at all. The only thing that can change, under historically differing conditions, is the form in which those laws assert themselves".[32] Meanwhile, the history of human society cannot be equated to purely natural processes. The change of nature is a spontaneous process, while human history is the active and conscious activity of people ruled by the law. The evolution of human history reflects the general law of historical development and reveals the general trend of historical development, thus with universal significance. But it does not mean that every specific country or nation can only take one development model. The general law of historical development is related with and differs from the stages of social development of each country or nation. The general law of historical development exists both in the process of world history development as a whole, and in the different social development stages of each nation or country. In researching the specific social development process of each country and nation, the typical and abstract characteristics of the general laws of historical development and the secondary factors, intermediate state and complex situation in the actual development process that are discarded when generalizing the general laws of historical development should be taken into account. The characteristics of the law of historical development mentioned above determines that the general rules and trends of the evolution of the social form do not exclude the special laws and circumstances the various nationalities and countries in their actual development, nor can they replace the analysis of the complicated historical conditions and the actual movement process in each country and nation. It is for this reason that Marx and Engels had never modeled the general law of social evolution in any specific country. On the contrary, they noticed the facts that Germany and the United States had entered into capitalist society without going through the feudal society. They oppose to turn the general law of social form evolution into formula that can be applied everywhere regardless of the specific the special historical conditions at specific historical stages or treat it as an insurmountable dogma. In 1877, Marx, in his *Letter to the Editorial Office of the Chronicle of the Motherland*,

31 Marx-Engels Collected Works, Vol. 5, Beijing, People's Publishing House, 2009, p. 9-10.
32 Marx-Engels Collected Works, Vol. 10, Beijing, People's Publishing House, 2009, p. 289.

refuted Mikhailovsky's misinterpretation of his historical development theory: "He must by all means transform my historical sketch of the development of capitalism in Western Europe into a historical-philosophical theory of universal development predetermined by fate for all nations, whatever their historic circumstances in which they find themselves may be, in order finally to achieve that economic formation which with the highest upswing of the productive forces of social work assures mankind its most universal development. But I beg his pardon. (That [view] does me at the same time too much honor and too much insult.)"[33] In 1881, in his reply to Zasulich, Marx clearly expressed his opposition to turning the path of Western European capitalism into a way that all nations were destined to go. He wrote: "'Historical inevitability' is limited to kind of Western European countries."[34]

Marxist founders' generalization of the general laws and trends of human society development fully embodies the dialectical unity of the uniformity of human social development and the diversity of national development. In their demonstration of the general laws and trends of historical development of human being, Marx and Engels had never excluded the particularity of social development path in each country or nation. On the contrary, they put the particularity and complexity of the development process of each country or nation as a prerequisite for the general law of historical development. When they studied the specific social development path of a single country or nation, they had never forgotten the restriction and influence of the universality of the law of historical development. In terms of diversity, the contradictory movement of productive forces and relations has different natures, levels, structures and forms in various countries or nations, so that the specific countries or nations are at different stages of socio-economic development. In terms of uniformity, the world market based on the international labor division links the nations and regions together, in which the contradictory movement of the productive forces and relations are out of the boundary of a region, a country or a nation and taking place all around the world. As the interaction between countries or nations is enhancing, "to lead to collisions in a country, this contradiction need not necessarily have reached its extreme limit in this particular country. The competition with industrially more advanced countries, brought about by the expansion of international intercourse, is sufficient to produce a similar contradiction in countries with a backward industry".[35] Therefore, the general law of historical development in the world determines that human society in general is evolving from a low level to a high level. But for those economically and culturally backward countries involved in the world capitalist system, they might achieve leaping development and do not have to start all again.

33 Marx-Engels Collected Works, Vol. 3, Beijing, People's Publishing House, 2009, p. 466.
34 Ibid., p. 570.
35 Marx-Engels Collected Works, Vol. 1, Beijing, People's Publishing House, 2009, p. 568.

2. Marx's and Engels' thoughts on the future social system

Marx and Engels called their future society theory as the "association of free individuals". In this "advanced stage" of society, i.e. the communist society, social productive forces are highly developed with very rich material wealth; there is no class difference and no difference between workers and farmers, urban and rural areas and physical labor and brainwork; the limit of labor division disappears and spontaneous labor division is replaced by conscious labor division; means of production are shared by all people who participate not only in the management but also the productive labor; social labor is planned to be distributed proportionally to each production chain; the primary need of human being is working through which they show and develop all of their physical strength and mental power; individual consumer goods are distributed according to one's needs; the free development of each person becomes the conditions for the free development of all people; and the state has completely died out and is replaced by social management. the arrival of such a stage has to be based on the development of productive forces and the self-perfection of the people, and go through a "lower stage" or "first stage" that is essentially similar to the above-mentioned stage. In 1875, in his *Critique of the Gotha Program*, Marx for the first time sketched the outline of this stage. Taking the *Critique of the Gotha Program* as the main line and summing up the related words in other works of Marx and Engels, it could be seen that the society later called the socialist society has the following basic characteristics: (1) creating a higher productivity than capitalism to make it more conducive to the development of social productive forces; (2) eliminating the capitalist private ownership and all private ownership, and the means of production belong to the whole society; (3) labor time is distributed according to plans in the whole society, and commodity currency relations disappear from social and economic life; (4) after the necessary deduction of the total product of the society for reproduction and public consumption, the individual consumer goods are distributed according to the amount of labor provided by each person, i.e. the principle of "do what you can and take what you deserve" featuring rewarding equal labor with equal products; (5) all classes and class differences are eliminated, and the conditions in which the bourgeoisie can neither exist nor rise again; (6) the state no longer has the political functions and the nature of being class oppression tools, retaining only its social management functions.

Marx and Engels knew that the socialist society would be born out of the capitalist society after a long period of pain. Therefore, even after the victory of the proletarian revolution, it has to go through a transition period from the capitalist society into a socialist society. The "transition period" a special stage of historical development: (1) socialist economic sectors coexist and compete with non-socialist economic sectors that gradually decline as the socialist economic sectors keep growing. (2) the class society will develop into classless society, and the problem that which side will win between the proletariat and the bourgeoisie has not yet been resolved due to the class struggle. (3) the function of the state will change from being a political/class state to public organ, i.e., which will undertake social management, and the practice of "revolutionary dictatorship of the proletariat" shows that the state will still remains to be the tool of class oppression. Since the transition from a capitalist society to a socialist society or the "first stage" of communism, it requires not only the profound transformation of the relations of production and the superstructure, but also the material and technological foundations for the "first stage" of communism. Therefore, one of the important tasks for this period is to develop social productive forces.

Critique of the Gotha Program is a representative text that contains the most insightful theories of the founders of the Marxism about the future society, and was also a letter for the German Party which was not written for publishing or the public. In 1891 when Marx had passed away for eight years, Engels for the first time published this manuscript. In his preface, Engels emphasized the significance of this letter to the criticism of opportunism, but did not mention the significance of Marx's discourse on future society. Because, in the view of Marx and Engels, their discussion of the future socio-economic characteristics is a description of a social form that has historically existed, nor a generalization of social practice that is actually existing, but a logical inference based on the economic facts of capitalism. In the process of judging and reasoning using concepts, it is necessary to abandon the non-essential specific things from the complicated special and discover the essential and inevitable links in the social economic development. Therefore, this discourse which is impossible to be systematic and fully explored could only be pure and general theoretical assumption to be tested and proven in social practices.

Living in the capitalist era of free competition, the mission of Marx and Engels given by history was neither to specifically plan the path to the future society, nor develop the blueprint of future society for countries with different levels of economy, but to take the developed capitalism in Western Europe as their research object, study the rising, development and historical trends of capitalism, and demonstrate the historical inevitability of the rising of socialist society, so as to find "scientific solution" to the problem of socialism replacing capitalism instead of "actual solution".

3. Marx's and Engels' exploration of the path of social development in the countries with backward economy and culture

Since the 1870s, the world economic and political situation had undergone new changes, and capitalist economic relations accelerated its extension into the economically and culturally backward countries outside of Western Europe. "'The bourgeoisie, with establishing and opening up the world market, has made both the production and consumption of all countries become universal' ...compel[ling] all nations, on pain of extinction, to adopt the bourgeois mode of production".[36] Under the impact of this so-called "cosmopolitanism", the economically and culturally backward countries are encountered with the issue of how to choose their own social and economic development path.

From *Marx's Letter to the Editorial Office of the Chronicle of the Motherland* in 1877 to Engels' *Postscript of On the Social Issues of Russia* in 1894, Marx and Engels put forward a series of important theoretical perspectives regarding the social development path for economically and culturally backward countries. In 1881, in order to answer the Russian female revolutionist Zasulich's request on prospect of Russian history, especially the fate of the Russian rural commune, in his Reply Letter to Vera Zasulich which he had revised four times, Marx took Russia as a typical object and proposed the theory of Caudine Forks which means that there is a possibility for the economically and culturally backward countries to leap over the capitalist system, namely the possibility of a development path that is different from the capitalist path.

From the perspective of the coexistence between Russian rural commune and the world market ruled by Western capitalist, Marx pointed out that, due to the rural commune prevalent in the countryside of Russia and "due its contemporaneity with capitalist production that it may appropriate the latter's all positive acquisitions without experiencing all its frightful misfortunes. And capitalist production is something that exists at the same time, so it can withstand capitalist production"[37]; "on the other hand, the contemporaneity of western production, which dominates the world market, allows Russia to incorporate into the Russian commune all the positive acquisitions devised by the capitalist system without passing through its Caudine Forks [i.e., undergo humiliation in defeat]".[38] That is to say, at a certain development stage of the capitalist world history, the Russian rural commune in the process of disintegration is likely to avoid all the unfortunate

36 Marx-Engels Collected Works, Vol. 2, Beijing, People's Publishing House, 2009, p. 35

37 Marx-Engels Collected Works, Vol. 3, Beijing, People's Publishing House, 2009, p. 571.

38 Ibid., p. 575.

disasters brought about by the capitalist system and become the factor of the Russian renaissance and the starting point of the "future society".

In Marx and Engels's view, to start and win the revolution in economically and culturally backward countries, there must be a prerequisite that revolution break out in the Western developed capitalist countries where the proletariat seize the power and provide strong support for the revolution in those countries with backward economy and culture. This is because the low level of productive forces leads to the fact that the economically and culturally backward countries lack the material and technological foundation for socialist transformation which could only be available in the Western developed countries with high degree of socialized production and fully developed capitalism. Because of the profound opposition between socialism and capitalism in social system and ideology, when the bourgeoisie dominates, it will never hand over the industrial achievements created accomplished by the capitalist industry to the economically and culturally backward countries so that they could lay the material and technical foundation for the socialism. Therefore, the victory of the Western proletarian revolution is the essential external conditions for the economically and culturally backward countries to develop into socialism.

In Marx's *Letter from Marx to Editor of the Otecestvenniye Zapisky* [Notes on the Fatherland] in 1877 and Engels' "On the Social Issues of Russia and Social Revolution" from 1874 to 1875, they took the Russian communes and Russian society as their research objects and preliminarily analyzed the social development path of the economically and culturally backward countries.

After the serfdom reform in 1861, the Russian communes and the Russian society encountered dramatic social changes, as the oppression of the feudal state and the rising and developing bourgeoisie exploitation pushed the Russian commune based on public land ownership to the brink of extinction. But whether it's the Russian commune or the Russian society, the basis of capitalism advancing into socialism was not the rural commune itself, because neither the capitalist mode of production nor the socialist mode of production can be built on the natural economy and small-scale agricultural production. Russian rural communes cannot directly grow into socialism. And secondly, it is an historical impossibility that a lower stage of economic development should solve the enigmas and conflicts which did not arise, and could not arise, until a far higher stage. All forms of gentile community which arose before commodity production and individual exchange have one thing in common with the future socialist society: that certain things, means of production, are subject to the common ownership and the common use of certain groups. This one shared feature does not, however, enable the lower form of society to engender out of itself the future socialist society, this final and most intrinsic product of capitalism. Any given economic formation has its own problems to solve, problems arising out of itself; to seek to solve those of another, utterly alien formation would be absolutely absurd".[39]

According to Marx, the reason why the Russian commune is likely to cross the Caudine Forks of capitalist system lies in its historical conditions. The Russian commune "Russia exists in a modern historical context: it is contemporaneous with a higher culture, and it is linked to a world market in which capitalist production is predominant".[40]

This particular historical condition determined that it might become "the fulcrum for social regeneration in Russia". But the transformation of the Russian commune can only be done by the Western industrial proletariat. "The victory of the West European proletariat over the bourgeoisie, and, linked to this, the replacement of capitalist production by socially managed production—that is the necessary precondition for raising the Russian commune to the same level (Engels)".[41]

In the *Afterword of Russia and Its Social Relations* in 1894, Engels more clearly pointed out: "The Russian revolution will also give the labour movement of the West fresh impetus and create new, better conditions in which to carry on the struggle, thus hastening the victory of the modern industrial proletariat, without which present-day Russia can never achieve a socialist transformation, whether proceeding from the commune or from capitalism."[42]

This analysis method then was further applied in studying other economically and culturally backward countries. "it is not only possible but certain that after the victory of the proletariat and the transfer of the means of production into common ownership among the West European peoples, the countries which have only just succumbed to capitalist production and have salvaged gentile institutions, or remnants thereof, have in these remnants of common ownership and in the corresponding popular customs a powerful means of appreciably shortening the process of development into a socialist society and of sparing themselves most of the suffering and struggles through which we in Western Europe must work our way. But the example and the active assistance of the hitherto capitalist West is an indispensable condition for this."[43]

Marx's and Engels's exploration on the possibility that economically and

39 Marx-Engels Collected Works, Vol. 4, Beijing, People's Publishing House, 2009, p. 458.
40 Marx-Engels Collected Works, Vol. 2, Beijing, People's Publishing House, 1963, p. 472.
41 Marx-Engels Collected Works, Vol. 4, Beijing, People's Publishing House, 2009, p. 457.
42 Ibid., p. 466
43 Ibid., p. 459.

culturally backward countries might leap over the Caudine Forks of capitalist system is a research of possibility under strictly set conditions. They considered the rural communes that coexisted with the capitalist production, connected with the world market ruled by capitalist production and possessed all the positive results created by the capitalist system as the "historical environment" for accelerating their own development and eventually transforming into communist society; considered the support and help for the economically and culturally backward countries from the developed capitalist countries, since they thought: "revolution "must take place simultaneously in all civilized countries – that is to say, at least in England, America, France, and Germany"[44], which would serve as the prerequisites for "the present public land ownership in Russia" to grow into "the starting point of communist development". Marx and Engels even envisaged, "If the Russian Revolution becomes the signal for a proletarian revolution in the West, so that both complement each other, the present Russian common ownership of land may serve as the starting point for a communist development. (Preface to Russian edition of the *Communist Manifesto*, 1882)."[45]

Based on the historical background of "history turning into world history", Marx and Engels had made a judgment that the social revolution transforming into the future society would inevitably have the worldwide characteristics. They argued that the victory of the proletarian revolution in developed capitalist countries would influence the former capitalist countries or backward capitalist countries by significantly changing the development process of these countries so that they could be led into the communist society by the developed countries without having to go through the stages of capitalist development or with a shortened capitalist stage. But they stressed that, when studying whether the economically and culturally backward countries have "historical conditions" or "historical environment" for leapfrog development, it is needed to fully consider the universal communication caused by the world market, and observe the connection between the economically and culturally backward countries and the developed capitalist countries in a global context. Without the historical environment and prerequisites for this issue, the Russian rural commune cannot become "the new fulcrum of Russian society" and there is no theoretical value and practical significance in the idea of "leaping over the Caudine Forks of capitalist system".

Marx and Engels' theory of the future society is an organic part of the Marxist theoretical system. It is based on the unity of history and logic, which is indisputably scientific and rigorous. It captures the essential economic characteristics of socialist society, reveals the general trend of social

44 Marx-Engels Collected Works, Vol. 1, Beijing, People's Publishing House, 2009, p. 687.
45 Marx-Engels Collected Works, Vol. 2, Beijing, People's Publishing House, 2009, p. 8.

development, and is of universal significance. However, the socialist doctrine founded by Marx and Engels is just a deduction based on the general laws of social development and certain conditions, rather than definite conclusions verified by practices. In particular, their exploration on the social development path for economically and culturally backward countries in their later years was only a kind of possibility under strictly set conditions and did not provide a definite and unswerving social development path for those countries. Its significance is not the idea of "leaping over the Caudine Forks of capitalist system", but rather that it provides a new theoretical perspective or approach for studying the social development path of economically and culturally backward countries. It determines that future society theories of Marxist founders cannot be applied directly to specific real life, and that the basic principles of socialism shall be concretized and recreated according to the actual situation. In this sense, what Marxism provides is "not any ready to hand doctrine, but provides a starting point or method for further study".[46] In other words, as Marx commented: "There is no royal road to science, and only those who do not dread the fatiguing climb of its steep paths have a chance of gaining its luminous summits".[47] Only by combining the universal principles of socialism with the special historical environment and the specific national conditions of each country can we find a practical development path of socialism.

(Dong Zhengping, Professor of College of Political Science and Law, Capital Normal University)

46 Marx-Engels Collected Works, Vol. 10, Beijing, People's Publishing House, 2009, p. 691.
47 Lenin's Monographs on Socialism, Beijing, People's Publishing House, 2009, p. 338.

"New Economic Policy" Utilizing Capitalism to Develop Socialism

With the rapid development of capitalism in Russia and the collapse of rural communes, the political and economic situation of Russian society had undergone great changes. Russia's autocratic system was facing a serious crisis, and the revolution is maturing. The victory of the October Revolution in 1917 marked the establishment of socialism as a social system in an economically and culturally backward country. The historical leap of socialism from theory to reality opened a new chapter in human society.

1. The great contrast between socialist theory and reality

Since the 1880s, the changes in social and revolutionary situation in Russia made the possibility of the Russian commune leaping over the Caudine Forks of capitalist system weaken and eventually gone. "In a short period of time established all the material basis for capitalist mode of production".[48] The young Russian bourgeoisie soon took the state in their own hands. "Russia is becoming more and more rapidly transformed into a capitalist industrialized country",[49] thus embarking on the capitalist development path. "The Russian commune has existed for hundreds of years without ever providing the impetus for the development of a higher form of common ownership out of itself"[50]; meanwhile, the crisis of the Western capitalist society, couldn't "give the Russian commune the means to enable itself to develop into this new form of society".[51] Thus, Russia's social development was faced with a new historical choice.

With the victory of the October Revolution, socialism had changed from theory to reality. However, the victory of the Russian October Revolution was neither the practice of the former capitalist countries leaping over the Caudine Forks of capitalist system, nor the successful case of social revolution in the way that combined the Eastern and Western revolutions, but the socialist revolution in a economically and culturally backward country in its own way. After the victory of the October Revolution in Russia, Lenin had hoped that the world socialist revolution would soon occur and prevail, which had failed to become true. Under the historical environment of that time, the socialist revolution and construction in Russia had not received the strong support from the victory of the western proletarian revolutions.

48 Marx-Engels Collected Works, Vol. 4, Beijing, People's Publishing House, 2009, p. 464.
49 Ibid., p. 466.
50 Ibid., pp. 456-457.
51 Ibid., p. 458.

On the contrary, it was encountered with armed intervention Western powers and long-term economic and technological blockade of imperialism.

The victory of the October Revolution confirmed Marx's and Engels' scientific assertions that capitalism will surely be replaced by socialism. But the concrete approach and form of socialism were quite different from what Marx and Engels had conceived. Because of the imbalance of economic and political development in the capitalism world, the socialist revolution found a weak link in capitalist chain and triumphed firstly in the economically and culturally backward Russia. The socialist system firstly emerged not in the most developed capitalist countries, but in an economically backward country where small-scale peasant economy dominated, which determined that, after obtaining the power, the proletariat had to build socialism with inadequate material and technological foundation and socialized production, and go through several transitional or intermediate stages to advance into the "first stage" of communism envisioned by the founders of Marxism, namely the mature or comparatively developed socialism. The great contrast between the socialist model in Marxist classics and the socialist reality had tasked the Bolshevik Party and Lenin a new subject: in an economically backward country like Russia where small-scale peasant economy dominated, how to transform into socialism after the victory of proletarian revolution?

Lenin argued, "For Russia, the times for advocating a socialism program based on books have passed, I am convinced that it is bygone forever, today we can only talk about socialism based on practice"[52]. Now it is all about practice and the theory is turning into practice. The theory is empowered, corrected and tested by practice. He particularly pointed out that the significance of the theory of development stages into the future society by the founders of Marxism is as follows: "Marx consistently applies materialist dialectics, the theory of development, and regards communism as something which develops out of capitalism. Instead of scholastically invented, 'concocted' definitions and fruitless disputes over words (What is socialism? What is communism?), Marx gives analysis of what might be called the stages of the economic maturity of communism".[53] According to Marx's view that there would be a transitional period of proletarian dictatorship between capitalism and socialism, Lenin pointed out the transitional nature of the Soviet economy determined that capitalism and socialist factors will be intricately coexisting in this transitional economy, so the fundamental characteristics of the transitional economy would take the form of mixed economy. Lenin said: "the term Socialist Soviet Republic implies the determination of Soviet power to achieve the transition to socialism, and not that the new economic

52 Lenin's Monographs on Socialism, Beijing, People's Publishing House, 2009, p. 399.
53 Ibid., p. 38.

system is recognized as a socialist order."[54] In this system there are capitalist and socialist components, parts and elements. It consists of "1) Natural economy: i.e. patriarchal production, almost totally consumed by its producers. 2) Small commodity production: "this includes the majority of those peasants who sell their grain". 3) Private capitalism: whose rebirth goes back to the NEP. 4) State capitalism: i.e. grain monopoly and national accounting of production, which the proletarian power strives to accomplish in the face of a multitude of difficulties. 5) Socialism: The strength of these five economic components is not equal, with the petty bourgeois spontaneous forces being dominant and only a small number of proletariat. And the petty bourgeoisie together with private capitalism are against any form of large-scale production, whether it is national capitalism or socialism. In light of the specific conditions in Russia, Lenin stressed: "We should start with the existing status of things"; "we should start with something we are absolutely certain."[55]

The starting point is that Russia is still a country where the small production mode of production is dominant. This kind of commodity economy develops slowly with low commodity rate and capital accumulation rate, so it is difficult to establish the material and technological foundation for socialism. This basic national condition of Soviet Union determined that the main task during the early transitional period is to fight spontaneous forces of the petty bourgeoisie. The decisive competition in this fight is in the economic field, and the key is that between the capitalist and socialist modes of production which one would earn the support from small-scale peasant economy. To win this competition, the proletariat must seek the form of economic ties between millions of small farmers and large industries, and find bonding point of socialist economy and small-scale peasant economy under proletarian dictatorship.

2. Advancing into socialism by utilizing capitalism

Before the October Revolution, Lenin began to conceive Russia's transition to socialism on the basis of Marx's and Engels' socialist doctrine. He argued that the imperialist war had accelerated the transformation from monopoly capitalism to state monopoly capitalism. "state-monopoly capitalism is the most complete material preparation for socialism."[56] "Socialism is merely the next step forward from state-capitalist monopoly. Or, in other words, socialism is merely state-capitalist monopoly which is made to serve the interests of the whole people and has to that extent ceased to be capitalist monopoly."[57] "The bourgeois state implements the functions of

54 Ibid., p. 111.

55 Lenin Complete Works, Chinese 2nd edition, Vol. 36, Beijing, People's Publishing House, 1985, p. 159.

56 Lenin's Monographs on Socialism, Beijing, People's Publishing House, 2009, p. 235.

57 Ibid., p. 234.

managing social and economic affairs "the organization shouldn't be broken, it doesn't need to be broken."[58] The proletarian revolution can only achieve its own goals by relying on the positive achievements of capitalism. He envisioned after the establishment of the Soviet government, the largest monopolies of all banks and capitalists and the land shall be nationalized; industrialists, businessmen and general business owners shall be forced to merge into a variety of joint organizations; food monopoly shall be implemented; all residents join the consumer cooperatives, and consumer goods shall be rationally distribute by the state; by using the banks, syndicate and other modern management agencies, the production and distribution of products shall be stringently calculated and supervised, so that the whole society would turn into a large factory or syndicate with equal labor and equal payment in which all citizens are the employees and workers.

After the October Revolution, with the signing of Brest-Litovsk Peace Treaty, the young Soviet regime got an extremely short period of time to catch its breath, during which it could begin to restore the economy. Lenin proposed the program for direct transition to socialism in Russia, mainly including: the capitalism, especially the production of small commodities, shall be incorporated into the national capitalist system; all residents join the consumer commune; trades shall be limited and gradually replaced with planned distribution of products under the unified national leadership; state-controlled direct industrial and agricultural products exchange system shall be established on the basis of industrial development; small farmers are guided to follow the joint tillage system.

However, when the plan of transition to socialism proposed in the spring of 1918 was not yet implemented, foreign armed intervention and domestic counter-revolutionary rebellion occurred. From the summer of 1918 to the beginning of 1921, the Soviet regime was forced to implement the wartime communist policy. With the increasing military victories, the demand within the Bolshevik Party to transform directly from capitalism into socialism was becoming more and more intense. The military victories led to the proletariat's intention of solving economic problems with the radical approach of "head-on collision". It means to transform the urban and rural economy in the war communism way and establish from top to bottom a production and consumption co-operatives covering the entire society based on the public ownership of the means of production. "we should, according to a nation-wide plan to maximize the integration of all economic activities across the country and maximize production."[59] The labor and consumption standards shall be rigorously calculated and supervised, and production and distribution of products adjusted in accordance with the principle of communism.

58 Lenin's Monographs on Socialism, Beijing, People's Publishing House, 2009, p. 44.
59 Lenin Complete Works, Chinese 2nd edition, Vol. 36, Beijing, People's Publishing House, 1985, p. 414.

The wartime communist policy integrated the limited financial, material and human resources, which met the demands of the domestic revolutionary war. But it had gone beyond the scope of contingency measures that had to be taken in the course of a war and become a system that "the production and distribution of products was directly adjusted by state orders according to communist principles in a small-scale farming country". It suffered a serious setback because it had gone beyond the stage of social development. In 1920, Russia's total grain output was reduced from 4.3 billion poods to 2.2 billion poods, only 51% of 1913 prior to the World War I; the number of livestock decreased by 40%; industrial production was only 1/7 of 1913; food and fuel shortage raged; transportation was stopped; and factories were shut down. As the foreign armed interference and the threat of domestic counter-revolutionary rebellion weakened, the increasingly prominent socio-economic contradictions triggered political crisis and the "direct transition" to socialism was hard to continue.

The failure of the wartime communist policy made Lenin realize that, "the direct transition to purely socialist forms, to purely socialist distribution, was beyond our available strength, and that if we were unable to effect a retreat so as to confine ourselves to easier tasks, we would face disaster."[60] From the economic point of view, the transition period means that there are both capitalist and socialist elements in the socio-economic structure. When the small peasant economy was dominant in the social and economic structure, it is impossible to directly transform into socialism. At the 10th Congress of the Russian Communist Party (Bolsheviks), Lenin summed up the experience and lessons of Russia's transition to socialism and highlighted the fact that Russia, a country with rather backward economy and the small peasant economy being dominant, shall take path to socialism different from the developed capitalist countries. He said, "it is no doubt that the transition from capitalism to socialism can take many different forms, depending on whether capitalist mode of production and irs relationship dominates or whether small-scale economy dominates."[61]

When there is neither developed large-scale industry nor developed large-scale agricultural production, it is impossible to advance directly into the communist economy. The "direct transition" approach simply would not work in Russia with small peasant economy being dominant. Unlike the "aggressive" approach of the developed capitalist countries, i.e. implementing the socialist principle of production and distribution in the simplest, quick and direct way, Russia shall take the "indirect", "careful and roundabout" and "reformist" approach and transform into socialism

60 Lenin Complete Works, Chinese 2nd edition, Vol. 43, Beijing, People's Publishing House, 1985, p. 278.

61 Lenin Complete Works, Chinese 2nd edition, Vol. 41, Beijing, People's Publishing House, 1986, p. 70.

through a series of intermediate links. He made it clear that, "The less developed a capitalist society is, the longer the time needed for transition to socialism."[62] In order to ensure the victory of socialism in Soviet Russia, retreat is necessary in a certain period of time. "we had suffered defeat in our attempt to introduce the socialist principles of production and distribution by 'direct assault', i.e., in the most direct way. The political situation in the spring of 1921 revealed to us that on a number of economic issues a retreat to the position of state capitalism, since the substitution of 'siege' tactics for 'direct assault', had become inevitable."[63]

If you want to "guarantee establisment of the the economic foundation of socialism, this is a must".[64] In the Soviet countries, "it is impossible to create and introduce socialism without learning from the the technology, engineering and culture created by large-scale capitalism."[65]

From the "direct transition" to the "indirect transition", from the wartime communist policy to the new economic policy, Lenin had significantly changed his understanding in respect to the transition period. He had realized that in the economically and culturally backward countries, it was impossible to transform directly into socialism by state political power. "It is necessary to take a series of special transitional approaches to carry out the socialist revolution." The new economic policy, being the combination of the socialist economy and the small-scale peasant economy, was the special transitional approach for economically and culturally backward countries to advance into socialism.

The new economic policy was not merely a retreat allowing the capitalism to exist and develop under certain historical conditions. Its profound meaning was that, after the working class of economically and culturally backward countries having taking the power, how they would lead the individual farmers accounting for the majority of the population to socialism, use commodity currency relations to develop social productive forces, and use capitalism to develop socialism, so as to gain the advantages compared with the capitalism and consolidate the newborn socialist regime. Lenin planned, without destroying the old economic structure, to carefully control the non-socialist economic sectors such as the small economy, small business and capitalism when they were rising, make them subject to national regulation, and slowly and gradually going toward socialism through a series of transitional stages. Lenin realized that it was impossible to try to completely ban or block the development of all private non-state exchanges, namely the development of capitalism. "If a political party tries to

62 Lenin Complete Works, 2nd Chinese version, Vol. 42, p. 183.

63 Lenin's Monographs on Socialism, Beijing, People's Publishing House, 2009, p. 280-81.

64 Ibid., p. 281.

65 Ibid., p. 133.

implement such a policy, then it is doing something stupid, it is a suicide."[66] Then the only reasonable policy is to incorporate capitalism into the state capitalism by which the government of proletariat dictatorship could set limitations and regulate its scope. Only through the state capitalism can the capitalist relations transform into socialism. It is wrong to counterpose capitalism and socialism in an abstract manner and argue unrealistically that "capitalism is a disaster and socialism means happiness". "Capitalism is a bane compared with socialism. Capitalism is a boon compared with medievalism, small production, and the evils of bureaucracy which spring from the dispersal of the small producers. In as much as we are as yet unable to pass directly from small production to socialism, some capitalism is inevitable as the elemental product of small production and exchange; so that we must utilize capitalism (particularly by directing it into the channels of state capitalism) as the intermediary link between small production and socialism, as a means, a path, and a method of increasing the productive forces."[67]

To build socialism, "with both hands we have to take everything that is good from other countries, or: Soviet goverment + the order of the Prussian railways + American technology and organization of trusts, American education, etc., etc., plus plus equals socialism."[68] "We have to admit that our entire view of socialism has changed radically."[69] The terms used by Lenin change our "whole" view and "fundamental" change in building socialism included fundamental changes in his understanding of using capitalism to transform into socialism during the transitional period. Of course, it should be noted that Lenin explored how to use the capitalism from the perspective of "advancing into" socialism. His "fundamental change" of the "whole view" was only about how to "transform" into socialism. He just affirmed that during the transition period of "a very long time" the commodity currency economy would be retained and state capitalism used, and never referred to the issue that whether the commodity currency economy and state capitalism would still exist in the socialist society after the end of transition period, so the changes of his whole outlook or overall understanding on the future socialism cannot be inferred. For instance, Lenin insisted that the market economy was still inherently, capitalist in nature. "Commodity exchange and freedom of trade inevitably imply the appearance of capitalists and capitalist relationships."[70] "Circulation is the freedom of trade, it is capitalism."[71] "The proletarian state may, without changing its own nature, permit freedom of trade and the development of capitalism only

66 Ibid., p. 219.
67 Lenin Collected Works, English ed., Vol. 32, p. 350.
68 Ibid., pp. 381-382.
69 Ibid., p. 354.
70 Lenin Complete Works, 2nd Chinese ed., Vol. 41, p. 269.
71 Ibid., p. 232.

within certain bounds, and only on the condition that the state regulates (supervises, controls, determines the forms and methods of, etc.) private trade and private capitalism."[72]

"We need to be familiar with free trade, compete with free trade, and use free trade ace and weapons to defeat the free trade."[73] The purpose of using capitalism is to overcome capitalism and build a socialist society. It can be seen that the change of Lenin's theory of transition to socialism in the new economic policy period was to explore how to use capitalism, especially national capitalism, to "advance" into socialism in a roundabout way. It is not to design a development model for the economically and culturally backward countries to build socialism, but to find the specific approach and special method for "advancing" into socialism under the special conditions in Russia. As Lenin led the economic construction for only a very short period of time, there was no adequate material for him to make a comprehensive and precise conclusion. So, his research was only preliminary. Even so, Lenin had considered the with the reality of social and economic development in Russia, made useful explorations on using capitalism to develop into socialism and put forward a number of creative ideas, the significance of which was beyond the new economic policy itself and the whole transition period, leaving an enlightening theoretical legacy for the later socialist countries to open up to the outside world and establish socialist market economic system.

3. "To build communism using the material basis created by capitalism"

The implementation of the new economic policy went through two stages of development. The first stage was the beginning of the policy implementation from March to October, 1921. At this stage, the main task of the new economic policy was to return to the form of state capitalism and commodity exchange, namely, through the exchange agencies in the form of state capitalism and in an organized way, to exchange products manufactured by state-owned enterprises and various state capitalist enterprises with the farmers. The second was the major implementation period after October 1921. At this stage, the main task was to go from state capitalism back to state regulation of business and currency circulation. This meant to continue to retreat, allowing farmers' free trade and private business development and having their development regulated by the state. The state regulation of business and currency circulation had become intermediate form of capitalism transforming into socialism.

72 Lenin's Monographs on Socialism, Beijing, People's Publishing House, 2009, p. 298.
73 Lenin Complete Works, 2nd Chinese ed., Vol. 41, p. 350.

The core of the new economic policy was to replace the system of collecting surplus grain with grain tax. The system of collecting surplus grain, which was implemented during the civil war, was to collect all the surplus grain from the farmers, except for the food rations, fodder and seeds. The collected food was directly assigned to front-line soldiers, urban workers and other residents by the Labor Defense Commission. In actual practice, the "surplus grain" was often not the amount of food after the farmers had kept enough rations, but the amount that was forced to give out according to the needs of the workers and the army. The farmers could only keep the left part after they paid the required amount. The gratuitous imposition of farmers' food led to sharp conflicts between farmers and workers, soldiers and the government. As their surplus food could not be properly compensated, they reduced food production, thus exacerbating the shortage of food supplies. The 10th Congress of the Russian Communist Party (Bolsheviks) held in March 1921, marked the transition of the Soviet regime from the wartime communist policy to the new economic policy. At this congress, Lenin proposed to replace the surplus grain collection system with the grain tax. In his view, food and fuel was needed to improve the living conditions of workers, and the living conditions of farmers shall be improved to increase food production, acquisition and transportation. Grain tax reflects the attitude of the working class to the peasant class. And the relationship between the two classes determined the fate of Russian socialism and was related to the issue of consolidating the worker-peasant alliance and proletarian dictatorship. The fact that the grain tax replaced the surplus grain collection system meant that the Soviet regime had begun to correct the relationship between the working class and the peasant class. It allows farmers to keep all the food, raw materials and feedstuff. Farmers' surplus grains and other agricultural products were allowed to exchange for industrial products, handicrafts and other agricultural products in the market. The Soviet regime collected the products of the state capitalist enterprises and the state-owned enterprises in their own hands and exchanged them to obtain the agricultural products needed for the development of the socialist economy from the farmers, "we are introducing the tax in kind, that is, we shall take the minimum of grain we require (for the army and the workers) in the form of a tax and obtain the rest in exchange for manufactured goods.[74]

To exchange for food with manufactured industrial products needed by the farmers, "That is the only kind of food policy that corresponds to the tasks of the proletariat, and can strengthen the foundations of socialism and lead to its complete victory."[75] The implementation of the grain tax was a concession to the small peasant economy, which gave the farmers a chance

74 Lenin's Monographs on Socialism, Beijing, People's Publishing House, 2009, p. 218.

75 Ibid., p. 217.

to catch their breath, mobilized their enthusiasm of production, promoted the development of large industries, and ensured the stability of the national economy. Its practical significance is as follows: "the New Economic Policy is important for us primarily as a means of testing whetherwe are really establishing a link with the peasant economy."[76] As the grain tax replaced the surplus grain collection system, the domestic free trade was becoming increasingly active; the commodity exchange went beyond the boundary of the local circulation; the commodity circulation driven by currency was further developed; and the private market was becoming more and more powerful. In order to improve the productivity of farmers and restore and develop the economy, "We must recognize that the retreat was insufficient, and further that a retreat is necessary, and that a shift from state capitalism to state regulation of trade and currency circulation is also necessary."[77] Free trades system between urban and rural areas shall be established using commodity-currency relations. The domestic businesses shall be activated with the correct national regulation. The commodity exchange with driven by currency shall be fully realized.

"Trade is the 'link' in the historical chain of events, in the transitional forms of our socialist construction in 1921-22, which we, the proletarian government, we, the ruling Communist Party, 'must grasp with all our might'. If we 'grasp' this link firmly enough now we shall certainly control the whole chain in the very near future. If we do not, we shall not control the whole chain, we shall not create the foundation for socialist social and economic relations."[78]

Thus, business had become the central part of the new economic policy and the suitable form of combining the private interests of commodity producers with the public interests of socialist construction.

The main way to implement the new economic policy was state capitalism. The Soviet state would sign agreements, covenants or contracts with domestic and foreign capitalists. The state leased a number of factories, enterprises, mines and forest to the capitalists. In accordance with the law and lease contract, the capitalists paid the state with their products and kept the profits. The leasehold would be taken back by the state when the contracts expired. In the transitional period of Russia, state capitalism, being "a special state capitalism", could be controlled and supervised by the proletarian state. It was "special", because the "state" was no longer bourgeois state, but the proletarian state. This kind of "special" state capitalism has its dual nature: on the one hand, as the result of concentrated and socialized production, it was an organized, planned and statistical form of production

76 Ibid., p. 315.
77 Ibid., p. 282.
78 Lenin's Monographs on Socialism, Beijing, People's Publishing House, 2009, p. 292.

and circulation that could be supervised by the state, which was conducive to the development of the Russian economy and could serve the socialism; on the other hand, it was a form of production and circulation operated in the capitalist way in order to gain profits, which meant it would pay the capitalists quite an amount of money at the expense of certain sacrifices, so it must be restricted to the scope of its activities.

During the period of the new economic policy, the specific forms of state capitalism included:

Firstly, the lease system. are perhaps the most simple and clear-cut form of state capitalism. It involves a formal written agreement with the most civilised, advanced, West European capitalism".[79] It meant that: "the state leases to the capitalist entrepreneur an industrial establishment, oilfields, forest tracts, land, etc., which belong to the state, the lease being very similar to a concession agreement."[80] According to the lease contract and the law, the capitalist paid tax to the state with part of their products and kept the left part as their profits. When the contract expired, the enterprise was recovered by the state. The lease system "cultivated" by the Soviet regime, in fact, was to restore production with the help of foreign capital and free trade in order to survive in the capitalist encirclement; to introduce Western advanced science and technology and the experience of managing socialized production and build socialism with materials inherited from the bourgeois; "the Soviet government strengthens large-scale production as against petty production, advanced production as against backward production, and machine production as against hand production. It also obtains a larger quantity of the products of large-scale industry (its share of the output), and strengthens state regulated economic relations as against the anarchy of petty-bourgeois relations."[81]

Secondly, the cooperation system. It was "a special state capitalism", a more complex form of transition. If the lease system was based on a large machine industry, the cooperation system was based on small handicraft industry and cooperation among farmers. It was a form that led the capitalism which has been developed as a result of the free trade of surplus grain into state capitalism. It was also a form that made the proletariat forge alliance with millions of small farmers and the smallest peasants and guide the transition from small-scale peasant economy to socialism. The cooperation system of the new economic policy period mainly referred to the trading cooperatives, as emphasized by Lenin "small commodity producer cooperative

79 Ibid., p. 221.

80 Lenin Complete Works, Chinese 2nd edition, Vol. 41, Beijing, People's Publishing House, 1985, p.150.

81 Lenin's Monographs on Socialism, Beijing, People's Publishing House, 2009, p. 221.

is typical in countries wherein smallholder farmers are prevalent."[82] For small commodity producers, this form (trading) in the circulation sphere was more acceptable, since "cooperatives can easily unite millions of peasants, all population and organize them".[83] Once the cooperation system succeeded, the deep-rooted old economic relations of pre- socialism and even precapitalism could be eradicated among the vast majority of the people.

Thirdly, commissions of buying and selling. Commission on buying and selling meant the state considered the capitalists as businessmen, let them sell the state commodities and purchase the products of small commodity producer, and pay then a certain amount of commission. These people were actually private contractors of state enterprises. When the Russian commodity economy was not yet well developed, the state capitalism's system of commission on buying and selling could speed up the circulation and exchange of industrial and agricultural products, link together the rural and urban areas, create favorable conditions for the restoration and development of large industries, and make up for the deficiencies of the Soviet business with capitalist business experience. But, for the exploitation and speculation of capitalists in businesses, "the need to reexamine revise all laws having to do with speculative activities."

He announced that punishments (actually punishments three times more severe than formerly) for all theft of public property and for all direct or indirect, open or secret evasion of state supervision, examination, and accounting."[84]

Fourthly, the renting system. It meant that the state rented state-owned enterprises, mines, forests and land to some domestic venture capitalists on the basis of signing the contract, collected rent and recovered the resources when the contract expired. The implementation of the state capitalist renting system was to utilize the operation and management ability of the bourgeois, restore the national economy as soon as possible, increase the number of goods and improve the lives of workers and farmers.

The implementation of the new economic policy saw remarkable effect. The Soviet regime gained adequate food; large-scale industries began to recover in some areas; inflation was contained; the financial situation was improving; and people's lives were gradually becoming stable. Through the implementation of national capitalism, the newborn socialist regime not only absorbed advanced science and technology and management experience of the capitalist large production and developed socialist large-scale industries, but also promoted the development of small-scale peasant

82 Ibid., p. 222.
83 Ibid., p. 222-23.
84 Ibid., p. 232.

economy which was gradually growing into large production on the basis of voluntary alliance. Russia's practice of utilizing capitalism to advance into socialism had solved a series of major problems of transition to socialism in economically and culturally backward countries such as the path, mode and steps, leaving a significant and far-reaching impact on the economic construction in those economically and culturally backward countries that subsequently took the socialist path.

(Dong Zhengping, Professor of Institute of Political Science and Law, Capital Normal University)

"Stalin Model" and Socialist Reform

The period from the 1930s to 1950s was very important in socialist construction in the history of the Soviet Union. It was a period of time of severe international situation and complicated domestic struggles. In the absence of any previous experience, Stalin led the Soviet people to carry out socialist construction and made valuable exploration on socialist theory and practice, forming the Soviet socialist model, also known as the "Stalin model". Soviet socialism was run exactly in accordance with this model. This model, as a concrete form of socialism in the Soviet Union, had left a great intellectual treasure for the socialist construction practices and theories of all subsequent socialist countries; meanwhile, it also had some serious flaws, which caused serious losses for the socialist construction practices and theories of all subsequent socialist countries.

1. The basic characteristics of "Stalin model"

"Stalin model" was characterized by a high degree of concentration, which was mainly reflected in the economy, politics and culture. The "Stalin model" had three main economic features. Firstly, the single socialist ownership, namely the public ownership. In the process of leading the socialist construction, Stalin thought that socialism could not be based on public and private ownership. On the basis of this perception, Stalin adopted the policy of limiting, excluding and eventually eliminating capitalist economic sectors while promoting high-speed industrialization. Through the agricultural collectivization movement, the rural capitalist element, namely the rich peasant economy, was limited, excluded and eventually eliminated. With the completion of socialist industrialization and agricultural collectivization, around 1936, the issue of "who defeat whom" was basically solved in the Soviet Union, and the socialist public ownership formed, which was embodied in national ownership by the whole people and collective farm ownership.

Secondly, the highly centralized planned economy. In leading the socialist economic construction of the Soviet Union, Stalin clearly pointed out that the imbalance in the development of capitalist economy was regulated by the spontaneous forces of the market, hence the frequent outbreak of economic crisis; the development of the socialist economy shall be adjusted by planned economy to avoid the economic crisis. Based on this understanding, after the 14th National Congress of CPSU (Bolshevik), Stalin reorganized the planning authorities strengthened the planning and leadership of the national economy. In industrial enterprises, the annual plan combining the production and finance was compiled, and people were encouraged to participate in production management and the development and implementation of the plan. In agriculture, because the decentralized small-scale peasant economy dominated, instead of implementing direct planning, the state could only regulate in the circulation area, including price, tax, credit, provision of machinery and forward purchasing contract, to guide it develop to the direction of enhanced planning. As the collectivization of agriculture was realized and the uncertainties in the national economy were greatly reduced, the national economic plan of the Soviet Union after the 1930s basically became a mandatory plan, which meant the planned economic system had been established in the Soviet Union. Although there was the market in this system, the regulatory role of the market mechanism was subject to great constraints.

Thirdly, the state had become the subject of economic activities, and the party led and determined the national economic policy. In the operation of this economic system, the socialist ownership of the whole people equaled the socialist state ownership by which the state controlled the ownership and management rights of the means of production. The socialist state not only played the role of protecting socialist ownership and generally regulating the economy, but also engaged in economy as the subject of economic activity. The party directly led the national economic activities, determined economic policies, and selected party members as the leaders of economic authorities at all levels to ensure and supervise the implementation of the party's guidelines and policies.

The "Stalin model" had two major political characteristics. Firstly, high centralization of power. It was mainly manifested firstly in no separation between the Party work and the government work and taking the party as the government itself. As for the relationship between the Soviet authorities and the Soviet congress, the legislative power was in the hands of the Supreme Soviet organ, and the Soviets at various levels had replaced the functions of the Soviet congresses at all levels. With regard to relation between the party and the government, Stalin believed that the party was the core of the state's power. "Cadres are the General Staff of the party and since our party is a ruling party, thus they are the Genaral Staff of the state leadership."[85]

The power of the various levels of the Soviet Union was concentrated in the Party department. Since the 16th National Congress of CPSU (Bolshevik), departments "leading production" were established in the Central Committee of the Party and the leading organs of Party organizations at all levels in the Soviet republics, provinces and regions. At that time there were Department of Agriculture, Department of Industry, Department

85 Stalin's Anthology (1934-1952), 1st edition, Beijing, People's Publishing House, 1985, p. 269.

of Transport, Department of Planning, Finance and Trade and Department of Culture in the Central Committee of CPSU (Bolshevik). After the 18th National Congress of CPSU (Bolshevik), department of school affairs was added. The party had the same set of departments as the government did, which led to no separation between the Party work and the government work. The party organs were nationalized; the Party agencies at all levels were performing the function of the government offices; and the Party directly intervened in the daily affairs of the government. Secondly, regarding the central and local relations, the local power was centralized to the central government; the authorities of administrative division approval and economic management were further centralized to the central Union; important decisions at all levels of society were made by the central Union. The central Union had the power to decide on national economic plans, to manage banks, and to manage industrial and agricultural institutions, enterprises and businesses with national significance. Thirdly, the highest power in the Party was centralized on one person, gradually forming individual dictatorship. In 1936, Soviet Constitution stipulated that the Soviet Union would implement the collective heads of state system, which in fact was not executed well. In May 1941, Stalin was the Party's general secretary and the chairman of the Council of People's Commissars. In June, he gained the title of the chairman of the National Defense Commission. His full control of the Party, government and military led to the serious consequences of personality cult.

Secondly, the administrative coercion. In the major affairs, remarks and decisions, administrative coercion was mostly applied. Stalin believed that, "the method of persuasion is the basic method for the party to lead the working class"[86], but when a few people could not be persuaded, that is "if a few don't get persuaded, if the minority refuses to voluntarily accord with the will of the majority, it should be forced to do so."[87] The National Congress of CPSU (Bolshevik) adopted the measure of handling the opposition view within the organization, and even annihilation, resulting in the weakening democracy within the party and the powerless democratic supervision. In 1934, in order to strengthen one-man management, the Soviet Union disbanded the mass supervision organization and canceled the Party supervisory committee and workers and farmers' procuratorate. The central supervisory committee that was elected in Party congress and parallel with the Central Committee was replaced by the supervisory committee that was appointed by the Central Committee of the Party; the workers and farmers' procuratorate was replaced by the Soviet supervisory commission led by Council of People's Commissars. The functions of the new supervisory

86 Stalin's Anthology, 1st edition, Beijing, People's Publishing House, 1979, p. 427.
87 Ibid., p. 428.

organs were only to monitor the implementation of the party and government resolutions. The regulations on the state supervision of the Council of People's Commissars passed in 1940 had no provision that encouraged the workers to participate in the supervision, which had turned people's supervision on the central organs, party cadres, state organs and its staff into top-down supervision. The essence of supervision had changed.

Culturally, the "Stalin model" had two major features. Firstly, great importance was attached to the education of Marxist-Leninist theory. In order to cultivate the moral quality of the new communist generations, Stalin personally guided and participated in the compilation of the Brief History of the CPSU (Bolshevik). He pointed out that, "The old habits and customs, traditions and prejudices inherited from the old society are most dangerous enemies of socialism. They—these traditions and habits—have a firm grip over millions of working people; at times they engulf whole strata of the proletariat; at times they present a great danger to the very existence of the proletarian dictatorship. That is why the struggle against these traditions and habits, their absolute eradication in all spheres of our activity, and, lastly, the education of the younger generations in the spirit of proletarian socialism, represent immediate tasks for our Party without the accomplishment of which socialism cannot triumph."[88] Since the 1930s, the Soviet Union had gradually set up courses such as philosophy, political economy and Marxism-Leninism, and called on people to systematically study Marxism-Leninism. It had played a positive role in upholding the guiding position of Marxism in the field of ideology. But in this process, there was a tendency to dogmatize Marxism and Leninism.

Secondly, much emphasis was put on developing the science and technology and strengthening cultural and educational undertakings. In order to speed up the development of science and technology and improve the cultural level of the working class and the working masses, Stalin put forward the slogan of "technology is everything in the transformation period", emphasizing the universal education for the workers. In the 1930s when the capitalism was in economic crisis and needed to explore the international market for its large number of scientific and technological achievements and equipments, the Soviet Union actively introduced foreign technologies and equipments. Meanwhile, the four years universal education was implemented. In the rural areas and industrial villages, seven years of compulsory education was implemented, giving millions of working people and their children access to education and scientific and cultural knowledge. However, the Soviet Union had attached the class properties to natural sciences. For instance, there were the proletarian biology and

88 Stalin Complete Works, 1st Chinese edition, Vol. 6, Beijing, People's Publishing House, 1956, p. 217.

bourgeois biology in the Soviet Union's natural science literature, which had put some biologist influence in the world into the ranks of bourgeois biology. This kind of philosophy and practice hindered the development of natural science.

2. The influence of the "Stalin Model" on the socialist countries

When the Soviet government was just established, the "Stalin model", as a product of specific historical conditions, was an important impetus for mobilizing the country's economic and political forces to deal with the imperialist encirclement and blockade and build the Soviet Union into a strong industrial power. It was the adoption of the "Stalin model" that the Soviet Union, through two five-year plans, implemented the industrialization and agricultural collectivization. The public ownership of the means of production dominated the national economy; the exploiting class was eliminated; and the society consisted of workers, collective farmers and intellectuals. It was the adoption of the "Stalin model" that the Soviet Union had established the guiding position of Marxism in the ideological field and the political system of proletarian dictatorship. Therefore, the implementation of "Stalin model" was adapted to the productive forces and construction tasks of the Soviet Union at that time.

However, with the change of socialism practice conditions, the drawbacks of Stalin model were becoming increasingly obvious, including the single form of ownership, the simple planned economic system, the overly emphasis on the development of heavy industry, the dictatorship of a few leaders, and the lack of sound supervision mechanism within the party, which had not only a negative impact on the Soviet Union's own socialist construction, but also an extensive and far-reaching impact on the subsequent socialist countries in Eastern Europe.

The socialist countries established after the Soviet Union adopted the "Stalin model" which had played a positive role in their socialist construction, laid a relatively solid material foundation for their large-scale socialist transformation and construction and provided important Political security. However, because this model was indiscriminately copied by those socialist countries regardless of their own national conditions, it had also adversely affected their construction and development of socialism. One of its main manifestations was that excessive pursuit of high speed and priority development of heavy industry caused imbalance of national economy, lagged development of light industry and agriculture and declining people's living standards. For instance, Romania copied the socialist development model of the Soviet Union, regardless of the demands of people's lives and national strength, in excessive pursuit of high accumulation, high indicators and high speed, causing large scale of industrial construction, negligence of agricultural production and serious imbalance of national economic proportion. During the administration of Ceausescu, about one-third of national income was spent on the accumulation and people's living standards were rising slowly. In Romania, the economy was feeble, technology backward and economic system highly centralized. A highly centralized Soviet socialist development model was also adopted in Poland. During the six-year plan (1950-1955), the industrial production developed; however, the overly emphasis on the development of heavy industry and the high accumulation rate had undermined the balance of the national economy. Agricultural production decreased and light industry and agricultural was lagging behind, which led to tight market supply and rising prices. It not only affected the healthy development of the entire national economy, but also directly affected the improvement of people's living standards. The second one was the enlargement of class struggle, individual arbitrariness, Party purging and the lack of democracy, causing a series of unjust cases. For instance, the integrated system of Party and government and family ruling were implemented in Romania. As for the leadership system, the posts at all level of Party organs and government offices were held by the same official; the secretaries of the party committee at all levels were also the leaders of the same level of administrative offices. There was no no separation between the Party work and the government work; the government functions were performed by the Party organs; and the power was highly centralized. For a long time, Ceausescu individually held the highest positions of the Party, government and military, resulting in personality cult and individual arbitrariness. In order to consolidate its dominance, Ceausescu appointed a large number of his family members, implementing the family ruling system. In the process of China's socialist construction, a highly centralized planned economic system was established, and left-leaning political mistakes were made. At the beginning of 1957, a small number of Rightist elements had attacked the Party and when countering this attack Mao Zedong made a false estimate on the fundamental social contradiction in the society and expanded the scope of the anti-rightist struggle. At the third plenary session of the eighth Central Committee of the CPC in 1957, Mao Zedong clearly pointed out that the main contradictions of the socialist society were the contradiction between the proletariat and the bourgeoisie and the contradiction between the socialist path and the capitalist path. In 1959, Mao Zedong wrongly launched a fight against "right opportunism". At the Lushan Meeting, Peng Dehuai and Zhang Wentian's criticism of the "Great Leap Forward" and the people's commune movement was evaluated and classified by Mao Zedong as the continuation of the fight between the bourgeoisie and the proletariat in the course of the socialist revolution in the past decade. The class struggle outside of the Party was extended into the Party and inner-party political life was deteriorated. In the early 1960s, Mao Zedong stressed that at the whole historical stage of the socialism development the bourgeoisie would exist and attempt to restore, which was the root cause of revisionism within the party. He believed that the class struggle must be focused on year after year, month after month, and day after day. Later the wrong slogans of "taking the class struggle as the top priority" and "class struggle solves all problems" were put forward. The class struggle was gradually intensified and eventually led to a decade of "Cultural Revolution". Since the 1950s, the Eurasian socialist countries had carried out reforms aiming at the drawbacks of the "Stalin model" and explored the socialist development path with their own characteristics. Some countries had failed in the exploration, leading to the collapse of socialism. The socialist China embodied the essence of socialism in its specific practice during the exploration process and explored a socialist development path with Chinese characteristics.

3. "Stalin Model" and the collapse of the Soviet Union

In the Soviet Union, after the death of Stalin, the successive leaders realized the drawbacks of the "Stalin model", but failed to fundamentally remove this model in the institutional reform. Khrushchev's institutional reform was to economically adjust the policy and restructure the administration and politically criticize personality cult of Stalin and correct the mistakes in the extension of counter-revolutionaries elimination. Different from Khrushchev, Brezhnev's institutional reform was bolder in economic reform by expanding the autonomy of enterprises, strengthening the role of economic leverage and linking the workers' interests with corporate profitability. But in politics, Brezhnev was more conservative and basically did not touch the drawbacks of highly-centralized political system. Although the successive leaders of CPSU after Stalin had all carried out institutional reforms, they were just establishing their own personality cult by eliminating the personality cult of Stalin. Individual arbitrariness was enhanced, instead of being weakened. In March 1985, Gorbachev served as general secretary of the Central Committee of CPSU. When Gorbachev came to power, the Soviet Union was stuck with difficulties and problems and the economy was in a state of stagnation. In the face of the Soviet Union situation, Gorbachev started from the reform of the economic system by promoting the reform of the state-owned enterprise and expanding the autonomy of the enterprises. The policies of self-compensation, self-funding, labor collective's self-governance and full economic accounting system were implemented; there was also macroeconomic management system reforms, including the abolition of the mandatory plan, the reform of the price system and financial credit system, and the diversification of the form of ownership. After three years (1983-1986) of economic reform, the Soviet Union's economic situation had been improved. However, at the plenary meeting of the Central Committee of CPSU in January 1987, Gorbachev thought that there was an "obstacle mechanism" in the Soviet society that hindered socio-economic development and technological progress, and the party and the people had to change their minds and abandon the old ways of thinking and practice patterns. In 1986, Gorbachev's "Perestroika: New Thinking for Our Country and the World" was published. In this book, he argued that the concepts and thinking methods under the guidance of Marxism-Leninism shall be abandoned and put forward the thinking of "the interests of human being above all". In 1988, Gorbachev explicitly summed up the new thinking as "humane democratic socialism" and made it the goal of the Soviet Communist Party. At the 28th Congress of the Communist Party of the Soviet Union in July 1990, after a heated debate, a series of documents were passed, including a Programmatic Statement entitled as "Towards a Humane and Democratic Socialism" and constitution of the Communist Party of the Soviet Union. In this way, "humane and democratic socialism" was written into the party program. Gorbachev's "humane and democratic socialism" aimed to explain that socialism was the principle and process of organizing social life that could be practiced under any social conditions. What he called as the "socialist principles" referred to the principles of humanitarianism and universal human values, the principles of democracy and freedom, the principle of social justice, patriotism and internationalism, which were based on ethical values.

What he called the "socialist process" was not limited to the socialist countries but included the developed capitalist countries where the socialist characteristics existed. The "humane and democratic socialism" actually neglected the distinction between capitalist and socialist social systems as well as the essential requirements of socialism, consequently with such principles the reform in the Soviet Union has slid into capitalism.

After the 28th Congress of the Communist Party of the Soviet Union, "humane and democratic socialism" was fully implemented in Soviet Union. Openness, democratization and socialist pluralism became the three "reform banners" of the CPSU.

The direction and goals of the Soviet Union's political system reform saw substantial changes. After its establishment, the opposition party of the Soviet often held large-scale rallies and seize the opportunity of local elections fight for the power. By the first half of 1991, among the 15 republics of Soviet Union, the CPSU had lost control of eight republics and several major cities including Moscow. At that time in the Soviet Union, the economy was plummeting; national income saw an absolute negative growth; the government was burdened with domestic and foreign debts; commodities were in short supply; prices were rising; people's living standards were declining; and about one-third of the population lived below the official poverty line. At the same time, social contradictions deepened; ethnic conflicts intensified; and the Republics were calling for independence. On August 19, 1991, Soviet Union Vice President Yanayev together with some Party, government and military leaders took the urgent measure of setting up an "emergency Committee" to restore order and stop the independence of the Republics, but they failed. After the "8·19" incident, the Soviet Union more openly implemented the capitalism. Russian President Boris Yeltsin took this opportunity to oppose and ban the activities of the Communist Party and later prohibited the Communist Party. Gorbachev made compromises and concessions. On August 23, he resigned from the post of General Secretary of the Central Committee of the CPSU and proposed voluntary dissolution of the Central Committee of the Soviet Union Communist Part. In this way, the Soviet Union that had existed for nearly a century collapsed.

Was it the drawbacks of "Stalin model" that had caused the disintegration of the Soviet Union? It can be argued that the rigidity of the "Stalin model" had led to the stagnation of the development of the Soviet Union's national economy, caused the political corruption and bureaucracy of the Soviet Union, and left Gorbachev with a mess to deal with. Therefore, the drawbacks of "Stalin model" had a certain impact on the collapse of the Soviet Union. But it could not directly lead to the disintegration of the Soviet Union. Because of the "Stalin model", the Soviet Union turned itself from a backward agricultural country into advanced industrial country within a short period of time. During the Second World War, the tanks and aircrafts of the Soviet Union were better in the number and quality than those of Japan. By the 1980s, the production of many industrial products had surpassed the United States and became the first in the world. Certainly, one of the biggest mistakes of the "Stalin model" was to have overly put emphasis on development of heavy industry and military industry and consumed too much valuable resources and technological strength, ignoring the development of the backward agriculture and light industry and affecting the improvement of people's living standards. The drawbacks of the Stalin model could be eliminated in the development of socialism. With its economic strength in steel, aerospace and military, the Soviet Union was able to produce light industrial products and change the backward state of agriculture.

During the disintegration of the Soviet Union, there were very few people in the leadership of the CPSU who truly wanted to maintain the socialist system and adhere to the socialist path. In 1991, a survey of the high-level party and government officials of the CPSU by a social issues research institute of the United States found that, 76.7% of these officials believed that the Soviet Union should implement capitalism, 12.3% of them had democratic socialist point of view, and some even made it clear that they were just a Party member, not a communist. The Soviet Union's reform only considered the interests of the persons in power who became not only managers of the means of production, but also the owner of the means of production. Their personal wealth was constantly expanding. After the disintegration of the Soviet Union, officials of the Soviet Communist Party at all levels became the "new elite" in Russia, who justifiably passed on the social wealth they had embezzled to their descendants. This situation showed that the CPSU had lost the public support and could no longer represent the majority of the people. It can be seen that the collapse of Soviet socialism was directly related to the qualitative change of the highest leadership. With so many high-level party and government officials who wanted to take the capitalist path, the collapse of Soviet socialism was doomed. The influence of the drawbacks of the "Stalin model" on the collapse of Soviet socialism was undoubtedly exerted through the qualitative change of the Soviet leaders. The fundamental reason for the collapse of Soviet socialism was to have blurred the essence of socialism and abandoned the socialist system.

In the development of socialism, we must adhere to the nature of socialism, the public ownership, the dominance of distribution according to work and the ultimate goal of common prosperity of all the people. Only by adhering to the essence of socialism can we absorb and introduce all the positive capitalist elements good for socialism to better develop socialism in the coexistence with capitalism, be free from capitalist containment, and resist the penetration of capitalism in spirit, culture, ideology and other aspects, thus smashing conspiracy of Western hostile forces using economic power to achieve their political purpose and ensuring the nature of the socialist country. Only by adhering to the essence of socialism can we uphold the principle of self-reliance in opening to the outside world, and earn wide respect and have a significant political influence in the world. Only by adhering to the essence of socialism can we reflect on the setbacks and mistakes in the development of Soviet socialism, sum up experience, enhance our abilities and avoid similar or bigger mistakes or greater setbacks. Only by upholding the essence of socialism can we guarantee that the overwhelming majority of the people can benefit from the achievements of socialist modernization.

(Zhang Leisheng, Professor of Institute of Marxism Studies, Renmin University of China)

All-round Development of Human Being and Socialism with Chinese Characteristics

The all-round development of human being is a core thought and fundamental principle of Marxism. At the new stage of the new century, the Communist Party of China, according to the Marxist theory of human's all-round development, reveals the importance of the all-round development of mankind to building a well-off society in an all-round and promoting the development of the cause of socialism, and explains a series of essential issues in implementing important thoughts of "Three Represents" and Scientific Outlook on Development, promoting the comprehensive development of the people on the path of socialism with Chinese characteristics and achieving the great rejuvenation of the Chinese nation, which have raised our understanding of socialism to a new level.

1. The all-round development of human being is the ideal goal of scientific socialism

Man is the subject of social history and the protagonist of the "performance" at the world stage. The development of human beings is not only the result of social and historical activities, but also the measure of social and historical progress. Therefore, the realization of all-round development of human being has become the pursuit and ideal goal of the visionary thinkers, politicians and other people with lofty ideals in all ages. As early as the ancient Greek period, the ideas of "perfect individual" and "humanitarian spirit" had formed. In the middle ages, the nature of man was alienated into mighty and all-knowing God, with the concept of all-round development of human being distorted. After the Renaissance, the humanists gradually broke the repression and bondage of religious theology on human nature, and directly affirmed the comprehensive development of people. As the American scholar Corliss Lamont said, "For the Renaissance, the ideal human being was no longer the ascetic monk, but a new type—the so-called universal or 'Renaissance man', who was a many-sided personality, delighting in every kind of this-earthly achievement."[89] Later, the utopian socialists condemned capitalism for turning man into the slave of machine and undermining human integrity. In the new society they envision, all people shall be well educated in morality, intelligence, physique and manner and become comprehensively developed. Marx and Engels not only inherited the outstanding achievements regarding all-round development of human being in the history of mankind, but also on the basis of dialectical and

89 Corliss Lamont, The Philosophy of Humanism, Humanist Press, Amherst-New York, 1997, p. 21.

historical materialism and scientific socialism further revealed the scientific implication and realistic conditions of the all-round development of human being, which had provided a sharp theoretical weapon for the liberation of the proletariat and all mankind. If you systematically study and grasp the relevant discussion of the Marxist classic writers, you will find that the all-round development of human being has multi-level connotations: The comprehensive development of personal activities. As individuals were confined to particular occupation or profession by the old division of labor, resulting in unbalanced personal development, Marx and Engels proposed that individuals shall adapt to different social demands and consider different occupations as changeable living manners, to achieve the comprehensive development. They believed that, individuals "are subordinated to division of labour, which makes him one-sided, cripples and determines him".[90] Therefore this old-style division of labor should be eliminated to let individuals develop in an all-round way.

(1) Fully developed individual, "fit for a variety of labours, ready to face any change of production, and to whom the different social functions he performs, are but so many modes of giving free scope to his own natural and acquired powers".[91]

(2) The comprehensive development of the individual's ability. Personal ability includes innate and acquired, physical and intellectual, truth-pursuing, kind and aesthetic abilities. In the view of Marx and Engels, "vocation, designation and task of every person is to achieve all-round development of his abilities, including, for example, the ability to think,"[92] and in this society "the development of members of society in all aspects will be attained"[93] They also oppose the prejudice treating people as pure labor and advocated that people's various talents shall be encouraged so that they to play their role, including sports, art and other creative talents.

(3) The overall formation and expansion of social relations between people. This means that people could free themselves from the limitations of division of labor, territory class, nation and state, and actively and extensively participate in social communications, so that people's social relations are diverse and universal and they really become the action, so that people's social relations are rich and universal, people really become "social individuals". Marx said that the comprehensiveness of the individual was not in the imagination or conception, but in his realistic and idealistic relations. Only by being more and more involved in social interaction in

90 Marx-Engels Complete Works, 1st Chinese Edition, Vol. 3, Beijing, People's Publishing House, 1960, p. 514.

91 Marx, Capital, Vol. 1, Beijing, China Social Sciences Press, 1983, p. 500.

92 Marx-Engels Complete Works, 1st Chinese edition, Volume 3, p. 330.

93 Marx-Engels Collected Works, Vol. 1, p. 689.

various fields at all levels, thus having universal exchange with the material and spiritual production of the whole world, can people be free from the limitations of individual, region and nation, and fully develop their various abilities and free personalities.

(4) The development of everyone, instead of only a few. In other words, "all-round development of human" is applicable to all members of society. The one-sided viewpoint that allows some people to develop but forbids others to do so shall be resisted. The founder of Marxism not only advocates that the free development of the individual is the condition of social or group development, but also stresses that social or group development is the prerequisite for personal development. The comprehensive development of mankind can never be achieved in the situation of the confrontation between men and the separation between individuals and the society; it can only be realized in the condition of harmony among people and between man and the society.

Marxism not only clarifies the scientific meaning of human's all-round development, but also closely links it with the evolution of social form and the reform of social system, to reveal the objective laws of social development and the realistic way of human's all-round development. In Marx's view, human development, being the process of unity with the social development, would generally go through three stages:

(1) In the pre-capitalist period, "human dependence" was the first social form. Under this social form, the level of productive forces was very low; self-sufficient natural economy dominates; people's relations in the production process, namely the relation between them and their relationship with the nature, are very narrow; human ability is only developing within the narrow range and isolated places.

(2) In the capitalist society, the independence of the people based on the substance-dependence is the second major form. Under this form, the free competition of the commodity economy dominates, personal dependence relation and hierarchical system are broken; in which a system of general social metabolism, of universal relations, of all-round needs and universal capacities is formed for the first time."[94]

This economic form on the one hand makes people's development be fettered by thing enslavement and capital ownership, on the other hand creates conditions for free personality and the comprehensive development of human. As Marx said, "Universally developed individuals, whose social relations, as their own communal [gemeinschaftlich] relations, are hence also subordinated to their own communal control, are no product of

94 Marx-Engels Collected Works, Vol. 8, Beijing, People's Publishing House, 2009, p. 52.

nature, but of history. The degree and the universality of the development of wealth where this individuality becomes possible supposes production on the basis of exchange values as a prior condition, whose universality produces not only the alienation of the individual from himself and from others, but also the universality and the comprehensiveness of his relations and capacities."[95]

(3) In the communist society, the free personality based on the comprehensive development of human and the social wealth created by their common social productive capacity is the third stage of human development. At this stage, private ownership and old-fashioned division of labor were eliminated; exploitation and oppression on people and the products' control over the producer have been overcome; and free and all-round development of human being develops into reality. As Engels said, "With the seizing of the means of production by society production of commodities is done away with, and, simultaneously, the mastery of the product over the producer. Anarchy in social production is replaced by systematic, definite organization."[96] "The laws of his own social action, hitherto standing face to face with man as laws of nature foreign to, and dominating him, will then be used with full understanding, and so mastered by him. Man's own social organisation, hitherto confronting him as a necessity imposed by nature and history, now becomes the result of his own free action...To accomplish this act of universal emancipation is the historical mission of the modern proletariat."[97]

Since the creation of scientific socialism, Marx and Engels had taken the all-round development of human being as an ideal goal and fundamental principle of socialism. As early as the 1840s, in the German Ideology, the founders of Marxism had pointed out: "the all-round realisation of the individual will only cease to be conceived as an ideal…when the impact of the world which stimulates the real development of the abilities of the individual is under the control of the individuals themselves, as the communists desire."[98]

In the Communist Manifesto, they again stressed, "In place of the old bourgeois society, with its classes and class antagonisms, we shall have an association, in which the free development of each is the condition for the free development of all."[99]

95 Ibid., p. 56.

96 Marx-Engels Collected Works, Vol. 3, Beijing, People's Publishing House, 2009, p. 564.

97 Ibid., p. 566.

98 Marx-Engels Collected Works, Vol. 3, Beijing, People's Publishing House, 2009, p. 330.

99 Marx-Engels Collected Works, Vol. 2, Beijing, People's Publishing House, 2009, p. 53.

In the Capital, Marx further generalized "Everyone's liberty and comprehensive development as the "Fundamental Principles"[100] of social form higher than capitalism. By the end of the nineteenth century, the Italian Canepa asked Engels to write an inscription for the forthcoming "New Era" weekly, to explain the basic characteristics of the new era of future socialism in order to distinguish from the old era Dante had described as "some is ruling and others suffering". In his reply, Engels wrote, "I intend to find out one from Marx's work, the inscription you are looking for... Marx is the only socialist in contemporary times who can compare with the great Florentines (Dante)."[101]

When quoting the above sentences, I couldn't find any other appropriate ones. This glorious thought of the founders of Marxism had pointed out the correct direction for the theory and practice of socialism. By the beginning of the 20th century, Lenin insisted that "not only to satisfy the needs of its members, but with the object of ensuring full well-being and free, all-round development for all the members of society,"[102] should be written into the program of Russian Social Democratic Labor Party. For more than a century, communists and progressive people in the world have made great progress in eliminating the exploitation and oppression on the proletariat and the working people and striving for liberation and all-round development, which has opened up a new era of human historical development.

2. The all-round development of human being is the essential requirement of socialism with Chinese characteristics

Human development, limited by economic, political and cultural development level, shall go through a long historical process. In the capitalist society, the capital has turned all the activities of people and their products into exchange value, which causes the appreciation of things and the devaluation of people. The capitalist system of production regards people as the tool for creating wealth. It focuses on people only for gaining more surplus value from people. Capitalist production facilities, organization and management system do not follow the principles of "human being the subject" and "human being the purpose", but serve for the needs of pursuing surplus value and monopoly profits. Therefore, although capitalism, to some extent, have promoted the development of science and technology and productive forces and let people get a certain degree of independence and personality liberation, it cannot consciously use material and spiritual productivity for the comprehensive development of human beings. Under

100 Marx-Engels Collected Works, Vol. 5, Beijing, People's Publishing House, 2009, p. 683.

101 Marx-Engels Collected Works, Vol. 10, Beijing, People's Publishing House, 2009, p. 666.

102 Lenin Complete Works, Chinese 2nd edition, Vol. 6, Beijing, People's Publishing House, 1986, p. 218.

the capitalist exploitation system, the development of the working class is bound to be unbalanced, instrumental and limited. The capitalists would be "the empty minded capitalists would be enslaved to his own capital and his insane craving for profits", And "the educated classes" are enslaved—in general—to their manifold species of local narrow-mindedness and to their own physical and mental short-sightedness enslaved".[103] Classic writers of Marxism have revealed that the future communist society will make "them give full play to their abilities and achieve all round development,"[104] to eventually achieve the ideal state of comprehensive development of the society and humans, clarified the essential characteristics of the socialist new society separating itself from the capitalist old society and its historical inevitability and superiority, and showed the ultimate concern of the scientific socialism for the future and destiny of human.

The highest ideal of the Chinese Communist Party is to build a communist society featuring as "from each according to his ability" and "to each according to his work". Whether it is in the past, present or future, this supreme ideal was, is and will always be the source of strength and spiritual pillar of Communists and progressives. And the construction of socialism with Chinese characteristics is the inevitable stage toward the highest ideal. Marxism shows that people's all-round development is not only a historical process that has different realization degree at different development stages, but also a value goal that shall be strived for in the socialist society till the realization of communism. As early as 1978, Deng Xiaoping made it clear: "Our schools are places for the training of competent personnel for socialist construction. Are there qualitative standards for such training? Yes, there are. They were stated by Comrade Mao Zedong: We should enable everyone who receives an education to develop morally, intellectually and physically and become a worker possessed of both socialist consciousness and a general education".[105] In 1985, he again stressed that, "while building a socialist society with Chinese characteristics, we must continue to promote not only material progress but also cultural and ideological progress. We must uphold the principle of the "five things to emphasize", "four things to beautify" and "three things to love" and encourage all our people to have lofty ideals and moral integrity, to become better educated and to cultivate a strong sense of discipline... What we are striving for is the cause of socialism, and our the ultimate goal is to achieve communism. On this issue, I hope that efforts should not be neglected at any time."[106]

---

103 Marx-Engels Collected Works, Vol. 9, People's Publishing House, Beijing, 2009. p. 309.

104 Marx-Engels Collected Works, Vol. 1, p. 689.

105 Deng Xiaoping Selected Works, 1994, 2nd edition, People's Publishing House, Beijing, p. 103.

106 Deng Xiaoping Selected Works, 1993, 1st edition, People's Publishing House, Beijing, p. 110.

Therefore, the "Four Things to Beautify" has become the fundamental standard for strengthening spiritual civilization aspect of building socialism and cultivating a comprehensively developed new generation of socialism. In 1992 when he made the Southern İnspection Tour, Deng Xiaoping further proposed, "the essence of socialism is to liberate and develop productive forces, eliminate exploitation, and polarization, and finally achieve common prosperity.

When judging whether the opening up policy is successful or not he proposed the criteria: "The chief criterion for making that judgement should be whether it promotes the growth of the productive forces in a socialist society, increases the overall strength of the socialist state and raises living standards."[107] From the unity between productive forces and production relations and the unity between the fundamental task and long-term goal, Deng Xiaoping clarified the material foundation, political guarantee and other social conditions for China at the present stage to promote the comprehensive development of human. At the conference in the celebration of the 80th anniversary of the founding of the Communist Party of China, Comrade Jiang Zemin declared, "We firmly believe that the basic principle of Marxism that human society will inevitably move towards communism. Communism can only be achieved on the basis of fully and highly developed socialist society. In the Communist society, there will be an overwhelming abundance of material wealth and people will have a very high realm of thought and be able to develop themselves freely and in an all-round way."[108] "Our various undertakings of building socialism with Chinese characteristics and all our work shall focus not only on people's material and cultural needs, but also on the improvement of people's quality, namely people's comprehensive development. This is the essential requirement of Marxism on building a new socialist society. We must continue to push forward the all-round development of human beings on the basis of developing the socialist material and spiritual civilization of the socialist society."[109] As we all know, people are the decisive force in production. It is necessary to constantly improve people's quality and ability in all aspects and promote their comprehensive development, in order to liberate and develop productive forces. The elimination of exploitation and polarization, the ultimate realization of common prosperity and liberating people from a variety of social constraints create the necessary social conditions for the all-round development of human. It is undoubtedly the enrichment and development of the Party's theory of the essence of socialism to solemnly incorporate the all-round development

107 Ibid., p. 372.

108 Selected Literature since the 15th National Congress, (Volume II), Beijing, People's Publishing House, 2003, p. 1924.

109 Selected Literature since the 15th National Congress (Volume II), p. 1925.

of human being into the programmatic document of Communist Party of China.

Regarding the all-round development of human being, we should adhereto the dialectical unity of ideals and reality, and the dialectical unity of maximum program and the minimum program. In other words, we can neither put forward the goal of the free and all-round development of each person which could only be achieved at the advanced stage of communism, nor publicize the "slim chance" of communism and ignore the practical requirements of the ideal goal and fundamental principle of all-round human development with the excuse of China's long-term socialist primary stage. Poverty is not socialism; there is no democracy without democracy. Similarly, if people's all-round development cannot be promoted, it is not real socialism. On the basis of the coordinated development of socialist economy, politics and culture, the continuous development of human being is the embodiment of the advanced nature of the Communist Party and the superiority of the socialist system. One of the reasons that socialism has failed in some countries is the serious hinderance of all-round development of people caused by rigid thinking and institutional structure, unreasonable economic structure, slow pace of improvement in people's lives and the flaws in establishing democracy and rule of law. Only by making all-round human development as the essential requirement and goal of socialism with Chinese characteristics can we really adhere to and develop Marxism and truly consolidate and develop socialism.

3. Socialism with Chinese characteristics is a realistic way to promote the all-round development of human being

On the one hand, the founders of Marxism affirmed the historical role of capitalism in the development of productive forces and human beings, and argued that the capitalism "has created the elements of a new economic system, also greatly promoted the productive forces of social and all-round development of all producers."[110] On the other hand, they had profoundly criticized the deformity of the men's development caused by capitalism, and believed that the labor was not free but alienated and people were having comprehensive development but unbalanced development. Only through the socialist revolution and construction can we completely clear the obstacles and open the way for the comprehensive development of mankind, because the fundamental reasons hindering the comprehensive development of human beings are the low productivity and the resulting spontaneous division of labor, private ownership, class opposition, class exploitation and class rule. When the great social revolution controls the fruits of the bourgeois era, the world market and modern productive forces,

110 Marx-Engels Collected Works, Vol. 3, People's Publishing House, Beijing, 2009. p. 465.

and made it all subject to the co-supervision of the most advanced peoples, human progress will not be like the horrible pagan God who only drinks the sweet wine with the glass made of the head of the murdered. The comprehensive development of man, the development of social economy, politics and culture and the improvement of people's life standards are interrelated and mutually promote each other.

Deng Xiaoping said clearly, "The socialist economy is based on public ownership, and socialist production is designed to meet the material and cultural needs of the people to the maximum extent possible—not to exploit them. These characteristics of the socialist system make it possible for the people of our country to share common political, economic and social ideals and moral standards." "If China abandoned that path, it would return to its semi-colonial and semi-feudal status, and the Chinese people would not have enough food and clothing, let alone become prosperous."[111]

China has a large population, a weak foundation and low per capita hold of resources. If we take the capitalist path, we will make the very few people get rich quickly and have our people fall into the abyss of poverty and turmoil. Under the conditions of the vast majority of people suffering shortage of food and clothing, sharp social contradictions and political turmoil, to pursue the all-round development of people is nothing else but fantasy. The fundamental reason why our party insists on sticking to the path of socialism with Chinese characteristics lies in the superiority of the socialist system and its guarantee for the country's prosperity, social progress and the comprehensive development of each person.

At the new stage of the new century, the CPC Central Committee propose to firmly establish and earnestly implement the people-oriented, comprehensive, coordinated and sustainable scientific development concept, and formulated a series of policies to comprehensively build a well-off society and promote the comprehensive development of human beings. In March 2004, Comrade Hu Jintao made it clear at the central symposium on the population, resources and environment that, "to adhere to the people-oriented idea is to take the all-round development of human being as the goal, promote development for the fundamental interests of the people, continuously meet the people's growing material and cultural needs, and effectively protect the people's economic, political and cultural rights, so that the achievements of development benefit all the people."[112] "We shall establish and implement the scientific concept of development, promote the comprehensive social progress and the all-round development of people on the basis of economic development, and promote the coordinated development

111 Deng Xiaoping Selected Works, 1st ed., Vol. 3, p. 206.

112 Selected Literature since the 16th National Congress, Volume I, Beijing, Central Party Literature Press, 2005, p. 850.

of socialist material civilization, political civilization and spiritual civilization."[113] This is a new achievement with great and far-reaching guiding significance achieved by the Chinese Communist Party's profound summarization of the historical experience of China's reform, opening up and modernization and the development lessons of other countries in the world, and deepening the understanding of communist party's ruling laws, socialist construction laws and human developing laws.

Economically, we must adhere to and improve the basic economic system with the socialist public ownership as the mainstay and the common development of diverse forms of ownership, the diversified distribution forms with distribution according to work being dominant and the socialist market economy system, so as to develop social productive forces and create a solid material and technological basis for the comprehensive development of people. In particular, we must adhere to the party's policy of enriching the people, strive to increase the income of urban and rural residents, constantly improve people's eating, wearing, living and traveling conditions, improve the social security system, upgrade medical and sanitation facilities, and improve people's life quality. We need to have all our people live a well-off life as soon as possible, keep moving towards a higher level and gradually realize the common prosperity of all the people. Only in this way can we ensure the sustained, rapid and healthy development of the national economy and that economic growth and prosperity is shared by the people.

Politically, we must uphold and improve the people's democratic dictatorship under the leadership of the working class and based on the alliance of workers and farmers, the system of people's congress and multi-party cooperation and political consultation system under the leadership of communist party and the system of regional national autonomy, promote socialist democracy, improve the socialist legal system and build a socialist country under the rule of law, so as to provide firm political security for the comprehensive development of mankind. In particular, we must actively and steadily push forward the reform of the political system, earnestly ensure people's right of being the masters of the country and manage the affairs of the country according to law, and give full play to the people's conscious initiative and great creativity. Only in this way can we create a centralized and democratic, disciplined and free, comfortable and lively political situation with both unified will and comfortable personal feeling.

Culturally, we must uphold the guiding position of Marxism, develop a national, scientific, and popular socialist culture oriented towards modernization, the world and the future, and strives to improve the ideological and moral quality and scientific and cultural quality of the whole nation, so as to

113 Ibid., p. 851.

create a good cultural environment for the comprehensive development of mankind. In particular, we must adhere to the implementation of the strategy of rejuvenating the country through science and education and develop science and education, so that people have the access to education and cultural achievements; we must strengthen the socialist spiritual civilization construction, carry forward the socialist humanitarian spirit, advocate the morality of unity, friendship, mutual cooperation and cooperation, and cultivate a new generation with ideal, morality, culture and discipline. Only in this way can we make people's cultural life more colorful and their spiritual world healthier and more meaningful.

Ecologically, we must adhere to the sustainable development strategy, rationally develop and utilize natural resources, maintain the production and living conditions and ecological balance, promote harmony between man and nature, so as to create a good natural environment for human's all-round development. Nature, the home of human, provides indispensable material resources and living environment for the survival and development of human beings. People's occupying and plundering the nature for the narrow and short-term interest of the individual or group will cause environmental pollution and ecological damage, and eventually destroy the natural foundation for the all-round development of human being. In March 2004, Comrade Hu Jintao stressed at the central symposium on the population, resources and environment that, "To establish and implement the scientific concept of development, we must strive to improve the quality and efficiency of economic growth, achieve the unity of speed, structure, quality and efficiency, maintain the coordination of the economic development, population, resources and environment, and continuously protect and enhance the sustainability of development."[114] This requires us to fully consider the capacity of resources and environment while promoting development, correctly handle the relations between economic development and population, resources and the environment, effectively control environmental pollution and waste of resources, take in to full account the current and future needs of development, and leave the future generations with sufficient development conditions and space. Only in this way can we achieve a virtuous circle of natural ecosystems and socio-economic systems and pioneer a path of civilized development featuring a thriving economy, an affluent life and a sound eco-system. In the harmonious coexistence between man and nature and the common progress of man and the society, the progressive realization of everyone's free and comprehensive development is the only way to build a new socialist civilization. Marx once pointed out that, the development of human talent "although this evolution of the species Man is accomplished at first at the expense of the majority of individual human

114 Selected Literature since the 16th National Congress of the CPC, Volume 1, p. 851.

beings and of certain human classes, it finally overcomes this antagonism and coincides with the evolution of the particular individual."[115] The fundamental purpose of our socialist revolution and construction is to overcome this resistance and realize the all-round development of man and society. Only with coordinated development of economy, politics and culture and mutual promotion of material civilization, political civilization and spiritual civilization can it be called the socialism with Chinese characteristics. Certainly, as the development of social productive forces, economy and culture, the all-round development of human being is also a gradually improving, never-ending historical process. We must proceed from the reality of our country, i.e., the primary stage of socialism, do a good job in every work related to reform, opening-up and modernization, and create the conditions for the realization of the free and all-round development of human beings.

(Luo Wendong, researcher of Academy of Marxism, Chinese Academy of Social Sciences)

115 Marx-Engels Collected Works, Vol. 34, People's Publishing House, Beijing, 2008. p. 127.

PART TWO

Innovations in the Theory of Socialism with Chinese Characteristics

Since the Reform and Opening-up, China has made great achievements in the development of socialism. Its fundamental reason lies in blazing the path of socialism with Chinese characteristics and establishing the theoretical system of socialism with Chinese characteristics. The path of socialism with Chinese characteristics is to, under the leadership of the Communist Party of China, based on basic national conditions and with economic construction as the central task, uphold the four basic principles, adhere to Reform and Opening-up, liberate and develop social productive forces, consolidate and improve the socialist system, develop socialist market economy, socialist democracy, advanced socialist culture and harmonious socialist society, and build a prosperous, democratic, civilized and harmonious modern socialist country. The critical reason why we can carve out this path is that we have upheld the basic principles of scientific socialism and endowed them with distinctive Chinese characteristics according to China's reality and the features of the times. The development of the Path of Socialism with Chinese Characteristics is the practical basis for establishing the Theoretical System of Socialism with Chinese Characteristics. The theoretical system of socialism with Chinese characteristics is the forerunner that paves the way for the path of socialism with Chinese characteristics. Since the Reform and Opening-up, the Communist Party of China has made important theoretical innovations in various aspects such as the theory of the main contradictions of socialism, the theory of the primary stage of socialism, the theory of socialist essence, the theory of socialist market economy, and the theory of socialist democratic politics. These theoretical innovations are integrated into the theoretical system of socialism with Chinese characteristics which includes Deng Xiaoping Theory, the important thinking of the "Three Represents" and Scientific Outlook on

Development. The theoretical system of socialism with Chinese characteristics has upheld and developed Marxism-Leninism and Mao Zedong Thought, and contained the wisdom and effort of the Chinese Communist Party in leading the people to explore. It is the latest achievement of localization of Marxism in China, the most valuable political and spiritual treasure and the common ideological foundation for the unity and efforts of the people of all nationalities. The formation of the theoretical system of socialism with Chinese characteristics shows that only exert strong vitality, creativity and inspiration when combined with national conditions and progressing with the times. In contemporary China, to uphold the theoretical system of socialism with Chinese characteristics is to truly adhere to Marxism.

On the Main Contradictions in the Socialist Society

Whether a proletarian party can correctly determine the focus of work and the fundamental task and continuously improve its ability to promote economic and social development after becoming the ruling party depends on its grasp of the historical status of the society and the scientific judgment of the main social contradictions in the society. For the past 60 years of ups and downs since the founding of new China, whether it is triumph or setbacks, it has been closely related with the Chinese Communist Party's understanding of the main contradictions in the socialist society.

1. The initial exploration of the main contradictions in the socialist society

At the beginning of the founding of new China, with the restoration of the national economy, the contradiction between the proletariat and the bourgeoisie, the contradiction between the socialist path and the capitalist path replaced the contradiction between the masses and the remnants of imperialism, feudalism and bureaucratic capitalism, becoming the main social contradiction. Under the guidance of the general line of the Party's transition period, the socialist transformation of China's means of production achieved a decisive victory and China entered the historical period of building socialism in an all-round way.

What is the main contradiction of our society after the establishment of the basic socialist system? At the 8th Congress of the CPC held in 1956, it was made clear that, socialist transformation had achieved a decisive victory, the contradiction between proletariat and the bourgeoisie in China had been basically resolved, and thousands of years of class exploitation system had been basically ended. "The main contradiction in our country has already become the contradiction between the demands of the people for the establishment of an advanced industrial country and the reality of the backward agricultural country, and the contradiction that people's needs for rapid economic and cultural development cannot be met by the current situation of our economy and culture. With the establishment of socialist system in China, the essence of this contradiction is the contradiction between the advanced socialist system and the backward social productive forces. Presently, the main task of the party and all the people is to concentrate on resolving this contradiction and transform China from a backward agricultural country into an advanced industrial country as soon as possible."[1]

1 Selected Literature since the Founding of New China, Vol. 9, Beijing, Central Party Literature Press,1994, pp. 341-342.

Although at the 8th Congress of the CPC, the expression of the main contradictions of the socialist society was not theoretically accurate enough, it had grasped the changes in the main social contradictions and the central task of concentrating on the development of social productive forces. Mao Zedong at first agreed on the judgments of the main social contradictions at the 8th Congress of the CPC. When he met with representatives of foreign parties, he repeatedly mentioned that Stalin's mistakes in expanding the class struggle were due to incompatibility of his knowledge with the objective reality.When the domestic exploitation class had been basically eliminated in the Soviet Union, the application of peaceful methods to protect and develop the productive forces was the right way to go, rather than solving the problem of developing productive forces through the class struggle.

However, after the end of the anti-rightist struggle in 1957, Mao Zedong changed the statement of main social contradictions at the 8th Congress of the CPC. In "On the Correct Handling of Contradictions among the People" published in June 1957, Mao Zedong wrote: "The class struggle between the proletariat and the bourgeoisie, the class struggle between the different political forces, and the class struggle in the ideological field between the proletariat and the bourgeoisie will continue to be long and tortuous and at times will even become very acute. The proletariat seeks to transform the world according to its own world outlook, and so does the bourgeoisie. In this respect, the question of which will win out, socialism or capitalism, is still not really settled."[2] At the Third Plenary Session of the 8th Central Committee of the CPC in October, 1957, Mao Zedong said, "The contradictions between the proletariat and the bourgeoisie and between the socialist path and capitalism path undoubtedly are the main contradictions of our society at present."[3] In 1962, in the Communiqué of the Tenth Plenary Session of the 8th Central Committee of the CPC, Mao Zedong put forward the basic line of the Party in the whole period of socialism, which was During the entire historical period of the proletarian revolution and proletarian dictatorship, and the period of transition from capitalism to communism which might take decades or even more, there would exist the class struggles between the proletariat and the bourgeoisie and between the socialism path and capitalism path. The overthrown reactionary class was reluctant to perish and always trying to come back,"[4] In this case, the class struggle was unavoidable. This class struggle would be inevitably reflected within the party. In 1963, Mao Zedong further proposed "the major task of class struggle". The fact that the class struggle was considered as the center

2 Mao Zedong Collected Works, Vol. 7, Beijing, People's Publishing House, 1999, p. 230.

3 Selected Literature since the Founding of New China, Vol. 10, Beijing, Central Party Literature Press,1994, pp. 606-607.

4 Selected Literature since the Founding of New China, Volume 15, Beijing, Central Party Literature Press,1997, p. 563.

of all work denied the major changes that had occurred in respect to the main social contradictions after the establishment of the basic system of socialism. The expansion of this class struggle developed into the "Cultural Revolution", eventually causing a serious disaster.

Mao Zedong's judgment on the main contradictions of the socialist society was swinging from right to wrong, which was caused by various objective and subjective reasons. But fundamentally, it was because of Mao Zedong's wrong view on what socialism should be and how to build socialism. It was Marx and Engels who developed socialism from utopia into the science world. The founders of scientific socialism living in the era of industrial revolution, based on the economic facts of the full development of the capitalist industry, made a series of logical inferences and predictions of the future society, revealing the general law of social development that socialism will inevitably replace the capitalism. However, Marx and Engels's account of the future socio-economic characteristics is neither a description of a social form that has historically existed, nor a generalization of a social practice that exists in reality. The historical task for Marx and Engels was to "Reveal all forms of conflicts and exploitation of the modern society, analyzed their evolution, has proved their historically temporary nature, finally that such a society would inevitably be replaced by a new form of society"[5], and that we should "scientifically" instead of "sentimentally and subjectively" treat the issue of socialism replacing capitalism. Obviously, their vision of the future society could not be systematic and was not fully discussed or expounded. It could only be abstract and general theoretical assumptions that cannot be applied into specific real life and need to be tested and proved in social practices and enriched and developed in the combination with the new historical environment and specific national conditions

As a great man who advocated the combination of Marxist universal truth and Chinese social practice, Mao Zedong hated dogmatism and had a strong sense of mission for pioneering a socialist construction path suitable for China's conditions. He repeatedly proposed to "learn the lessons of the Soviet Union" and tried to correct Stalin and the Chinese Communist Party's wrong tendency of unrealistic pursuit of quick results beyond the development stages. Unfortunately, Mao Zedong's correct understanding and practice did not consistently go on. After 1956, he not only blurred the difference between the period of overall socialist construction and the previous transition period by regarding the whole socialist stage before entering into communism as the transitional period, but also lost all touch with the reality of China's productive forces in the choice of the mode of socialist overall goal. Regarding the ownership structure, economic system and

5 Lenin's Monographs on Dialectical Materialism and Historical Materialism, Beijing, People's Publishing House, 2009, p. 213.

consumer goods distribution, he "abode by" the individual conclusions of the classic socialism, and basically copied the "Stalin model". For instance, the implementation of public ownership featuring large in size and collective in nature, putting the commodity economy into "capitalist category", emphasizing "plan first, price second", and regarding distribution according to work and wage system as "bourgeois rights". He even followed the experience of the revolutionary war and advocated the use of mass movement to development the economy, carry on revolution and promote production. Even when he suffered from great setbacks and had to face social contradictions and conflicts, he did not focus on the contradiction between backward social production and the growing material and cultural needs of the people, but concentrated on the impact of class struggle on economic construction, and attempted to accelerate the liberation of productive forces through the reaction of production relations. The long-term deviation of the party and government work resulted in two serious consequences. Firstly, the development of social productive forces was ignored, leading to the long-term backwardness of the country. Secondly, the people's material and cultural life improvement was neglected, causing the long-time poverty of the broad masses of the people. Mao Zedong thought that he had found a new way of building socialism in line with Marxism and different from the "Stalin Model" that could develop socialist productive forces faster and better. In fact, he was just continuing the mistakes of Stalin and the socialist construction of the Soviet Union. As Deng Xiaoping later summed up, Mao Zedong's major mistake in the major social contradictions and fundamental task of socialist society was having neglected the development of social productive forces; it is not that he did not want to develop productive forces, but that "the methods used were not all correct".[6]

2. Correct understanding of the main contradictions in the primary stage of socialism

Based on the historical reflection on the practice of Chinese socialism, Deng Xiaoping began to explore the path of building socialism with Chinese characteristics. After the Third Plenary Session of the 11th Central Committee of the Communist Party of China (CPC) in 1978, Deng Xiaoping repeatedly raised the question: "What is socialism and what is Marxism? We were not quite clear about this in the past."[7] Therefore, the most important lesson is that, "we have a clear understanding of what socialism is and how to develop and build it."[8] Deng Xiaoping's rethinking of socialism is related with the historical lessons he concluded that going beyond the stage

6 Deng Xiaoping Selected Works, 1st ed., Vol. 3, p. 116.

7 Ibid., p. 137.

8 Ibid., p. 369.

of social development would lead to wrong understanding of the main social contradictions and his personal judgment was that people's material and cultural life has not been fundamentally improved because of neglecting the development of productive forces.

The replacement of capitalism with socialism is the general law of the development of human history. As a new social form, socialism should be based on mature commodity economy and inherit and use highly developed productive forces of capitalism. In other words, only when the capitalist mode of production develop into the internal relations within the whole social production in the form of commodity production, the workers could equally and directly use and possess the material conditions of production in the social production, "and all the springs of co-operative wealth flow more abundantly", the possession and distribution relation of the whole society could be correspondingly established. At this time, in the association of individuals who have controlled the conditions for their free development, "It is not only possible to ensure that all members of society can live affluent material and cultural lives day by day, but it will be also possible to guarantee them the conditions wherein they can freely develop and utilize their physical and mental strengths."[9]

However, the socialism in contemporary practice is not the "natural birth" out of the highly developed capitalism, but basically born out of colonial or semi-colonial, feudal or semi-feudal countries. It determines that there would be a long way to go for China to advance from socialism to the future society described by the founders of Marxism. Therefore, unlike the proletarian revolution in developed countries, we need to inevitably go through a special stage of social development, and complete in the socialist system the industrialization and the production commercialization, socialization and modernization, which have been completed in developed countries through the capitalist mode of production. In this stage of social development, the economic relations of the future society envisioned by Marx and Engels are still hard to achieve; all forms of non-public economy are very common; distribution according to work and distribution based on productive factors co-exist; and market mechanism plays a fundamental and dominant role in resource allocation. The concepts such as the so-called "underdeveloped" socialism, "unqualified" socialism, "developing" socialism, in fact, are to explain: firstly, after the establishment of the basic system of socialism in China, the nature of our country is not semi-colonial and semi-feudal, or new-democratic, or the transition from capitalism to socialism, or capitalist, but socialist; secondly, China's socialism at this stage is neither the first stage of communism envisioned by Marx and Engels, nor the "developed socialism" that has been advertised by the former Soviet socialist countries,

9 Marx and Engels Collected Works, Vol. 3, People's Publishing House, Beijing, 2008, p. 563-64.

but the "primary stage" of socialism. Denying the fact that under certain historical conditions we can skip a normal and fully developed capitalist stage and embark on the socialist path and advocating a comprehensive "westernization" and privatization are the ideological roots of the right-leaning mistakes. Ignoring the "existing and inherited" backward social production conditions and believing that without the full development of productive forces we can go beyond the socialization of production by reforming the productive relationship and advance into the socialism, the first stage of communism, are the ideological roots of left-leaning errors.

In the face of years of slow economic development or even stagnation caused by the "poor transition" beyond the development stage, Deng Xiaoping painfully pointed out: for many years we have suffered a major loss. After our socialist transformation was basically completed, we still focused on the "class struggle" and neglected the development of productive forces. To adhere to socialism, the first thing is to get rid of poverty and backwardness. "poverty is not socialism, that socialism means eliminating poverty. Unless you are developing the productive forces and raising people's living standards, you cannot say that you are building socialism"[10] It is necessary to abandon the policy of "taking the class struggle as the top priority" and scientifically judge the main contradictions of society at the current stage on the basis of clearly grasping the historical orientation, to set things right. At the theory-discussing meeting held in early 1979, Deng Xiaoping clearly put forward that, "The level of our productive forces is very low and is far from meeting the needs of our people and country. This is the principal contradiction in the current period, and to resolve it is our central task."[11] Based on Deng Xiaoping's thought, in the Resolutions for Certain Historical Issues of the Party since the Establishment of the PRC, passed in the 6th Plenary Session of the 11th Central Committee of the CPC in 1981, the major contradiction of Chinese socialist society was more simply stated: "After the socialist transformation was basically completed, the principal contradiction within the country was no longer the contradiction between the working class and the bourgeoisie but between the demand of the people for rapid economic and cultural development and the existing state of our economy and culture which fell short of the needs of the people; that the chief task confronting the whole nation was to concentrate all efforts on developing the productive forces, industrializing the country and gradually meeting the people's incessantly growing material and cultural needs."[12]

10 Deng Xiaoping Selected Works, Vol. 3, 1st ed., People's Publishing House, 1994, p. 116.

11 Deng Xiaoping Selected Works, Vol. 2, 2nd ed., People's Publishing House, 1993, p. 182.

12 Selected Works of Important Documents since the Third Plenary Session of the Eleventh Central Committee, Beijing, CPC Central Party School Press, 1981, p. 186.

It was further pointed out in the 13th Congress of the CPC that, "It will be at least 100 years from the 1950s when the socialist transformation of private ownership of the means of production was basically completed, to the time when socialist modernization will have been accomplished for the most part, and all these years belong to the initial stage of socialism."[13] Production and demand is the eternal contradiction of the human society. It is this contradictory movement that drives the state alternation of economy from unbalanced to balanced, and constantly improves the efficiency of resource allocation. However, the main contradiction in the primary stage of socialism does not mean the opposite and unified relation between production and demand, but the contradiction between people's growing material and cultural needs and the backward production. Because for a country with backward productive forces, dominant small-scale peasant economy, underdeveloped commodity economy and unbalanced regional development, when it embarks on the socialist path, the nature of socialism determines that "the growing material and cultural needs of the people" must be met. But as the superiority of the socialist system is limited by the "backward social production", people's growing material and cultural needs cannot be timely and fully met. This is the inevitable main contradiction that must be solved by economically and culturally backward countries after from the establishment of the basic system of socialism to the basic realization of the socialist modernization. Only by facing squarely this major reality and basic national condition at the primary stage of socialism can we clearly understand its long-term and arduous nature and develop the correct lines principles and policies. Based on the scientific judgment of the main contradictions in the primary stage of socialism, after the successful switch of the party and state's focus, our party has established the basic line of building socialism with Chinese characteristics, which is to adhere to Reform and Opening-up and the four cardinal principles and concentrate on the central task of economic construction. Because fundamental task of socialism is to constantly liberate and develop social productive forces.

Practice shows that after the socialist transformation of the means of production is basically completed, the exploiting class has been eliminated as a class; the main social contradiction is no longer the class struggle, but the contradiction between people's growing material and cultural needs and the backward social production. Therefore, when a real Marxist political party is in power, it must be committed to the development of productive forces, gradually improve the people's living standards, and achieve common prosperity, thus display the superiority of the socialist system.

13 Selected Works of Important Documents since the Thirteenth National Congress (I), Beijing, People's Publishing House, 1993, p. 12.

Otherwise, the economic development will be slow or even stagnant; people will be living in poverty; and the society will not be stable. Development "is not just an economic issue, it's actually a political issue."[14], "the key to solving all problems in the country is to push development and rely on our own development."[15] We cannot consolidate and improve the socialist system and enhance the socialist cohesion and persuasiveness without development. We cannot enhance comprehensive national strength, gradually eliminate poverty and improve people's lives without development. We cannot solve various domestic contradictions, maintain social stability and achieve national long-term stability without development. We cannot implement the "one country, two system" policy and complete the great cause of reunification of the motherland without development. We cannot fight against hegemonism and safeguard national independence and sovereignty without development. And we cannot eliminate the exploitation and polarization and ultimately achieve common prosperity without development. All in all, development is the overriding requirement.

3. Striving for development based on China's main contradiction at present stage

Since the Reform and Opening-up, guided by the basic line of building socialism with Chinese characteristics with "one central task and two basic points" as the core content, we have correctly grasped the main contradictions in the primary stage of socialism, ruled out from the "left" and the right interference, overcome the difficulties and risks, and achieved universally recognized great achievements in socialist construction. According to statistics, in the past 33 years from 1978 to 2011, China has maintained a high-speed economic growth with annual average speed close to 10%, a miracle in the world's economic growth. China's GDP increased from ¥362.4 billion in 1978 to ¥471.546 billion in 2011; the total economic output ranks second in the world; comprehensive national strength has been significantly increased. China's per capita GDP rose from ¥379 in 1978 to ¥34,999 in 2011; urban and rural residents' material and cultural life has been greatly improved. As of 2011, the national foreign exchange reserves reached $3.18 trillion, ranking first in the world. Total foreign trade value has amounted to $364.21 billion, becoming the world's largest exporter and the second largest importer. In a country with a population of about 20% of the world's total, the historic breakthrough from poverty adequate food and clothing to prosperity within just a few decades has been achieved, which is major feat in human history and fully shows that the Chinese Communist Party's judgment on the main contradictions at the primary stage of socialism and the missions set are totally correct.

14 Deng Xiaoping Selected Works, 1st ed., Volume 3, p. 354.

15 Ibid., p. 265.

However, we must clearly see that although since the Reform and Opening-up China's economy has seen great achievements, the basic national condition that we are and will be in the primary stages of socialism for a long time and there is still a long way to go before entering into the "mature" or "developed" society. First of all, though China is among the ranks of the world's largest economic powers, it is far from the world's foremost economic power; it still takes a long time to achieve the modernization with the goal of industrialization. According to the data published by the International Monetary Fund, in 2011 China's per capita GDP was $5414, which puts it among the middle-income developing countries according to the World Bank standards and ranks the bottom. It will need the unremitting efforts of more than several generations to completely eliminate poverty. Secondly, in China at a rapid growth period, the economy is unbalanced, and there is giant gap between urban and rural areas, and among regions and social groups. From the perspective of urban-rural relations, the contradiction of urban-rural dual structure in China is very prominent; urbanization is far behind the process of industrialization. There is large income gap between urban and rural residents. As for the regional disparities, GDP proportion of the eastern region in the national total has been rising; while the proportion of the Midwest is declining. The area of the western region accounts for 71.3% of the country's population and the population 28.6% of the country's total. However, the proportion of its GDP accounts for less than 17% of the national total; and the per capita GDP is only 2/3 of the national average, less than half of the average in the eastern region. Seeing from the income levels of different social classes, according to the sampling survey by relevant departments, in 2010 the per capita disposable income of the highest 10% income group is ¥13,322, 2.8 times the national average; while the per capita disposable income of the lowest 10% income group is ¥1397, only 29% of the national average. The ratio of per capita income between high and low income groups is 9.5:1.

Lastly, though China is blessed with vast territory and abundant resources the per capita resources is extremely scarce. The extensive economic growth with high input, high consumption and low efficiency is unsustainable. China is a country with a large population. The per capita hold of resources that are of strategic significance to the national economy and people's life such as land, fresh water and minerals is less than half of the world's average level. The high economic growth achieved by the extensive input of capital, labor, natural resources and other production factors is at the expense of great resource consumption and environmental damages.

China is currently in the midst of an important strategic opportunity. In 2003, China's per capita GDP exceeded $1,000, reaching the level of lower middle-income developing countries. In 2011, China's per capita GDP reached $5,414, entering the ranks of middle-income developing countries. By 2020 when the goal of building a well-off society in an all-round is realized, China's per capita GDP will likely be close to $10,000, entering the ranks of upper middle-income developing countries. International development experience shows that when low-income developing countries enter into the ranks of middle-income developing countries, it means they also enter the stage to accelerate the industrialization and marketization. At this stage, economic development is both full of hope and risk. On the one hand, with the rapid economic growth, income keeps rising; the consumption structure is improved significantly; urban and rural residents' consumption gradually change from food and clothing to well-off consumption to rich consumption; the growth of the material and cultural needs of the people presents the characteristics of quantity expansion and quality improvement. On the other hand, the fast-growing economy, while providing the necessary material security for social development, drives the diversification of various interests; the contradiction between man and nature become prominent, and people's social relations tend to be complicated. As the contradictions and conflicts increase, the social risks increase. We must focus on controlling the population and improve resource utilization efficiency and the ecological environment, to ease the population, resources, and environmental constraints. We shall effectively curb the development gap, reduce unemployment and improve social security, in order to alleviate the social conflicts caused by structural differentiation. Once the above-mentioned contradictions are mishandled, it might lead to intensified conflicts, economic recession and even social instability, thus valuable development opportunities will be missed.

In the face of profound changes in economic and social development, the CPC Central Committee has focused on seizing the important strategic opportunities and put forward historical task of constructing socialist harmonious society at the hope of creating a new situation of socialism with Chinese characteristics. At the Sixteenth CPC National Congress in 2002, "a more harmonious society" for the first time was written into the party's programmatic documents and became one of the goals of building a well-off society in an all-around way. At the Third Plenary Session of the 16th CPC Central Committee in 2003, "to adhere to the people-oriented principle, uphold the comprehensive, coordinated and sustainable development view and promote the all-round development of economy, society and people" became the guiding principle of China's overall economic and social development. At the Fourth Plenary Session of the 16th CPC Central Committee in 2004, it was proposed that, "we shall adapt to the profound social changes, put the construction of a harmonious society in an important position, and focus on stimulating social vitality and promoting social equity and justice." At the 5th Plenary Session of the 16th CPC Central

Committee in 2005, it was required that, "we shall uphold the Scientific Outlook on Development in the economic and social development and guide the economic and social development into a comprehensive, coordinated and sustainable development track." At the 17th National Congress of the Communist Party of China in 2007, it was made clear that, "the first essence of the Scientific Outlook on Development is development; its core is people-oriented principle; its basic requirement is being comprehensive, coordinated and sustainable; and the fundamental method is overall planning and all-round consideration."

To promote scientific development, we must seize the main contradiction of our country at present stage, adhere to the central task of economic construction, and take keeping liberating and developing social productive forces as a fundamental task. The reason why economic construction is in the center of socialist harmonious society is not only that the development of productive forces is the final decisive force of the development of human society and the material basis of comprehensive social progress and human development, but also that the inharmonious factor in current economy is caused by the underdeveloped productive forces. Only through the development of productive forces can we better solve the contradictions and problems on the way forward. There will be no impetus for political construction, cultural construction, social construction and ecological civilization construction without the economic construction and the highly-developed productive forces. In the process of building a socialist harmonious society, prevent the mistake of neglecting the economic construction because of concentrating on the political construction, cultural construction, social construction and ecological civilization construction. Only by focusing on promoting the economic development can we maximumly satisfy the growing material and cultural needs of people, and continuously promote the socialist political construction, cultural construction, social construction and ecological civilization construction.

(Dong Zhengping, Professor of College of Political Science and Law, Capital Normal University)

The Essence of Socialism and the Issue of Fairness & Efficiency

How should we understand the essence of socialism in China at present-stage? This issue that had been discussed in the academic community for a certain time in the past but currently the debate has almost faded. However, in the process of building a well-off society in an all-round way and realizing modernization and building a socialist harmonious society, we cannot avoid facing this question when thinking about the future of Chinese society. Whether it is to understand the nature of socialism from the relationship between nature and characteristics, or from the unity of productivity and production relations, or the unity of means and objectives, to solve the contradictions and practical problems in current Chinese society, the fundamental way is to understand the nature of socialism from the unity of efficiency and fairness, so as to ensure that our well-off society truly embodies the essence of socialism and that Chinese society truly becomes a socialist society with Chinese characteristics.

1. Evaluating the development and liberation of productive forces as the essence of socialism from the perspective of efficiency and fairness

"To liberate and develop productive forces, eliminate exploitation and polarization and eventually realize common prosperity" is Deng Xiaoping's scientific summary of the essence of socialism, under the reality of the contemporary world and the development at the primary stage of China's socialism, based on the combination of the basic principles of Marxism and the new characteristics of the changing times and the economic, political and cultural development in China. The primary contribution of this generalization is to consider the liberation and development of productive forces as the essential requirements of socialism, which show clearly the reason and principles of the existence of socialism.

In general, people regard "liberating and developing productive forces" as the content of productive forces in the nature of socialism. If we see this content from the perspective of efficiency and fairness, we will find that in the content of productive forces of the socialist essence, it is not only about the efficiency, but also the fairness. Efficiency and fairness exist not only in the society of people, but also in the social and economic activities. The so-called efficiency refers to the ratio of activities and goals achieved, namely the ratio of inputs and outputs. In the development of market economy, the efficiency is usually associated with the effective use and allocation of resources. In other words, it means to produce more goods and services meeting the social demands with the least consumption of resources. The purpose is to obtain the optimum benefit. The definition of efficiency proposed by Western mathematical economist Pareto is a widely accepted definition. He argues that when there is no other way, the resource allocation is optimal and efficient if it benefits at least one person without causing damage to anyone else. Pareto's optimal state is difficult to achieve in real life, but it shows at the most basic level that efficiency is a reflection of the optimal allocation of resources, and that the pursuit of efficiency must be fair without causing damages to most people's interests. The socialist essence's emphasis on "liberating and developing productive forces" first shows that the development of socialism must be efficient, which means that "According to our experience, in order to build socialism we must first of all develop the productive forces, which is our main task."[16]; "To uphold the socialist system, the most fundamental thing is to develop productive forces." "The superiority of socialism will ultimately be demonstrated in the better development of productive forces".[17]

However, for the socialist system established on the basis of the backward economy and culture, and for a socialist country that have made mistakes in socialist construction, it is not just about developing productive forces, but also about liberating productive forces. The liberation of productive forces in fact means that the development of socialism shall emphasize fairness. The so-called fairness means that interest relationship among people and the principles, systems, practices and behavior of the interest relationship are all in line with the needs of social development. It is a value judgment. Fairness is both historical and objective. There is neither an eternal fairness nor fairness with the same connotation. Fairness varies according to the social and historical conditions and different social natures. In different societies, different classes have different interpretations of fairness. Therefore, fairness is the conceptual expression of the existing economic relations. It develops and changes with the development and changes of social and economic relations. In terms of the reality of China's economic relations, in line with the requirements of the development of the socialist market economy, fairness must be consistent with the efficiency. The emphasized content of "liberating and developing productive forces" in the essence of socialism also we should pay attention to fairness in the pursuit of efficiency, which means that in the development of productive forces we must reform productive relations fettering the development of productive forces and the superstructure unsuitable for the economic foundation. Deng Xiaoping said: "In the past, we only stressed expansion of the productive forces under socialism, without mentioning the need to liberate

16 Deng Xiaoping Selected Works, 2nd ed., Vol. 2, p. 314.
17 Deng Xiaoping Selected Works, 1st ed., Vol. 3, p. 149.

them through reform. That conception was incomplete. Both the liberation and the expansion of the productive forces are essential."[18]

Efficiency and fairness are unified. Efficiency is the basis and premise of fairness; there is no fairness without efficiency. Efficiency must be unified in the fairness. We shall focus on fairness in pursuit of efficiency, because fairness will promote the improvement of efficiency. The unity of the liberation and development of productive forces as the essence of socialism, on the one hand, reflects the unity of efficiency and fairness, which shows that only through the liberation and development of productive forces can the essence of socialism be truly reflected. On the other hand, it also corrects the erroneous ideas and practices that neglect the development of productive forces and efficiency, emphasizes that the primary stage of socialism we must focus on both the liberation and development of productive forces, and shows that the socialist system is more favorable to people to build and develop socialism.

"Liberating and developing productive forces" is not only about resource allocation, but also the development and utilization of resources, which contains the issue of efficiency and fairness. In terms of resource allocation, efficiency depends on the ability and tool of the subject, and also directly depends on the way it works, and even more the enthusiasm, initiative and creativity of people's activities. The dynamic factors influencing the efficiency, namely the enthusiasm, initiative and creativity of people's activities, is usually determined by fairness. The more reasonable the degree of social justice, the more consistent a social member's contribution with his gains, the higher the enthusiasm, initiative and creativity of his work become; otherwise, it becomes the lower. Fairness, to a certain extent, improves the efficiency by encourage man's enthusiasm, initiative and creativity. Fairness has become the fundamental guarantee of efficiency. In terms of resource development and utilization, efficiency must be unified with fairness. Modern society is facing increasing population, resources, environmental pressures, so we shall not concentrate only on efficiency regardless of the fairness. There is no doubt that the relationship between man and nature is manifested as productive forces. If we focus only on efficiency without concerns of the environmental protection and the development and utilization of resources, there will be a lot of unfairness, such as intragenerational unfairness and intergenerational unfairness. This unfairness would bring about serious disaster to the people and cause far-reaching and turmoil and damage to the society. For the development and utilization of natural resources in the development of productive forces in China, if we focus only on the efficiency regardless of fairness, we will inevitably suffer the punishment of disasters such as drought, water and soil erosion

18 Deng Xiaoping Selected Works, 1st ed., Vol. 3, p. 370.

and sand storm, causing damages to more people. Therefore, the liberation and development of productive forces requires focus both on efficiency and fairness.

It is of great significance to the construction of a well-off society in an all-round way to see the liberation and development of productive forces in the essence of socialism from the perspective of efficiency and fairness. Through the concerted efforts of the whole Party and the people of all ethnic groups, we have achieved the first and second goals of the "three-step" strategy of modernization in the end of the 20th century; people's lives have generally reached a well-off standard. However, the current level of well-off society is still low, which means that we must vigorously develop productive forces and improve the level of per capita income to build a comprehensively well-off society. The notable features the well-off society include higher productivity, higher per capita GNP, higher living standards of people, and enhanced comprehensive national strength, especially the economic strength. To eliminate the gap between the low level in reality and the high level of a comprehensively well-off society, we must follow the theory of socialism essence put forward by Deng Xiaoping, adhere to the central task of economic construction, adapt to the requirements of the development of productive forces, and continue to liberate and develop productive forces. Therefore, in building a comprehensively well-off society, the first thing is to develop a reasonable indicator system. Building build well-off society in an all-round way requires not only the rigid indicator, but also the flexible one. It needs not only the quantitative economic indicators, but also the quantitative indicators for system, institutional and mechanism securities, social stability and legal security. We need to enrich and perfect the "Basic Standards for People's Well-off Living Standards" formulated by National Bureau of Statistics and other authorities into the standard of building a well-off society in an all-round way. The guarantee of system, institutional and mechanism security in building a well-off society in an all-round way requires us to understand the content of the productive forces in the essence of socialism from the perspective of efficiency and fairness. Only in this way can the essence of socialism be fulfilled.

2. Evaluating the link of productive forces as the essence of socialism from the perspective of efficiency and fairness

People generally consider "the elimination of exploitation and polarization between the rich and the poor and the final achievement of common prosperity" as the content regarding productive relations in the essence of socialism. Obviously, it is consistent with the content of productive forces.

In the socialist society, only by "the liberation and development of productive force can the "the elimination of exploitation and polarization between the rich and the poor and the final achievement of common prosperity" be achieved. In other words, only when "the elimination of exploitation and polarization between the rich and the poor and the final achievement of common prosperity" is achieved in a socialist society can the productive forces be greatly liberated and developed. The unity of the two makes us avoid the drawbacks of understanding the essence of socialism from the perspective of productive forces or relations. It shows that "the liberation and development of productive force" is the premise and means of "the elimination of exploitation and polarization between the rich and the poor and the final achievement of common prosperity". "The elimination of exploitation and polarization between the rich and the poor and the final achievement of common prosperity" is limited by the level of "the liberation and development of productive forces", and their higher level also will promote it.

If we see the link of productive forces being the essence of socialism from the perspective of efficiency and fairness, we can clearly find that "common prosperity" is the core of the essence of socialism. Deng Xiaoping has repeatedly stressed that, "Achievement of common prosperity characterizes socialism, which cannot produce an exploiting class."[19]; "One of the features distinguishing socialism from capitalism is that socialism means common prosperity, not polarization of income"[20]; "there is no such thing as poor socialism. Socialism is characterized not by poverty but by prosperity–the common prosperity of all."[21] The content of "the elimination of exploitation and polarization between the rich and the poor and the final achievement of common prosperity" in the essence of socialism clarify the fundamental difference between socialism and capitalism, and the difference between purposes of the liberation and development of productive force in socialism and capitalism. In the content of "the elimination of exploitation and polarization between the rich and the poor and the final achievement of common prosperity" regarding productive relations in the essence of socialism, all laborers finally achieve common prosperity, which fully embodies the significance of fairness. Of course, fairness is not average, because the average focuses on the equality in quantity, which means that people with different contributions enjoy the same amount of economic development achievements. Fairness is not equality in the general sense, because equality is not always fair. Fairness is a special kind of equality. It is the equality with quantity difference. In line with the requirements of the development of socialist society, fairness must be the fair income distribution based on equal

19 Deng Xiaoping Selected Works, 2nd ed., Vol. 2, p. 236.

20 Deng Xiaoping Selected Works, 1st ed., Vol. 3, p. 123.

21 Ibid., p. 265.

starting point and opportunity. It must be that there is no polarization in the society. "The elimination of exploitation and polarization between the rich and the poor and the final achievement of common prosperity" stresses the importance of efficiency while fully embodying fairness. In socialist society, the natural conditions, the difference between people's physical and intellectual strength will inevitably lead to the income gap, but it does not equal to polarization. The existence of the income gap is based on the premise that part of the people in some region through honest labor, intelligence, lawful business operations and investment of production factors become prosperous first. It is the recognition and compensation for people with different labor skills and contributions, so it is reasonable and legitimate. The purpose of allowing the existence of income gap is to have those prosperous people demonstrate, help and encourage others to embark on a path of common prosperity. "This is a shortcut path we can take to speed up development and attain common prosperity."[22] It is also only practical way for all people to achieve common prosperity. The transformation from the prosperity of part of the people or regions to the common prosperity of all shows the high degree of unity of fairness and efficiency. It is impossible to achieve social equity without highly developed productive forces and high economic efficiency. Meanwhile, the fairness also improves efficiency. But we must maintain a reasonable degree of fairness. Specifically, when the society is extremely unfair, it will result in the unequal phenomena of the poor getting poorer and the rich getting richer weaken the enthusiasm initiative and creativity of the workers, affect the improvement of efficiency and even lead to an "inefficient" state of the whole society. Only by recognizing that fairness is equality with quantity difference with the premise that there is a certain income gap can we better improve efficiency.

"The elimination of exploitation and polarization between the rich and the poor and the final achievement of common prosperity", as the content regarding productive relations in the essence of socialism, further embodies the significance of fairness in the essence of socialism on the basis of the liberation and development of productive force. The common prosperity of all workers means that the fairness is realized and that the achievements of social and economic development are share by all. Common prosperity, fairness and sharing are closely related. Common prosperity itself is a kind of sharing; while sharing emphasizes that fairness is equality with quantity difference. But it cannot be ignored that the premise of common prosperity, fairness and sharing must be the development of productive forces, the improvement of efficiency and the participation and promotion of all laborers in social and economic development. Here, we clearly see that fairness and efficiency are always unified. All laborers are not only the interest subjects

22 Deng Xiaoping Selected Works, 1st ed., Vol. 3, p. 166.

of the socialist economic development, but also the practical subject and value subject of the socialist economic development. The goal of development is to achieve common prosperity and fairness and share the achievements of social and economic development. And the purpose of achieving common prosperity, fairness and sharing is to better develop productivity, improve efficiency and show all workers' ability in engaging in and promoting social and economic development. All the workers make efforts for the socialist economic development and strive for their own interests and liberation, at the hope of being the master of their own affairs and achieving equality and common prosperity.

Seeing the productive relations in the essence of socialism from the perspective of efficiency and fairness is of great significance to the construction of a well-off society in an all-round way. In addition to the characteristic of high level, the well-off society in an all-round way also has the characteristics of being balanced and comprehensive, with common prosperity as its core content. As Deng Xiaoping said, "As China is a socialist country, our national revenue will be distributed in a way that benefits all the people. There will be neither people who are too rich nor people who are too poor, and everyone will have an easier life."[23]

In entering the overall well-off stage, our goal is to "let some people and some regions get rich first" and others will be brought along to prosperity. But fundamentally, the goal of building a well-off society in an all-round way is to make the majority of people or regions become rich and truly achieve common prosperity. This is the process of demonstrating the essence of socialism and the superiority of the socialist system. Most of the rich people refer to the people who account for a large proportion and enjoy the benefits. Viewing from the current situation of our country, 30 million people in rural areas and 20 million urban people have not yet solved the problem of food and clothing. Building a well-off society in an all-round way is to let these people become rich, so that the high-level well-off society benefits of more than one billion people and the achievements of social and economic development and common prosperity could be shared by all out people accounting for 1/4 of the world's population. Therefore, only by studying how to achieve the elimination of exploitation and polarization between the rich and the poor and the final achievement of common prosperity in the process of building a well-off society in an all-round way, the issue of balancing the efficiency and fairness, and the issue of how to expand the proportion of middle-income group and improve the level of low income group, can we make this process more suitable for the requirements of the development of socialism with Chinese characteristics and truly achieve a sharing and progressive well-off society. Most regions that have become

23 Deng Xiaoping Selected Works, 1st ed., Vol. 3, pp. 161-62.

rich show the degree of realization of well-off society. In the whole country, the degree of realization of the well-off society is not balanced. For all regions and urban and rural areas, the starting point for building a moderately prosperous society is different. How will the regions and urban and rural areas with a high degree of realization of well-off society take new measures to achieve the goal of building a well-off society in an all-round way on the basis of their existing advantages of economic level, material life, population quality, spiritual life and living environment? How will they encourage and bring along the backward regions to get close to the threshold of a well-off level as soon as possible and achieve the overall goal of building a well-off an all-around way? Obviously, the key point of the problem lies in the central and western regions and the rural areas, especially in the villages of the vast Midwest regions. The development of the central and western regions and the rural areas determines the process of building a comprehensively well-off society and the modernization process. It is impossible to achieve a comprehensively well-off society and modernization without the development in the central and western regions and the rural areas. Changing the imbalance of China's development, the rural backwardness and the uncoordinated status of China's economy, politics and culture is the requirements of building a comprehensively well-off society and reflect the essence of socialism. Therefore, the study of rural, agricultural and farmer issues, the study of development of the west regions, the study of how to develop rural economy, establish modern agriculture and increase farmers' income in order to let the majority of farmers reach the well-off society, and how to develop the western region so as to achieve coordinated regional development, have become a major aspect reflecting the essential requirement of socialism in the process of building a comprehensively well-off society. To achieve common prosperity in the process of building a comprehensively well-off society requires us to understand the productive relations in the essence of socialism from the perspective of efficiency and fairness. Only in this way can the essence of socialism be fulfilled.

3. Evaluating the realization of the essence of socialism from the perspective of efficiency and fairness

Viewing the essence of socialism from the perspective of efficiency and fairness, we believe that the theoretical content of the essence of socialism contains the unity of efficiency and fairness. Properly dealing with the relationship between efficiency and fairness means the realization of the essence of socialism. However, in the understanding of the essence of socialism, we cannot match productive forces and production relations with efficiency and fairness. Whether it is the content of the productive forces or relations, it in fact contains both of them.

The real significance of studying the essence of socialism lies in the realization of the essence of socialism. The true significance of viewing the essence of socialism from the perspective of efficiency and fairness lies in the realization of the essence of socialism by proper handling the relationship between efficiency and fairness. At present, there are some serious unfair problems in the development of socialist economy in our country. The most prominent is that unbalanced development of economy between urban and rural areas, among regions and different classes lead to the imbalanced hold of resources, thus creating a large disparity of resources and services such as basic quality of life, culture and education level and health care services. To make our society truly become a high level and comprehensive well-off society with balanced development and truly fulfill the essence of socialism, it is important to solve the problem of the giant gap between urban and rural areas, among regions and social classes, and uphold the unity of efficiency and fairness.

In terms of urban-rural gap, China's agricultural production capacity has increased significantly; the rural industrial structure tends to be optimized; the per capita income of farmers has increased by 50 times from 1978 to 2010; the overall living standards of farmers continue to improve. But, compared with the industry, the level of agricultural productivity is still relatively low; the level of urbanization in rural areas is still relatively backward; the modern civilized conditions and degree in rural areas such as culture, science and technology, education, health and sports are far behind that of the cities; The per capita net income of farmers is far behind the growth of per capita disposable income of urban residents; there are still 30 million people in rural areas who have not solved the problem of food and clothing; there is a large gap between urban and rural economic development. Urban and rural economic development gap is eminently reflected in lagging agricultural development, low level of urbanization in rural areas and low income of the farmers.

To properly handle the relationship between efficiency and fairness in dealing with the gap between urban and rural areas, we must start from enhancing the foundational position of agriculture, developing the rural economy, promoting the process of urbanization, increasing the income of farmers and protecting the interests of farmers. To strengthen the foundational status of agriculture and develop modern agriculture, we must speed up the technological innovation of agriculture, and transform the land and labor resources based agricultural growth into technology and knowledge-based agricultural growth. We shall comprehensively upgrade agricultural and rural economic structure, adjust the rural region layout, optimize the allocation of resources, and build advantageous region of production and industrial belt. We need to actively promote the industrialization of agriculture management, integrate the agricultural production, processing and sales, and unify the scattered household production and market demands, and improve the organization of farmers and comprehensive agricultural benefits when entering the market. To development rural economy and promote urbanization, we must address the problem of rural surplus labor, develop township enterprises and rural service industry, and build small towns with urban functions. We need to develop small towns, spread urban culture and value in rural areas, improve the quality of farmers, promote agricultural science and technology, and drive forward development of rural cultural undertakings. In order to increase the income of farmers and protect their interests, we need to deepen the rural reform. We shall uphold the basic policies of the party in the rural areas and maintain and constantly improve the household contract management system. We also shall reform the rural financial system, improve rural financial services, establish rural financial system that is adapted to socialist market economy system and promotes rural economic development. We shall promote rural tax reform, reduce the burden on farmers, protect their interests, and increase government support and protection of agriculture, including investment in rural infrastructure and public agricultural services such as technology promotion service system and information service system, increase direct subsidies to farmers, and intensify efforts to alleviate poverty and support rural education.

In terms of regional disparities, since the Reform and Opening-up, China has seen rapid economic development. With the deepening of the economic system reform and the continuous improvement of the level of opening up to the outside world, the economic development gap between eastern and central & western regions becomes larger. Its main manifestations include: the economic growth in the eastern coastal areas is faster than that in the central and western regions; income level of urban residents in the eastern region was significantly higher than that in the central and western regions, and the income gap widens year by year. The widening gap in regional economic development will eventually affect the national unity of a country and the development of the national economy as a whole and endanger social stability. Therefore, we should understand that disparity is caused in the development due to different development speeds. It is a matter of earlier and later prosperity. We should also recognize the damage caused by the widening gap and take positive measures starting from the perspective of efficiency and fairness to narrow the gap. To narrow the regional gap, we should mainly focus on the optimization and upgrading of some industries among regions and the improvement of urbanization level. Viewing from the optimization and upgrading of some industries among regions, the eastern region should develop high-tech industries, cultivate new industries and knowledge-intensive industries, accelerate the upgrading of industrial structure, transfer the original leading industries to the central and western regions, open up channels for the central and western regions, promote the central and western regions to a higher stage of technological development, support northeastern region and other old industrial bases in their adjustment and transformation with more financial and material resources, so as to become the leader of economic development. The western region should develop new industries and comparative advantage industries, promote intensive processing of the raw materials and turn resource advantage into economic advantage. Geographically the central regions of China can make full use of the science and technology, talent and capital advantages in the eastern regions, focus on the transformation of their traditional industries, and cultivate new economic growth point and promote the industrialization process. Through the optimization and upgrading of some industries among regions, we can gradually create a good situation with accelerated economic growth in the eastern region and economic take-off in the central and western regions. From the perspective of enhancing the level of urbanization, in China the current urbanization level is low; the city layout is not reasonable; the urbanization degree in the eastern region is higher than that in the western regions. To change this situation, we must take the rural urbanization as an intermediate link and develop small towns. The development of small towns with the city's industrial agglomeration effect and population aggregation effect could not only establish new production factors gathering and diffusion centers in the central and western regions, so that the extremely rich resources in agriculture, forestry and animal husbandry can be transformed into real productive forces in a timely manner; but also promote industrial transformation, optimization and upgrading in the central and western regions and build a number of new cities to adjust the layout of China's cities and promote the improvement of urbanization in the central and western regions. It could also gather industries of finance, services, transportation, communications and education in the central and western regions cultivate all kinds of personnel at all levels, making it a place of economic restructuring and industrial structure optimization and upgrading, so as to achieve leapfrog development in the central and western regions and narrow the gap with the development level of the eastern region.

In terms of class gap, since Reform and Opening-up, China's social class composition has undergone new changes. There are many kinds of social groups, including entrepreneurs and technical personnel in private technology enterprises, management and technical personnel employed in foreign-funded enterprises, self-employed entrepreneurs, private business owners, intermediary organizations, practitioners and freelancers. The emergence of new social groups exposed the intensification of social differentiation, which is prominently manifested in widening income gap. The widening income gap among different social groups is not all the result of the current quite reasonable institutional arrangement. There are unreasonable, contingent and unlawful factors that cause the gaps. The unfair income distribution directly affects production efficiency, the rational use of resources and the efficiency of macro-resource allocation. It is time for the problem to be solved.

To solve the problem of income distribution gap, the key is to correctly handle the relationship between efficiency and fairness. Firstly, residents of all social classes enjoy fair opportunities, to ensure a fair starting point. For the rural surplus labor that have migrated to cities to work and the urban laid-off workers, we shall improve their basic education and vocational training to ensure that they will be employed and have access to middle-income groups. For the children of all the urban and rural residents, we need to completely solve the problem of inadequate funding for compulsory education and organize professional training to ensure that they enjoy fair starting point. Secondly, we need to protect the legitimate income according to the law, standardize the social distribution order and prohibit illegal income. It is necessary to combine the labor remuneration with the contribution by rewarding the diligent and punishing the lazy and strengthen the supervision of income distribution in the monopoly industry. Anti-monopoly has become a necessary condition for solving the widening income gap caused by monopoly, establishing economic order of fair trade and fair competition and promoting the improvement of production efficiency and resource allocation efficiency. The reasonable adjustment of the high income in oil, telecommunications and finance industry is an important part of the correct handling of efficiency and fairness in income distribution. We shall also encourage and protect the acquirement of wealth by legitimate business and labor, establish power restraint, supervision, checks and balances mechanism, prevent and eliminate the breeding and corruption from the source, and resolutely ban and punish according to law all kinds of illegal income including the embezzlement of public property, tax evasion and power-for-money deals. Lastly, we need to support the low-income groups and keep reducing poverty-stricken population in the economic development. We should establish a "safety net" nationwide to ensure the basic subsistence, the medical treatment and the education of the poor children and the basic needs for the survival of people living in extreme poverty. This is an important measure to prevent polarization. We should also adjust the tax structure and increase personal income tax rate for the high-income group. We should also reform the rural tax policy design, gradually eliminate the unfair urban and rural dual tax structure, implement unified urban and rural tax system from the perspective of efficiency and fairness, levy tax on the high-income groups, and provide tax exemption and subsidy for the low-income groups, so as to control the expansion of personal income gap.

(Zhang Leisheng, Professor of Institute of Marxism, Renmin University of China)

Economic System and Socialist Market Economy

Market economy, as an economic form, always exists and develops in a certain economic system. People's understanding and study on the relationship between market economy and economic system keep being deepened with the development of practice. In Marxist economics, the relationship between public ownership and market economy has gone through a process of development from opposition to unity. Based on the pure public ownership and socialized mass production, Marx concluded the opposition between the public ownership and the market economy. In their practices, Lenin and Stalin put forward that under the conditions of real socialist public ownership the commodity economy must be applied to develop the socialist economy. In China's socialist practice, Deng Xiaoping founded a new theory of the socialist market economy which realized the unity of public ownership and market economy. This achievement fully implies that the Marxist theory develops with development of practice with the theoretical quality of advancing with the times.

1. The relationship between economic system and economic form

Economic system is the institutional structure established by the dominant class or group to achieve their own interests and goals and ensure the smooth operation of the society and economy. The establishment of an economic system is the result of the combination of various factors, with the level of productive forces being the most fundamental one. Marxist theory of productivity determining production relations (economic system) is derived from the law of the evolution of human socio-economic system. Certainly, in addition to the fundamental factors of productivity, the establishment of an economic system is also influenced by other factors, such as politics, ideology, class struggle and social conditions. Therefore, the establishment and change of an economic system in a country is not just a simple relationship between productive forces and relations, but a very complex issue that requires in-depth research to make a specific statement. The basic principle of productive forces determining productive relation is also validated in the long history of human beings.

The development of human society has gone through a variety of socio-economic systems. If separated according to its basic nature, these systems could be categorized into public ownership and private ownership systems. The fundamental difference between these two different types of economic system is that the physical conditions of production belong to different owners. If the physical conditions of production belong to the individual, it is the private ownership. If the physical conditions of production belong to all or part of the workers, it is the public ownership. The ownership of physical conditions of production is important, because it determines the status of people in the production process, the different possessions of production results and ultimately the different economic interests. The economic system, as a legal norm, is mandatory. Once an economic system is established, it defines the different interests of people in social and economic activities.

Economic form is the way the socio-economic operates. Its essence is in what way the social resources would be allocated. On the one hand, the way of the economic operation is directly related with the development of productive forces. The level of development of productive forces is closely linked to the degree of socialization of production. The development of socialization of production is mainly reflected in the social division of labor and cooperation; a high degree of socialization of production means developed social division of labor and close cooperative relations. In this sense, the way of economic operation first of all shall meet the objective requirements of the development of productive forces. On the other hand, the mode of economic operation involves the interests of the economic entities. In other words, what kind of economic operation can more fully mobilize the enthusiasm of economic entities? The main mode of economic operation is to solve this problem: how to solve the problem of economic efficiency according to the objective requirements of the development of productive forces and the objective laws of economic activities.

When human society into enters into the stage of more developed productive forces and economy (after the feudal society), the economic operation can basically be divided into two kinds: the planned economy and the market economy. If the social resources are mainly allocated through the planning which plays a dominant role in economy, it is planned economy. Otherwise, it is called the market economy. Resource allocation is a problem that any society must solve; and it is necessary to find more efficient way of resource allocation. Therefore, in terms of resource allocation, it is common in societies of different economic systems. The one who implement more efficient allocation of resources will be able to gain more economic benefits.

Economic system and economic form or the ways of resource allocation are the major problems that should be solved in any social and economic development processes. Although both belong to different levels of economic problems, but there are internal links between them. No matter what the economic system, the problem of resource allocation must be solved properly. Therefore, the issue of choosing economic form emerges. No matter what way of allocation of resources is applied, its economic operation is carried out in a certain economic system. So, you have to find out how to better integrate the economic form with the economic system. Therefore, in the relationship between the economic system and the economic form, looking from the perspective of economic system, the question is how to make a proper concrete form of economic system that would meet the requirements of the resource allocation mode by the way of reforms; if we look from the perspective of economic form, the question is how to design it so that it can better adapt to the basic nature of the economic system

Looking from the perspective of public ownership system, its basic institutional characteristics are established and should be upheld. When we discuss the question of which way of resources allocation can better adapt to the basic nature of the economic system: the planned economy or market economy. Whether the public economy system should choose the planned economy or whether the private economic system should choose the market economy. The theoretical answer to this question has deepened with the development of practice. For a very long historical stage in the past, since the socialist countries implemented the planned economy, and the capitalist countries implemented the market economy, both the Marxist economists and the bourgeois economists have believed that public economic system better matches the planned economy, and private ownership system the market economy. This former understanding of economic theory has also changed with the development of practice. After the 1960s, the economic reform explorations by the socialist countries, to a certain extent, broke through the framework of the planned economic system and introduced the operating mechanism of the market economy; while with the development of the monopoly in the capitalist countries the means of planned economy became more prominent. Consequently. with these new developments planning and market no longer seemed to be in strict contradiction. And, economists began to think that the distinction and opposition between public ownership and the private ownership should have the former simple matching in respect to the way of resources allocation. Consequently, the traditional theoretical conception of opposite relation between the economic system and the economic form has gradually weakened in the new practice.

Besides, the introduction and development of China's economic reform has made great progress in the understanding of the relationship between economic system and economic form in Marxism both in terms of the practice and theory. The socialist market economy was gradually made the major part of the socialist economy with Chinese characteristics, which is an innovation in economics theory redefining the relationship between public ownership and market economy. Therefore, the understanding of the socialist market economy, in essence, is to understand the relationship between the public ownership and market economy.

2. Marx's and Engels' theoretical understanding of the relationship between public ownership and market economy

In the era of Marx and Engels, public ownership had not existed and run as a real system, so its relationship with market economy was not their direct research object. The idea about this issue resulted from their in-depth study of the capitalist economic movement. Therefore, to understand Marx's and Engels' thought on the relationship between public ownership and market economy, we must first systematically grasp their theory of capitalist economic movement and development. Marx and Engels' thought on the relationship between public ownership and market economy is based on the following two theories:

Firstly, the theory of the development law of capitalist production relations. Marx and Engels have argued that with the continuous development of social productive forces, the basic contradiction of capitalist society is the antagonism between the high sociality in socialized mass production and the capitalist private ownership of means of production. And without changing the nature of capitalist production relations, this contradiction would not be ultimately resolved, no adjustment in the capitalist production relations, can resolve it, this contradiction can only be resolved by a new production relationship, namely the public ownership.

Secondly, the theory of development requirements of socialized mass production. Marx and Engels believed that the basic characteristic of capitalist social productive forces is the socialized mass production. To be able to adapt to the development of this kind of social productive forces, both the nature of production relations and the economic operation mechanism should meet these requirements, namely the establishment of a planned economy and the operation mechanism of planned economy. Therefore, in the replacement of capitalist production relations with a new production relationship, it is necessary to simultaneously establish a new economic system and economic operation mechanism.

Based on the above two theories, Marx and Engels have argued that the characteristics of production relations and economic operation of the future society will be fundamentally different from capitalism. Only such arrangement can overcome the basic contradiction and problems that arise in the operation process of capitalist economy and such arrangement will effectively solve the inherent defects of the capitalist economy featured by the market regulation operation mechanism. So, it is bound to involve the relationship between public ownership and the market economy. Marx and Engels' study on this issue was based on the contradiction between productive forces and relations, which was specifically analyzed in the following 4 levels:

Level 1	level of productive forces	extremely backward	relatively developed	highly developed
Level 2	nature of productive relations	primitive public ownership	private ownerships	public ownership
Level 3	economic form	sharing economy	commodity economy (market)	product economy
Level 4	operation features	tribal coordination	market regulation	planned adjustment

The first level reflects the different levels of development of productive forces. The development level of productive forces in the development of human society so far is divided into three types : extremely backward level of productive forces; relatively developed productive forces; and highly developed productive forces.

The second level reflects the different nature of the productive relations. The production relations of different nature are determined by the different levels of productive forces development. Primitive public ownership is related with the extremely backward level of productive forces. Various private ownerships including slavery, feudalism and capitalism are related with different degrees of relatively developed productive forces. Public ownership including socialism and communism is related with highly developed productive forces.

The third level reflects the different economic forms taken. The nature of the different production relations determines the different economic forms. Primitive public ownership determines the sharing economy. Various private ownerships determine commodity economy. Public ownership determines product economy.

The fourth level reflects the characteristics of different economic operations. Related with different economic forms, there are characteristics for different economic operations. Sharing economy determines the characteristic of tribal coordination. Commodity economy determines the characteristic of market regulation. And product economy determines the characteristic of planned adjustment. Based on Marx and Engels' analysis logic of these four levels, the following two formulas could be concluded:

(1) Private ownership (capitalist) commodity economy with market regulation

(2) Public ownership (socialist) product economy with planned adjustment

From these two formulas, we can see that under the effect of the basic contradiction between productive forces and relations, there will be two kinds of different production relations, i.e. private ownership and public ownership. There are relevant economic forms and operation modes for these two productive relations. So, the antagonism between private ownership (capitalism) and public ownership (socialism) extends to the antagonism between the market economy and the planned economy. Market regulation and planned adjustment is opposed, because the commodity economy (market economy) and the product economy are opposed. The root cause of the opposition between the commodity economy and the product economy relies on the opposition between private ownership (capitalism) and public ownership (socialism).

In Anti-Dühring Engels pointed out"The seizure of the means of production by society eliminates commodity production and with it eliminates the domination of the product over the producer. The anarchy within social production is replaced by consciously planned organization."[24] "From the moment when society enters into possession of the means of production and uses them in direct association for production, the labour of each individual, however varied its specifically useful character may be, becomes at the start and directly social labour. The quantity of social labour contained in a product need not then be established in a roundabout way; daily experience shows in a direct way how much of it is required on the average." Under these conditions: "People will be able to manage everything very simply, without the intervention of much-vaunted "value" [25]

From the above discussion of Marx and Engels, we can see that one of their basic views is that the relationship between public ownership and commodity economy is contradictory, thus the market regulation and the characteristics of public ownership economy are also opposed. These views and conclusions, being clear in precondition of assumption, rigorous in logic and tenable in theoretical reasoning, are theoretically solid. It is also because of this point that the view of the opposition between public ownership and commodity economy and market regulation has been dominant in the socialist economic theory. In the traditional socialist economic theory, "the two equals" (i.e., the planned economy equals socialism; the market economy equals capitalism) is fundamentally based on the Marx and Engels' thought.

24 Marx-Engels Collected Works, Vol. 9, p. 300.

25 Ibid., pp. 326-327.

3. Lenin's and Stalin's theoretical understanding of the relationship between public ownership and market economy

Lenin was the first practitioner of Marx's and Engels' theory of socialist economy. It has been a huge leap forward from theory to practice. The connotation of this leap contains two aspects: the original theory could be tested by practice; justified new judgments on the theory could only be made after practice, so as to enrich and develop the theory. Lenin as a great revolutionary and practitioner had constantly amended his views and understanding and put forward new ideas and thoughts in his practice, so that the socialist economic theory in Marxism could be enriched and developed.

In the years from the victory of the October Revolution to the early 1920s, the economic construction of the first socialist country led by Lenin had experienced the two stages of "wartime communism" and "New Economic Policy". On the basis of practice, Lenin's new development of the socialist economic theory is embodied in the relationship between socialism and commodity economy. In the process of socialist practice, Lenin realized, for socialism established on the basis of the backwardness of productive forces and economic development, it would be possible to achieve the development of socialist economy by eliminating commodity and monetary relations. Therefore, although Lenin was not able to fundamentally solve the problem of the relationship between socialism and the commodity economy (in the new economic policy period, Lenin still theoretically believed that the commodity economy and trade freedom would lead back to capitalism), he had realized that commodity and currency relations must be maintained in the practice of real socialism. In the On Tax in Kind , Lenin clearly pointed out that if a political party attempted to completely ban and block all private, non-state trade exchanges, namely the development of business or the capitalist development policies, "this means doing stupid things, it's a suicide, since such a policy will not work economically, such policies of any will inevitably lead to failure."[26]

From the above-mentioned discourse of Lenin, it can be seen that, after the practice of "wartime communism" and "New Economic Policy", Lenin has a clear understanding of the relationship between socialism and commodity economy, which is in an economically and culturally backward country with small farmers accounting for the majority of the population it is impossible to achieve the socialist economic development by eliminating the commodity and currency relations. Therefore, in order to advance into communism, commodity and currency relations must be applied in the

26 Lenin's Monographs on Socialism, Beijing, People's Publishing House, 2009, p. 219.

actual socialism. These new thoughts put forward by Lenin prompted people to re-understand the original Marxist theory.

As Lenin pointed out, "Now we are entitled to say that for us the mere growth of cooperation (with the "slight" exception mentioned above) is identical with the growth of socialism, and at the same time we have to admit that there has been a radical modification in our whole outlook on socialism (*On Cooperation*)"[27].

However, we need to notice that because Lenin's socialist practice only lasted a few years, the problems of socialist economic development had not been fully exposed, and there was no full understanding of the objective laws of the socialist economic development, it was impossible for Lenin to theoretically solve all the problems in the development of socialist economy. Especially about the relationship between socialism and commodity economy, Lenin only discussed that under the specific conditions in Russia the elimination of commodity and currency relations was not feasible, so the commodity and currency relations must be maintained and developed in practice. Consequently, the issue of the relationship between socialism and commodity economy was not theoretically solved, which means the opposition between socialism and commodity economy was still considered as the basic viewpoint of the socialist economic theory in Marxism.

From the 1920s to the early 1950s, through the socialist economic construction and development of nearly 30 years, Stalin had a more profound understanding of the law of socialist economic development. During this period, the theory of the relationship between socialism and commodity economy was the most important theoretical contribution of Stalin. However, due to historical and realistic limitations the development of the times and other restrictions, Stalin's understanding of the socialist commodity economy, was still far from being complete which caused some major mistakes in the Soviet Union and other socialist countries.

Stalin's theory of the relationship between socialism and commodity economy is the most important contribution to the Marxist theory of socialist economy. Because Stalin for the first time theoretically demonstrated the objective necessity of the existence and development of commodity production and exchange in the socialist economy, which significantly drove forward the socialist economic theory of Marxism.

Stalin's theoretical exploration has first modified Marx's two conditions for the existence and development of commodity economy, namely social division of labor and private ownership. Stalin believed that the existence of commodity production and exchange is not necessarily associated with

27 Lenin, "On Cooperation", March 1923.

private ownership; it can also be associated with public ownership. As for Stalin, commodity production cannot be regarded as something which exists independently, instead it will inevitably adapt to the surrounding economic conditions; In fact commodity production has a longer history than capitalist production. It is wrong to think that after the dominance of the public ownership of the means of production has been established and systems of wage labor and exploitation have been eliminated, commodity production should be eliminated. Stalin pointed out that in Soviet Union there were objective economic conditions for commodity production. This economic condition was the existence of two kinds of socialist public ownership in the sphere of fmeans of production, namely, ownership of the whole people and the collective ownership. These two kinds of public ownership are different economic entities; they separately own their products; the exchange between them leads to change of ownership. Therefore, this is a relationship of commodity production and commodity exchange.

Based on the fact that there are two kinds of public ownership in socialism, Stalin demonstrated the objectivity of the existence of commodity production under the conditions of socialism and that the socialist economy and commodity production can coexist from the perspective of objective economic conditions. In fact, it theoretically demonstrated that the private ownership is no longer necessary the condition for commodity economy. Two public ownerships have replaced the private ownership as the condition for commodity economy. Therefore, the commodity economy could well be associated with public ownership and socialism. This thought of Stalin is undoubtedly a major development of Marxist theory of socialist economy. It has largely solved a major fundamental problem that has long plagued the development of socialist economy, which is how to treat the commodity economy in the process of socialist economic development. It has also to a large extent solved the contradiction of commodity economy in the theory and practice of socialist economy.

According to Stalin's theory, the products exchanged among the entities owned by the whole people are not commodities. Because this kind of exchange does not involve the transfer of ownership, in essence, they are not commodities. But because they have to take the form of goods to be counted and priced, in practice it made use of the "shell" of commodity. Stalin's theory of "commodity shell", for a long period of time, had a direct impact on the socialist economic development, especially on the means of production in the economic sector under ownership by the whole people. Stalin's theory of commodity production under socialist conditions contains dual features: firstly, a major development of Marxist economics and theoretically no longer considering the commodity production and exchange as opposed with socialism; secondly, his theory was not complete and did not theoretically solve the issue whether the socialist economy is commodity economy, which led to the fact that the various contradictions in socialist practice cannot be fundamentally resolved.

4. Mao Zedong and Deng Xiaoping's theoretical understanding of the relationship between public ownership and market economy

After the establishment of the socialist system in China, whether to implement commodity production and commodity exchange in the early days of new China was not a problem. Because with the conditions back then, there were various ownerships and the public ownership economy was not dominant. In the whole society, the socio-economic relations needed to be dealt with according to the commodity production and economic laws. However, with the establishment of a highly centralized planned economic system and the completion of the "three major reforms", the economic and institutional conditions of the whole society have undergone major changes. Under the new economic conditions, how to use the basic theory of Marxism to understand the problem of commodity production in the process of socialist economic construction in China has become an important issue that must be clarified theoretically. Meanwhile, after several years of operation, a lot of problems exposed under the highly centralized planned economic system. It needed theoretical discussion and study to solve the problems of this system.

Against some people's proposition that commodity production should be eliminated, Mao Zedong pointed out that, "some people intent to eliminate the commodity production which they considered as a capitalist thing and they are anxious about it. They yearn for communism and tend to abandon exchange and trade". Some of our economists, known as Marxist economists, are more "left" and advocate the elimination of commodity production and the administrative allocation of products. This is wrong and goes against the objective laws. They have not realized the distinction between the natures of the socialist commodity production and the capitalist commodity production, the importance of commodity production under the socialist system, the law of value at the current primary stage of socialism and the positive effects of price and currency in commodity production and circulation. It shows that they have no idea of how the proletariat should treat the 500 million farmers in the countryside. After the founding of the People's Republic of China until the completion of socialist transformation, we shall use commodity production and commodity exchange to unite hundreds of millions of farmers. After the socialist transformation is basically completed, we still need to use commodity production and commodity exchange to unite 500 million farmers. With the people's communes, socialist commodity production and commodity exchange should develop in a more planned way. Some people want to immediately announce the people's communes as the ownership by the whole people, abolish the commodity production and exchange, and implement allocation of materials. This is to deprive the farmers. Regarding Stalin's theory of extinction of commodity production, Mao Zedong stressed that, in addition to the condition of ownership by the whole people, there is also the condition of highly developed productive forces and abundant products, so Stalin's understanding on the condition for the commodity economy was incomplete. For Stalin, the existence of two kinds of ownership (collective farms and SOEs) was the main premise of commodity production and commodities. But this understanding was flawed, in fact the necessity the commodity production is ultimately related with the level of social productive forces. Therefore, even if the transition to a single socialist ownership of the whole people is achieved, there will be commodity production and commodity exchange in some fields when the products are not abundant yet. Mao Zedong's thought can be seen as a development and enrichment of Stalin's theory of socialist commodity production.

With the holding of the third plenary session of the 11th CPC central committee in 1978, China embarked on the path of Reform and Opening-up. The mission of reform is to break the highly centralized planned economic system, which will necessarily involve a basic theoretical issue, namely the relationship between socialism and commodity economy. The second generation of the central collective leadership, with Deng Xiaoping as the core, insisted on combining the basic principles of Marxism with China's reality and exploring a path of socialism with Chinese characteristics. First of all, they theoretically resolved the issue of the relationship between socialism and commodity economy. In the Decision of the Central Committee of the Communist Party of China on Economic Restructuring passed at the third plenary session of the 12th CPC Central Committee in October 1984, the first theoretical innovation on this issue was achieved, namely the theory of socialist planned commodity economy. The development of Marxist economics by this theory is mainly reflected in the following two aspects:

Firstly, it proves that commodity economy is an insurmountable stage of socialist economic development. Marx and Engels believed that the socialist economy is based on the full development of the capitalist commodity economy, so that the development of the socialist economy can skip the stage of commodity economy and directly advance into the product economy stage. However, both the practice of China's socialist economic development and the practice of other socialist countries have proved that by denying commodity economy and promoting product economy the socialist economic development goals cannot be achieved. The establishment of the theory of socialist commodity economy fundamentally changed the traditional view that socialism can directly enter the stage of product economy and turn people's understanding of the characteristics of socialist economy back to reality. Commodity economy is one of the basic economic forms of human social development and also an insurmountable stage of socialist economic development. Socialism can only achieve its own development goals through the form of commodity economy. So, it must vigorously develop the commodity economy.

Secondly, it demonstrates that the socialist and commodity economy are inherently unified. In the past practice of socialism, commodity production and commodity exchange never withdrew from the field of economic activity. However, from Marx to Stalin, from the Soviet model to the Chinese system, the commodity economy has been theoretically considered as opposed to socialist economy, and commodity production and commodity exchange are reluctantly maintained in socialism. The establishment of the theory of socialist commodity economy theoretically demonstrated that under the conditions of real socialism, the existence of commodity economy objectively inherent in the socialist economy. As an economic form, commodity economy itself is neutral and could be applied in different socio-economic systems. The economic nature of socialism can be combined with commodity economy; and the implementation of commodity economy will never affect the economic nature of socialism.

However, with the deepening of reform, the position and function of the market in resources allocation and economic activities has become a unavoidable problem that must be resolved theoretically. On the one hand, this is because from the beginning China's reform was carried out according to the principle of expanding the regulation range and influence of the market and reducing the proportion of planning in the economic activities. By the late 1980s, the proportion of market regulation in economic activity had exceeded the planned regulation. If we cannot theoretically give a clear positioning of the market allocation of resources, the further development of reform will inevitably be affected. On the other hand, there is a great disagreement about the understanding of the planned commodity economy. Whether the characteristics of the socialist economy should be considered as "commodity economy" or "planned economy", there are various views that are hard to be unified. If we cannot fundamentally solve this theoretical problem, it is difficult to make breakthroughs for the whole reform. The development of reform requires a theoretical breakthrough in the issue of the relationship between socialism and market economy.

According to Deng Xiaoping's thought that the market economy might develop in the socialism society, socialist market economy theory was put forward at the 14th Congress of the CPC. This theory holds that the planned economy is not equal to socialism and that there is also planning in capitalism; market economy is not equal to capitalism, and there is also market in socialism. Planning and market are both economic means. The different proportion of planning and market does not mean the essential difference between socialism and capitalism. This fundamentally freed us from the ideological restraints of considering the planned economy and the market economy as basic social systems and innovated and developed Marxist economics. It is embodied in the following three aspects:

Firstly, the combination of socialism and market economy will not change the economic nature of socialism. The proposition is based on the theoretical innovation of the planned economy and the market economy. For a long time, the planned economy and the market economy has been theoretically associated with different social systems. From the objective requirements of socialized production, the issue of efficient allocation of resources shall be solved in any society. In the development of human society, planning and market are two basic ways of allocating resources. As a way of resource allocation, they themselves do not have institutional attributes, and therefore do not belong to the scope of the basic social system. The essence of the combination of socialism and market economy is to have the market play a fundamental role in the allocation of resources. It does not involve changes in the economic nature of the society. This shows that the planned economy and market economy are the ways of resource allocation, establishing the basic premise for the socialist market economy theory.

Secondly, the market economy in general is more conducive to the development of productive forces than the planned economy. As means of economic regulation, planning and market have their advantages and strengths, and shortcomings and defects as well. In the context of socialized mass production and the existence of complex economic relations, the market economy has a greater adaptability and a more significant advantage in promoting economic development, thus having a higher efficiency. On the whole, the market is more efficient than planning when applied as the basic means of resource allocation. Therefore, we must take the development path of socialist market economy.

Thirdly, the socialist market economic system is combined with the basic system of socialism. As a way of resource allocation, market economy has no system attribute. But when it is combined with socialism, it must embody the characteristics of the basic system of socialism. The combination of the development of market economy and upholding the basic system of socialism is the main content of building a socialist economy with Chinese characteristics. The market economy might develop in the socialism society. But it does not equal to socialism. Only by embarking on the path of market economy under the premise of adhering to the basic system of socialism can real socialist market economy be established. In the past 160 years from the mid-19th century when the Marxism was born till today, the world has undergone tremendous changes, and the Marxist theory itself is constantly moving forward. The scientific socialism first put forward by Marx and his in-depth study of the market economy theory has completed the process from the opposition to unity in this long history. The socialist market economy and the theory of socialism with Chinese characteristics created by the Chinese Communists marked the development of Marxism to a new stage. It shows to the world that advancing with the times is the theoretical quality of Marxism.

(Gu Yumin, Professor of Institute of Marxism,
Fudan University, Shanghai)

The Innovation Rendered by the Theory of "Three Represents" to the Theory of Scientific Socialism

In the 1990s, the third generation of the central collective leadership, with Comrade Jiang Zemin as the core, in the face of new changes in the international and domestic situation, adhered to the theoretical theme of building socialism with Chinese characteristics under the guidance of Marxism, summed up the new features and experience of the Reform and Opening-up and modernization under the new situation, put forward a series of interrelated new ideas, views and conclusions in the aspect of politics, economy, culture, reform, development, stability, domestic and foreign affairs, national defense and the governance of party, state and military, which have formed the important thought of "Three Represents". The important thinking of the "Three Represents" has further answered the question of "what is socialism and how to build socialism", and creatively answered the question of "what kind of party to build and how to build the party", deepening the understanding of the socialism with Chinese characteristics and push forward the scientific socialism theory to a new stage.

1. Emphasizing the "comprehensive social development" and deepening the understanding of the law of human society development

The socialist society is a fully developed and comprehensive society, which is the scientific conclusion that Marx and Engels draws from the critique of deformed capitalist development. However, when the socialist system was established in some countries with economic and cultural backwardness, in order to resist the strangulation of imperialism and accelerate the process of modernization, the highly centralized economic and political system had been established. This system had played an important role in the development of socialism; but with the development of history, more and more limitations and drawbacks were exposed. In the course of socialist construction in our country, we had not only experienced the situation of neglecting the development of productive forces, one-sided pursuit of the change of production relations and emphasizing the role of superstructure and spirit, but also seen the situation of one-sided pursuit of economic development, considering economy being everything and neglecting the construction of political civilization and spiritual civilization. These had affected the healthy development and the superiority of socialism, and damaged the appeal of socialism among our people. Since the Third Plenary Session of the 11th CPC Central Committee, Deng Xiaoping led the Chinese Communist Party to formulate the basic line of "one center and two basic points", put forward the basic principle of "focusing on material and spiritual civilization at the same time and attach sufficient importance to both", and gradually developed the general strategy of taking economic construction as the central task and promoting comprehensive social development. Under the guidance of Deng Xiaoping Theory, our party has established the goal of "building our country into a prosperous, democratic and civilized socialist modernized country".

After entering the 1990s, the international and domestic development put forward new requirements for China's economic and social development. The issue of comprehensive development is increasingly concerned by people around the world. Domestically, there were great achievements and many problems in China's reform and construction in the 80s. Compared with the economic development, social development was generally slow; investment in science, education, culture, health and other social undertakings was not sufficient; the level of infrastructure was still relatively low; and various public services and welfare undertakings cannot fully meet the needs of the people for production and life. Although the national economic strength has been enhanced, sustainable development is still subject to the limitations of low quality of national economy, population and environment. Meanwhile, in the process of social transformation, China needs to not only develop the economy, but also solve a series of social problems brought about by the rapid economic development. In view of the new changes in the international and domestic situation, the third generation of the central collective leadership of the party, on the basis of China's reality, focused on the comprehensive development of society, and more consciously take the comprehensive and coordinated social development into the overall development strategy of socialism with Chinese characteristics. At the celebration of the 40th anniversary of the founding of the People's Republic of China in September 1989, Comrade Jiang Zemin pointed out that, "Socialism not only needs to achieve economic prosperity, but also the overall and all-round progress of society."

In October 1991when he visited Zhejiang, he pointed out, "both the promotion of economic development and the overall progress of society are the essential requirements of socialism."[28] In Provincial and Ministerial Cadres' Advanced Studies Class of Party School of the CPC Central Committee in June 1992, Comrade Jiang Zemin said, "the undertakings of socialist modernization are carried out in a coordinated and comprehensive way. We need to not only promote the economic construction, but also improve people's ideological, moral, scientific and cultural qualities, social order and social morality, so as to promote the comprehensive progress of society and the overall development of social civilization."[29]

28 Jiang Zemin on Socialism with Chinese Characteristics (excerpts), Beijing, Central Party Literature Press, 2002, p. 379.

29 Selected Literature since the 13th National Congress of the CPC, Volume II, Beijing, People's Publishing House, 1993, p. 2080.

In October 1996, at the Sixth Plenary Session of the 14th CPC Central Committee, he pointed out, "The socialist society develops and progresses comprehensively. Socialist modernization is the cause of the coordinated development of material civilization and spiritual civilization. It is impossible to achieve socialism with Chinese characteristics without any aspect."[30] In 1997, at the 15th Congress of the CPC, based on the requirements of the socialist modernization with Chinese characteristic, a great blueprint was drawn in the field of politics, economy, military, diplomacy and culture for the comprehensive development of China's modernization and all-round social progress. Comrade Jiang Zemin's discussion fully integrated the overall and coordinative development into China's socialist modernization strategy, effectively strengthened economic, political and cultural construction, so that with the cooperation among all factors the goal of economic development and social progress will be achieved. At the 16th Congress of the CPC in 2002, Comrade Jiang Zemin made clear the goal of building a well-off society in his report, which is to "Further develop the economy, improve democracy, advance science and education, enrich culture, foster social harmony and upgrade the texture of life for the people."[31]

These thoughts profoundly reflect the deepening understanding of the law of the development of human society by the third generation of the central collective leadership. The important thinking of the 'Three Represents' embodies the requirements of the comprehensive development of society. "Representing the requirements of the development of China's advanced productive forces" embodies the ideal and value goals of developing socialist economy and building a socialist material civilization. "Representing the progressing direction of advanced Chinese culture" embodies the ideal and value goals of developing socialist culture and building a socialist spiritual civilization. "Representing the fundamental interests of China's most majority of people", emphasizing considering the interests of the people, demands and practice as the highest standards of value and evaluation, embodies the Party's aim the nature of our country. The important thought of "Three Represents" reveals the way of self-improvement and development of the socialist system from the perspective of the comprehensive development of society, and demonstrated that only with a solid material foundation, strong cultural support and extensive public support can the self-improvement and development of the socialist system be achieved.

30 Selected Literature since the 14th National Congress of the CPC, Volume II, Beijing, People's Publishing House, 1999, p. 2027.

31 Selected Literature since the 16th National Congress of the CPC, 2003, Vol. 1, p. 14.

2. Highlighting the comprehensive development of people and deepening the understanding of the essence of socialism

The essence of socialism is the fundamental attribute inherent in socialism itself, which determines the features, nature and development of socialism. The realization of the essence of socialism is the dynamic process of the gradual development of the socialist history. The important thinking of the 'Three Represents' guided the real socialist path toward the core values and ultimate goals of human social development, which is to realize the free and comprehensive development of human beings. It deepens the understanding of the essence of socialism and further enriches and develops the theory of scientific socialism.

The free and comprehensive development of human beings is the fundamental orientation and highest value of social development and the highest value standard measuring the social development and historical progress. The founders of Marxism believe that communism, as a process of social revolution, has the ultimate goal of realizing people's free and comprehensive development. In the past, various social forms have a progressive effect on advancing the development of people as a whole. But in these social forms, human development was unbalanced, unjust and unreasonable, and the development of some people was under the premise of the deprivation of others' development rights. Therefore, they are destined to be replaced by a more advanced social form, namely the communist society. Seeking the free and comprehensive development of human beings is not only an ideal goal for the future development of socialist society, but also the value goal that the socialist society should uphold.

The third generation of the central collective leadership of the party adhered to the basic principles of Marxism, upheld the Marxist scientific spirit, fully considered China's reality, systematically and profoundly elaborated the idea of promoting the all-round development of human from the perspective of deepening the understanding of socialist construction laws and the laws of human society development. Comrade Jiang Zemin pointed out that, all our undertakings of building socialism with Chinese characteristics and other works shall focus on material and cultural needs of the people and the improvement of people's quality. In other words, we must strive to promote the comprehensive development of the people, which is the essential requirement of Marxism on building a new socialist society. We must continue to push forward the all-round development of mankind on the basis of the development of socialist material and spiritual civilization.[32]

32 Jiang Zemin, "Three Represents", Beijing, Central Party Literature Press, 2001, p. 179.

The idea regarding the realization of the comprehensive development of human beings in the important thinking of the 'Three Represents' which mainly includes the following contents:

Firstly, it illustrates the necessity to achieve the all-round development of man. The comprehensive development of man is the essential requirement of socialism, so to promote the comprehensive development of human beings should be a major part of the socialist construction. The socialist system is a people-oriented system. To realize the free and comprehensive development of man is the essence of socialism. Socialism can truly transcend capitalism only if it reaches a greater degree of free and comprehensive human development. In the Party's practice of leading the socialist revolution and construction, only by fully reflecting the fundamental interests and aspirations of the people and focusing on promoting the all-round development of human beings, can our undertakings be successful, and the superiority of socialism fully realized. With more comprehensive development and higher the enthusiasm and initiative of people, more social material and cultural wealth will be created, and people's lives improved more.

Secondly, it analyzes the possibility of achieving all-round human development. Currently China has entered a new stage of building a well-off society in an all-round way and accelerating the construction of socialist modernization. The economic and cultural conditions that promote the comprehensive development of human beings are basically in place. Since the Reform and Opening-up, our comprehensive national strength has been greatly enhanced; people's material and cultural living standards have improved significantly; and we are moving towards a new stage of building a well-off society in an all-round way and accelerating the process of socialist modernization. The great development of productive forces and the rapid progress of society provide adequate conditions for free and comprehensive development of the people and require higher quality of the people. Only by continuously promoting free and comprehensive development of people based on the economic and social development can people's enthusiasm and creativity be fully mobilized to contribute the socialist modernization.

Thirdly, it proposes the main approach to the comprehensive development of human beings. The important thinking of the 'Three Represents' not only emphasizes the urgency and importance of promoting the all-round development of human beings, but also puts forward, from the aspects of economy, politics and culture, the major issue we must solve in our efforts in promoting the comprehensive development of human beings, namely economically building a well-off society in an all-round way and continuously improving people's living standards. Politically, we should guarantee that people manage their own affairs in accordance with the law, and give full play to people's initiative and creativity, to achieve the interests and aspirations of the people. Culturally, we should improve the ideological, moral, scientific and cultural qualities of the whole nation, to achieve the all-round development of people's ideological and spiritual life. In term of the relationship between man and nature, we should achieve the harmony between man and nature, so that people work and live in a beautiful ecological environment. In term of the relationship between human development and economic and social development, we should coordinate people's comprehensive development with the all-round development of society, economy, politics and culture, promote social development on the basis of people's comprehensive development, and promote people's comprehensive development based on social development. This makes people's comprehensive development on the agenda of socialist modernization.

3. Considering the primary stage of socialism as the beginning of socialism and deepening the understanding of the primary stage of socialism

The developing stages of socialism have always been an important theoretical issue for scientific socialism. In the course of the development of socialist history, the Communist Parties of various countries had some correct understanding of this issue and many mistakes as well. The theory of the primary stage of socialism first proposed by Deng Xiaoping as the foundation of Deng Xiaoping's theory is the innovation made by Chinese communists.

After the Fourth Plenary Session of the 13th CPC Central Committee, the third generation of the central collective leadership of the party further enriched and developed the theory of the primary stage of socialism. In the report of the 14th National Congress of the CPC, Comrade Jiang Zemin listed the theory of the primary stage of socialism as the major content of the theory of socialism with Chinese characteristics. The report of the 15th Party Congress further elaborated on the theory of the primary stage of socialism. There were many new ideas and original expressions, which are embodied in:

Firstly, it scientifically demonstrates that the theory of the primary stage of socialism is the cornerstone of Deng Xiaoping's theory and creatively expounds the status of the theory of socialism in the scientific system of Deng Xiaoping's theory and its guiding significance to the practice of socialist construction. At the same time, Comrade Jiang Zemin also mentioned that the first 20 years of the 21st century is the stage of building a well-off society in an all-round way, which deepened Deng Xiaoping's thought on the phased and step-by-step modernization, enriched our party's theory of the primary stage of socialism, accorded with China's reality and people's demands.

Secondly, it expounds the theoretical connotation of the primary stage of socialism, and the social nature, basic characteristics, historical tasks and development process of the primary stage of socialism. In the report at the 15th National Congress of the Communist Party, Comrade Jiang Zemin first summed up the basic characteristics of the primary stage of socialism from nine aspects, which outlined the basic features and historical tasks of this historical stage.

Thirdly, based on the essence of Deng Xiaoping's theory on the primary stage of socialism, it raised the most realistic and urgent question of how to build socialism in the primary stage of socialism, for the first time clearly put forward the basic programs of the Party at the primary stage of socialism, creatively revealed socialist economy, politics and culture at the primary stage of socialism and the basic goals and policies at this stage. There are new expressions and original ideas in each aspect mentioned above. All of these lifted the theory of the primary stage of socialism to a new level, laying a solid foundation for the socialist economic theory.

Fourthly, it deepens and develops the understanding of the long-term of socialist development. Deng Xiaoping pointed out: "We have been building socialism for only a few decades and are still in the primary stage. It will take a very long historical period to consolidate and develop the socialist system, and it will require persistent struggle by many generations, a dozen or even several dozens."[33] Comrade Jiang Zemin pointed out, it must be understood that the realization of communism is a very long historical process. In the past, our understanding of this problem was superficial and simple. After so many years of practice, our understanding of this issue is more comprehensive and profound.[34] Socialism is the lower stage of communism; the long-term nature of socialism determines the same nature of communism. Especially in the socialist primary stage of China, the socialist period of history will be longer. This clear understanding determines that "We believe in the unity of the minimum and maximum programs." The comrades of the whole Party and all the people in China should not only have the lofty ideals of communism, but also do well in all our work at present stage.

Fifthly, it elaborated the unity of the party's minimum program and the maximum program. The issue of minimum and the maximum program is the major theoretical question that all proletarian parties must answer. Comrade Jiang Zemin believes that the communist society is a society with extremely abundant material wealth, greatly improved people's spiritual realm and free and comprehensive development of everyone. The Communist Party of China (CPC) is engaged in the cause of revolution and construction in a country with backward economy and culture. We need

33 Deng Xiaoping Selected Works, 1st ed., Vol. 3, p. 379-380.

34 See Jiang Zemin, "Three Represents", p. 177.

to, based on the actual situation and the main contradictions, fundamental tasks and international and domestic conditions at each stage, scientifically develop the minimum Party programs for various historical periods, in order to mobilize all positive factors, unite all forces and create conditions for the achievement of the maximum program of the Party. Comrade Jiang Zemin pointed out, comrades of the whole Party should not only establish the lofty ideals of communism, strengthen their beliefs, discipline and push oneself with high moral standards, but also make unremitting efforts to realize the basic program of the Party at present stage and do well in all their work. If we focus only on the present and neglect the ideals, we will lose the direction of progress. If we overlook out actual work and always talk\ about the ideals, we will be divorced from reality.[35] To uphold the unity of the minimum program and the maximum program reflects the deep insight of Chinese Communist Party on the law of social development and their clear understanding of the reality of revolution and construction.

4. Putting forward the idea that Development is the CPC's top priority in governing and rejuvenating the country and deepening the understanding of the law of socialist development

Development is the ultimate solution to the current issues we are faced with. Deng Xiaoping has always attached great importance to the liberation and development of productive forces. He considered it as a major part of the essence of socialism. In view of the wrong concepts in the past such as "poor socialism", "taking the class struggle as the top priority" and ignoring the development of productive forces, on the basis of summing up the experiences and lessons of socialist construction, Deng Xiaoping put forward the famous thesis of "Development is a top priority." The third generation of the central collective leadership of the party adhered to Deng Xiaoping's thinking on the liberation and development of productive forces, led the whole party and all the people withstood the difficulties and risks, actively promote the development of China's social productive forces, kept driving forward the cause of socialism with Chinese characteristics, and made world-acclaimed achievements.

In the course of practice, the Communist Party of China has continuously deepened its understanding of the importance of development and put forward the important thinking that development is the CPC's top priority in governing and rejuvenating the country. From an international point of view, first of all, the world multi-polarization is developing amidst twists and turns. As a socialist country with a population of 1.3 billion and a developing

35 Ibid., p. 178.

country, it is necessary for China to make development a top priority in order to become a strong pole in the world's multi-polarization trend and continuously enhance China's international status. Secondly, economic globalization continues to accelerate. China shall make development a top priority so as to seize the opportunity and change the situations of "northern countries stronger than southern ones", "western countries stronger than the eastern ones" and "capitalist countries stronger than the socialist ones", in the economic globalization dominated by western developed capitalist countries. Thirdly, science and technology have been making continuous progress. In order to narrow the gap with the developed countries and achieve China's modernization as soon as possible, we must focus on the development of the first productive forces of science and technology, implement the strategy of rejuvenating the country through science and education and vigorously develop science, technology and education. Lastly, in today's world the comprehensive national strength competition is becoming increasingly fierce. Without development, we will have no future; without development, we will fall behind and be in a weak position in international competition.

Domestically, after entering the new century, China has entered a new stage of building a well-off society in an all-round way and accelerating the socialist modernization. On the whole, the first two decades of the 21st century is an important strategic opportunity that must be firmly grasped for more accomplishments. To further solve the contradiction between the growing material and cultural needs of the people and the backward social production and comprehensively build a well-off society that has benefits more than one billion people depend on development. To further enhance the comprehensive national strength and achieve the great rejuvenation of the Chinese nation depend on development. To solve various domestic problems and maintain the sustained and stable situation depend on development. The development of socialist democracy, the improvement of socialist legal system and the construction of a high degree of socialist political civilization depend on development. Strengthening the construction of socialist spiritual civilization and enhancing comprehensive quality of the Chinese nation depend on development. To consolidate the party's ruling position, maintain the party's advanced nature and enhance the cohesion and persuasiveness of socialism with Chinese characteristics depend on development. Early settlement of the Taiwan issue and the realization of the complete reunification of our motherland depend on development. In conclusion, development is the key to constantly solving all problems.

The third generation of the central leadership of the party also stressed that regarding development as the top priority of the Party in governing arid rejuvenating the country requires us to solve the problems in development with development mentality and reforms and properly handle the relationship between reform, development and stability. In the process of development, there will be various problems. But only with the development can these problems be fundamentally resolved. On the one hand, we must uphold the theme of development, solve the problems in development with developing foresight, ideas and approaches, promote all the ideas, practices and systems suitable for development and resolutely remove all ideas, practices and system defects hindering development. On the other hand, it is necessary to correctly handle the relationship between reform, development and stability and integrate reform intensity, development speed and social acceptance. We should not only promote reform and development while maintain a stable political environment and social order, but also achieve social stability in the reform and development.

Regarding development as the top priority of the Party in governing and rejuvenating the nation inherits Deng Xiaoping's theory on the nature of the socialism, but also adds new contents of the new era, highlighting the important position of development in the ruling content, process and basis of the party and is of great guiding significance for further clarifying the party's governing mission, improving governing ability and enhancing the ruling position. From the perspective of the party's ruling content, the party is encountering various complicated problems and needs to deal with many affairs. But only development is the top priority; other affairs shall be adapted to the development without any influence or interference on the promotion and implementation of the "top priority". From the perspective of ruling process, the implementation of each decision-making and the introduction of each important policy should focus on development and be conducive to development. The purpose of the ruling party is to solve the development problem; the ruling measure shall aim at development; the effectiveness of ruling shall be tested by developing achievements; and the long-term stability of the ruling relies on development. From the perspective of the party's advanced nature, the most important thing is to promote the development of social history. Because "the party's advanced nature is concrete and historical, which should be measured in promoting the development of China's advanced productive forces and advanced culture, the efforts of safeguarding and realizing fundamental interests of the overwhelming majority of the people, and ultimately the practical role of the party in promoting the historical progress."[36]

The thought of regarding development as the top priority of the party work in governing and rejuvenating the country not only enriches and develops the Marxist theory of development and deepens the understanding of the law of socialist development, but also lay the foundation for the Scientific Outlook on Development.

36 Jiang Zemin on Socialism with Chinese Characteristics (excerpts), p. 584.

5. Formulating the basic program at the primary stage of socialism and enriching and developing the theory of socialism with Chinese characteristics

Based on Deng Xiaoping Theory and the basic line of the Party, focusing on the goal of building a prosperous, democratic and civilized socialist country, the 15th National Congress of the Communist Party of China further clarifies what the socialist economy, politics and culture with Chinese characteristics at the primary stage of socialism and how to build them, and put forward the basic program of the party at the at the primary stage of socialism. The party's basic program at the primary stage of socialism is a major party of the party's basic theory and the extension of the party's basic line in the aspects of economy, politics and culture.

Firstly, it put forward the construction of socialist economy with Chinese characteristics and promoting China's economic development with socialist market economy. With what kind of economic system should we promote the improvement of social productive forces and rapid economic development is a key issue for China's socialist modernization. Deng Xiaoping put forward that market economy can develop in socialist country, which has laid a theoretical foundation for the implementation of the socialist market economic system. Under the guidance of Deng Xiaoping Theory, the third generation of the central collective leadership of the party made their contributions to socialist market economy theory. In Provincial and Ministerial Cadres' Advanced Studies Class of Party School of the CPC Central Committee in June 1992, based on Deng Xiaoping's idea of developing market economy in the socialist society, Comrade Jiang Zemin for the first time put forward the thought of establishing a socialist market economic system. In October 1992, the 14th Congress of the CPC formally decided that the goal of China's economic system reform is to establish a socialist market economic system. The Third Plenary Session of the 14th CPC Central Committee held in November 1993 passed the "Resolution on Several Issues Concerning the Establishment of a Socialist Market Economic System", which systematizes and specifies the goals, requirements and principles established in the 14th Congress of the CPC and sketches out the basic framework of Socialist Market Economic System. In 1997, the 15th Congress of the CPC further emphasized that the construction of a socialist economy with Chinese characteristics was to develop market economy and continuously liberate and develop productive forces under the socialist conditions. The 15th Congress of the CPC put forward a series of new ideas and statements on how to establish a relatively perfect socialist market economic system. In the 21st century, the 16th Congress of the CPC proposed that the major task of economic construction and reform in the first 20 years of the 21st century is to improve the socialist market economic system.

Since the Fourth Plenary Session of the 13th CPC Central Committee, our party's explorations on the construction of a socialist market economic system could be summed as in the following:

Firstly, it explained the historical inevitability of establishing a socialist market economic system; secondly, it clarified the basic concept of the socialist market economy and emphasized that "China's socialist market economic system is integrated with the basic system of socialism"; thirdly, it built the basic framework of the socialist market economy, assuring the smooth operation and development of the new socialist market economy system; fourthly, it summarized the basic characteristics of the socialist market economy. The theory of socialist market economy cannot be found in the works of Marxist classic writers. It is entirely the theory of the Chinese Communist Party. Through hard explorations, the third generation of the central leadership of the party has pushed the socialist market economic theory created by Deng Xiaoping to a new development stage.

Secondly, it proposed the construction of socialist politics with Chinese characteristics and promoting China's political development with the rule of law. There is no socialism or socialist modernization without democracy and legal system, which is an important idea of Deng Xiaoping. Under the guidance of Deng Xiaoping Theory, in the report of the 14th National Congress of CPC in 1992, "actively promoting the reform of the political system and achieving significant development of socialist democracy and legal system" was made as the major task of the reform and construction in the 1990s. In 1997, the 15th National Congress of the Communist Party of China put forward the important task of "governing the country by law and building a socialist country under the rule of law". In 2002, the 16th National Congress of the Communist Party of China made "developing socialist democracy and building socialist political civilization" as an important goal of building a well-off society in an all-round way. The 16th National Congress of CPC also put forward specific measures to construct the socialist political civilization through the reform of the political system based on the reality of the socialist modernization.

Since the Fourth Plenary Session of the 13th CPC Central Committee, the party's third-generation of central collective leadership has actively explored the development of socialist democracy and the construction of socialist political civilization, and put forward a series of new ideas, opinions and judgments, providing us with a new understanding of the political development of Chinese-style modernization. Firstly, it points out the direction of the construction of socialist democracy in China and emphasizes that the construction of socialist politics with Chinese characteristics is to, under the premise of upholding the four basic principles, continue to promote the political system reform, perfect the socialist democratic system, improve the socialist legal system, and build a socialist country under the rule of law. We must consider our national conditions, sum up our practical experience and learn from the useful achievements of human political civilization, but never copy the Western political system. Secondly, it clarifies the main task of our political system reform. Comrade Jiang Zemin pointed out that promoting the reform of the political system should be conducive to enhancing the vitality of the party and the state, show the characteristics and advantages of the socialist system, fully mobilize the enthusiasm and creativity of the people, safeguard national unity and social stability, and promote economic development and social progress. We should focus on strengthening the system construction and realizing the institutionalization, standardization and proceduralization of socialist democratic politics. Thirdly, it put forward the governing strategy combining "rule of law" and "rule by virtue". Comrade Jiang Zemin pointed out that in the process of building socialism with Chinese characteristics and developing a socialist market economy, we must not only unswervingly strengthen the socialist legal system construction to rule the country according to law, but also unswervingly strengthen the socialist moral construction to rule the country by virtue.[37] This is another great step forward in the strategy of governing the country, which is a major development of the leadership and ruling mode of the Chinese Communist Party. Lastly, it creatively put forward the important idea of building socialist political civilization and makes the coordinated development of the socialist material civilization, political civilization and spiritual civilization as the goal of the new century, which organically integrated the development of socialist economy, politics and culture.

Thirdly, it proposed the construction of the culture of socialism with Chinese characteristics and promoting the development of Chinese culture with spiritual civilization. Since the 4th Plenary Session of the 13th CPC Central Committee, the third generation of the central leading collective of the Party has learned the lessons of various problems caused by ignoring the construction of socialist spiritual civilization in the first ten years of Reform and Opening-up and attached great importance to the cultural and spiritual civilization construction with Chinese characteristics. On the basis of the resolution of the Sixth Plenary Session of the 12th Central Committee of the Communist Party of China on the guiding principles of the construction of socialist spiritual civilization, the Sixth Plenary Session of the 14th CPC Central Committee held in October 1996 passed Resolution on the Issues in Strengthening Socialist Spiritual Civilization, which determines the guiding ideology, objectives and tasks, basic principles and major measures for strengthening the spiritual civilization construction under the new situation and creates new dimension for socialist spiritual civilization construction. The report of the 15th National Congress of the

37 Jiang Zemin, "Three Represents", pp. 134-135.

Communist Party of China sets out the program of socialist cultural construction with Chinese characteristics. Comrade Jiang Zemin pointed out that the socialist culture with Chinese characteristics is an important force to unite and inspire the people of all ethnic groups throughout the country and an important symbol of comprehensive national strength. It provides a new perspective for the whole party to attach importance to cultural construction.

In order to strengthen the construction of spiritual civilization in the new period, Comrade Jiang Zemin timely put forward a series of new ideas, opinions and requirements for Chinese cultural modernization. Firstly, the socialist culture with Chinese characteristics must represent the direction of advanced culture. It was clearly stated in the report of the 16th CPC National Congress that, "in contemporary China, the development of advanced culture is to develop a scientific and popular socialist culture oriented towards modernization, the world and the future, so as to constantly enrich people's spiritual world and enhancing people's spirit power". Secondly, carrying forward and cultivating the national spirit is the key to the modernization of Chinese culture. The development of socialist culture with Chinese characteristics and the construction of socialist spiritual civilization essentially is the construction of national spirit. Comrade Jiang Zemin believed that spiritual power is also an important part of comprehensive national strength. He stressed that whether there is high national spirit is a major standard measuring the comprehensive national strength of a country. To truly achieve a comprehensive and well-off socialist modernization, we must carry forward and cultivate the national spirit into through the whole process of spiritual civilization construction, so that all the people always maintain a high-spirited state of mind. Lastly, innovation is the driving force of cultural modernization. In the face of the competition of all kinds of ideology and culture in the world, the socialist culture with Chinese characteristics must carry out the policy of encouraging blossoming and contending of all, promote reform, opening up and modernization construction, focus on the forefront of world cultural development, carry forward the fine tradition of national culture, learn from the strengths of all nations in the world, and constantly innovate.

In conclusion, under the guidance of Marxism-Leninism, based on Deng Xiaoping's theory, the important thought of "Three Represents" more comprehensively and systematically answered the questions on development path, development stage, fundamental purpose, driving force, external conditions and political guarantee, deepened our party's understanding of the law of human society development, the law of socialist construction and the development law of the ruling party, and enriched and developed the theory of scientific socialism.

(Qin Xuan, Professor of Institute of Marxism Studies, Renmin University of China)

Scientific Outlook on Development Guiding China's Economic and Social Development

The 3rd Plenary Session of the 16th CPC Central Committee proposed to adhere to people-oriented conception and establish a comprehensive, coordinated and sustainable development view; the Fifth Plenary Session proposed to unswervingly guide the overall situation of economic and social development with Scientific Outlook on Development; the 17th National Congress of the Communist Party of China put forward that Scientific Outlook on Development is an important guiding principle for China's economic and social development. Scientific Outlook on Development has become a major strategic thought that must be upheld and carried out in the development of socialism with Chinese characteristics. It marked the important changes in the development concept of our party and the government, and the great innovation in the development mode. It has made a profound impact on China's economic and social development.

1. Scientific Outlook on Development marks the change of development concept

From the first day of the founding of new China, the party and the government regarded development as the overriding theme and fully engaged in the development of socialism. However, for the issues of how to achieve development, what ideas to guide the development, what kind of economic and social development path should be taken and how to deal with a series of relations during the development process, it went through a continuous process of exploration.

In the course of leading the development of socialism in China, based on the reality that China was an economically and culturally backward country and that the socialist system lacked a solid material foundation, according to the goal of building China into an industrialized country, Mao Zedong put forward the basic guiding ideology on economic and social development. There were three distinct characteristics of this guiding ideology: firstly, to rapidly develop socialism with the spirit of "great leap forward". The high speed was considered as the most important indicator of development; the rapid growth of some individual indicators was regarded as the major goal of development; the guiding ideology of development was highlighted in being fast and focusing on catching up. Secondly, it took the mode of unbalanced development of some industries and gave priority to heavy industry. All the forces of the country were concentrated on the development of heavy industry which was ensured at the expense of agriculture and light industry, in order to rapidly achieve the goal of socialist industrialization.

It believed that the material basis of socialism lay in the development of heavy industry and developed heavy industry equaled a developed economy and a developed country. Thirdly, it promoted the development with mass movement. The mass movement was considered as the major driving force of economic development. It attempted to vigorously drive forward the economic development with mass movements. There were two modes of drive economic development with mass movement. One was to engage in large-scale economic construction and mobilize the masses to engage in an industry so that the extraordinary development of this industry would drive the development of the whole economy, for instance, the "great leap forward" campaign in 1958. The other one was to drive economic development through large-scale political campaign, for instance, the campaigns of "learning from Daqing in industry" and "learning from Dazhai in agriculture" during the Cultural Revolution. The characteristics of Mao Zedong's guiding ideology on the issue of development was directly related with economic development stage of China back then, the degree of understanding of the law of economic development and short time of socialist economic development. Therefore, when reviewing the limitations of the past guiding ideology today, we should also realize the objectivity of its formation. In fact, the deepening of understanding on the guiding ideology of economic and social development is inseparable from the practice development.

With the launching of Reform and Opening-up, China's economic and social development has entered a new historical period. Through the summary of more than 30 years of economic and social development, especially in the late 1950s and early 1960s as well as the twists and turns and lessons learned in the Cultural Revolution, the Party Central Committee represented by Deng Xiaoping kept deepening their understanding of the objective laws of economic and social development and put forward a series of new ideas on economic and social development. There are several major characteristics. Firstly, it set the basic line for economic and social development, which is to focus on the central task of economic construction and adhere to the Four Cardinal principles and Reform and Opening-up policy and established the guiding ideology for social development at the primary stage of Chinese socialism. This basic line clearly put forward the general guiding ideology that development should focus on economic construction guaranteed by upholding four cardinal principles and driven by the Reform and Opening-up policy, establishing a new concept of development. Secondly, it put forward the strategic thinking of non-balanced development. Deng Xiaoping proposed that some region with favorable conditions should get rich first and then bring along and support other regions. There could be some special policies for these regions to provide them with more room for development. In the process of Reform and Opening-up and the development of the socialist market economy, it is necessary to carry out experimental exploration in some areas which would provide demonstration effect to other places on the basis of accumulated experience. This idea embodies the new concept of development of promoting national development with local development. Thirdly, it put forward the idea that development is of overriding importance and economy should continuously move forward. In the event of fluctuations and difficulties in economic and social development, we must always unswervingly put development as the priority and the prerequisite for solving all difficulties and problems. Only with development can we gain the initiative. Economic development should maintain a high speed and reach a new level every few years. Only in this way can we more quickly narrow the gap with the developed countries. Development is of overriding importance and economy should continuously move forward become a distinctive feature of the new concept of development. Fourthly, it put forward the strategic thinking of grasping both material and spiritual civilization at the same time and attaching sufficient importance to both. Development is not only about the construction of material civilization, but also the spiritual civilization. Based on the mutual promotion between the constructions of material civilization and spiritual civilization, Deng Xiaoping put forward a general ideology for development. The formation of this guiding ideology shows that our understanding of development has extended from the construction of material civilization to that of spiritual civilization, then to that of the whole society. This is a major new feature of Deng Xiaoping's development concept.

Deng Xiaoping's concept of economic and social development was formed in China's Reform and Opening-up course and during the development of socialist market economy. This concept and the theory of socialism with Chinese characteristics he created became the guiding ideology of China's economic and social development during this period. Under the guidance of this concept, China's development has made remarkable progress. Practice has proved that Deng Xiaoping's thoughts on economic and social development reflect the deepening of our party's understanding of the development concept. After entering the mid-1990s, on the basis of more than ten years of sustained high economic growth, the party had a more profound understanding of the development. The third generation of the central collective leadership with Comrade Jiang Zemin as the core further emphasized the importance of development and brought development to a higher level. It was mainly manifested in several aspects. Firstly, it put forward that development is the first priority of the party in governing and rejuvenating the country. Comrade Jiang Zemin pointed out, "that development is of overriding importance is a strategic idea that we must always adhere to. We shall view this issue economically and politically.

For more than two decades, the principles and policies were supported by our people; we withstood the test of various international and domestic issues; and China's international prestige and influence has been continuously enhanced. These are all closely related with the rapid development of China's social productive forces, the significantly enhancement of our national strength and continuous improvement of people's lives."[38] This shows that if a ruling party cannot regard development as the top priority in governing and rejuvenating the country, it can neither take on the task of rejuvenating the country nor show its ability to govern. That development is of overriding importance economically recognized the importance of development. That development is the first priority of the party in governing and rejuvenating the country politically recognized the significance of development. Viewing the development issue from the perspective of unity between economy and politics marks the comprehensiveness of our party's understanding of development.

Secondly, it proposed that development is the key to solve all the problems in China. Comrade Jiang Zemin pointed out, "the key of solving all the problems in China is development. Solving people's ideological issues, convincing those who do not believe in socialism and enhancing people's faith and confidence in the future of socialism and our country ultimately rely on development. In considering the strategy of China's development at the beginning of the new century, the central government stressed the need to focus on development, which was a major decision based on this most basic principle. The party, the government and all our people shall seize every minute and make every effort to focus on the central task of economic construction, vigorously promote economic and social development and continuously enhance our economic strength, national defense and national cohesion."[39] It further shows that when our things go well or when we are encountered with difficulties and problems, we should firmly adhere to development.

Thirdly, it put forward that the purpose of development is to realize the fundamental interests of the vast majority of the people. The core content of the important thinking of the 'Three Represents' put forward by Comrade Jiang Zemin is to always represent the fundamental interests of the overwhelming majority of the people. It contains a new understanding of the purpose and stance of development. The understanding of the issue such as the purpose of development is not always clear. The important thinking of the 'Three Represents' clearly defines in nature that when the purpose of development is the fundamental interests of the people, it is in line with the party's aim. Development itself is not a goal, but only a means. The purpose

38 Jiang Zemin on Socialism with Chinese Characteristics (excerpts), p. 92.
39 Ibid., p. 93.

of development is to improve people's living standards and life quality and achieve the fundamental interests of the people. As Comrade Jiang Zemin said, "that our party must always represent the fundamental interests of the overwhelming majority of the people of China means that party's theory, line, program, principles, policies and work must take the people's fundamental interests as the starting point and purpose, give full play to people's enthusiasm and initiative, and let people enjoy real economic, political and cultural interests on the basis of continuous social development."[40]

It is an important manifestation of the deepening of our party's understanding of the development by taking the important thinking of the 'Three Represents' as the guiding ideology of the Party. A ruling party should not only regard development as the top priority of the Party in governing and rejuvenating the country, but also take people's fundamental interests of the overwhelming majority as the starting point and purpose of development. The 16th National Congress of the Communist Party of China put forward the goal of building a well-off society in an all-round way. In order to achieve this goal, we need to maintain sustainable economic development, improve the quality and efficiency of economic development, achieve the coordinated development of man and nature, and realize comprehensive social progress on the basis of economic development. So, it is necessary to maintain the rapid economic development, and properly solve all the deep-seated contradictions and problems in the process of development. It leads to a higher requirement for development, which is to maintain scientific, people-oriented, comprehensive, coordinated, sustainable and balanced development. The Party Central Committee with Comrade Hu Jintao as the general secretary proposed to take Scientific Outlook on Development as the major guiding principle for economic and social development and important strategic thinking for development of socialism with Chinese characteristics, which established a new concept of development whivh we must uphold in the new historical conditions.Upholding the Scientific Outlook on Development to guide the overall economic and social development requires us to change our development concept.

The changes include:

Firstly, the economic development must focus on "steadiness", "sustainability" and "innovation". To maintain a rapid economic development has always been an important principle for us. The high growth for many years has been a great achievement in China's economic development. In the new round of economic development process, in accordance with the requirements of the scientific outlook on development, in order to achieve steady economic development, we need to change guiding ideology from speed

40 Ibid., p. 581.

first to quality and efficiency, which is an improvement of understanding of economic development. Steadiness means high quality and avoidance of ups and downs. It also means that development is no longer just about current speed, but also the long-term speed. This change in the concept of development makes our understanding of development more comprehensive and mature.

Economic development must be sustainable, which is a new concept of human understanding of the law of economic development. When economic development is at a low level, people's understanding of development is relatively superficial. They only focus on the immediate benefits in economic development and pursue short-term goals. The cost of resources, environment and ecology is not considered as the major indicator of economic development. The sustainable concept has not yet been established. Scientific development concept is to require people to not only focus on the output but also the cost in the process of development. Especially under the situation that China's land, fresh water, energy, mineral resources and environmental conditions are seriously limiting development, we must change our economic development mode, take a resource-saving and environment- friendly development path, and maintain the harmony between economic development and population, resources and environment. The establishment of such a concept of development is a conceptual guarantee for achieving sustainable development and marks that our guiding ideology of development has reached a new level.

To achieve sustainable development, we must rely on scientific and technological progress and the improvement of the quality of labor and improve our capability of independent innovation, which is our deepened understanding of the driving force for development. In the economic globalization, when the economy of a country reaches to a certain stage, in order to achieve sustainable development, it must solve the issue of driving force for development. With weak economic foundation, low level of technology, low quality of labor, China's economic development relied on the input of resources. This kind of economic development will gradually lose its momentum, so it is hard to achieve sustainable economic development. The Scientific Outlook on Development is to put the improvement of innovative ability to a prominent position, understand development from the perspective of its driving force, lay a solid foundation of developing the country through science and education and strengthening the country through talents and vigorously improve the original innovation capability, integrated innovation capability and the ability of introduction, absorbing and re-innovation, so that economic development is based on scientific and technological progress and improvement of labor quality. This change in the concept of development makes our understanding of development law more profound.

Secondly, we must focus on “balance” in the development course. For a variety of reasons, in the past 20 years of development, we allowed some regions with favorable conditions to get rich first. The advantage of implementing this strategy is that the development of some regions could demonstrate and lead the development of other regions in our country. However, it will cause the widening gap among regions and between urban and rural areas, leading to uncoordinated development. When the level of economic development is low and the gap among regions and between urban and rural areas is not that large, this uncoordinated situation would not affect the whole development. But, when economic development has crossed the take-off phase and especially when building a well-off society in an all-round way is taken as our goal, this uncoordinated situation would cause serious problems in the development. It is also an issue that must be solved for building a well-off society in an all-round way. At present, the hard part of China’s comprehensive construction of a well-off society is the rural areas and western regions. The main factors restricting the building of a well-off society in an all-round way are the backward development of rural areas and the slow development of the western region. Therefore, it is impossible to achieve the goal of comprehensively building prosperous society without development of rural and western regions. There will be no national prosperity without prosperity in rural area. There will be no national modernization without modernization in western regions. Scientific Outlook on Development requires us to establish the concept of coordinated development, take into consideration of the overall situation of socialist modernization and coordinate urban, rural and regional development. The key is to properly solve the “three rural issues” and establish a regional systematic development mechanism featuring complementary advantages and positive interaction between eastern, middle and western areas. Coordination is an issue that must be properly handled in the development of a big country. It means smooth development and easement of contradictions in development process. To consciously lift the coordination to the level of guiding ideology indicates that our development concept is more in line with China’s reality and the development law of a large country.

Thirdly, social development must focus on “harmony”. Development must be comprehensive. It is not just about economic development, but also comprehensive social development and progress. Economic development is the foundation, but it is not the only goal. Only with economic development and comprehensive social progress can it be a higher level of more substantial development. Viewing from the general situation of the development of countries, it is in line with the law to focus on economic development first and then pay more attention to social development when the economic development reaches to a certain stage. The development firstly refers to economic development. Without the prerequisite of economic development, there will be no solid foundation for social development and comprehensive social progress. However, if the development is confined to economic development ignoring social development, it will lose its true meaning. The ultimate goal of development is to achieve comprehensive social progress, so that the whole society can be in a state of harmony. We cannot focus only on the economic development and allow social contradictions to intensify and make whole society fall into disharmony. If this is the case, the fruits of economic development will not be shared by the whole society and result of economic development won't lead to the overall progress of society.

The threes aspects of changes in development concept required by Scientific Outlook on Development are the profound understanding of the development by Chinese Communist Party under the new historical conditions. To guide economic and social development with Scientific Outlook on Development that is in line with requirements of the times, people's interests and development law reflects that the Chinese Communist Party is advancing with the times in its concept of development.

2. Scientific Outlook on Development becoming an important guideline for economic and social development

Scientific Outlook on Development is an important guideline for China's economic and social development and a major strategic thought that must be adhered to and implemented in the development of socialism with Chinese characteristics. It is the new generalization and development of status and significance of Scientific Outlook on Development by the CPC. This is because Scientific Outlook on Development reveals the law of economic and social development, that of socialist modernization and the ruling law of Communist Party of China.

Scientific Outlook on Development accurately reveals the law of economic and social development. Society is an organism composed of productive forces, production relations, economic basis and superstructure. They are interrelated and interact to promote the development of human society. In the course of the development of socialism with Chinese characteristics, the dialectical unity of economic construction, political construction, cultural construction and social construction fully embodies the contradiction between productive forces and production relations, and economic basis and superstructure. n the overall development of economy, politics, culture and society, Scientific Outlook on Development emphasizes people-oriented development, reflecting the purpose of development is to promote the comprehensive development of people, meet the people's growing material and cultural needs, safeguard people's economic, political and cultural rights and interests, and make sure the fruits of development benefit all the people. Scientific Outlook on Development emphasizes the overall coordination and sustainability, reflecting development should continue to strengthen the material basis for harmonious socialist society, enhance political security for the construction of a harmonious socialist society, consolidate the its spiritual support, and create favorable social conditions for the construction of a socialist harmonious society. The scientific connotation and spiritual essence of Scientific Outlook on Development are the concrete manifestations of the basic principles of Marxism in the relationship between productive forces and relations and economic basis and superstructure, becoming an important guideline for promoting economic and social development.

The fact that Scientific Outlook on Development can accurately reveal the law of economic and social development is closely linked with the correct grasp of scientific methods of thinking. The scientific way of thinking is to be pragmatic. Adhere to the pragmatic thinking and political style is to uphold the Marxist world view and methodology, uphold the party's scientific spirit of being practical and realistic, and uphold the ideological character and work style of being practical, telling the truth and doing a solid work. Only by adhering to the thinking method and political character of being realistic and pragmatic can we scientifically summarize the development experience, face the practical problems, plan for the future development, thoroughly implement the Scientific Outlook on Development and reflect the regular requirements of economic and social development.

Scientific Outlook on Development accurately reveals the law of socialist modernization. In the discussion of "what is socialism and how to build socialism", socialism has experienced ups and downs. There were both successful experience and lessons from failure. The catastrophic events in the development of socialism such as the drastic changes in Eastern Europe and collapse of the Soviet Union affected the socialist countries' exploration, understanding and grasp of the law of construction. We need to understand the historical process of the emergence and development of socialism, grasp the great historical contribution of the socialism development to the development of human history, sum up the lessons learned in socialist construction, and more importantly adhere to socialism, take the socialist path, carry out socialist reform and explore socialist development path suitable for national reality. Scientific Outlook on Development, on the basis of grasping the objective laws of economic and social development, deepens the understanding of the Communist Party of China on the law of socialist modernization.

In the history of the development of socialism in China, at the beginning of the founding of new China, the Communist Party of China clearly proposed to explore the law of socialist modernization. The first generation of CPC leadership with Mao Zedong as the core made a preliminary exploration on the development path suitable for China's conditions and put forward a series of important theoretical views on the socialist construction. After the Reform and Opening-up, the second generation of the central collective leadership with Deng Xiaoping as the core clearly put forward the historical task of building socialism with Chinese characteristics, formulated basic line of the primary stage of socialism and a series of major policies, and implemented the "Three Steps" development strategy for socialist modernization. The party's third generation of the central collective leadership with Comrade Jiang Zemin as the core proposed to guide socialist construction with Deng Xiaoping Theory and the important thinking of "Three Represents", developed and implemented the strategies of developing the country through science and education, sustainable development and western development, adhere to the development approach to solve the problems, and further enriched the theory and practice of socialist modernization. Since the beginning of the 21st century, the Party Central Committee with Comrade Hu Jintao as the general secretary clearly put forward the Scientific Outlook on Development, which was a great achievement in Communist Party of China's exploration on the law of socialist modernization. From the preliminary exploration of Mao Zedong to Deng Xiaoping's socialism with Chinese characteristics, to Comrade Jiang Zemin's insisting on using the development approach to solve the problems, to the Scientific Outlook on Development, it is reflected the gradual deepening of the exploration and understanding on socialist construction law by Chinese Communist Party.

Scientific Outlook on Development accurately reveals the development law of the Communist Party of China as a ruling party. Comrade Jiang Zemin pointed out: Our Party has a history of 80 years. It has had the great practice of creating and developing Mao Zedong Thought and Deng Xiaoping Theory. It has historical experience, both positive and negative and both Chinese and foreign, in developing socialism. We will be able to make fresh contribution to enriching and developing Marxism as long as we remain in the forefront of the times, base ourselves on the present practice, try to understand the characteristics of the times, study major issues of immediate importance in accordance with the basic theory of Marxism, deepen our understanding of the laws governing the rule of the country by the Communist Party and the development of socialism and human society, and draw upon all scientific and new experience, thoughts and achievements.[41]

41 See Jiang Zemin, "A Speech at the Celebration of the 80th Anniversary of the Founding of the Communist Party of China", Beijing, People's Publishing House, 2001, p. 29.

In the new historical period, based on the nature, purpose, content and requirements of socialist development, General Secretary Hu Jintao put forward the Scientific Outlook on Development, which has a series of requirements, such as the implementation of the policies for building the socialism with Chinese characteristics, the achievements of socialism with Chinese characteristics shared by all, the development path of socialism with Chinese characteristics, being practical and realistic, breaking the shackles of old thinking and promoting the comprehensive and coordinated development of socialism with Chinese characteristics. It represents the Chinese Communist Party's new concept of governing, reflects the basic law of governing by Chinese Communist Party, and marks to a certain extent that the governing concept of Chinese Communist Party has reached a new height. To implement the Scientific Outlook on Development means to strengthen the ability of the Chinese Communist Party to lead the development according to the new demands of the development of the party and people and enhance the ability of the party in leading people in grasping the overall situation, thus enhance coordinating and planning.

3. To incorporate economic and social development into scientific development

To guide China's economic and social development with Scientific Outlook on Development means to incorporate the economic and social development into the track of scientific development. The key is the choice of scientific development path.

Building a new socialist countryside is a major way of balancing urban and rural development. In accordance with the requirement of balancing urban and rural development by Scientific Outlook on Development, we must change the current urban-rural dual economic structure. The priority is to solve the problem of rural development. "Three Rural Problems of China" actually refers to the issues of agriculture, farmers and rural areas. The incompatibility between three rural issues and national modernization is specifically manifested in farmer's lower income compared with urban residents, weak position of agriculture compared with other industries and serious lag behind development in rural areas compared with cities. Therefore, in the process of building a well-off society in an all-round way, the key is to change the situation in rural areas.

It takes new ideas to solve the "three rural issues". In the past, the various policies and measures by the state to support the agriculture have played an important role. However, these policies and measures are mostly individual and local. Therefore, at present, the deep-seated contradiction that restricts the development of agriculture and rural areas has not yet been eliminated;

long-term mechanism promoting sustained and stable income increase for farmers has not formed; backward rural economic and social development has not fundamentally changed; and institutional mechanism for urban and rural development has not been fully established. It is difficult to fundamentally solve the problem of rural development.

Considering the construction of a new socialist countryside as an important way of coordinating urban and rural development means to generally take it as a major task of the party. We need to comprehensively take farmers' income increase, agricultural development and comprehensive progress in rural areas into consideration, and regard the policies of industry nurturing agriculture, city supporting village and giving more and asking for less as a systems engineering. Through the construction of a new socialist countryside, we will fundamentally solve the "three rural" issues and truly balance urban and rural development. The construction of a new socialist countryside is comprehensive in terms of its content, including economic construction, democratic political construction and spiritual civilization. Specifically, the first thing is to strengthen the rural productive forces, improve the comprehensive production capacity of grain, accelerate the progress of agricultural science and technology, and speed up the transformation of agricultural growth. Industry should nurture the agriculture and provide more substantial support to agriculture. In particular, the science and technology sector enhance support to agriculture. The progress of science and technology will fundamentally change the situation of agricultural productivity. As productive forces is the foundation, only by comprehensively improving agricultural productive forces can the gap between agriculture and other industries be narrowed. Secondly, increasing farmers' income shall be the central task of agricultural and rural work. Due to the particularity of agricultural production, the improvement of productive forces does not necessarily increase farmers' income. Farmers' income growth is also related with policy and market. Therefore, it is necessary to implement policies that can guarantee farmers' income growth, support farmers with policies and improve farmers' ability to resist market risks. Meanwhile, we must also encourage and support farmers to transfer employment, so that farmers can have more ways to increase income and a long-term mechanism for farmers to increase income would be established.

Thirdly, to expand democracy at the grassroots level in rural areas and the practice of self-administration should be a major part of democratic political construction. When building a new socialist countryside, we should focus on both economic construction and democracy construction. The goal of democratic political construction is to ensure that the masses of farmers are exercising their right as masters according to law, so that they can enjoy the achievements of political civilization construction while acquiring the fruits of material civilization construction. Village self-governance, transparency of village affairs, sound legal system and democratic management are the goals democracy construction in our task of building a new socialist countryside.

Fourthly, strengthening the construction of spiritual civilization and accelerating the development of rural education and cultural undertakings shall be a major part of cultural construction. Cultural backwardness in rural areas is a major factor for the backwardness in those rural areas. When building a new socialist countryside, we must cultivate and train new farmers, which is the foundation of construction of new countryside. The foundation of nurturing new farmers lies in the development of educational and cultural undertakings. We need to increase the government's investment in rural education, culture and health and change the situation of lagging behind rural social undertakings, so that farmers can have a comprehensive development on the basis of enjoying material civilization, political civilization and spiritual civilization. To promote the optimization and upgrading of industrial structure is an important way to change the mode of economic development. As a developing country, when its economic development reaches to a certain stage, transforming economic development mode is a prominent problem that must be solved. Generally speaking, in countries with relatively low levels of economic development, when the economy is taking off, the development mode is often extensive. The rapid economic growth is at the expense of large-scale investment and the consumption of a large number of resources. It will cause low efficiency, less benefit, significantly increase environmental pressure and unsustainable overall situation of development.

The development required by Scientific Outlook on Development aims to restrict the consumption of a large amount of resources and restrict such development which is at the expense of ecological environment, aims a development that is sustainable. This kind of development can only be achieved on the basis of the transformation of the economic development mode. The transformation of economic development mode should be realized through the optimization and upgrading of industrial structure. The transformation from the extensive growth mode to the intensive growth mode is related with the industrial structure. When the low-end industries dominate, the technological content is low; economic growth is mainly driven by input of production factors and the consumption of resources; the growth is extensive. To take the intensive economic growth path, we must improve the technological level of industries. On the one hand, low-end industries should develop into high-end industries. On the other hand, we should transform the traditional industries, so that they could take a new development path. Without the optimization and upgrading of industrial structure, the transformation of economic development mode will lack realistic foundation.

To speed up the transformation of economic development mode, we must promote the optimization and upgrading of industrial structure. Firstly, we need to consolidate and strengthen the basic position of agriculture. The strengthening of the basic position of agriculture must be based on the promotion of modern agriculture. Modern agriculture is characterized by extensive use of modern science and technology, the use of modern production tools and specialization, intensification and socialization of agricultural production. To strengthen the construction of modern agriculture, we need to adjust the agricultural production structure, build industrial zone with advantageous agricultural product actively develop the second and tertiary industries and agricultural products processing industry in rural areas. We shall strive to improve the organic composition of agriculture, improve resource utilization and land production rate and develop circular economy, so that agricultural development could go on the track of intensive production and a solid foundation could be laid for the transformation of the entire economic development mode. Secondly, we need to reorganize and transform the traditional industries, promote industrialization through informationization, and take the new path of industrialization development. A major part of optimization and upgrading of industrial structure is to transform traditional industries. In China, it's not that the traditional industries have no development prospects, but that it is necessary to change the traditional industry development model and road. It is important to transform the traditional industries with modern science and technology, so that the look of the traditional industry could be changed. Based on the continuous improvement of scientific and technological level, we should drive the optimization and upgrading of the information technology and create new growth points for the transformation of economic development mode. Thirdly, we should develop high-tech industries and advanced manufacturing. The development of high-tech industry is another important content to realize the optimization and upgrading of industrial structure. High-tech industry represents the direction of industrial development and is the key to change the mode of economic development. Whether a country's industrial structure is advanced is largely reflected by the proportion of high-tech industries. High-tech industry itself means a new way of development, because it mainly relies on science and technology to promote economic development. Therefore, accelerating the development of high-tech industries would inject new vitality to industry structure optimization and upgrading. Fourthly, we shall accelerate the development of modern service industry and improve the proportion of service industry. Compared with other countries in the world, development of China's service industry is lagging behind. One of the characteristics of the modern economy is the increasing proportion of service industry. The development of the service industry reflects not only its own degree of development, but also means that the whole industry is specialized, the degree of socialization is raised and the efficiency of economic development is improved. In particular, the development of modern service industry is an essential condition and basic characteristic of modern economic development. To rapidly improve the proportion of service industry in the whole industry is a major part in narrowing the gap between China and developed countries and a main indicator of whether the industrial structure is optimized and upgraded. Accelerating the development of the service industry will create favorable conditions for the transformation of the economic development mode.

Building a socialist harmonious society is an important way to realize people–oriented, comprehensive, coordinated and sustainable development. The construction of a socialist harmonious society is an important manifestation of people-oriented concept and Scientific Outlook on Development. It is deepened understanding of development on the basis of economic and social development and the unity of value and goals. The party's understanding of building a socialist harmonious society is deepened in practice. When proposing the comprehensive construction of a well-off society, a more harmonious society was for the first time taken as one of the six goals. In the discussion of strengthening the party's ability to govern, building a harmonious society was considered as one of five major capacities of the party's governance. In planning the cause of building socialism with Chinese characteristics, the construction of a harmonious society was regarded as one of the four major aspects. This is the enrichment and development of the Marxist theory of social construction by the CPC Central Committee with Comrade Hu Jintao as General Secretary.

The people-oriented, comprehensive, coordinated and sustainable development is the core content of Scientific Outlook on Development. To achieve this requirement of Scientific Outlook on Development, we must create a favorable social environment, which is a socialist harmonious society. The socialist harmonious society shall be one with democracy and order, equality and justice, credit and friendliness, vitality and stability in which human and nature have a harmonious relationship. Social harmony means social stability, cohesion and vitality. With these conditions, we can achieve a comprehensive, coordinated and sustainable development. In this sense, we might say that building a socialist harmonious society is an important way to achieve people-oriented, comprehensive, coordinated and sustainable development. Its specific content can be summarized as the following aspects:

Firstly, a new type of social management pattern would be established. To build a socialist harmonious society, we must promote the innovation of social management system. The core content is to establish a new social management system that is compatible with socialist market economy, democratic politics, advanced culture and harmonious society. Under this system, the party committee is at the core position; the government is fully responsible for social management under the leadership of the party; social organizations fulfill some of the functions of social management in cooperation with the government; people are encouraged to participate in social management; a comprehensive force of social management and service would be formed to promote the harmonious development of society. It is the update of management philosophy and innovation in management mode. A new social management model would be established to lay a solid foundation of social management for the sustainable development.

Secondly, we need to strengthen the construction of harmonious community and harmonious village and enhance social foundation. Harmonious communities and villages is the basis of a harmonious society. With the continuous improvement of market economy and democracy, communities and villages as the grassroots organization of society are the basic foothold of building a harmonious society. We should take the construction of harmonious communities and villages as the starting point for the construction of a harmonious socialist society, implement more favorable policies of social construction, management and services at the grassroots level, vigorously strengthen the basic work of urban communities at the grassroots level, comprehensively promote the construction of new socialist countryside, so that each community and village could become a cell for a harmonious society and a solid social foundation could be laid for sustainable development.

Thirdly, we shall effectively solve the problems most concerned by our people. The foundation of a harmonious society is the harmony of interests. In building a harmonious society, we must solve the issues of people's vital interests. Employment is the basic thing in people's life. It is not only economic and political issue, but also social issue. We should put employment increase at the important position in economic and social development, make the employment increase as the integration point in coordinating economic and social development, and achieve positive and interactive development between economic growth and employment increase. Perfecting the social security system is an important guarantee for social harmony and stability and national long-term stability. In view of the existing problems in the current social security system, speed up the improvement of insurance systems of basic pension, basic medical care, unemployment, work injury and maternity for urban workers, and development various social welfare undertakings such as social welfare, social relief, special care and social assistance. Sorting out distribution relationship and reasonable adjustment of income distribution is the policy basis for promoting social harmony. Under premise of implementing the policy of distribution according to the contribution of the production factors, we should attach more importance to social equity, strengthen the government's function in regulating income distribution, enhance supervision of distribution structure and standardize the system of distribution, so the income distribution mode of "small in the ends and big in the middle" could be established. Accelerating the development of cultural undertakings and industries is an important guarantee and necessary requirement for building a harmonious society. Social development is the purpose of economic development; people's development is the center of social development; and spiritual culture is the core of people's development. We must attach great importance to cultural construction. In market economy, cultural products and services not only have the attributes of goods, but also the characteristics of social welfare. We shall give priority to the social effect of cultural products and services. A law-based cultural management system and a dynamic cultural products production and management mechanism should be established to provide more and better cultural products for the people. When the issues concerned by people are solved and interests well-coordinated, favorable social conditions for the sustainable economic and social development can be created.

(Gu Yumin, Professor of Institute of Marxism, Fudan University, Shanghai)

Building a Socialist Harmonious Society

Since the 16th CPC National Congress, in the process of thinking about how to build a well-off society in an all-round way, the Party Central Committee with Comrade Hu Jintao as the general secretary put forward the idea of building a socialist harmonious society. The construction of a socialist harmonious society is the inheritance and development of Marxism-Leninism, Mao Zedong Thought, Deng Xiaoping Theory and the important thinking of the "Three Represents". It is the deepened understanding of the law of socialist construction under the new situation, which reflects that Chinese Communist Party has a new understanding of the development law of socialism with Chinese characteristics and new understanding of the laws, ability, strategy and way of governance. It provides an important ideological guidance for us to seize and make good use of important strategic opportunities and achieve the grand goal of building a well-off society in an all-round way.

1. The proposition of building a socialist harmonious society

The first 20 years of the 21st century is an important period of strategic opportunity that our country must seize to concentrate on building a well-off society at a higher level that benefits more than one billion people. The Party Central Committee with Comrade Hu Jintao as the general secretary summed up the experience of social development in the world, analyzed new situations and problems facing China's social development, and put forward the development idea with the goal of building a socialist harmonious society. No important ideas are out of imagination. There are two aspects of conditions: certain ideological and cultural conditions; realistic requirements of economic and political relations. In term of ideological and cultural conditions, there is a large number of "social harmony"ideas in the traditional Chinese culture, such as "Harmony is most precious" by Confucius, "mutual love" and "love without distinction" by Mo-tse, "to abandon boats, cars, weapons, to keep a record of events with knots, to have people satisfied with their food, clothes, house and customs" in the idea of "a small country with a small population" by Lao-tzu, "Heaven, Earth and I come into being together, and all things and I are one" by Zhuang-zi, "to respect the elderly of your own family and other families and love the children of your own family and other families"by Mencius, the ideal society in the Book of Rites where righteous governing principles are implemented, the country owned by all, virtuous people elected to govern, people in mutual trust and harmony and treat their own and others' relatives and children well, the elderly live a peaceful life in old age, the youth given full play their power, the young well educated, the widowed, the orphan, the childless old people and the disabled well protected" and Kang Youwei's social ideal of "people loving each other, all being equal and the whole world as one community". Among China's traditional "social harmony" ideas the Confucianism and Taoism are the most influential. Confucianism focuses on the society, ethics and the harmony among people and between man and society, regardless of the nature. Taoism focuses on the nature and the harmony between nature and society, regardless of society. In the West, utopian socialism thinkers also attached importance to social harmony. For instance, in 1803 in the Harmonious World, the French utopian socialist Fourier put forward that the existing unreasonable capitalist system would be replaced by a "harmonious system"; in 1824, British utopian socialist Owen had a communist experiment named as "new harmony" in Indiana of the United States; in 1842 in Guarantees of Harmony and Freedom, the German utopian communist Weitling explained the socialist society as "harmonious and free" society and the harmony in the new society would be "universal". These are the ideological and theoretical origins of the idea of building a socialist harmonious society. From Marx to Mao Zedong and Deng Xiaoping, they all have harmonious thoughts. Although they did mention the word of "harmony", their views on the comprehensive development of society contained the idea of social harmony, which was the direct theoretical basis for the idea of building a socialist harmonious society. In term of the realistic economic and political relations, in the last 30 years of the 20th century, especially since the reform and development in the 1990s, China's economy has reached a new level. In 2005 the GDP has reached more than ¥50 trillion; the people's living standards continue to improve. The historical experience of social development in the world shows that there are two possibilities for economic and social development in countries with per capita GDP ranging from $1,000 to $3,000, either entering the gold development period or the period of conflicts. If the right measures are taken, it will continue to develop, maintain a longer economic growth, and smoothly realize industrialization and modernization. If wrong measures are taken, various social conflicts will intensify, and the situation of Latin-Americanization will happen. At present, China's reform and development is in a critical period; it has also entered the internationally recognized crossroads for development; there are some prominent problems needed to be solved. Comrade Hu Jintao pointed out that with the continuous development of China's socialist market economy, with the improvement of the basic economic system featuring keeping public ownership as the mainstay of the economy and allowing diverse forms of ownership to develop and the distribution system featuring distribution according to work being dominant and the coexistence of a variety of modes of distribution, with the accelerating industrialization, urbanization and economic restructuring, with the accelerating reforms in social organization form, employment structure and social structure, there are some new characteristics in China's economic and social development that must be carefully understood. We are and will be facing for a long time some prominent problems urgently needed to be solved, mainly including the more prominent imbalance between urban and rural areas, economy and society and among regions, more complex social interest relationships, conflicts among all kinds of ideology and culture, corruption and serious crimes, which have serious impact on social stability and harmony. These are the contradictions and problems that we must properly deal with. Internationally, peace and development remain the themes of our era, and international situation continues to be in profound and complex changes. The trend of world multi-polarization and economic globalization is developing; scientific and technological progress continue to drive forward the overall level of world's productive forces International industrial upgrading and transfer speed up; all countries focus on economic development and international economic and technological cooperation; Regional economic integration is accelerating; Economic ties and interdependence are significantly deepened; world economic development is in the midst of an important opportunity. These factors have brought a rare opportunity and favorable conditions for our reform and development. But the world is not in peace; there are various complicated contradictions; instable and uncertain factors affecting peace and development still exist; the global economic development is unbalanced; the gap between North and South continues to widen; energy resources and environment restrict the economic development; trade protectionism has new forms; world economic development is facing many difficulties and problems. As the old international economic order has not fundamentally changed, world power imbalance is hard to fundamentally change in the short term. The trend of economic globalization not only promotes the development of the world economy, but also brings challenges and risks to countries, especially the developing countries. Developing countries are facing severe pressure on economy, politics, culture, information and military affairs. Traditional and non-traditional security threats are intertwined; Ethnic and religious conflicts and borders, territorial disputes rise from time to time; Terrorist activities are still rampant; Regional and international security situation is not promising. It is the necessary requirements of building a socialist harmonious society to firmly grasp the initiative to deal with the international situation and affairs, hold high the banner of peace, development and cooperation, observe and handle calmly, create a strategic situation conducive to our country and strive for a long period of favorable international environment for China's modernization.

2. The theoretical basis of building a socialist harmonious society

The idea of building a socialist harmonious society put forward by Communist Party of China is an important measure to solve the social problems, resolve social contradictions and deal with the challenges in socialist modernization. The solution to these problems is politically a strategic initiative and theoretically the result of innovation. The basic theory of building a socialist harmonious society is the foundation or starting point of the socialist harmonious society, and a deepened understanding of the theory of Marxism and socialist construction. The basic theory of building a socialist harmonious society can be divided into three levels: philosophy, system and practice. It is the unity of uniqueness and multidimensionality.

The theory of philosophy, namely the world view and methodology of dialectical materialism and historical materialism, is the most fundamental theoretical characteristics of Marxism and the deepest theoretical basis for building a socialist harmonious society. According to the basic theory of Marxism, the socialist harmonious society is not without contradictions. Contradictory movement is the basic driving force of social development. "The process of building a socialist harmonious society is the process of continuously advancing while handling various contradictions and constantly eliminating the factors of disharmony and increasing the harmonious factors. With China's reform and development entering a crucial period, contradictions among the people more frequently happen in a variety of forms. This is the phenomenon that cannot be completed avoided in the profound transformation of our society. The key is that we must face up to the contradictions, find the correct and effective ways to resolve them and establish a mechanism properly handling the contradictions, instead of allowing the accumulation and development of contradictions to affect overall situation of national reform and development. We should deeply analyze the causes of the contradictions among the people at present stage, especially the deep-seated reasons, and focus on reducing the contradictions among the people from the source."[42] All the understanding activities and practical activities of building a socialist harmonious society must be consciously guided by dialectical materialism and historical materialism.

Institutional theory refers to the theory of Marxism on the construction of socialist society, especially the theory of the basic system. The harmonious society advocated by our Party is called socialist harmonious society. The socialist system is a major prerequisite. At the seminar of improving the ability in building a socialist harmonious society for provincial and

42 Selected Literature since the 16th National Congress of the CPC, Volume II, Central Party Literature Press, Beijing, 2006, pp. 714-715.

ministerial level leading cadres in 2005, Comrade Hu Jintao made brief scientific discussion on the Marxist theory of socialist social construction. These discussions could be summarized into four points.

Firstly, the construction of a socialist harmonious society is associated with the eradication of classes and private ownership. The harmonious society advocated by Marxism is the harmony in a new social system that is different from capitalist society and better than it.

Secondly, the building of a socialist harmonious society is entirely for the people and for the most fundamental interests of most people; meanwhile, it needs to fully rely on the people and give full play to their enthusiasm and creativity in building a harmonious society.

Thirdly, it is necessary to correctly understand and deal with social contradictions, especially contradictions among the people, establish a lively political situation, prevent the contradictions among the people from transforming into antagonistic ones.

Fourthly, it is necessary to promote the coordinated development of material civilization, political civilization and spiritual civilization, the harmony between man and nature, and the comprehensive development of human. Based on the combination of theory, history and reality, these basic points systematically analyzed the socialist social construction theories in Marxist-Leninism, Mao Zedong Thought, Deng Xiaoping Theory and the important thought of "Three Represents", clarified the relationship of succession and advancing with the times between them, grasped the internal unity and development among them, and distinguished what the basic principles of Marxism should be adhered to for a long time, what theories should be developed by combining with the new reality, what doctrinal understanding of Marxism should be eradicated, and what wrong view that remains under the cloak of Marxism should be revealed. Thus, the practice of building a socialist harmonious society should be supported by the theoretical history and scientific principles of socialist social (societal) construction.

The theory of practical operation level means the six important principles summed up by Comrade Hu Jintao that must be upheld in the construction of socialist harmonious society : (1) We must adhere to the guiding ideology of Deng Xiaoping Theory and "Three Represents" = basic system of socialism and the path of socialism with Chinese characteristics; (2) We must establish and implement the scientific concept of development, persist in taking economy construction as the central task, adhere to "five balances", and promote the comprehensive development of socialist material civilization, political civilization, spiritual civilization and harmonious society construction; (3) we must adhere to the people-oriented principle, always take the fundamental interests of the majority of the people as the fundamental starting point and goal of the work of the party and the government; (4) We must respect people's creativity and stimulate the creativity of the whole society through deepening reform, innovation system and mobilizing all positive factors; (5) we must focus on social equity, correctly reflect and take care of the interests of different social groups, properly handle contradictions among the people and other social contradictions, and skillfully coordinate interest relationship of all aspects; (6) We must correctly handle the relationship between reform, development and stability, persist in unifying the intensity of reform, the speed of development and social acceptance, maintain the inter-coordination and mutual promotion among reform, development and stability, and ensure people's happy life and work, social and political stability and national long-term stability. These six important principles are the most direct guiding ideology of building a socialist harmonious society. The internal relations and unity among the three levels mentioned above form theoretical basis of the ideological system of building a socialist harmonious society.

3. The basic characteristics of the socialist harmonious society

"The socialist harmonious society we aim to build should be one with democracy and order, equality and justice, credit and friendliness, vitality and stability in which human and nature have a harmonious relationship."[43] This definition of a socialist harmonious society scientifically expresses the basic characteristics of the socialist harmonious society in China, and theoretically answers the question of what kind of society in which everyone can do his best in his proper place and live in harmony with others. The "six basic characteristics" of building a socialist harmonious society are the realistic requirements of accurately grasping the development of our social history, the scientific summarization of the practical experience of China's socialist social construction, the specific manifestation of the basic experience in building socialism with Chinese characteristics by our party since the 4th Plenary Session of the 13th CPC Central Committee, the enrichment and development of Marxist theory on the construction of socialist society in the new century, and a new understanding of the basic characteristics of socialist society.

The "six basic characteristics" of the socialist harmonious society summarized by Comrade Hu Jintao are based on the basic principles of Marxism, the practical experience of China's socialist social construction, the new requirements of China's economic and social development in the new century and new stage, and the new trend and features in our society. It is a vivid expression of the Marxist theory of building a socialist harmonious society.

43 Selected Literature since the 16th National Congress of the CPC, Volume II, p. 706.

The essence of the basic principles of Marxism is its position, views and methods. But the application of Marxist positions, views and methods is always associated with specific things and historical circumstances. It takes a systematic and comprehensive study to grasp it. The basic principle of Marxism is the scientific summary of the essence and development of human society. The basic characteristic of the socialist harmonious society resulted from the exploration of relevant expositions of the basic characteristics of socialism in Marx and Engels' various literatures, revealing of their scientific connotation, basic requirements and internal relations, and systematization of them. The basic principles of Marxism must be combined with our specific historical reality and our own practical experience. Our party attaches great importance to summing up practical experience. At each party congress and every plenary session of the central committee, we would sum up the experience of that period. These basic experiences are precious. On the basis of the summary of our party's endeavor in 80 plus years, especially since the 4th Plenary Session of the 13th CPC Central Committee, the report of the 16th Party Congress concluded ten basic experiences of the socialist construction with Chinese characteristics. With down to earth attitude, these ten basic experiences strategically conclude a set of theories, directions, programs, principles and policies for building socialism with Chinese characteristics. It also integrates upholding Deng Xiaoping Theory with promoting theoretical innovation and summing up the past and carrying forward the revolutionary tradition with specifying the future and enhancing the spirit of times. These rich and fresh practical experiences, together with the concentrated expression of our party's historical experience, are the development forms of Marxism-Leninism, Mao Zedong Thought and Deng Xiaoping Theory, reflecting the important thinking of "Three Represents" which are the new requirements of the development and changes in contemporary world and China for the work of the party and government. This is an important basis for Comrade Hu Jintao's summary of the "six basic characteristics" of the socialist harmonious society. "Six basic characteristics" is a scientific summary of China's socialist social construction and the embodiment of the new progress of socialist social construction theory and practice and the advancement of Marxism in China.

The connotation of "six basic characteristics" is as in the following: (1) Democracy and the rule of law. It means that socialist democracy should be fully developed, the basic strategy of governing the country effectively to be implemented, and positive factors widely mobilized. This is mainly the harmony in political relationships and political life of the society. (2) Fairness and justice. It means the interests of all sectors of society should be properly coordinated, the contradictions among the people and other social contradictions properly dealt with, and social fairness and justice effectively maintained and realized. This is mainly the harmony in social economic relations and economic life, and the harmony in extensive social life and interpersonal relationship. (3) Sincerity and friendliness. It means all people should help each other, be honest and trustworthy, equal and friendly, and get along well. This is mainly the harmony in ethic aspect and interpersonal relationship of the society. (4) Full of vitality. It means all the desire of innovation favorable to social progress should be respected, all creative activities supported, creative talent given full play, and all creative achievements affirmed. These should promote a vibrant social situation featuring harmony in interpersonal relationship, self-relations and the relations between man and society. (5) Stability and order. It means sound organizational structure, improved social management, good social order, peaceful life and work of people and social security. This is mainly comprehensive harmony in social economy, politics, culture and relations. (6) Harmony between man and nature. It means developing eco-friendly production, prosperous life and sound ecology. This is harmony between man and nature.

"Six basic characteristics" are interrelated and interactive. They are fully embodied and unified in the process of building a well-off society in an all-round way. Realizing and building a harmonious society, as a social ideal, is the common pursuit of mankind which has existed since ancient times. Although these ideas bear the features of different times and the class status of the proposers, they to a certain extent reflect people's yearning for a better life. However, the harmonious society is a comprehensive social reality relationship, which is impossible to achieve in the old system with class oppression and class exploitation of and in the society with class contradictions and class struggle. Therefore, the construction of a harmonious society shall be based on establishing, adhering to and improving the socialist system. In contemporary China, economically, this fundamental premise is to maintain the basic economic system featuring public ownership in a dominant position and diverse forms of ownership developing side by side; politically to uphold socialist democratic political system featuring the leadership of the CPC and people being the masters of the country; and ideologically and culturally uphold the guiding position of Marxism and maintain the advanced nature and diversity of socialist culture. To sum up, it is necessary to uphold the four basic principles of the party, since the four basic principles of the party is the embodiment of socialist basic system and its essential characteristics. The construction of a socialist harmonious society put forward by our party is based on the deepened understanding of the laws of governance by the communist party, laws of socialist construction and the laws of human society development. Or in general, it is based on understanding of the law of building socialism with Chinese characteristics. Comrade Hu Jintao has made it very clear by saying that, "on the basis of combining the basic principles of Marxism with China's reality, we achieved the victory of the new democratic revolution, founded the new China where people are the masters of the country, and established the socialist system, which created the political foundation for building a socialist harmonious society."[44] To build a socialist harmonious society, we must uphold Deng Xiaoping Theory and the important Thought of Three Represents and adhere to the basic system of socialism and the path of socialism with Chinese characteristics."[45]

The socialist harmonious society is the comprehensive harmony in social relations, which is different from the partial harmony enountered in the hitherto social relations in history. In Chinese and foreign history, partial harmony in social relations was achieved under the control of the dominant exploiting class during a certain period of time. This kind of harmony has provided a temporary stability within the ruling class, which accorded with the requirements of the development of productive forces at that time and was conductive to social progress to a certain extend and to the social production realized by the working people. However, before the establishment of the socialist system, it was impossible to establish a comprehensively harmonious society that encompasses the whole social relations and the relationship between man and nature. During the long ages of class societies, from the slave-ownership society to the capitalist system, the past societies were based on "exploitation of one class by another, all their development included constant contradictions. Every progress in production, at the same time, has been a step backwards in the living conditions of the most members of the oppressed class."[46] Based on the scientific analysis of this historical phenomenon, especially the characteristics of class and class struggle in capitalist society, the founders of Marxism discussed the great historical mission of the proletariat. They pointed out that if the proletariat cannot emancipate the whole society from exploitation, oppression, and class struggle, they cannot liberate themselves. Marx wrote: "In place of the old bourgeois society, with its classes and class antagonisms, we shall have an association, in which the free development of each is the condition for the free development of all."[47] From the Marxist point of view, only in the society where class oppositions are eliminated can the harmony of all social relations be achieved and a harmonious society established. Since the fundamental interests of the people of the socialist society are the same, the non-antagonistic contradictions among the people are dominant in the

44 Selected Literature since the 16th National Congress of the CPC, Volume II, p. 703.

45 Ibid., p. 707.

46 Marx and Engels Collected Works, Vol. 4, pp.196-197.

47 Marx and Engels Collected Works, Vol.2, p. 53.

society, which makes it possible to achieve a comprehensive harmonious relationship in this society. Under the system of proletarian dictatorship or people's democratic dictatorship, contradictions between us and the enemy will be restrained. In general, it would not worsen to a stage that will negatively affect the harmony in social relations. Therefore, we should uphold the socialist nature of the harmonious society we are aiming to build.

4. Correctly dealing with the contradictions of socialist society and promoting the construction of socialist harmonious society

In the historical process of profound changes in our society, in the face of complex contradictions, the issues of whether we can build a society in which all the people can do their best in the society and live in harmony and how to build a socialist harmonious society are not only a major test for governing capacity of our party, but also a new enrichment in the law of socialist construction.

The socialist harmonious society cannot emerge spontaneously; it takes a process of constantly resolving the contradictions to realize it. There are two different types of contradictions in the socialist society. One is confrontal contradiction between us and the enemy; the other one is the non-antogonistic contradiction among the people. Two different types of contradictions should be resolved in different ways. We should distinguish the nature of two different types of contradictions and properly deal with them in different ways, in order to establish a harmonious socialist relationship and build a socialist harmonious society.

The implementation of proletarian dictatorship against the hostile forces and handling of the contradictions between us and the enemy with dictatorship is an indispensable condition for the building of a socialist harmonious society. At the primary stage of socialism, although class contradiction is not the main contradiction of society, the class struggle will exist for a long time and be intensified under certain conditions because of western countries' infiltration, subversion and peaceful evolution strategies against China, and some negative domestic factors and negative international influence. Only by resolute struggle against anti-socialist activities of the hostile forces can political and social stability be maintained. "It is right to consolidate the people's power by employing the force of the people's democratic dictatorship. There is nothing wrong in that."[48]

In China, the dominant social contradictions are always the ones among the people, instead of the ones between us and the enemy. Correctly dealing

48 Deng Xiaoping Selected Works, Vol. 3, 1st ed., p. 379.

with the contradictions among the people is the key to building a harmonious society and the permanent task of the socialist society. The first thing in correctly dealing with the contradictions among the people is to properly handle the contradictions in ownership structure. In terms of ownership structure, with 30 years of reform practice, we have established a basic economic system featuring public ownership being dominant and diverse forms of ownership developing in tandem. This is in line with the development of productive forces and development requirements at primary stage of socialism. The public ownership of the means of production is the essential feature of socialism. As the main pillar, public ownership is able to determine the social nature of our society. We must unswervingly uphold the dominant position of public ownership. But it should be noted that non-public economic sectors have a positive effect on the national economic development at the primary stage of socialism. As an important part of the socialist market economy, it is conducive to the development of production, income increase of the people, expanding employment and meeting various needs of people. There is no doubt that there is contradiction between the public sector of the economy and the non-public economy. The natures of the two are different and there is a fundamental difference between them, which is a major manifestation of current contradictions among people. Under the present conditions, this contradiction should be properly dealt with in the framework of upholding the dominant position of public ownership and encouraging and guiding the development of non-public economy sector. On the one hand, we must unswervingly consolidate and develop the public sector of economy, develop and strengthen the state-owned economy, and enhance China's economic strength, national defense and national cohesion. On the other hand, we must unswervingly encourage, support and guide the development of non-public economy, fully mobilize the enthusiasm of all sectors of people in the society, and accelerate the development of productive forces. We must not focus on one aspect only. We should integrate upholding the dominant position of public ownership and promoting the development of non-public ownership economy sector in the process of socialist modernization, so that they can play their respective advantages in the market competition and promote the development of each other.

Correctly handling the contradictions among the people requires us to properly solve the issues in distribution. In the primary stage of socialism, we implement the distribution system featuring distribution according to labor contribution being dominant and coexistence of various distribution forms, which is compatible with the basic economic system of socialism and meets the objective requirements its development. But, as Deng Xiaoping pointed out, "After China developed to a certain stage, the distribution problem should be re-considered. If only a few people get rich, we will end with capitalism."[49] "Unfair distribution of income would lead to polarization. After a certain period of time, severe issues will emerge. We need to solve this problem. In the past, we focused on the development issue. Now we see that the problems after we have achieved development are no less than during the development."[50] To solve the problem of distribution is "even harder than solving the problems of development".[51] At present, the gaps among regions and between urban and rural areas and people's income gap are widening, which is not in line with the essential socialist aim of gradual realization of common prosperity. If we don't solve the problem of unfair distribution and allow the income gap widen and polarization worsen, contradictions will be intensified which wil negatively affect social stability. Correctly dealing with the contradictions among the people in the field of distribution is an urgent thing in building a harmonious society. The Communist Party of China is the ruling party; and the solving of contradictions among the people depends on the correct understanding of the party. Constantly improving the party's ability to correctly handle the contradictions among the people is a major issue in implementing the decision of the 4th Plenary Session of the 16th CPC Central Committee, strengthening the construction of party's governance ability and building a harmonious society. In dealing with the contradictions among the people, we must uphold the guiding ideology of Deng Xiaoping Theory and the important thought of "Three Represents" and adhere to the basic system of socialism and the road of socialism with Chinese characteristics; we must establish and implement the scientific concept of development, adhere to the central task of grasping the task of economic construction and maintain the "five balances"; we must also adhere to the people-oriented principle, always take the fundamental interests of the broad masses of people as a fundamental starting point and foothold, continue to meet the people's growing material and cultural needs on the basis of economic development, and promote the comprehensive development of people; we must respect people's creativity, mobilize all positive factors, and stimulate the creativity of the whole society; we should attach importance to social fairness, correctly reflect and take into consideration the interests of different social groups, and properly coordinate and balance their interest; we must correctly handle the relationship of reform, development and stability, integrate the following: the depth of the reform, its development pace and social acceptance, maintain mutual coordination and promotion among reform, development and stability, ensure that people work and live happily, ensure social stability and overall long-term stability. These are the basic principles that must be adhered to

49 Deng Xiaoping Selected Works (1975-1997), Volume II, Central Party Literature Press, Beijing, 2004, pp. 1356-1357.

50 Ibid, pp. 1356-1357.

51 Ibid. p. 1364.

in dealing with the contradictions among the people. We must establish the idea of believing in and relying on people, maintain close ties with them and follow the people-oriented line, which is the key in correctly handling the contradictions among the people. In term of working methods, we shall be good at making overall plans and take all factors into consideration. The contradictions among the people are mainly concentrated in the field of interest relations. Due to the development level of productive forces and other conditions, under the conditions of socialism there are still personal interests and principle of distribution according to work needs to be implemented. We must pay attention to and protect everyone's individual personal interests. But in addition to personal interests, there are also national interests and collective group interests. We should give consideration to all three aspects of interests. When there is contradiction among them, personal interests should be subject to national interests and collective interests. Even for non-public economic sectors which are featured by distribution according to factors of production, to a certain extent, should be subject to this principle, due to the need for maintaining influence of the dominant public ownership economy sector and due to need to uphold the laws of the socialist state. Deng Xiaoping pointed out: "Under the socialist system, personal interests must be subordinated to collective ones, the interests of the part to those of the whole, and immediate to long-term interests. In other words, partial interests must be subordinated to overall interests, and minor interests to major ones. Our advocacy and practice of these principles in no way means that we can ignore personal, local/partial or immediate interests. In the final analysis, under the socialist system there is a unity of personal interests and collective interests, unity between the interests of the part and those of the whole, and of immediate and long-term interests. We must adjust the relations between these various types of interests in accordance with the principle of taking them all into proper consideration."[52] To deal with the interest relations among people under the socialism conditions, it is possible to form harmonious relationship in the society. If we only focus on personal interests and handle the interest relations among the social groups according to the capitalist hypothesis of "human nature being selfish", there will appear antagonistic relationships among people and it will be impossible to properly handle the contradictions among the people and build a harmonious society. In order to ensure the smooth progress of building a socialist harmonious society, we must pay attention to restrict the interference of neoliberalism. Neo-liberalism, as an ideology or theory that reflects the fundamental economic and political interests of international monopoly capitalist, has a serious negative impact on the world economy and politics. The international monopoly bourgeoisie, led by the United States, will always aim to "westernize" and divide us, introduce new

52 Deng Xiaoping Selected Works (1975-1997), 2nd ed., Vol. II, pp. 175.

liberal theories and policies into our system. and will aim penetrate into the spheres of ideology, politics, economy and culture. When we are building a socialist harmonious society and adhering to the socialist political direction, neo-liberalism will surely aim to interfere and sabotage in order to achieve its aspirations and demands. Neoliberal theories and policies are fundamentally antagonistic to our theory of building a socialist harmonious society. If we do not guard against, resist and overcome its negative effect, there will be anarchy in our society, the construction of socialist spiritual civilization will inevitably encounter setbacks, and democracy and order, equality and justice, tolerance, sincerity, friendliness, vitality and stability and harmony between man and nature, i.e. the requirements of harmonious socialist society cannot be achieved.

5. Strengthening social investigation and theoretical research thus improving the ability to build a socialist harmonious society

To improve the ability and capacity of building a socialist harmonious society, we must deepen our understanding of the laws of building a socialist harmonious society. This is not only an objective requirement of building a socialist harmonious society, but also a major issue of promoting the localization of Marxism in China in the new century. There are various ways (the number of ways are increasing in our research and practice) of deepening the understanding of the laws of building a socialist harmonious society. Three aspects will be discussed below:

Firstly, we should carry out investigation and research. Investigation and research are the method, tool and means of the subject trying to relate with the object, or the intermediary and link between theory and reality. If I express this in the general sense, "the methods decide the fate of research", in studying the laws of building a socialist harmonious society, the investigation and research method determines whether we can carry forward the scientific spirit and grasp the truth; because the scientific method of investigation and research is the embodiment of upholding scientific spirit. Its essence lies in seeking the truth. So, we should attach great importance to investigation and research. Investigation and research involve a wide range of content, such as the situation and the practical work regarding construction and management of socialist harmonious society, the development and changes in social structure (including changes in social interests structure, class structure, urban and rural structure, regional structure, population structure, employment structure, social organization structure, and so on), and social stability (including public security and social order). Through investigations, we can get historical, realistic and concrete materials with which we can present analytical and insightful research results. Understanding the characteristics and laws of the development of socialist harmonious society in contemporary China is the premise to solve the major and prominent problems in our development, also to establish effective social relationship mechanisms and working mechanism, and also to formulate and improve policies and measures.

Secondly, we should strengthen the theoretical analysis. Lenin said that understanding is a process "from phenomenon to the essence, from the shallower to the deeper essence".[53] In this process, the theoretical analysis is to grasp the general relationships among the things as a whole. When ignoring the theoretical analysis and cannot grasp the overall situation, we might not be able to separate essence and phenomenon, so that the nature of study object will be hidden behind a large number of non-essential or accidental factors and we wll not be able to reveal any scientific laws. Lenin pointed out: "In the field of social phenomena... no single phenomenon can be understood if it is taken in isolation, if the representative facts are not grasped in their wholeness, not from the connection, and if the facts are piecemeal and randomly selected, Then they can only be a kind of play, or even worse than a child's play."[54]

To master the facts by looking from the overall situation and connections means to discard the dross and select the essential, eliminate the false and retain the true, proceed from the exterior to the interior and from one point to another in dealing with a large amount of data or facts and in order to advance from "vivid intuition to abstract thinking". To carry out proper theoretical research on the construction of a socialist harmonious society and strengthen the theoretical analysis, we should focus on the 9 issues proposed by Comrade Hu Jintao, namely, (1) How to effectively integrate social relations and promote positive interaction of various social forces; (2) How to establish and perfect laws and regulations on social construction and management and construct a strong legal guarantee for a harmonious socialist society; (3) How to effectively safeguard and realize social fairness and justice, and ensure that the achievements of reform and development are shared by all; (4) How to fully play the positive role of the grassroots self-government organizations, people's organizations, social organizations, industry organizations and intermediary organizations under the leadership of the party and form and mobilize the joint forces of social management; (5) How to strengthen the ideological and moral construction of the whole society, and further develop a good social atmosphere and interpersonal relationships; (6) How to understand and grasp the

53 Lenin's Monographs on Dialectical Materialism and Historical Materialism, p. 140.

54 Lenin, Complete Works, 2nd Chinese ed., vol. 28, Beijing, People's Publishing House, 1990, p. 364.

characteristics and laws of the rising of contradictions among the people under new situation and establish an effective mechanism of correctly handling the contradictions among the people; (7) How to establish social coordination mechanisms to promote self-management and self-service of society members and social organizations; (8) How to establish and improve the effective mechanism of maintaining public safety, to guarantee happy and peaceful life and work of the people; (9) How to promote coordinated development among material civilization, political civilization and spiritual civilization and the harmonious development of man and nature.[55] These above are overall, forward-looking, strategic issues of major significance. The in-depth theoretical analysis and fruitful research results by investigation and research on these problems is of great significance to are of great significance to deepening the cognition of the laws of building a socialist harmonious society and providing theoretical guidance for social practice.

Thirdly, we shoul strengthen and improve the party's leadership in theoretical research. In contemporary China, the key to doing a good job in all spheres lies in the party's leadership. So is the situation with theoretical research. In order to strengthen and improve the party's leadership in theoretical research of building a socialist harmonious society, we should focus on manifold aspects of things. First, we should put the theoretical research of building a socialist harmonious society into an important position. We should fully understand that theoretical research is a major part in the overall situation of building a harmonious socialist society. It is the foundational construction regarding the fundamental nature of the harmonious society and fundamental path of socialist construction. Comrade Hu Jintao pointed out that, building a socialist harmonious society is related with the fundamental interests of the overwhelming majority of the people, with the consolidation of the social basis of the party's governance, with the realization of the historical mission of party's governance, the overall situation of building a well-off society in an all-round way, the success of the party's cause and the long-term stability of the whole country. We should understand and organize the theoretical research work from the strategic height of the interwoven connections among these "four relations". Secondly, we should properly mobilize all the positive forces. The forces of theoretical research include both the theorists and the comrades engaged in the departments of practical work, which need to be coordinated by the party. We should establish a Marxist theory research system incorporating the center of Marxism Academy attached to Chinese Academy of Social Sciences, the research bases in the major key comprehensive universities directly attached to the Ministry of Education and Academies of Social Sciences in all provinces, and party and government departments, further mobilize the

55 Selected Literature since the 16th National Congress of the CPC, Volume II, pp. 718-719.

research strength of Marxist theory in China in order to carry out coordinated and planned theoretical research, which will significantly promote the deepened understanding of the laws of building a socialist harmonious society. Thirdly, the leading cadres should take the initiative. In theoretical research, the leading cadres should take the initiative in understanding the situation, grasping the direction, mastering the policies, coordinating relations, gathering and accumulating strength, to provide adequate material and spiritual support.

(Mei Rongzheng, Professor of Institute of Marxism of Wuhan University; Zhang Qianyuan, associate professor of Institute of Marxism of Wuhan University)

PART THREE

The Exploration of the CPC on the Law of Governance throughout Socialist Construction

Unity of the Path of Socialism with Chinese Characteristics, the Theoretical System of Socialism with Chinese Characteristics and the Institutional System of Socialism with Chinese Characteristics

For the development of socialism with Chinese characteristics, the key is to constantly adhere to and develop path of socialism with Chinese characteristics, the theoretical system of socialism with Chinese characteristics and the institutional system of socialism with Chinese characteristics.

In the 18th Congress of the CPC, Hu Jintao, has mentioned: "unswervingly follow the path of socialism with Chinese characteristics in order to build a moderately prosperous society in all respects," In the Congress report, he expounded on the unity of the three and made a profound exposition on the relations between them. He clearly stated: "The path of socialism with Chinese characteristics, the theoretical system of socialism with Chinese characteristics and the institutional system of socialism with Chinese characteristics are the fundamental accomplishments made by the Communist Party of China (CPC) and Chinese people in the course of arduous struggle over the past 90-plus years."[1]

About the relations between the three he said: "The path of socialism with Chinese characteristics is the way to reach the goal, the theoretical system of socialism with Chinese characteristics offers a guide to action, and the institutional system of socialism with Chinese characteristics provides the fundamental guarantee. The three function as an integral whole in the great practice of building socialism with Chinese characteristic." He stressed: "this is the salient feature of the long-term endeavors of the CPC in leading the people to build socialism."[2]

Deep understanding of the incisive summary of the comprehensive and profound socialist development with Chinese characteristics performs great theoretical and practical significance for the implementation of the spirit of the 18th Congress of the CPC and building a moderately prosperous society.

1 Hu Jintao, "Firmly march on the path of socialism with Chinese characteristics and strive to complete the building a moderately prosperous society in all respects", Beijing, People's Publishing House, 2012, p. 11.

2 Ibid., p. 12.

1. The path of socialism with Chinese characteristics is the approach to realize socialist modernization

In recent years, the path of socialism with Chinese characteristics as a theoretical concept, attracts more and more interest in our academia. Some scholars interpret it as socialist modernization with Chinese characteristics, some as building socialism with Chinese characteristics, and some others as socialism explored by the CPC after the 16th National Congress of the CPC.

The 18th Congress of the CPC gave a clear explanation on the connotation of the term "path": taking the path of socialism with Chinese characteristics means China must, under the leadership of the CPC and based on China's realities, take economic development as the central task and adhere to the Four Cardinal Principles and the policy of Reform and Opening-up. It means China must release and develop the productive forces, develop the socialist market economy, socialist democracy, an advanced socialist culture and a harmonious socialist society, and promote socialist ecological progress. It also means China must promote all-round development of the people, achieve prosperity for all, and make China a modern socialist country that is prosperous, strong, democratic, culturally advanced and harmonious."[3] The above statements do not only reveal the essential requirements of the socialist path with Chinese characteristics, but also expounds on the value target of the path of socialism with Chinese characteristics.

Firstly, the most important requirement and the nature of taking the path of socialism with Chinese is to base ourselves on the national realities and conditions. The CPC, when leading the socialist revolution and construction, has continued to achieve numerous victories by always basing itself on the scientific analysis of China's realities. As early as 1939, during the New Democratic Revolution, Mao Zedong had pointed out: "a clear understanding of the nature of Chinese society, that is, of Chinese conditions, is therefore the key to a clear understanding of all the problems of the Chinese revolution."[4]

Over the long years, before making major decisions, the CPC has always kept in mind the importance of comprehensively analyzing and taking into consideration of the current conditions of China. The 18th Congress of the CPC emphasized that most important reality and condition that China's still being under the primary stage of socialism and has summarized the work in the past five years from both positive and negative aspects. The statements which reflected the current situation, did not only mention that China has

3 Ibid., p. 11.

4 Mao Zedong Selected Works, 2nd Ed., Vol. 2, Beijing, People's Publishing House, 1991, p. 633.

made a lot of significant achievements, but also clearly recognized that there are still many aspects to be improved: "we must be keenly aware that there is still much room for improvement in our work and there are a lot of difficulties and problems on our road ahead." The socialism with Chinese characteristics is developed by constantly renewing the incomplete understanding of China's reality. Thus, correctly examining and grasping the basic national conditions, is the most important factor to achieve successes when following the path of socialism with Chinese characteristics.

Second, is to adhere to the basic line of the Party.

"One Central Task and Two Basic Points" is the core content of the CPC's basic line and the lifeblood of the CPC and China, it is the political guarantee when promoting the path of socialism with Chinese characteristics. Taking economic construction as the central task is the material basis for the path of socialism with Chinese characteristics and adhering to the Four Cardinal Principles is the political cornerstone of the path of socialism with Chinese characteristics. Adhering to Reform and Opening-up is the lifeblood of the path of socialism with Chinese characteristics. The basic line of the CPC lays a solid material foundation for enhancing the China's prosperity and national strength when taking the path of socialism with Chinese characteristics. Deng Xiaoping said, "The basic line governs one hundred years and must not be shaken."[5] With profound meaning, the basic line shows China the direction to unswervingly take the path of socialism with Chinese characteristics. Following are the value targets of the path of socialism with Chinese characteristics: First is to promote the all-round comprehensive development of people. All-round development of people is the essential requirement of socialism. Marx and Engels pointed out that in the future society, "we shall have an association in which the free development of each individual is the precondition for the free development of all."[6]

Marx further stressed that the future society is "a society in which the full and free development of each individual forms the ruling principle."[7] Full and free development of people is an important measurement of social progress, it is the highest goal that Marxism struggles to pursue. Accordingly, in the current Chinese society, the path of socialism with Chinese characteristics is the only way to promote the comprehensive development of individuals. Second, is gradually realizing the common prosperity of the people. The ideal of common prosperity is the goal and inspiration of humankind for thousands of years. Adhering to marching on the path of common prosperity for all, has always been the conviction of the CPC.

5 Deng Xiaoping Selected Works, 1st ed., Vol. 3, pp. 370-371.

6 Marx-Engels Collected Works, Vol. 2, p. 53.

7 Marx-Engels Collected Works, Vol. 5, p. 683.

To unswervingly lead the path of common prosperity, is the solemn promise of the CPC to the Chinese people. We keep on the socialist path in order to attain the ultimate goal of common prosperity. Consequently, the path of socialism with Chinese characteristics is the only way to create a better life for the people. Third is to build a prosperous, democratic, civilized and harmonious modern socialist country. A century after the foundation of the People's Republic of China (PRC), the CPC set a goal of building a prosperous, democratic, civilized and harmonious modern socialist country, after scientifically and comprehensive understanding objective laws of socialist modernization and fully analyzing realities of current China. The goal can be achieved only by keeping to and adhering to the path of socialism with Chinese characteristics. In a word, the path of socialism with Chinese characteristics is the only way to achieve socialist modernization.

The essential requirement and value target of the path of socialism with Chinese characteristics indicate that it is the proper way to promote the all-round development of the people, gradually achieve common prosperity of the people, and build a prosperous, democratic, civilized and harmonious modern socialist country. If China had not taken up this path, it would be impossible to achieve the national rejuvenation and social development, nor the better life for all people or the socialist modernization. The reason is that the path of socialism with Chinese characteristics was generated by combining Marxism with China's socialist construction practice that is, it is the product of following China's own way. Combining theory with practice is a fundamental principle of Marxism, which has been fully grasped by the Communist Party of China which has combined the theories such as the theory of the primary stage of socialism and Marxist theory on oriental society with the development practice of socialism in China, thus opening up a new path of socialism with Chinese characteristics.

The path of socialism with Chinese characteristics not only persists in the basic principles of Marxist scientific socialism, but also insists on the right course of socialism. Just as mentioned by Deng Xiaoping "This history teaches us that capitalism would lead China nowhere and that we must follow the socialist path." namely China's modernization can be realized only through socialism, not capitalism.

Thus, adhering to Marxism and upholding the socialist path has become the core concept of the CPC. Significant achievements in social and economic development that have been made since the implementation of Reform and Opening-up in China prove that, the path of socialism with Chinese characteristics not only adhered to socialism but also has extended the conception of it, manifesting that the path of socialism with Chinese characteristics is the perfect combination of socialism concept and China's reality. The key to the success of the path of socialism with Chinese characteristics, on the one side is the result of adhering to the leadership of the CPC and the basic system of socialism, on the other hand, of firmly grasping the development direction of modernization to develop socialist market economy, democratic politics, advanced culture; not only adhering to the basic line of the CPC when unremittingly striving to resolve the principal contradiction of the socialist society, but also vigorously implementing the people-oriented principle to promote economic construction, political construction, cultural construction, social construction, ecological civilization construction, consequently realizing the coordinated and sustainable economic and social development. The path of socialism with Chinese characteristics is an important way to establish and develop the theoretical system of socialism with Chinese characteristics and to uphold and complete the institutional system of socialism with Chinese characteristics. The path of socialism with Chinese characteristics is a process of long-term exploration and meticulous work led by the Communist Party of China with Chinese people.

When the People's Republic of China (PRC) was founded in 1949, Mao Zedong led the Chinese people to achieve the establishment of the new democracy and the socialist system, as well as the initial practice of socialist construction, which laid the foundation for the formation of this path. And in the historical process of Reform and Opening-up, Deng Xiaoping as the representative of the CPC has opened up this path. One of the important products of these series of practices was the theoretical system of socialism with Chinese characteristics.

The formation of this "theoretical system" and the exploration of this new "path" is closely linked. On the one hand, the formation of the theoretical system of socialism with Chinese characteristics is based on the exploration of the path of socialism with Chinese characteristics; on the other hand, practicing and exploring the path of socialism with Chinese characteristics has promoted the continuous development of the theoretical system of socialism with Chinese characteristics.

The experience and lessons as well as successes and failures in the practice of the path of socialism with Chinese characteristics inspires the development of the theoretical system of socialism with Chinese characteristics. Therefore, we can say that the path of socialism with Chinese characteristics leads the formation and development of the theoretical system of socialism with Chinese characteristics. Similarly, the establishment of the institutional system of socialism has fundamentally changed the historical fate of China, guided Chinese people to choose and adhere to the path of socialism with Chinese characteristics, which in turn has constantly promoted the completion of the institutional system with Chinese characteristics. In that sense, the path of socialism with Chinese characteristics is the approach to improve the socialist system.

2. The theoretical system of socialism with Chinese characteristics is the guide to action

The report of the 13th Party Congress in 1987, for the first time clearly introduced the concept of "the theory of socialism with Chinese characteristics" (the theory of building socialism with Chinese characteristics) and later the CPC has constantly enriched and completed its understanding of this concept by refining it for several times. The concept of the "theoretical system of socialism with Chinese characteristics" was proposed and briefly expounded in the 13th Party Congress. And it was comprehensively expounded in the 18th Party Congress: "The system of theories of socialism with Chinese characteristics is a system of scientific theories that includes Deng Xiaoping Theory, the important thought of Three Represents and the Scientific Outlook on Development, and this system represents the Party's adherence to and development of Marxism- Leninism and Mao Zedong Thought."[8]

The process from expounding "the theory on building socialism with Chinese characteristics" to the formation of "the theoretical system of socialism with Chinese characteristics" is in fact a process in which the CPC deepened and refined the understanding of basic issues such as "what is socialism and how to build it" and "what kind of party to build and how to build it" and "what kind of development should be realized and how to realize it" and it is also a process in which China have deepened its understanding of the laws of governance by the Communist Party, laws of building socialism, and laws of the development of human society.

The theoretical system of socialism with Chinese characteristics requires not only adhering to the basic principles of Marxism, but also insisting on distinctive Chinese characteristics. This system includes practical characteristics, theoretical characteristics, national characteristics, characteristics of the times, thus constitutes a complete scientific theoretical system.

Practical characteristics of the theoretical system of socialism with Chinese characteristics refers to treating Marxism with a scientific attitude, incessantly making breakthroughs in order to break free from the dogmatic understanding of Marxism, and putting forward a series of new ideas, new thoughts and new conclusions. Meanwhile, it refers to focusing on the practical problems of China's Reform and Opening-up and its modernization drive and on what China is doing. In a word, China emphasizes the application of the Marxist theory, demonstrating an attitude of problem awareness.

8 Hu Jintao, "Unswervingly Advance along the Path of Socialism with Chinese Characteristics for Building A Moderately Prosperous Society in All Respects", p. 12.

The theoretical feature of the theoretical system of socialism with Chinese characteristics refers that it is the achievements resulting from CPC's theoretical innovation by adapting Marxism to Chinese conditions in the new historical period of Reform and Opening-up. It is also the result of CPC's efforts to forge ahead, explore the truth, and its efforts to grasp the law for the purpose of pursuing China's prosperity. It's the only correct theory for China to go ahead along the path of socialism with Chinese characteristics and achieve the great rejuvenation of the Chinese nation. In its relation to Marxism- Leninism and Mao Zedong Though, it has the same strain as well as the nature of keeping up with the times. It is a scientific system of theories that is inherited from Marxism-Leninism but is the embodiment of Marxist theory as further enriched and developed with new ideas and viewpoints.

The national feature of the theoretical system of socialism with Chinese characteristics refers that it fully considers the requirements of China's realities and local uniqueness, reflecting Chinese manner, Chinese style and Chinese characteristics, so that Marxism can further take root in the Chinese soil and flourish further. It is by no means to make a last-ditch defense of specific conclusions or to discard Marxist theory, but rather to adhere to the basic principles of Marxism and put forward brand-new ideas that manifest the nation's outstanding wisdom and the practical experience of Chinese communists. It never means China should exclude itself from the international experience and stay out of the development trend of world progress and development, but should closely link China's development to the realization of socialist modernization, the great rejuvenation of the Chinese nation and the development and changes of the world. The time feature of the theoretical system of socialism with Chinese characteristics mainly refers that China should adhere to the scientific attitude of advancing and developing Marxism with times and always track and study the development and change of reality, pay close attention to every new achievement in science and technology and each breakthrough in natural sciences. China should also handle the contemporary issues and innovate thoughts and theories in the actual process of combining the basic principles of Marxism with China's concrete reality and characteristics of the times.

The four features of the theoretical system of socialism with Chinese characteristics fully demonstrate that the theoretical system of socialism with Chinese characteristics constitute a new breakthrough in the development of the theory of Marxist scientific socialism. It is certainly the newly developed Marxism. In contemporary China, the hope for China's development depends upon the adherence to the theoretical system of socialism with Chinese characteristics. Only if the theoretical system of socialism with Chinese characteristics is taken as the guide to actions, can China have a beautiful feature. Theoretical system of socialism with Chinese characteristics offers a guide to the CPC to open up and adhere to the path of socialism with Chinese characteristics. In the course of 30 years of Reform and Opening-up, when following the path of socialism with Chinese characteristics, China has encountered a lot of difficulties and problems, to which the theoretical system of socialism with Chinese characteristics have offered solutions. For example, when people were confused and had doubts on the future of socialism, and felt the urgent need to answer the issue of "what is socialism, and how to build it", notions in the socialist theory system such as the nature of socialism, the theory of primary stage of Socialism, and the theory of socialist market economy have provided Chinese people with explicit and systematic understanding on the issues of how to build and develop socialism, laying the theoretical foundation for perpetuating the path of socialism with Chinese characteristics.

Another example is as the following: when the historical background and the social environment that the CPC was faced with have unprecedentedly changed and the historic mission shouldered by the party has undergone major unprecedented changes, "what kind of party to build, how to build it" came to the fore as a key issue to be handled during the marching on the path of socialism with Chinese characteristics. Theories embodied in the theoretical system of socialism with Chinese characteristics such as the Important Thought of "Three Represents" and ideas about the CPC's construction have enhanced the confidence of Chinese people in the CPC's governance of China as well as have enabled Chinese people to be aware of the importance of the socialist path with Chinese characteristics in raising the CPC's ability and capacity of ruling.

Besides, due to changes of times, transformation of society, uncertainty of institutional transition and dual influences of socialist market economy, diversification of economic sectors, diversification of economic interests, social organizations and employment patterns have occurred. At the same time, there appeared the issues of unreasonable economic structure, disorderliness related to distribution relations, and the growth pace in the farmers' income has slowed down. By putting forward brilliant elucidation related to "what kind of development should be achieved and how to develop", the theoretical system of socialism with Chinese characteristics has become the important theoretical guide to the path of socialism with Chinese characteristics, providing solutions towards how to understand and solve these problems mentioned above.

Theoretical system of socialism with Chinese characteristics clearly defines the goals, values and the essential requirements of the path of socialism with Chinese characteristics, therefore it is the guiding ideology of China in following the path of socialism with Chinese characteristics.

The theoretical system of socialism with Chinese characteristics serves as a guide to China's action when this country constantly improves the socialist system with Chinese characteristics forward.

The last 30 years saw the formation and development of the theoretical system of socialism with Chinese characteristics as well as big changes and major adjustments in China, during when peace and development have become the theme of the times. Meanwhile the Western capitalist world saw various new changes, world socialist movement has suffered a serious setback, the development of economic globalization has accelerated, and multi-polarization trend has become increasingly evident, especially the new scientific and technological revolution occurred, consequently the applications of the new discoveries and innovations brought by it have greatly promoted the world-wide advances in productive forces, and production pattern. Consequently, the lifestyle of people and socio-economic life have undergone unprecedented and profound changes, leading to changes in the global economic and interest patterns upon which world's political configuration has undergone unprecedented major changes. In the presence of such profound and huge transformations, the theoretical system of socialism with Chinese characteristics studies such issues as social development, development of people, scientific development, political civilization and peaceful development. This fully reflects that the CPC insists on observing and examining the world with broad vision, examines and self-improves itself with the requirements of the new era, plans the overall situation with strategic thinking and pays close attention to the development trend of world civilization, attaches importance to observing, thinking and solving problems through considering the realities of both China and the world. Besides, the CPC is good at absorbing the scientific and rational elements from different civilizations, eliminating the irrational factors of the socialist system, and constantly insisting on consolidating and improving the socialist system. It is during the past 30 years of the formation and development of the theoretical system of socialism with Chinese Characteristics that, China has developed a series of theoretical systems on how to build socialism, on how to construct the Party, and how to develop the country. Theoretical system of socialism with Chinese characteristics has offered creative ideas and solutions on the important issue of how to build socialism. Based on this theoretical system, the CPC has broken the fetters of the conventional concepts arguing that "Market economy that is exclusive to capitalism is not applicable to socialism" and developed this idea forward by proposing that "the planning is not the definitive factor to differ socialism from capitalism" and the idea that "developing a market economy does not mean practicing capitalism, socialism can also practice market economy" thus formed the basic economic system of socialism.

As to the important issue of how to build the party, the CPC always takes the fundamental interests of the overwhelming majority of the people in China as the first consideration in the formulation of the theoretical systems that embrace different nationalities as well as balance different strata and different interest groups in the society, thus forming the fundamental political system of socialism. As to the crucial issue of how to develop the country, the CPC always unremittingly implements the people-oriented principle (the ruling party's most important priority should be to focus on bringing tangible development and benefits to the common people) and emphasize scientific development approach, thus forming a series of specific economic, political, cultural, and social institutions that comply with the fundamental political system, basic political systems and the basic economic system. Under the new historical conditions, in order to uphold and improve the socialist system with Chinese characteristics, the CPC adheres to the theoretical system of socialism with Chinese characteristics as a guide to action.

3. The socialist system with Chinese characteristics is the fundamental institutional guarantee

Marx said: "Assume a particular stage of development in production, commerce and consumption and you will have a corresponding social constitution, a corresponding organization of the family, corresponding organization of orders (estates) or of classes, in a word a corresponding civil society."[9] Any system (social constitution/formation) is the product of practice, thus the socialist system with Chinese characteristics is based on the practice of socialism with Chinese characteristics. An institutional system is always fundamental, comprehensive, stable and lasting, thus a sound institutional system is crucial for a magnificent future of the Party and state. In the long years of revolution, construction and reform process, the Communist Party of China, adhering to the basic principles of Marxism and combining them with the actual realities of Chinese society and the Chinese revolution, the socialist system was first established. Based on this socialist system, and the actual circumstances of China's socialist construction the CPC has explored and developed a comprehensive understanding on the laws of socialist construction, laws of rule by the communist party (in power) and the laws of development of human society, thus establishing a socialist system with Chinese characteristics that has strong vitality. The CPC's 18th congress gave a clear and a systematic explanation of the connotation of Chinese socialist system: "Chinese socialist system includes: the system of people's congresses that is China's fundamental political

9 Marx-Engels Collected Works, Vol. 10, p. 43.

system; the basic political systems that include the system of multiparty cooperation and political consultation under the leadership of the CPC, the system of regional ethnic autonomy, and the system of community-level self-governance, the socialist system of laws with Chinese characteristics; the basic economic system with public ownership as primary with diverse others types of ownership developing in tandem; and specific economic, political, cultural, and social institutions based on the fundamental political system, basic political systems and the basic economic system."[10]

This statement not only demonstrates that the socialist system with Chinese characteristics is a set of interrelated, interconnected set of systems, but also reveals that the CPC has developed a set of standardized institutional systems in various specific fields such as economy, politics, and societal life. The socialist system with Chinese characteristics as an integrated set of institutions is a fundamental institution, which includes the basic systems, specific systems and a socialist system of laws (legal system) with Chinese characteristics. Firstly, in these institutional systems, the basic systems play a decisive role. They reflect the nature, the content and the fundamental characteristics of the institutional system and manifest the prescriptive property of the institutional system.

People's Congress system as the fundamental (political) system refers to the organizational form of state power, reflects the essential characteristics of the state, namely that people are the masters of the country, which directly reflects the nature of the social system. It determines the basic principles and the direction of the social development activities of the country, acting as the foundation and origin of China's institutional systems.

Secondly, the basic systems not only embody the fundamental system, but also constitute the basis and starting point for the development of the specific systems (institutions). As the components of the whole institutional system with China's socialist characteristics, the basic system of China includes the basic political system and the basic economic system. The basic political system that includes the system of multi-party cooperation and political consultation under the leadership of the Communist Party of China, is not only a political party system which bears Chinese characteristics but also anew creation in the world history relating to the relations among political parties and the political party system; as the right choice for solving ethnic problems and also interest relations among them, the system of regional ethnic autonomy is in line with China's national conditions and conforms to the notion of ethnic unity, reflects the CPC's adherence to the principle of ethnic equality, mutual assistance, cooperation and the principle of striving for common prosperity; the system of community-level (grass-roots)

10 See Hu Jintao's Report, "Unswervingly Advance along the Path of Socialism with Chinese Characteristics for Building A Moderately Prosperous Society in All Respects", p. 12.

self-governance is an important foundation to expand grassroots democracy, namely developing socialist democratic politics with Chinese characteristics. In terms of the basic economic system, with public ownership as its main component part, this basic economic system allows and promotes the development of diverse forms of ownership, so as to mobilize the masses of the people and the enthusiasm of all sectors of society, and enhance the vitality of economic development which is an important guarantee. This basic economic system enables China's development to proceed along the socialist direction which is also an important guarantee of social progress.

Third, specific institutions (systems) are based on the fundamental (political) system and the two basic systems. Deriving from the fundamental system and the two basic systems, specific institutions are restricted and controlled by them. In reverse, the specific institutions promote the completion of both the fundamental system and the two basic systems. The specific institutions (systems) with Chinese characteristics include the specific socialist economic institutions (systems), political systems, cultural systems, social systems determined by the fundamental institutions and the basic system; in turn they serve them.

Fourth, China's socialist system of laws (the whole legal system) has established the socialist system in its legal form. This legal system includes the Constitution as its core and leading factor, and it is supplemented by the domestic legal system as the backbone, plus also supplemented by the administrative regulations and the local regulations which are parts of the whole law system, ensuring that all aspects of the country's economic construction, political construction, cultural construction, social construction and social life and ecological civilization proceed in a lawful way.

These four aspects of the socialist system with Chinese characteristics constitute an interrelated, interconnected organic whole. Adhering to the socialist system with Chinese characteristics, is the fundamental guarantee for the development and progress of contemporary China, and also embodies the characteristics and advantages of socialism with Chinese characteristics. In fact, there can be either no path or theoretical system of socialism with Chinese characteristics without being carried by the institutional system of socialism with Chinese characteristics, or the institutional system of socialism with Chinese characteristics departed from the path or theoretical system of socialism with Chinese characteristics cannot exist. Thus, path of socialism with Chinese characteristics, the theoretical system, and the institutional system form the unity of the three. That is, any one of the three separated from the unity is meaningless. The socialist system with Chinese characteristics provides the fundamental guarantee for China to take the path of socialism with Chinese characteristics. Historical facts prove that the socialist system with Chinese characteristics is the product of Chinese

Communist Party's practice in leading the people of all ethnic groups in China in adhering to the socialist path with Chinese characteristics. On the other hand, during the process of marching on the path of socialism with Chinese characteristics, the socialist system with Chinese characteristics plays a fundamental role in meeting the essential requirements and in achieving value goals of the socialist path with Chinese characteristics. For example, the spontaneity, blindness, and the blind pursuit of personal self- interests brought by allowing the operation of the market economy is restrained by the fundamental and basic systems of the whole socialist system. Thus, to further improve the socialist market economy, China has to develop the initial formation of the social security system and enhance the macro-control system that can curb these above drawbacks of the market economy. Another example, the irrational factor of unfair income distribution is also restricted and adjusted by the socialist system. Distribution according to work is dominant distribution mode and supplemented by a variety of modes of distribution that coexist in China's whole distribution system (institution). This distribution institution can to a certain extent, help to solve the issues of increasing income gap among certain groups in China.

Thus, the socialist system with Chinese characteristics not only ensures people's basic economic rights and life conditions, but also promotes the development of human's potential and creativity. The socialist system with Chinese characteristics not only mobilizes all positive factors serving the development of productive forces and enhancing the country's comprehensive national strength, but also can benefit the development and liberation of productive forces and promote coordinated economic and social development. It is not only conductive to the maintenance and promotion of fairness and justice in the society and conductive to achieve common prosperity for all the people, but also helps us to concentrate our resources to accomplish large undertakings and to effectively cope with various risks and challenges on the path ahead. The socialist system with Chinese characteristics is conducive to safeguarding national solidarity, social stability, social harmony, national unity, all of which can provide guarantee for adhering to the path of socialism with Chinese characteristics. The socialist system with Chinese characteristics is the fundamental guarantee for the improvement and development of the theoretical system of socialism with Chinese characteristics. We all know that any system is the expression of the theoretical structure, thus the nature of the theory determines the nature of the system. Historical facts have proved that the formation of the socialist system with Chinese characteristics is guided by the theoretical system of socialism with Chinese characteristics which is formed by our Party in the historical process of reform and opening. However, with the development of practice, theories need continuously to be developed. The socialist system with Chinese characteristics plays an important role in promoting and safeguarding the improvement and development of the theoretical system of socialism with Chinese characteristics. In other words, the improvement and development of the theoretical system of socialism with Chinese characteristics should take the socialist system with Chinese characteristics as the carrier. Without the carrier, the theoretical system of socialism with Chinese characteristics will lose its meaning of existence, and we will be left with nothing. The development of practice is an endless, ever continuing progress, and we are in the constant pursuit of truth, innovation and development of theory. Accordingly, with the development of the great practice of socialism with Chinese characteristics, the path of socialism with Chinese characteristics will continue to be developed and enriched, and also the theoretical system of socialism with Chinese characteristics will continue to be enriched and will become more perfect, the socialist institutional system with Chinese characteristics will be continuously improved, these three are highly complementary.

(Zhang Leisheng, Professor of Institute of Marxism Studies, Renmin University of China)

The Socialist Market Economy and the Construction of the CPC's Ruling Capacity

The establishment of a socialist market economic system is a pioneering undertaking in the development of socialism. In pursuing this pioneering undertaking, only by putting forward and implement correct theory, path, route, principles and policies in accordance with the development and changes of market economy, and timely adjusting and changing its leadership system and style can the ruling Communist Party of China truly undertake the responsibility of leading the healthy development of socialist market economy, lead the people of all ethnic groups of the country in building a well-off society in an all-round way under the condition of domestic and foreign opportunities and challenges, further promote modernization and realize the great rejuvenation of the Chinese nation.

1. The establishment of the goal of the socialist market economic system is the embodiment of the improvement of the party's governance ability

The theory of socialist market economy is a major innovation of socialist economic theory. It is the result of deepening the understanding of how to develop socialist economy and an embodiment of the improvement of the party's governance ability. Marxism believes that everything that people strive for is related to their interests. If the ruling party cannot take on the responsibility of leading the economic development, no victory will lead to any results and falling back to the old system will be inevitable. As early as the 1840s, in *The German Ideology*, Marx and Engels has made it clear that the communist society must be based on the prerequisite of huge improvement in respect to productive forces, "is an absolutely necessary practical premise because without it want is merely made general, and with destitution the struggle for necessities and all the old filthy business would necessarily be reproduced".[11] Therefore, after gaining the political domination and depriving the capitalists, the proletariat must increase the total amount of productive forces as quickly as possible. While emphasizing the importance of productive forces development to the future society, Marx and Engels also foresaw the future economic operation of the society based on a profound analysis of the capitalist mode of production. They argued that the contradictions and drawbacks in the capitalist market economy, such as the anarchy of the whole social production, the materialization of human relations, cannot be solved within the capitalist society; and the fundamental way to solve these contradictions is to replace blind working

11 Marx-Engels Collected Works, Vol. 1, p. 538.

market regulation with conscious and planned production, to achieve the unity between personal interests and social interests, and between personal rationality and social rationality. Thus, they come to the conclusion that there is no commodity monetary relationship in the future society, and socialism and market economy cannot be combined. After the victory of the October Revolution, based on the reality of Russian socialist revolution and construction, Lenin also highlighted the development of productive forces. He pointed out that labor productivity is fundamentally the most important thing to make the new social system successful. Capitalism created labor productivity which could not be created under the serfdom of socialism. Capitalism can be and will certainly be defeated, because socialism can create new and much higher labor productivity. Thus, after taking the state power, the most important and most fundamental thing for the proletariat is to increase the number of products and greatly improve social productive forces. In the concrete practice of building a socialist economy, the Russian Communist Party (Bolshevik) tried to establish a centralized planned economy without commodity currency relations and market exchange. They eliminated currency with the most radical measures. Here, the elimination of commodity currency relations and market mechanisms is not just a theoretical forecast, but a policy proposition and action program. The demise of commodity currency relations is no longer a natural historical process or an abstract theoretical derivation, but a result achieved by violence and power of proletarian dictatorship. The combination of ideological understanding and the wartime environment resulted in a highly centralized and materialized wartime communist policy. However, with the end of the war, this attempt of direct transition to communism in the way of the Red Guards attack failed and was replaced by the new economic policy featuring commodity currency relations and market mechanisms. But this has not changed the basic trend towards a transition to a socialist planned economy.

In the Stalin period, the traditional planned economic system and planned economic theory were finally established. The establishment of this model reflects the Marxist classic writers' planned economy thought that there is no commodity currency in socialist society. Different from Marx and Engels' vision, commodity currencies and market mechanisms had been completely eliminated in a highly centralized planned economy. But they only played a small role. In the general guiding ideology, the plan and the market were still opposed. The planned economy based on the mandatory plan was seen as the essence of the socialist economic system; the market mechanism is constrained as the dissident factor to socialism. This model had a decisive influence on the development of socialism in the world. China, Eastern Europe and other socialist countries were imitating the Soviet Union to establish a highly centralized planned economic system.

It is undeniable that under certain historical conditions, this system had played a positive role in ensuring and promoting the national construction and achieving the coordinated development of the national economy, thus laying a solid material foundation for consolidating the socialist system. But with the socio-economic development, the drawbacks of this system were gradually exposed. To eliminate the obstacles to the productive forces and explore a new path suited to their own development has become an urgent problem needed to be solved by the ruling Communist Party. In the process of socialist construction in China, the Chinese Communists, represented by Mao Zedong, based on the lessons of the Soviet Union, made in-depth thinking and bold exploration of China's economic operation, and put forward a series of valuable theoretical points of view. For example, in term of commodity economic development, Mao Zedong believed that there was still commodity economy in socialist society and its fundamental reason was that there was ownership by the whole people and collective ownership at that stage. As long as there are two different ownerships, commodity production and commodity exchange are extremely necessary and useful. Therefore, we must fully understand the positive role of socialist commodity production and exchange. We shall make use of commodity production, commodity exchange and the law of value for the development of socialism. For those opinions denying commodity economy, Mao

Zedong pointed out that they feared commodity production only because of their fear of capitalism. The nature of commodity production depends on what economic system it is associated with. If it is associated with capitalist system, it is capitalist commodity production. If it is associated with socialist system, it is socialist commodity production that serves for socialist construction. In addition, for the "communist style" of "egalitarianism and indiscriminate transfer of resources" in people's commune campaign and wrong words and deeds denying commodity production and equivalent exchange, Mao Zedong proposed that "the law of value is a great school". In the process of exploring the laws of the socialist economy, Mao Zedong put forward some valuable theoretical points of view. These ideas represented the highest level of the Chinese Communist Party's exploration of the socialist commodity economy. They provided valuable theoretical wealth for the establishment of the socialist market economic system.

It is undeniable that, due to the limitations of historical conditions, the party's first generation of central leadership had made some mistakes in socialist economic construction. Having the courage to correct the mistakes and further explore the development path suited to China's national conditions has become the arduous task for the party's new generation of central collective leadership. After the Third Plenary Session of the 11th CPC Central Committee, the second generation of the central collective leadership of the Party with Deng Xiaoping as the core, under the guidance of emancipating the mind and seeking truth from facts, broke the rigid dogma, made more in-depth thinking and presented new answers to the questions of "what is socialism and how to build socialism". The essence of socialism is to liberate and develop the productive forces, to eliminate exploitation and polarization and to achieve common prosperity. The fundamental task of socialism is to develop productive forces. "For economic system reform, the only way is to develop productive forces".[12] In the process of deepening understanding, the 14th CPC National Congress proposed that market economy could also be developed in socialist system. "The planned is not equal to socialism, as capitalism also has plans; Market economy is not equal to capitalism, as socialism also has markets. Planning and market are economic means."[13] Socialism can be combined with the market economy. The birth of the theory of socialist market economy changed the views, content and system structure of socialist economic theory, marking that the party's capacity in leading socialist construction has reached to a higher level.

2. The new requirements of the socialist market economy to the party members' ability and quality

The establishment and development of the socialist market economic system is the result of the improvement of the party's ability to govern. Meanwhile, it also has new requirements for the party's ability to govern. The party's ability to govern is directly reflected in the leadership and governance ability of party committees at all levels and leading cadres, and the capacity and quality of all party members. Therefore, strengthening the theoretical accomplishment of the party members and improving their ability to deal with the new contradictions and problems brought by the market economy has become the basic part to strengthen the party's ability to govern.

It takes the guidance of correct theories to lead the healthy development of socialist market economy. For China, the market economy is a new thing that has different operation mode from the planned economy. To understand the operational characteristics of the market economy and raise the consciousness of doing things in accordance with the objective law of the market economy has become a new issue for the ruling party. The task of understanding the particularity of socialist market economy has higher requirements for the party members' theoretical quality. The socialist market economy is the combination of the basic system of socialism and the

12 Deng Xiaoping Selected Works, 1st ed., Vol. 3, p. 138.
13 Ibid., p. 373.

market economy. Essentially, it is to achieve is the organic combination of socialist public ownership and market economy and ensure the socialist nature of market economy. To promote the development of market economy and ensure the socialist nature of its development requires the party members to strengthen their theoretical studies. It is necessary to understand the general rules of the market economy and grasp the special nature of the socialist market economy. They need to understand the Western market economy theory and focus on learning the basic theory of Marxist. Of course, we cannot require all party members to become experts who know well all the theories. But without certain theoretical accomplishments, it is difficult to hold the right position in major issues of principle and truly understand and implement the relevant policies of the party. In particular, as China is more integrated with the international market, international factors have more influence on domestic economy and the operation of market economy is increasingly complex. Some people, on the excuse of integration with international economy, blindly copy the Western market economy theory, advocate liberalization, privatization and marketization, and ignore the particularity of socialist market economy, which inevitably lead to the development of market economy deviated from the socialist direction going against the original intention of Reform and Opening-up. Therefore, the party members must strive to improve their own theoretical quality, especially their understanding of basic principles of Marxism. Only with certain theoretical basis can we better integrate the socialist market economy into the world economy, be fully aware of the foundation and applicable circumstances of the principles, concepts and categories of the Western market economy theory while learning from it, so as to avoid copimism regardless of the fundamental difference of systems, avoid the theoretical confusion and economic fluctuations, and better make use of market economy for developing socialism. The development of the socialist market economy not only have theoretical requirements for the party members, but also requires that they could correctly deal with the new contradictions and problems brought by the market economy from. The market economy itself has the insurmountable defects of spontaneity, blindness, selfishness and injustice distribution. The particularity of the development of market economy in the primary stage of socialism has made some contradictions more prominent. In the field of distribution, all kinds of statistics show that the gap between rich and poor in the whole society is gradually widening, and many conflicts or contradictions of economic interests are emerging. Distribution according to work, as the most important distribution principle of the socialist economy and the party's major approach of adjusting economic interests among people, has been impacted and misinterpreted because of various reasons. This requires that the ruling party, which stands for the fundamental interests of the overwhelming majority of the people, must uphold the dominant position of distribution according to work, proceed from the overall situation and correctly handle the relationship between the overall interests of the whole society and long-term interests and partial interests of different regions and social groups and immediate interests. In particular, we should focus on the interests of the disadvantaged groups. We shall take various practical measures to effectively regulate income disparities in reform and development and lay a solid foundation for the realization of common prosperity. It is also necessary to see that a reasonable, legitimate and modest income gap is the inevitable product of breaking the egalitarian distribution and developing the socialist market economy. It is conducive to mobilizing the enthusiasm of the masses and promoting the development of the productive forces. Therefore, in dealing with the income gap, we must not stubbornly adhere to the egalitarianism; otherwise, we will repeat the mistakes in history. Only by coordinating the interests of all parties can we mobilize the enthusiasm and creativity of the whole society to create wealth, give full play to all sources of social wealth, and consolidate the mass base for the ruling party. In the field of ideology, the self-interest and profit-orientation of market economy also lead to issues such as money worship, lack of credibility and moral decline. Some party members and cadres concentrate on money which has become their only goal. This not only seriously distorts the party's purpose and violate the party character, but also have great impact on ideology of the whole society, resulting in shaken faith and lack of ideal among the people. The one-sided understanding of the competitiveness of market economy has also led to the lack of comprehensive and coordinated development of some places, organizations and party members. They only want freedom, regardless of discipline. They only focus on the present situation, without any long-term plan. The spirit of collectivism was neglected and centralization and unification of the party seriously undermined. Under the impact of market economy, some party organizations become weak and undisciplined, and have lost their conviction and strength for realizing the party's ideals. These discordant situations are incompatible with the ideals of the party. So, we must start from the realistic problems and better practice the "Three Represents" by strengthening the party education, in order to set a good example for the people. We shall innovate on theories, find the best connecting point between ideal and reality, help people solve the problems of spiritual pillar and power, and more effectively resist the infiltration of Western hostile forces in the ideological field.

More importantly, the development of a market economy poses a challenge to the material basis of the party's ruling. Socialism is based on the system of public ownership of the means of production. The public ownership economy is the material basis for the party to consolidate its ruling position. Once the public economy has been impacted, socialism will lose its foundation and the party's ruling position will be inevitably threatened. Under the planned economic system, public ownership is dominant, with only a small proportion of non-public economy. Under the condition of socialist market economy, public ownership and non-public ownership sectors such as individual economy, private economy and foreign capital are all equal market players. The dominant position of the public ownership economy is achieved through equal competition with other economic sectors. Judging from our current reform, the public ownership economy still occupies the dominant position. But we should also see the deep-seated problems in the reform of public ownership and the contrast in economic vitality and development speed between public ownership and non-public ownership economy. The latest data show that since the Reform and Opening-up, the average annual growth rate of China's non-public economy is more than 20%. The number of privately or individually-owned businesses has increased from 100,000 in 1978 to 37.56 million; the number of private enterprises has increased from 90,000 in 1989 to 9.676 million; and the number of foreign-invested enterprises has increased from none to 446,000. Fixed assets investment of non-public ownership economy is more than 60% of the national total. The GDP created by non-public sectors account for more than half of the national total. The foreign trade of non-public sectors account for 60% of the national total. And the non-public sectors provide more than 80% of urban jobs and more than 90% of new jobs. How to correctly understand these realistic problems, how to develop public ownership economy in equal competition, and how to avoid the "left" ideological influence and the tendency of falling into privatization have become the new subjects that needs deep and serious thinking by the party members.

In general, the development of the socialist market economy demands new requirements for the ability and quality of party members in the aspects of theories and practices. Therefore, to improve the ability and quality of party members has become a system construction involving various aspects. When explaining this issue, the 16th party congress clearly put forward that the Party committees and leading cadres at all levels should meet the requirements of the new situation and new tasks, constantly improve the ability to scientifically judge the situation, control market economy, cope with the complex situation, govern according to law and grasp the overall situation, which has pointed out the starting point for party members to improve their ability and quality.

3. To establish the party's leadership system and working mechanism adapted to socialist market economy

To improve the capacity and quality of the party members is the basic part of strengthening the party's ability to govern. In accordance with the requirements of the development of the socialist market economy, to constantly improve the institutional mechanisms and ways of the party in leading the economic work is the key to improve party's ability to govern. It difficult for party members to fully play their ability and the party's ruling efficiency cannot be improved, without perfect leadership system and working mechanism.

How to lead the healthy development of the socialist economy is the issue that the Party has been exploring for many years. Since the founding of new China, due to the specific historical conditions and social factors, there was no separation between the Party work and the government (state) work and the government was replaced by the party committees in China. Because of no separation between the Party work and the government work and organizational overlapping, the party controlled the affairs that should've been managed by enterprises, public institutions and social organizations. The mixed functions of the government and enterprises under the planned economic system have further deepened the degree of party's direct intervention to the economy. Therefore, at the beginning of Reform and Opening-up, Deng Xiaoping made it clear that the relationship between the party and the government should be handled through reform. "Separation of the functions of the Party and the government comes under the heading of political reform, and that raises the question of how a Party committee should exercise leadership".[14]

"Separation of government and enterprise, both involves economic system reform, and political system reform".[15] Properly handling the relationship between government and enterprises is the major task in reforms of economic system and administrative system. Aiming at determining the power of responsibilities of the party and state organs, Deng Xiaoping's ideas pointed out the direction for the reform at that time and now.

With the deepening of the reform, especially the development of the socialist market economy, some achievements have been made in separating the party, government and enterprise. But we also encountered new problems. Under the condition of market economy, the market players decide on their own the expansion or reduction of the production and demands according to signals such as the price, supply & demand and competition. The market plays a fundamental role in the allocation of resources. This requires the government to change itself from the managers controlling everything in the

14 Selected Works Deng Xiaoping, Vol. 3, 1st ed., p. 177.

15 Ibid., p. 192.

planned economy into the macro manager of socialist market economy, and shift focus of their work to providing services for market players and creating favorable environment for development. The new changes of government functions under the conditions of market economy will inevitably require adjustments on the party's decision-making mechanism, law enforcement system, supervision mechanism and mechanism in appointing and dismissal of cadres. Only in this way can we further rationalize the relationship between party and government, provide an important impetus for the party's ability to govern, and improve the level of the party's economic work. Macro decision-making is a key part of the party's leadership over economic construction and an important manifestation of the party's ability to govern. The history of China's economic construction shows that scientific and democratic decision-making is the important prerequisite for reducing and avoiding mistakes. When the macro decision-making is correct, the national economy will run smoothly; when it is wrong, the national economy will fluctuate. Under the highly centralized planned economy, the excessive concentration of power in the party committees, the party's overall control of business affairs and bureaucracy will inevitably have a certain impact on the scientific and democratic macro-decision-making. Under the conditions of the socialist market economy, the market plays a fundamental role in the economic operation and the enterprises exist as independent market players. It not only has higher requirements for the party's macro decision-making capacity, but also more urgently requires the party the free itself from the trivial specific issues, and focus on controlling the direction, major issues and key policies. Therefore, the scientific and democratic macro-decision making shall be attached great importance. We must constantly improve the democratic decision-making mechanism through the continuous development of inner-party democracy, the expansion of socialist democracy and the establishment and improvement of major decision-making rules and procedures of decision-making organs at all levels. We shall ensure the correctness of macro-decision-making and improve the effectiveness of macro-control by scientific decision-making methods and democratic decision-making process. In accordance with the inherent requirements and operational characteristics of the socialist market economy, to constantly improve the party's ability to govern according to law is also a major task for the party. Market economy is the economy ruled by law, under which all economic activities should be legalized. Promoting economic legislation and running the socialist market economy on the track of law is an important way for the party to lead the economic work. But for a long time, because of no separation between the Party work and the government work and the government being replaced by the party, the legalization in market economy has been limited to a certain extent. It not only lowers the efficiency of economic legislation and increases the cost of legalization of the market economy, but also interferes with the normal legal procedures, so that "rule of man" often is more powerful than "rule of law". Therefore, our party must further improve the way of leadership and governance in accordance with the law, establish a legal system compatible with the market economy, gradually change the way of promoting economic development by instructions and leadership to the normal operation mode of relying on laws, systems and working mechanism of functional departments, and putting the exercise of power by the Party and government within the framework of the law, (putting power in a lawful cage).

The socialist market economy requires us to improve the party's ability to govern according to law. We cannot realize this goal without power restriction supervisory mechanism adapted to market economy. In the economic field, the party's ability to govern according to law is embodied in the party's ability of macroeconomic regulation and control. In essence, the process of macroeconomic regulation and control means that the ruling party's intervention of the economy by public power. If the macro-control cannot be under the constraints of laws and regulations and there is no corresponding monitoring mechanism, it will inevitably lead to power corruption and ultimately affect the party's ability to govern. Therefore, it is necessary to establish a power control and supervision mechanism featuring reasonable structure, rational configuration and strict procedures in accordance with the characteristics of power operation under the market economy, to ensure that the power given by the people is used for the benefit of the people. The views put forward in the 4th Plenary Session of the 16th CPC Central Committee such as the establishment and improvement of the patrol system, strengthening social supervision and establishment and improvement of reporting system of leading cadres' major personal matters have pointed out the right direction for strengthening the construction of the party's supervision mechanism under the conditions of socialist market economy.

In addition, the profound changes in social structure in the process o socialist market economy have also brought a lot of new issues and requirements for the party's grassroots organizations. We need to have new ideas to figure out how to adjust the organizational settings, improve the work style, innovate activities content, expand coverage and enhance cohesion, so that the party's grassroots organizations truly become the organizer, promoters and practitioners of the important thinking of the "Three Represents". The openness of the market economy strengthens the connection between domestic and world economy and brings us favorable development opportunities. But it also brings various risks. To cope with the challenges of economic globalization and build a mechanism improving the party's ability to resist risks is an issue that requires the party's in-depth study.

(Li Yufeng, associate professor of Institute of Marxism, Renmin University of China)

Correctly Grasping the Party's Ruling Experience in the Process of Socialist Construction

The socialist system is a new social system in human history, which represents the development direction of human history. In the process of socialist construction, the ruling Communist Parties in some countries have lost their ruling status and the nature of the social system has undergone fundamental changes. In sharp contrast, China's socialist construction is showing infinite vitality. Systematic summary and scientific understanding of the ruling experience of the Communist Party of China is of great significance to further improve the party's ability to govern, realize the party's self-improvement and development, and promote the cause under the leadership of the Party.

1. To constantly enrich and develop Marxism in practice

Thought is a guide to action. The ruling effect of a ruling party depends to a large extent on whether the guiding ideology of the ruling party is scientific and whether the ruling party can treat this guiding ideology scientifically. Marxism is the inheritance and development of the outstanding cultural heritage of all mankind. It is the revolutionary truth that is produced and proved in practice. It is the scientific world view and methodology. Since the birth of the Communist Party of China, Marxism has been written solemnly on their banner and used to guide the practice. It can be said that through the history of China's revolution and construction led by the party they have been upholding the guiding position of Marxism. The practice of Chinese revolution and construction has proved that when the Marxist guiding position is truly adhered to, the socialist revolution and construction will succeed; when the guiding position of Marxism is weakened or broken, the socialist revolution and construction will suffer setbacks. This is also an important experience of the socialist revolution and construction in the world. The victory of the Russian October Revolution and the establishment of a large number of people's democratic countries after the Second World War marked the victory of scientific socialism advancing from theory to practice. The bankruptcy of "Second international" and the later drastic changes in Eastern Europe and collapse of the Soviet Union to a large extent was due to the abandonment of guiding position of Marxism. In the name of "exploring the new socialist model", the soviet eastern European countries actually abandoned Marxism and diverted to the banner of democratic socialism. Losing the banner of Marxism means to lose the soul of the Marxist political party, which inevitably leads to the ending of party, state and socialism. This is a painful historical lesson.

Positive and negative facts are warning us that, in the current complex situation of conflicts among various ideologies and cultures, we must uphold the guiding position of Marxism and hold firm our guiding ideology. If we abandon guiding position of Marxism and implement diversified guiding ideologies, the party, the country and the nation will suffer serious damages. But we must also realize that upholding Marxism does not mean to treat it as dogma. The Marxist worldview is not a doctrine, but a method. It provides not ready-made dogma, but a starting point for further research and a method for study. The quality of Marxism's advancing with the times determines that it is evolving with the development of the times. Only by developing Marxism in practice can we truly adhere to Marxism.

Specifically in China, upholding Marxism means that we shall at any time adhere to the principle of combining Marxism and China's reality, and constantly enrich and develop Marxism. In this regard, as early as in the democratic revolution period, Mao Zedong had made it clear that the whole party must "learn to apply Marxist-Leninist theory in China's specific environment", "use it according to the characteristics of China", and "make Marxism concrete in China". It is under the guidance of this thinking that Chinese Communist Party found the way of "countryside surrounding cities and taking the political power by armed forces" and won the victory of socialist revolution. It is also under the guidance of this thinking that the ruling Communist Party of China could quickly restore the national economy and consolidate the regime featuring people being the masters in a relatively short period of time. Of course, in the process of socialist construction, due to various interference factors, there have been ultra-left thought that dogmatized Marxism. This not only led to the decline of the party's ability to govern, but also caused serious harm to the socialist construction.

Since the Reform and Opening-up, our party has resumed its scientific attitude towards Marxism, established the ideological line of emancipating the mind, seeking truth from facts and advancing with the times, and developed Marxist theory under the new historical conditions. The Chinese Communists, represented by Deng Xiaoping, based on summing up the positive and negative experiences since the founding of new China, and based on the study of international experience and the world situation, have made the scientific conclusion of China being in the primary stage of socialism, set the goal of building socialist market economic system, profoundly revealed the essence of socialism, blazed a correct path of building socialism suitable for China's reality, created socialist theories with Chinese characteristics, and realized another historic leap in combining Marxism with China's reality in the new period of socialism.

Since the Fourth Plenary Session of the 13th CPC Central Committee, the Chinese Communists, represented by Comrade Jiang Zemin, have held high the great banner of Deng Xiaoping Theory, focused on the theme of building socialism with Chinese characteristics, innovated Marxist theories with the wisdom of the whole party, and gradually formed the scientific theory of "Three Represents", which further answered the question of "what is socialism and how to build socialism" and creatively answered the question of "what kind of party to build and how to build the party". The formation of the important thinking of the "Three Represents" shows that our party has reached a new theoretical level in understanding the laws of communist party's governance, socialist construction and human society development. Since the 16th CPC National Congress, the Party Central Committee with Comrade Hu Jintao as general secretary upheld Deng Xiaoping Theory and the important thinking of "Three Represents", and put forward a series of major strategic thinking including Scientific Outlook on Development in the great practices of leading the whole party and the people to comprehensively build a well-off society and create a new situation in building socialism with Chinese characteristics, which creatively answered the questions "what kind of development we are to achieve and how to achieve it" and open up a new sphere for the development of Marxism.

Deng Xiaoping Theory, "Three Represents" and Scientific Outlook on Development have presented some words that have never been said before. We did not forget the "ancestors", but repeatedly stressed that "ancestors cannot be forgotten". It means to inherit and adhere to Marxism and take Marxism as the guidance for solving the new problems. At present, China's socialist construction has advanced to a new stage, and the world has undergone tremendous changes. In the face of the new situation and the new environment at home and abroad, there is no ready answer to how to build socialism with Chinese characteristics and realize the great rejuvenation of the Chinese nation in the books of our "ancestors". The New Practice of Socialism Construction with Chinese Characteristics calls for theoretical innovation of Marxism. "We shall not forget the ancestors, but we should also innovate". This is the summary of our party's ruling experience and the principle that we must adhere to in the future reform and opening-up practice. Only by treating Marxism with a scientific attitude and continuously make theoretical innovation of Marxism can we combine upholding Marxism with development, innovate in upholding, develop in innovation, and better promote the healthy development of socialism.

2. To constantly promote the self-improvement and development of socialism in reform

In the 1980s or 1990s, some countries in Eastern Europe changed their path and abandoned Marxism and socialism. The Soviet Communist Party was also forced to declare the dissolution; the Soviet Union, the first socialist country in the world, announced the disintegration; world socialist movement encountered serious setbacks. Accordingly, some Westerners asserted that, “Socialism has failed, and it will disappear from the earth”. Did socialism really fail? The answer is no. The remarkable achievement of China’s socialist construction is a convincing proof. The Fourth Plenary Session of the 16th CPC Central Committee made it clearer that only socialism can save China and only socialism with Chinese characteristics can develop China. This is the inevitable result of the Chinese Communist Party’s relentless exploration of the path of national rejuvenation and common prosperity.

Only socialism can save China, which is the truth that has been proved by history. Only socialism with Chinese characteristics can develop China, which is a summary of the valuable experience gained in the development of new China for more than 60 years. After the founding of new China, the ruling Communist Party of China made useful exploration on the issues of “what is socialism and how to build socialism”. There were so many great achievements of our Party’s exploration on “what is socialism and how to build socialism”, including the completion of three socialist transformation campaigns, the publication of On the Ten Major Relationships and On the Correct Handling of Contradictions among the People and analysis and discussion on the main contradictions of socialism in the 8th CPC National Congress. There was misunderstanding of the historical stage of social development, and wrong theories of one-sided emphasis on the relations of production and focusing on “the top priority of class struggle”, but it did not mean we were to give up socialism. Those were wrong understanding due to limitations of knowledge on the basis of upholding socialism. This is different in nature from the abandonment of socialism in socialist countries of Eastern Europe and the Soviet Union.

After the Third Plenary Session of the 11th CPC Central Committee, our Party profoundly reflected the problems in the process of socialist construction, continued to explore the question of “what is socialism and how to build socialism”, and gradually established the theory of building socialism with Chinese characteristics, which has brought its understanding of socialism to a new stage. Deng Xiaoping repeatedly stressed that in the past we had no idea of what socialism is and how to build and develop socialism. This is the fundamental reason of the twists and turns and mistakes in the socialist construction. "The socialist system we have established is a good one, and we must adhere to it. The realization of socialism and communism was the lofty ideal we Marxists set for ourselves during the revolutionary years. Now that we are trying to reform the economy, we shall continue to keep to the socialist path and to uphold the ideal of communism. This is something our younger generation in particular must understand. But the problem is: what is socialism and how is it to be built? The most important lesson we have learned, among a great many others, is that we must be clear about those questions."[16]

With the deepening and development of socialist reform, based on repeated thinking, continuous exploration and multiple arguments, in 1992, Deng Xiaoping profoundly revealed in his South Tour speech that the essence of socialism is to liberate and develop productive forces, abolish exploitation and polarization, and achieve common prosperity, which has answered the questions of "what is socialism and how to build socialism".

For the great impact of drastic changes in Eastern Europe and the disintegration of the Soviet Union, and for those voices saying socialism has failed, Deng Xiaoping clearly said: If we did not adhere to socialism, implement the policies of reform and opening to the outside world, develop the economy and raise living standards, we would find ourselves in a blind alley."[17] The Fourth Plenary Session of the 14th CPC Central Committee elaborated the "twelve relations" of the modernization construction. The 15th National Congress of the Party elaborated on the basic program of the Party in the primary stage of socialism. The important thinking of the 'Three Represents' profoundly reveals the law of the construction of the ruling party in socialist countries. Scientific Outlook on Development profoundly answered the major problems of what kind of development we are to achieve and how to develop under the new conditions. These theories have greatly deepened our understanding of the socialist path.

That only socialism can save China and only socialism with Chinese characteristics can develop China are the scientific conclusions that is already or being proved. The firm belief in socialism and communism is inspiring generations to fight for it. Today, under the guidance of the theory of socialism with Chinese characteristics, Chinese society has undergone tremendous changes and the people's life has realized the historical leap from adequate or ample food and clothing to prosperity. With the further improvement and development of the socialist system, the superiority of the socialist system will undoubtedly be more fully demonstrated to the world and socialism will be full of greater vitality.

16 Deng Xiaoping, Selected Works Vol. 3, 1st ed., p. 316.

17 Ibid., p. 370.

3. To focus on development while scientifically grasping the main contradiction of socialism

Whether there is any contradiction in the socialist society and what is the main contradiction of the socialist society are the major issues for the ruling party of the socialist countries. Being able to correctly understand and treat this issue related to the key work of the ruling party and the socialist countries. It is the key to consolidation and health development of socialist system. The ruling parties of the socialist countries have made great efforts to explore this issue and put forward their own solutions.

After the founding of new China, the Chinese Communist Party has also made unremitting efforts to solve this problem. On the basis of deeply studying China's own experiences and lessons, especially on the basis of profound experiences and lessons of some socialist countries in Eastern Europe, the 8th CPC National Congress explained the contradictions and major contradictions of the socialist society. In term of major contradictions, the 8th CPC National Congress put forward that the main contradiction in China is no longer the contradiction between the proletariat and the bourgeoisie, but the contradiction between the people's demands for the establishment of an advanced industrial country and the reality of a backward agricultural country, and the contradiction between people's need for rapid economic and cultural development and the current situation of economy and culture. Therefore, the party and the country's focus should be shifted from the class struggle to economic construction. This is a correct analysis of the main contradictions of the Chinese society and the central work of the party after the establishment of the socialist system. However, with the changes of the international and domestic situation, the class struggle has been gradually exaggerated as the main contradiction of the socialist society, which led China's economic and social development into a stage of twists and turns. In particular, it should be noted that in this period, there were many deficiencies in people's understanding of development. On the one hand, development was considered equal to economic growth. On the other hand, development was considered equal to industrial development which meant development of heavy industry at that time. It caused the issues of unbalanced economic structure and speed in the beginning of economic take-off. On the basis of scientific conclusion of experience and lessons, the Sixth Plenary Session of the 11th CPC Central Committee clearly stated that the main contradiction of the socialist society is the contradiction between the growing material and cultural needs of the people and the backward nature of social production, and the focus of the work of the party and the state should be transferred to the socialist modernization. "In a socialist country, after a true Marxist party is in power, it must commit itself to developing productive forces and gradually improve the people's living standards on this basis."[18] According to the new judgment on the international and domestic situation, Deng Xiaoping put forward that peace and development are the two major themes of the contemporary world. He pointed out that development is both a need for world historical development and a common need of the peoples of the world. If we cannot understand the objectivity and urgency of this need, we will fall behind in the development of the times, and cannot achieve the goal of standing proudly in the world, let alone upholding and developing socialism. He believed that the key to a powerful socialism and to demonstrate its superiority would be development. "Why do the people support us? Because over the last ten years our economy has been developing and developing visibly… This is not only an economic problem but also a political one."[19] In short, "Development is overriding priority".

That development is overriding priority and we must insist on using the development approach to solve the problems in progress have become the leading thought in promoting China's reform. In the past 30 years of Reform and Opening-up, our party has maintained the central task of economic construction, vigorously promoted socialist modernization, and made great achievements in economic construction and social undertakings. In the new stage of the new century, the third generation of the central collective leadership of the party has further enriched and developed the idea of "development is the top priority" and put forward the new proposition of "making development the top priority of the party in governing and rejuvenating the country". The theory of making development the top priority of the party in governing and rejuvenating the country profoundly reveals that development is the core content and foundation of our party's governance. Only by taking the development of productive forces as the priority and unswervingly focusing on economic construction can Communist Party of China lay solid foundation for the comprehensive progress of socialism and provide a strong material guarantee for the ultimate realization of communism.

In view of some new problems in the process of reform, such as the widening gap between urban and rural areas, the uneven regional economic development, he uncoordinated economic and social development, the increasing pressure on resources and environment, the Third Plenary Session of the 16th CPC Central Committee on the basis of the reality of China's current economic and social development put forward the Scientific Outlook on Development featuring adhering to the people-oriented principle, establishing comprehensive, coordinated and sustainable development view, and promoting the overall development of economy, society

18 Deng Xiaoping Selected Works, vol. 3, 1st ed., p. 28.

19 Ibid., p. 354.

and people, which enriched and innovated the connotation, driving force, law and path of development. Scientific Outlook on Development not only emphasizes the fundamental issue of development, but also pointed out that the development must be scientific, people-oriented, comprehensive coordinated and sustainable, which is an innovation of development conception. Scientific Outlook on Development means that the party's understanding of development has reached a new level and also marks a new sublimation of our party's ruling philosophy. Only by firmly upholding and implementing Scientific Outlook on Development can we have the important guiding ideology and basic working principles for properly dealing with many contradictions in economic and social development, truly reflect the purpose of development by giving people more benefits, understand the overall situation of economic and social development, successfully realize the grand goal of building a moderately prosperous society, and continue to create new situations of socialism with Chinese characteristics.

4. To strengthen the party building with the spirit of reform on the basis of upholding the party's fundamental purpose

On the constantly changing international stage, whether the ruling party of a country can consolidate its ruling position to a large extent depends on two aspects: one is that whether it has continuously strengthened its own construction to keep up with the times; the other one is that whether it can win the support of the broad masses of people. In this regard, we can analyze from both positive and negative perspectives. The Communist Party of the Soviet Union used to have more than 18 million party members and being the ruling party for more than 70 years. However, it fell in a very short period of time and handed over the power in a surprisingly smooth way. For the reasons for the failure of Communist Party of the Soviet Union although people have different opinions, the above two aspects fundamentally explain the problem.

The Soviet Communist Party is an advanced organization armed with Marxism. The Marxist theoretical quality of advancing with the times requires that it make theoretical innovation and system reforms according to the changing governance environment to meet the requirements of the environment and the task and improve the ruling effect. However, dogmatism imprisoned innovation of theories which did not advance with the development of practices. Seemingly the Marxism-Leninism was upheld; in fact, it was out of touch with reality. The highly centralized system of the Soviet Union formed in a certain historical context has played a major role. But this system featuring rule by persons in a highly centralized manner, lifelong tenure and cadre appointment had not changed according to the changes of times and reform requirements, resulting in structural crisis in the internal operation mechanism and ultimately becoming a systematic obstacle.

"Formalization of the work of party organizations" and "bureaucratization of cadres of the party and state" made the party a part of state institution and a power above the society. "Individualization of state power" and "absence of supervision mechanism" hindered the supervision of the power by relevant organs and people and led to a rampant corruption problem.

The problems of the party's own construction have a direct impact on the relationship between the party and the people. Before the collapse of the Soviet Union, an investigation report titled "Who the Soviet communist party actually represents" showed that 7% of the people saw it as the representative of the working people, 4% thought it as the representative of the workers, 11% saw it as the representative of all party members, and 85% regarded it as the representative of bureaucrats, leading cadres and government officials. The extreme mistrust against of the party organization led to the fact that when Gorbachev declared the dissolution of the Soviet Communist Party, almost no one objected the change and campaigned for the party to remain in power. This is in sharp contrast with people's voluntary sacrifice when the Soviet Communist Party took power.

The lesson of the Communist Party of the Soviet Union losing its ruling position warns us that, in order to consolidate the ruling position and improve the ruling performance, we must constantly strengthen the building of the ruling party and establish flesh and blood ties with the people to win their support. In fact, the ruling Communist Party of China has been following this thinking and perfecting governance style and improving the ability and level of governance in the constantly changing governance environment. As early as the Second Plenary Session of the 7th CPC Central Committee, Mao Zedong warned the whole party, "To win countrywide victory is only the first step in a long march of ten thousand li... The Chinese revolution is great, but the road after the revolution will be longer, the work greater and more arduous. This must be made clear now in the Party. The comrades must be helped to remain modest, prudent and free from arrogance and rashness in their style of work. The comrades must be helped to preserve the style of plain living and hard struggle."[20] The idea of "Two Inevitabilities" is of great significance in the early days of the founding of New China and the construction of the ruling party today. In the early 1950s, for the domestic situation at the early days of the founding of new China, our party carried out the rectification movement within the party and implemented reorganization in the grassroots organizations of the party, conducted the Three-anti and Five-anti Campaigns, which purified and consolidated the party's organization, strengthened the party's ability to govern, and created one of the best times in the history of our party. In

20 Mao Zedong Selected Works, 2nd ed., Vol. 4, Beijing, People's Publishing House, 1991, pp. 1438-39.

order to uphold the correct leadership of the party to the cause of socialism, Mao Zedong and Liu Shaoqi also put forward such issues as constantly improving the party's leadership, improving the party's leadership style, carrying forward the mass line in Party's work, improving democratic centralism, and opposing personality cult. Since the Reform and Opening-up, Comrade Deng Xiaoping and Jiang Zemin have published many important expositions on these issues and put forward the important thinking of the party's system construction, laying a theoretical foundation for institutionally and systematically improving the party's leadership.

After entering the new stage in the new century, the new practice of socialism with Chinese characteristics once again calls for theoretical innovation. Regarding the issue of "what kind of party we are to build and how to build it", the party put forward the important thinking of "Three Represents". The important thinking of the Three Represents not only reveals foundation for building our Party, the cornerstone for its governance and the source of its strength, but also points out the direction of the Party's construction and puts forward higher requirements for the Party. The Fourth Plenary Session of the 16th CPC Central Committee put forward the idea that we must adhere to scientific governance, democratic governance and rule by law. This is a major change in the party's leadership and governance and the inevitable requirement of implementing the basic strategy of governing the country according to law, developing socialist democratic politics and building a socialist political civilization. The Fourth Plenary Session of the 17th CPC Central Committee answered a number of major issues of strengthening and improving the party building under the new situation and put forward the action plan and guidelines for party building in the present and future eras.

While strengthening the party's construction in the aspects of ideology, institution and system, the party should always maintain close ties with the people. The people are the masters of the socialist state and the fundamental force that determines the fate of our future. At any time, we should put the interests of the people to the first rank and serve the people wholeheartedly, which is the political essence of Marxist parties. Deng Xiaoping has repeatedly stressed that all the work, principles and policies of the party shall be aimed at winning the people's satisfaction and support. "as adhering to the line of Reform and Opening-up and who had some achievements in that respect should be praised. This would convince the people that we are wholeheartedly committed to that line. The masses judge from practice. When they come to the conclusion that socialism is good and that Reform and Opening-up policy are good, our cause will flourish forever."[21] The Party is built for the public and it exercises state power for the people.

21 Deng Xiaoping Selected Works, Vol. 3, 1st ed., p. 381.

The government must function by the mandate of the people, empathize with the feelings of the people, and work for the well-being of the people. There is no small thing when talking about people's interests. The highest virtue is to love and benefit the people.These simple words reflect the party's people-oriented thinking and conduct in the new era. This is also the party's most essential understanding about the rule of law. Reviewing the success or failure of the ruling proletarian party in the process of socialism can make us more scientifically understand the experience of the Communist Party of China over the past 60 years. These experiences are a comprehensive, profound and constitute the scientific summary of successful experience of our party's governance for more than 60 years. Looking from the perspective of current times, it improves our theoretical thinking and answers the questions we face in reality and illuminates the future path of creating the new situations of socialism with Chinese characteristics. These experiences are our party's valuable wealth and important guiding principles for the party to strengthen the construction of its ruling ability. It is of far-reaching significance for future success of the cause the party and state which we pursue.

(Li Yufeng, associate professor of Institute of Marxism, Renmin University of China)

Reforms Initiated by Various Parties of the World in the Contemporary Era

Since the British bourgeois revolution, party politics has a history of three centuries. If analyzed form the aspect of more complete political party formation in the United States, they have a history of a century and a half. After the Second World War, party politics spread from a few countries to the whole world. At present, except for a few countries, most of more than 200 countries and regions in the world implement party politics. In the process of technological revolution and globalization, party politics in the world have experienced profound changes.These changes are highlighted in three aspects: party system, party organization and governing strategy. To sum up and sort out the laws of the reform of contemporary political parties and to compare with and learn from the experiences and lessons of other political parties is of great significance to strengthen the ruling ability of the Communist Party of China and improve the ruling quality.

1. The choice of party system

The first issue of party politics is the party system. The most common classification of the party system is single-party system, two-party system and multi-party system according to the number of the ruling parties or potential ruling parties. Single-party system means one party is in power; two-party system means two parties are in power in turn; and multi-party system means more than two parties are involved in governance. Of course, there is other classification of party system, for instance, Sartori has classified party system into competitive party system and non-competitive party system.

Western developed countries have different party systems. Britain implemented parliamentarism of two-party system. The first two parties in the UK. were the Whigs and the Tories, which was later followed by the Liberal Party and the Conservative Party. At the beginning of the 20th century, after the rise of the Labor Party, the Labor Party and the Conservative Party began a long-term rotation in ruling. The United States implements presidential system with two-party system. After differentiation and combination, the early parties in America developed into the pattern of ruling in turn by Democrats and Republicans after the Civil War. In the past, the Democratic Party had an overwhelming advantage in the southern states. After the Second World War, the Republicans developed in the south, and the two parties were evenly distributed throughout the country. France implements a semi-presidential multi-party system. After the French bourgeois revolution, republic and autocracy rules repeated alternately. Although there were many competing parties, France didn't have the powerful parties with long tradition like in Britain and the United States. The current pattern of political parties in France was formed during the Fifth Republic. In the contemporary multi-party system of France, the political parties with important influence are Rally for the Republic, Union for French Democracy, the Socialist party and Communist Party. The first two parties form the right wing and the latter two parties the left wing. Germany implements a parliamentary multiparty system. In the first half of the 20th century, after the chaotic multi-party system of Weimar Republic and after fascist dictatorship, the present multi-party system was established in Germany based on the reflection of history. The political parties that play a leading role in Germany are Christian Democratic Union and Social Democratic party. There are also Christian Social Union, Free Democratic Party and recently rising Green Party. Under Germany's multi-party system, the two core parties respectively ally the small parties to form a coalition government. After the Second World War, "one-party dominance" has been the case in Japan. The Liberal Democratic Party has been in power since 1955 until the first time when it was out of office in 1993. Today, Japan has a lot of political parties in the parliament; its party system is changing. But compared with other parties, the Liberal Democratic Party still has a certain advantage.

The political system of developing countries is more diverse and varied. Today's developing countries are basically implementing party politics. The independence of Latin American countries is relatively earlier. In the long-term battle among various forces military rule faded and party politics eventually dominated. After the revolution and independence, and after experiencing military regimes and dictatorships, party politics is also a common choice in Asian countries. Even in the most under-developed Africa, party politics is universal, except for very few countries. Compared with the developed countries, the party systems in developing countries are quite different. The party systems in some countries are still not mature and in the process of exploration and formation. Some new independent countries copied the western party systems at the beginning of their founding,they copied the western countries or the Soviet Union. The countries imitating the western countries are implementing multiparty system; those whivh imitated the Soviet Union implemented single-party system. A more prominent feature of the party system of developing countries was the dominance of one-party system in a period of time. It is reflected in the newly established countries that abondoned the colonial rule after the Second World War. For instance, in more than 50 African independent countries, 37 had implemented one-party system. In addition to the one-party system that has been widely practiced, in some countries there were seemingly many parties but in fact only one party was in power, for example People's Action

Party in Singapore, Institutional Revolutionary Party in Mexico, Umno in Malaysia, and Congress Party in India after the independence. These one-party systems in developing countries have played a unique role in safeguarding national independence, achieving national integration, maintaining social stability and promoting economic development. Of course, there occued many problems under this kind of system. Long-term ruling of one party and lack of competition lead to serious corruption and foster individual autocracy.

After the 1990s, many developing countries were involved in the multi-party trend under the influence of internal and external factors. The party systems in some major developing countries began to change. In Mexico, Institutional Revolutionary Party had been in power for 71 years from 1929 to 2000. However, in the 2000 it was forced to step down in the 2000 presidential election. In Indonesia, Golkar had been in power for a long period of time. After Suharto stepped down, many parties began to compete. Even in the countries whose party system has not fundamentally changed, such as Singapore and Malaysia, the advantages of the ruling party are shrinking and the opposition parties are rising. From the experience of above developed countries and developing countries, we can see that various party systems coexist in the world today. The formation of each party system has its special reason, a certain internal rationality and certain advantages and disadvantages. The party system implemented in a country depends on many complex factors. Firstly, the basic system of the state. In the capitalist countries, two-party system and multi-party system are commonly implemented, with the exception of one-party system in some countries. In socialist countries, it is mainly one-party system and multi-party cooperation system led by one party. In Britain, the birthplace of modern capitalism, two-party system was implemented in the early days. The Soviet Union was the first socialist country in the world and implemented one-party system after its establishment. Their party systems deeply influenced the latecomers who chose between the two systems (socialism or capitalism). Secondly, the level of social development. Today, the party systems in the developed countries are quite different from those in developing countries. It is basically two-party and multi-party system in developed countries. The party system of developing countries is generally immature and still changing. One-party system used to be implemented in developing countries. After the end of the Cold War, and under the influence of the new world trend, many countries shifted to multi-party system. Thirdly, the electoral system. In general, election system favoring the majority is not favorable for the survival of small parties, but it is conducive to the formation of the two-party system. The electoral system in Britain and the United States is an important cornerstone for the stability their Two-party system. Proportional representation system is an important reason for the formation and continuation of multiparty system. The Western countries mostly implement proportional election system which can partly promote small parties. Fourthly, historical and cultural factors. Party system is not so much a choice as a historical heritage. There are special historical reasons for the formation of political parties in each country. Cultural factors include religious factors which have profound impact on the formation of political parties.

2. Changes in party organization

The contemporary society is becoming more and more complicated with accelerating social changes, which constantly impact the survival and development of political parties. Firstly, the class structure changes. After the Second World War, with the rapid development of the scientific and technological revolution and the profound adjustment of the economic structure, the class, stratum and interest groups of the developed countries have undergone new changes, and the social basis of the political parties has changed. The political parties, especially the left-wing parties with more striking class nature, have been impacted by this change. In the process of accelerating modernization, the class structure in developing countries has also undergone dramatic changes. The number of traditional farmers are decreasing, while the working class and the middle class are increasing. The changes of party system in some developing countries also have a profound internal relationship with this situation. Secondly, the expansion of social organization. Today, a large number of interest groups have emerged. These groups are becoming more organized and orderly. They tend to skip the parties and directly lobby with the parliament or government and propose their views and ideas. This has weakened the party's original commitment to express public opinion. In developed countries, there are also a large number of civil society organizations. These organizations focus on specific activities such as human rights, environmental protection and local rights, and participate in social movements such as anti-war, anti-nuclear and anti-globalization. Their social impact is constantly expanding, and gradually penetrates the traditional fields of political activities. Thirdly, the development of democratic forms. Under indirect democracy, political parties are the bridge between the public and the government. With the help of new technologies, especially information technology, direct democracy featuring democratic participation is being revitalized, which undermines the political parties' functions of mobilization and participation. Some Western political figures no longer rely entirely on political party organizations, but directly communicate with the voters through television, Internet and other mass media. People also skip the political parties and directly participate in democracy. Fourthly, the weakening party identity. With the development of society, the relationship between political parties and class has become increasingly complicated. The connection between the party and the class is no longer obvious but has become increasingly blurred. People are becoming more self-conscious and more independent from the political parties. They do not firmly stick with one political party. For instance, the US voters could vote for the Republican Party today, Democratic Party tomorrow and the Republican Party again the day after tomorrow. Voters pay more attention to the candidate, not the party to which he/she belongs.

In the face of a variety of impacts and increasingly complex situations, any political party needs to respond effectively. In order to survive and develop, and especially to compete for and maintain ruling position, the political parties need to advance with the times and constantly adjust and reform themselves.

Firstly, it is reflected in how political parties treat the class. A political party is an organization that reflects the interests, wishes and demands of the classes. Modern political parties have emerged from the need of class struggle, whose essence is the representation of class interests. In today's world, various types of political parties in all countries reflect in different extent the class tendencies. In all political parties, the Communist Party emphasizes its class attributes the most. The class nature of socialist party is also relatively clear. Even a typical bourgeois party has a certain class tendency. For instance, in the United States, there are more voters from lower middle class than those from the upper class in the Democratic Party and there are obviously more rich people supporting the Republican Party than those supporting the Democratic Party. Of course, some political parties are not based on class, but based on consensus on major issues, such as the rising green party. There are also political parties based on religion. One of the trends in contemporary development is that many political parties, especially the ruling parties are trying to expand their class base and even go beyond class. Political parties adapt to the requirements of governance, make appropriate decorations to hide their own class nature, and do everything possible to advertise that they represent the interests of the majority of the people or the whole people. Because after seizing the ruling power the political party should rely on the public power to remain as the government party, therefore it has to show a certain degree of public character to win the public. Otherwise, it will be considered as a selfish party and cannot maintain effective or long-term ruling position. Some of the past class-based political parties such as the Socialist Party tried to dilute their own class attributes, so that it can be accepted by different social classes and groups. Some of the ruling parties in developing countries have extensive class nature. Institutional Revolutionary Party in Mexico implements the

"Corporatism" organization system which aims to incorporate the workers, farmers, people and soldiers. The Indian National Congress party is a mass party that includes workers, peasants and craftsmen. The Golkar in Indonesia divides the society into several functional groups, incorporates these groups into their own organizations, thereby claiming to represent the interests of the whole society.

Second, it is reflected in how political parties treat ideology issues. According to their programs and political principles, political parties can be divided into principled political parties, programmatic parties and expedient political parties. The so-called principled parties are those parties whose purpose is to promote and ultimately achieve a set of principles or pursue for ideologies. The Communist Party and the early Social Democrats belong to this type. The so-called programmatic type of parties are those who have their own clear goals which are mainly limited to a certain range. The Social Democratic Party and Christian Democratic Party after the Second World War belong to this type. The so-called expedient party refers to those whose purpose is to take power and other goals but whose policies can be changed at any time[22], such as the Democratic Party and Republican Party of the United States. From these distinctions we can see that ideology does not have the same role and effect on various types of political parties. However, the traditional parties generally have their own ideology. Because it is hard for a political party identify itself without a certain ideology. There are several major systems of ideology in today's world, such as Marxism, conservatism, social democracy, Christian democracy, and ecology thought. Currently, the mainstream ideologies, which are influential in the West, are social democracy and neo-conservatism. The ideology of political parties in developing countries is peculiar. Many of their ideologies are a mixture of socialism, capitalism, nationalism, and various religious beliefs. The ideologies of contemporary political parties tend to be intermediate. After the Second World War, the ideologies of the mainstream political parties in the West tend to converge. This is a reflection of their consensus on the basic social system and the major problems, their response to the rise of the middle class, and their ruling strategy. The parties with neutral ideology have advantages in gaining public support. And for the parties with radical ideology, it is hard to gain the majority of social recognition and gain the ruling position. In order to maintain better governance, the mainstream left and right political parties have to study and learn from the ideas, policies and development experience of their competitors, leading to the the phenomenon of "left wing not being left and right wing not being right" in some countries.

22 Wang Changjiang, A Study on the Ruling Law of Modern Political Parties, Shanghai, Shanghai People's Publishing House, 2002, pp. 63-64.

Thirdly, it is reflected in the party's organizational change. In accordance with the intensification of organizational discipline, political parties can be divided into strict organizational standards type, loose type and mixed type. The political parties with strict organizational standards type are strict in disciplines and have a large number of provisions in the party constitution. It not only has strict requirements for representative of the party, but also has established requirements for ordinary party members. The Communist Party and some Western Social Democratic Parties belong to this type. Political parties with loose standards type do not pay attention to organizational discipline. In particular, they don't have written provisions. The two parties of the United States are the typical examples. Ordinary party members do not even have to go through the procedures to join a party. The representatives could go beyond their party when voting. Mixed type is in the middle. The political parties this type generally have requirements for the high-level members and representatives. But their provisions are not for the whole party. For instance, the People's Action Party in Singapore. There are two notable features of contemporary political party organizational change. First, strengthening the inner-party democracy. With the deepening development of contemporary democratic ideas, all political parties attach great importance to the issue of democratization within the party. In term of organizational change, the Western Socialist Parties tend to be more decentralized, democratic, diversified and open. Even some of the traditional bourgeois parties also began to strengthen the building of inner-party democracy. For instance, the British Conservative Party began to elect the party leader. The emerging Green parties attach greater importance to democracy within the party, especially democratic participation and direct democracy at the grassroots level. Political parties in developing countries are also moving towards organizational democratization. Secondly, the selection of outstanding talents. Today, the party leaders have significant influence over the organization. The rise and fall of Western parties depends to a large extent on the success or failure of the elections. The important factor in the success of the election lies in the candidate. If the candidates with influence and charisma win the election, they will effectively promote the development of political parties. Many Western political parties incorporate outstanding talents into the party through organized activities and present them as their candidates in the elections. For political parties in the developing countries, talent is more important. Because the state institution and legal system are incomplete and immature, role of individuals have great impacts. Whether political parties in developing countries can absorb outstanding talents into their own organizations to a large extent determines their survival, development and governance capacity.

3. The exploration of the ruling strategy

A political party is a group that is organized to seize power. Any political party wants to be in power for a long period of time. The government control is of great significance to the survival and development of a political party. Some Western parties even regard governance as the fundamental purpose of their own existence. Through the ruling, political parties can use their public power to implement their own political ideas, and use the institutional authority to expand their political influence and appeal.

There are many ways for political parties to gain a ruling position, including legitimate ways, violent or abnormal extraordinary illegal ways and the way of founding an independent state. The legitimate way means that, without changing state system and regime, political parties compete for and obtain the ruling position in the framework of existing constitutional, legal and political rules. Political parties in Western developed countries usually take office in this way. The abnormal extraordinary way means that the political parties which do not recognize the existing political system seize the ruling power through abnormal extraordinary means and change the existing system. The governance by the Communist Party after the success of the revolution belongs to this type. The way of founding a state means that in some developing countries, political parties take power in the process of founding the state. In those countries which won independence from colonial powers are the "founding father" types of political parties, this is the most typical example.[23] Under normal circumstances, contemporary political parties aim to obtain power through legal channels and compete for the office in the framework of the established rules.

A political party must first win power. In the multi-party system of free elections in the West, all legitimate political parties have the right to win power, but many political parties have never been given this opportunity. Because the political parties need to win the elections in order to take power. For winning the election, they need the support of the public. In the countries with multi-party democratic election, the public opinion is displayed directly and periodically through elections. If it is recognized and supported in the elections by the voters, the party has the opportunity to take office. If it fails in the election for several occasions, the party may decline. In order to win the election and win seats in the parliament, the Western parties try to expand their ties with the voters in the organization and make corresponding adjustments according to the people's demands and moods in their policies. Today, many developing countries have also embarked on a multiparty and democratic electoral path. In order to seek votes, these political parties also take more and more measures which respond to public opinion from

23 Ibid., pp. 70-73.

the aspects of organization and policy. It is important to note that one of the keys to win public support today is to promote economic development. For developing countries, the importance of developing the economy is self-evident. In a poor society, whoever can more effectively solve the problem of people's subsistence and housing issues will be more advantegous in public. In the case of economic globalization, the competition among countries is becoming increasingly intense. Whether the economy could develop smoothly is a major issue for the developed countries. The ruling party should seek a suitable development model, formulate a clear development strategy and promote economic development according to the domestic and international economic environment. Some long term ruling political parties, such as Sweden Social Democratic Party and People's Action Party of Singapore, have made outstanding economic achievements. It is also important to note that the ruling party should not only devote itself to the development of the economy, but also pay attention to the equitable sharing of economic results. Sweden Social Democratic Party had committed itself to narrowing the gap between rich and poor, which is an important factor for winning the support of the middle and lower classes. During the administration of Vajpayee from the People's Party in India, the party has made remarkable economic achievements. Their campaign slogan for the election was "Shining India". Although India has undergone enormous changes from many aspects, ordinary people have not benefited from it. The middle and lower classes were dissatisfied with social injustice. In the 2004 election, People's Party's dream of maintaining the office was broken. In the economic reforms of the 1980s, Mexican Institutional Revolutionary Party gradually adopted neo-liberal economic policies, resulting in serious economic turmoil and social chaos, which widened the gap between the rich and poor. While promoting economic reform, this Mexican party did not solve the problem of social justice and lost the support of the people and also lost its reputation.

A party not only needs to seize power, but should also govern the state scientifically. Scientific governance requires properly dealing with the following key issues:

Firstly, the relationship between the ruling party and the government shall be properly handled. The ruling party's control over public (state) power is mainly the control of its cadres, personnel and control on policy affairs, instead of all-round control. Personnel control means that the party recommends personnel for government posts. Affairs control means that party has control upon its policies and principles. However, the ruling party should maintain a moderate control over the government or state. Western ruling parties generally do not greatly interfere with and intervene in the specific operations and affairs of the government. The head of government or ministers have vast space for his independent decision making. A political party is not a national authority itself and should not give direct orders to the state authority. The ruling party usually administrates the state through intermediate links. Most of the ruling parties mainly guide the government indirectly and pay attention to the appropriate distinction between the front desk government and the backstage party. For the legitimate ruling party, the constitutional law has the highest priority. The ruling party should pay attention to handling the relationship among leading the legislation work, taking the lead in observing the constitutional law and administrate according to laws. The laws and systems of the developing countries are not yet sound, so there are no adequate systems that restrain the ruling party. Especially, for those countries that have been long ruled by one party, rule by individual man is prevalent. If the ruling party does not indulge with the specific government affairs, instead concentrate with the party affairs, it can streamline the party's institutions and improve efficiency.

Secondly, government affairs should be scientifically managed. In terms of governance, the ruling party should grasp the whole situation. Different countries have different governance experiences. Contemporarily, there are different types of governance, such as welfare state model and liberal model. When choosing the macro model, the characteristics of the times and national conditions shall be carefully considered. Whether the decision-making is scientific and whether a party is widely recognized and supported is directly related to its performance. There is a trend of policy specialization among Western political parties. The ruling party generally has special policy research institutions to draft policy decisions for the party leaders and party organizations. Many Western political parties also support think tanks, advisory bodies, research institutes and special commisions outside the party as adviser and assistant for decision-making. For the decision-making process, the parties should also expand democratic participation in order to enhance the quality of decision-making and enhance party members' sense of identity.

Thirdly, special attention shall be paid to maintain an honest and upright government. This is even more necesarry for political parties wich hold power for longer years. Power has inherent nature of limitless expansion and corrosiveness.Since the 1990s, the collapse of the long-term ruling big ,old parties is related with corruption. Liberal Democratic Party in Japan has maintained a long-term rule, resulting in a trinity relationship of "politics, bureaucrats and finance". The leading party members of the long-term ruling Indian National Congress party are keen on securing the official state posts to obtain material interests. In order to remain honest and avoid corruption, the ruling party must be effectively supervised. These supervisory initiatives include: (1) Constitutional and legal norms. The constitutions of many foreign countries has stipulations for the behavior of political parties. Some countries have also enacted specific laws on political parties, such as in Germany. (2) The restraint of the power system. Western judicial institutions are quite independent. They are not only independent from the administrative and legislative bodies, but also independent from the parties, and objectively supervise the parties' activities. (3) Supervision of the opposition party. The existence of the opposition party is a lasting challenge for the ruling party and to a certain extent prevents the ruling party from abusing its powers. (4) Media supervision. It mainly reflects public opinions and exerts psychological pressure on power holders. With the rapid development of IT, information and communication technology, the media and public opinion play an increasingly important role in curbing the power abuse of the ruling parties.

4. Enlightenment for China

China's history, culture, social system, the level of development is different from other countries, so we cannot copy the practices and measures of the political parties in these countries. But when building the socialist modernization under the background of globalization and opening up, we should study and learn from the experience and lessons of other countries, so as to broaden our vision and better understand laws of the construction of Chinese political parties.

There are the following enlightenments for China's party construction in understanding the changes of world political parties:

Firstly, China's political party system must conform to national conditions. There are several basic realities behind the development of the world political party system. Firstly, it is complicated. The situation in developed countries is different from developing countries. And there are differences among developed countries and developing countries. Secondly, it is still in a change process. It is also not completely stable in developed countries. And developing countries are in a period of great change. Thirdly, the developing countries have their particularities and cannot be completely understood from the western perspective. There is not a unified, universally applicable political party model in today's world. The party system should vary according to different countries and adjust itself to changing times. The most important thing for all countries is to have a party system suitable for their national conditions and try to utilize advantages and avoid disadvantage of a certain party system. China's political party system has developed in the long-term revolutionary struggle and has been gradually improved in socialist construction and also in Reform and Opening-up period. Under its system, China has achieved remarkable achievements in national independence, national unity, economic development and social stability. After the end of the Cold War Era, some developing countries adopted the multiparty system, leading to huge chaos and even catastrophe. China as a developing socialist country must learn from this lesson. Therefore, in view of China's current development level and cultural background, adhering to multi-party political consultation system under the leadership of the CPC is conducive utilize the existing advantages thus accelerate the realization of socialist modernization.

Secondly, the Chinese Communist Party must keep pace with the times. With great changes in our times, there are some common new trends in the organizational transformation of the world's political parties, such as expanding party's mass base, updating the party's ideology and strengthening the party's organizational structure. While China's modernization and Reform and Opening-up are speeded up, the Chinese Communist Party in particular stresses the principle of advancing with times. In term of class basis, the Communist Party of China is committed to represent the fundamental interests of the overwhelming majority of the people. It is not only the vanguard of the Chinese working class, but also the vanguard of the Chinese people and the Chinese nation. In term of guiding ideology, the Communist Party of China adheres to the theory of Marxism-Leninism, Mao Zedong Thought, Deng Xiaoping Theory, the important thinking of the "Three Represents" and the Scientific Concept of Development, work on new practices and development, focus on the theoretical deliberation of major issues, and constantly open up the new realms in the enrichment of Marxist theories. In term of organizational construction, the Chinese Communist Party adheres to the principle of democratic centralism and is committed to carry forward the inner-party democracy and recruit and cultivate talents.

Thirdly, the Chinese Communist Party must improve its ability to govern. Competing for and maintaining power is a top priority for the mainstream political parties in all countries. The basic strategy of the world's political parties is to win public support, develop the economy, safeguard justice and maintain scientific governance. The ruling position of the Communist Party of China is neither innate, nor once and for all. After entering the 21st century, new and profound changes have taken place in the international situation; domestic reform and development process are at a crucial stage; The Communist Party of China must earnestly learn from the lessons and successful experience of some ruling parties of the world and improve its ability to govern. The party should serve, maintain and develop the fundamental interests of the broad masses of the people, since the support of the people is the source of the party's power and the foundation for its victory. The party should also firmly establish the strategic thinking of seizing opportunities and accelerating the development, focus on the central task of economic construction, uphold the people-oriented, comprehensive, coordinated and sustainable scientific development concept, and better promote economic and social development. We should build a ruling party serving the interests of the people and governing for the people. The party should maintain scientific and democratic administration by law. And it should become a pragmatic, pioneering, innovative, diligent, efficient and honest and upright ruling party.

(Tao Wenzhao, Professor of Institute of Marxism Studies, Renmin University of China)

A Study of the Ruling Experience and Lessons of the Communist Party of the Soviet Union

On August 24, 1991, when the Soviet Communist Party announced "self-dissolution", "Great Bolshevik Party" ended its 74 years of rule. The Fourth Plenary Session of the 16th CPC Central Committee stressed that the whole party should "profoundly learn from the experiences and failures of some of the ruling parties in the world and more consciously strengthen its ruling capacity, and always maintain sound governance for the people."[24] Therefore, summing up the ruling experience and lessons of the Communist Party of the Soviet Union is of great significance to strengthen the Party's construction in the new era, consolidate the ruling position of the party and improve the ruling qualities.

1. Improving scientific ruling ability under the guidance of Marxism-Leninism

The socialist revolution and construction are a brand new undertaking and must be guided by scientific theories. Through the analysis of free capitalism, Marx and Engels revealed that capitalism will surely perish and communism will prevail. However, Marx and Engels also stressed that the conditions of communism replacing capitalism, as follows: "No social order is ever destroyed before all the productive forces for which it is sufficient have been developed, and new superior relations of production never replace older ones before the material conditions for their existence have matured within the womb of the old society."[25] According to the objective situation of the 19th century, Marx and Engels argued that the proletarian socialist revolution could only be achieved in developed capitalist countries, or at least in several major capitalist countries in Europe and in the United States. How to carry out the socialist revolution under the premise that the material conditions are not yet ripe has become a major theoretical and practical issue for the Russian communists.

With creative use of Marxist epistemology and based on a comprehensive analysis of the new situation and new problems in the era of imperialism, Lenin demonstrated the law of unbalanced economic and political development of capitalism and concluded that the socialist revolution might first succeed in a single country or several countries. In August 1915, in the article of *On the Slogan for a United States of Europe*, Lenin pointed out:

24 The Decision of the Central Committee of the CPC on Strengthening the Construction of the Party's Ruling Ability, see http://www.gov.cn/test/2008/08/20/content_1075279.htm, 2008/08/2.

25 Marx-Engels Collected Works, Vol. 2, p. 592.

"Under capitalism the smooth economic growth of individual enterprises or individual states is impossible."[26] "Uneven economic and political development is an absolute law of capitalism. Hence, the victory of socialism is possible first in several or even in a single capitalist country alone. After expropriating the capitalists and organising their own socialist production, the victorious proletariat of that country will arise against the rest of the world—the capitalist world—attracting to its cause the oppressed classes of other countries, stirring uprisings in those countries against the capitalists, and in case of need even violent armed struggle can bu used against the exploiting classes and against capitalist states.."[27] The genius conclusion of "Socialism may first succeed in a few or even in a single capitalist country" revealed the objective laws of socialist revolution's outbreak and victory of socialist revolutions in the imperialism era, which indicates the glorious prospects for the the victory of the socialist revolution, and became a theoretical guide for the victory of the Socialist October Revolution in Russia. The victory of the October Revolution is the result of theoretical innovation under new historical conditions and embodies the enrichment of Marxism.

After the victory of October Revolution, to answer the question of how to build socialism in backward Russia, Lenin made important explorations. First of all, according to the grim situation facing Soviet Russia, the War Communism policy featuring the "system of collecting surplus grain forcedly" was implemented. In the face of the severe economic plight of being short of food and industrial goods after the end of the civil war in 1920, especially with the severe economic and political crisis in the spring of 1921, Lenin summed up the lessons of the War Communism policies in a timely manner. At the end of December 1920, Lenin wrote "Opinions on Economic Construction Tasks" and proposed "taxation = surplus grain collection system" (tax-in-kind)[28], which showed that Lenin was considering the application of tax-in-kind instead of forced surplus grain collection from the farmers. In March 1921, at the 10th Congress of the Russian Communist Party (Bolshevik) Lenin made a "Report on Replacing the System of Collecting Surplus Grain with Taxes", in which Lenin for the first time clearly put forward the concept of NEP and the "issue of replacing War Communism policy with NEP". thus put the socialist transformation and construction work back to the right track in accordance with the objective law.

According to Lenin's proposal, the Congress passed two important resolutions: replacing the system of collecting surplus grain forcedly with

26 Lenin's Monographs on Socialism, p. 3.

27 Ibid., p. 4.

28 Lenin, Complete Works, 2nd Chinese ed., Vol. 40, Beijing, People's Publishing House, 1986, p. 401.

tax-in-kind; transition from War Communism policy to the implementation of the NEP. The NEP of Lenin stipulates that the tax-in-kind should be implemented instead of forced surplus grain collection system; in the cities, private capitalists were allowed to set up small businesses and carry out private trade; some enterprises were allowed to be leased to foreign capitalists but which would be run under the supervision of the Soviet regime. The key and core of the NEP (new economic policy) was the implementation of the tax-in-kind. The so-called tax-in-kind means that farmers pay a certain amount of grain in accordance with the amount of arable land they run as an agricultural tax, keep the remaining grain and other by-products that could be freely traded in the market by themselves. The prominent features of the new economic policy embody the recognition of reality and being realistic. In a country where small peasant economy is dominant, how to treat farmers becomes a basic prerequisite for solving the problem of socialism construction. Therefore, Lenin believed that the economic autonomy of small farmer producers and small private ownership should be recognized and that their products cannot be forcedly collected free of charge. "The correct policy of the proletariat exercising its dictatorship in a small-peasant country is to obtain grain in exchange for the manufactured goods which the peasant needs. That is the only kind of food and grain collecting policy that corresponds to the undertaking or task of the proletariat and can strengthen the foundations of socialism and lead to its complete victory. The tax in kind is a transition to this policy."[29]

After entering the NEP period, the Soviet Union fundamentally changed the original leadership concept and the way of socialist construction and economic operation, shifted to the business principle featuring planned use of commodity and currency relations, implemented economic accounting system, abandoned the highly centralized "Gosplan central planning system", and started began the "unified leadership and hierarchical management" system in the state enterprises, including the one-man management system.

Since 1926, the Soviet Union suspended the implementation of the New Economic Policy, entered the historical period of the establishment of the socialist economic base (1926-1932) and started the completion of the socialist transformation of the national economy (1933-1937), and carried out a large-scale industrialization and agricultural collectivization. By 1937, with the implementation of the two five-year plans, the tasks of industrialization and agricultural collectivization were basically completed; an independent industrial system was established; the whole national economy was transformed on the basis of new technologies; consequently the Soviet Union became a powerful socialist state. During this period

29 Lenin's Monographs on Socialism, p. 217.

the Soviet Union's socialist construction has made great achievements, but there were many mistakes as well. In particular, the highly centralized economic system established by the Soviet Union in the early 1930s, was once considered the only feasible model for the socialist economic system and was copied in many socialist countries. Over the next 50 years, the Soviet Union had always insisted on the basic principles of this system and firmly defended it, so its economic system didn't change fundamentally. A rigid system stems from the rigidity of theory. Without theoretical innovation and enrichment tof Marxism based on the new changes, the rigit theory was also one reason for the perishmen of the CPSU.

2. To keep pace with the times and improve the ability in leading the economic and social development

Marxism tells us that capitalism will be replaced by communism, because with the development of capitalism to a certain stage there will emerge a state when the old relations of production will become the shackles for the development of productive forces. So, new productive relations and a new social system will be necessarily demanded which can accomodate more advanced level of productive forces. Whether a social system is viable first of all depends on whether such a system is conducive to the liberation and development of productive forces, conductive to improving the overall national strength and improving people's living standards. After the victory of the October Revolution, the Soviet Communist Party had no clear understanding of "what socialism is and how to build it" and tended to rush directly into communism. The implementation of the War Communistm policy although it was forced by the harsh environment at home and abroad, was essentially a direct transition to communism by leaping over the socialist economy. In the concrete practice, Lenin put forward various concepts, including the "developed socialist society", "complete socialist society", "building socialism", "building the primary form of socialism", the primary stage", "middle stage" and "highest stage" of communism. After depriving the landlord capitalists, there was only the possibility for building a primary form of socialism. Even in the third year after the overthrow of the bourgeoisie, it was only possşble to implement the initial steps for the transition from capitalism to socialism, namely transition to the primary stage of communism.

The War Communism policy, which the party was forced to implement was considered as an opportunity to move directly to communism. On the issue of the eradication of free trade and the direct transition to communism, Lenin made practical conclusions in his later speeches. He considered the systems of forced collecting of surplus grain and state monopoly as the mistake of direct transition to "communist production and distribution". It was wrong to implement the systems of forced collecting of surplus grain and state monopoly on trade, because back then there were five economic sectors in Russia, and among them small-scale peasant economy was dominant, the economy was lagging behind, and socialist large-scale industry was not yet working smoothly due to various reasons. To assume that the direct transition to communist society could be achieved was clearly not suitable for the development of social productive forces and Russia's economic conditions. The production and exchange policies which go beyond the level of social and economic development has led to heavy burden on the farmers, depressing their enthusiasm and hindering the development of productive forces. In summing up the experience of "War Communism" policy, Lenin pointed out, "It is necessary to adopt a gradualist, and prudent manner of action".[30] Therefore, it is necessary to transit into socialism in an indirect or roundabout way. "it has become evident that we had suffered defeat in our attempt to introduce the communist principles of production and distribution by "direct assault", i.e., in the shortest, quickest and most direct way. The political situation in the spring of 1921 revealed to us that on a number of economic issues a retreat to the position of state capitalism, the substitution of "siege" tactics that serve "direct assault" against capitalism, was inevitable."[31]

However, the "impulse" and the idea of direct transition to communism had not been effectively surmounted. because, with the achievment of industrialization and agricultural collectivization, the Soviet Union established a highly centralized economic management system. Stalin insisted that the policy of rapid development of industry must be adopted and that industrialization cannot be achieved "at the pace of a tortoise walk".[32] Stalin believed that it was necessary and possible for Soviet Union's economy to rapidly catch up with the advanced capitalist countries. He said: it took about 200 years or less for the feudal economic system to prove it superiority over the slave economic system. It took about 100 years or less for capitalist economic system to prove it superiority over the feudal economic system. Contemporary technology shows unprecedented progress, and the pace of development is extremely fast. In addition, under the Soviet Union leadership, people are not parasites, but producers. This makes the socialist economic system, develop extremely fast and prove its superiority over the capitalist economic system in a short period of time."[33]

30 Lenin's Monographs on Socialism, p. 253.

31 Ibid., p. 280.

32 Stalin Complete Works, Chinese 1st ed., Vol. 11, Beijing, People's Publishing House, 1955, p. 217.

33 Ibid.

In the early stages of agricultural collectivization movement, Stalin basically followed the fundamental principles of Marxism on agricultural cooperation. However, Stalin's correct guiding ideology only functioned for a short period of time and was soon replaced by overall and prompt collectivization. In fact, administrative means were taken to enforce the "overall and rapid collectivization". From the end of 1929 to the beginning of 1930, the overall collectivization campaign in the rural areas of Soviet Union was pushed forcedly. Overall collectivization brought the Soviet Union's agricultural collectivization into a new stage. From June to September 1930, the number of farmers who joined the collective farms increased from 1 million to 1.91 million households. After the autumn of that year, the agricultural collectivization movement was further pushed to a comprehensive agricultural collectivization. In other words, the farmers joined the collective farm not by small groups, but by the whole village, whole township and whole region. They soon became collective farmers in the basic production organization of collective farms. The overall collectivization swept the rural areas like a storm. When achieving collectivization by large-scale revolutionary mass movements, the reality and farmers' mental preparation for joining the collective farm were neglected. This process was extremely accelerated by the party will.

The highly centralized traditional socialist system formed in transition to communism was seriously flawed. The most prominent features were too much centralization, over control, lack of internal driving force in state enterprises for developing production and for improving their operation, and lack of enthusiasm and management initiative. Its effect to economy was the low efficiency of enterprises, which negatively affected the development of the entire national economy. With the economic development, social division of labor becomes more refined and economic relations become more complex. The drawbacks of the rigid administrative management of economy and enterprises' lacking enthusiasm became more and more obvious. In particular, in the era of scientific and technological revolution, informationization (IT) developed greatly and the world began to change faster. If the enterprises lack the ability to give flexible and timely responses to extrenal developments and do not pay attention to efficiency, they will not be able to adjust to the demands of the new times. The development of productive forces itself nurtures the needs for reforming the economic system. Since the 1950s, the Soviet Union began to explore the issue of economic reform. There were three major reforms, including the restructuring of industry and construction sector in 1957, economic reform in 1965 and the attempt to perfect the economic mechanisms in 1979. These reforms had their own characteristics, but generally had little effect.

At the beginning of November 1967, Brezhnev mentioned the concept of "advanced socialist society" for the first time in his report which celebrated the 50th anniversary of the October Revolution. In 1970, in the report in memory of the 100th anniversary of Lenin's birth, Brezhnev reiterated that the Soviet Union had built an "advanced socialist society". In March 1971, Brezhnev in the 24th congress of the Soviet Communist Party, claimed: "The Soviets has built an advanced socialist society with their efforts. Lenin discussed this society as the future of our country in 1918."[34] Since then, the Soviet Union's theoretical authority led by Suslov made a more comprehensive discussion on "advanced socialism" from the aspects of economy, society, politics and culture. There was a boom of study projects on "advanced socialism" among the Soviet theoretical circles. In 1977, the new constitution of the Soviet Union stated, "The Soviet Union has built an advanced socialist society." "The advanced socialist society is a qualitative stage on the road to communism."

Due to the rapid transition to communism and the due to pride in the achievements made, the flaws of the economic structure could not be corrected for a long time and the extensive mode of economic growth could not be reformed. The lack of correct judgment on the impact of the new technological revolution had led to a decline in the level of development of Soviet productive forces. Under the impact of the wave of world science and technology revolution, in May 1973, a working group led by Krilenko prepared a report regarding conducting technological revolution in the Soviet Union for the Central Plenum which was presented to General Secretary Brezhnev. But Brezhnev was not interested. This report stayed in Brezhnev's safe box until his death.[35] In the book Age of Extremes, Hobsbawm pointed out that the isolation from the capitalist world system has hindered the development of the Soviet economy, and led to its decline in the international market. In 1960, the Soviet Union mainly exported processed products such as machinery and transportation vehicles and metal equipment. But since 1985, it mainly exported primary products such as energy. Machinery and other processed products accounted for about 60% of its imports. The Communist Party of the Soviet Union could not advance with the times and represent the development of advanced productive forces, so it was inevitable that it would perish by the advance of the times.

3. To overcome bureaucracy and improve the ability in solving people's major demands

The Communist Party is the vanguard of the working class and the faithful representative of the people's interests. Only by trusting and relying

34 Compilation of the main documents of the 24th Congress of the Communist Party of the Soviet Union, Beijing, Joint Publishing, 1976, p. 59.

35 Arbatov, Inside Story of Soviet Union Politics—Witness of the Insider, Xinhua Publishing House, Beijing, 1992, pp. 218-219.

on the people and accepting their criticism and supervision can it win the trust and support of the people. After the victory of the October Revolution, regarding the relationship between the Russian Communist Party and the people, Lenin pointed out: "Only the Communist Party, if it is really the vanguard of the revolutionary class, if it contains all the best representatives of that class, if it consists of fully class-conscious and devoted Communists who have been educated and steeled by the experience of stubborn revolutionary struggle, if this Party has succeeded in linking itself inseparably with the whole life of its class and, through it, with the whole mass of exploited, and if it has succeeded in inspiring the complete confidence of this class and this mass—only such a party is capable of leading the proletariat in the most ruthless, resolute and final struggle against all the forces of capitalism. On the other hand, only under the leadership of such a party can the proletariat develop the full might of its revolutionary onslaught and nullify the inevitable apathy and, partly, resistance of the small minority of the labour aristocracy corrupted by capitalism, and of the old trade-union and co-operative leaders, etc.—only then will it be able to display its full strength, which, owing to the very economic structure of capitalist society, is immeasurably greater than the proportion of the population it constitutes"[36].

Lenin stressed that, "We communists are but a drop in the ocean, a drop in the ocean of the people. We shall be able to lead the people along the path we have chosen only if we correctly determine it not only from the standpoint of its direction in world history."[37]

In Lenin's view, the Russian Communist Party and the people should be inseparable. After the Russian Communist seized the power, to maintain close contact with the people, there was not only the need to realize the correct leadership of the party, but also the need to consolidate the Soviet state power and build socialism. Lenin pointed out that the three basic conditions for the correct leadership of the party include the following: Firstly, by the class consciousness of the proletarian vanguard and by its devotion to the revolution, by its stamina, self-sacrifice and heroism. Secondly, by its ability to link itself with, to keep in close touch with, and to a certain extent, if you like, to merge with the broadest masses of the working people—primarily with the proletariat, but also with the non-proletarian sections of the labouring masses."[38]

Without the active support of the people, the correct leadership of the party is out of the question. Accordingly, for Lenin "The new regime is the dictatorship of the majority, it relies entirely on the trust invested by

36 Lenin Complete Works, Chinese 2nd ed., Vol. 39, Beijing, People's Publishing House, 1986, p. 182.

37 Lenin's Monographs on Socialism, p. 340.

38 Lenin's Monographs on the Proletarian Party, pp. 245-246.

the masses, this new regime can be completely maintained by the unrestricted, broadest and most powerfully attracting the participation of people in administrating the political power."[39] Since the nascent socialist system represents the advanced production relationship, "the creativity of the grass root masses is the basic motive factor of the new social life."[40] "Lively, *creative* socialism is the product of the *masses* themselves"[41]. Without the support of the broad masses of the people, the cause of socialism led by the Communist Party cannot be achieved.

Facts prove that it was due to the Soviet Communist Party's close contacts with the people in the early stages of the revolution that the theory of consolidating the political regime was established. At the beginning of the establishment of the Soviet regime, various reactionary forces carried out sabotages and subversive actions. Since the occurance of revolutions in the developed western countires Lenin and the Bolshevik Party had invested their hopes for a victory but no victory occured, so they changed the policy based on such expectation, all in all they couldn't get support from the western proleteriat winning victory in the West. There was the question within the party that whether the Bolshevik regime can be consolidated under such conditions. Lenin pointed out, "Only those who believe in the people, only those who aim to rely to the fountain of people's creativity, can win and maintain the political power."[42]

In July 1918, Russia entered the period of civil war. The Russian Communist Party and the Soviet regime, relying on the theory of basing themselves on the support of the masses of workers and peasants, established the Red Army, fought bravely, won victory in the civil war and defended the new Soviet regime. In November 1919, in *Fight Against the Fuel Crisis—A Letter to the Party Organizations at All Levels*, Lenin analyzed the reasons of this victory, "Firstly, by the class consciousness of the proletarian vanguard and by its devotion to the revolution, by its stamina, self-sacrifice and heroism. Secondly, by its ability to link itself with, to keep in close touch with, and to a certain extent, if you like, to merge with the broadest masses of the working people—primarily with the proletarian, but also with the non-proletarian, labouring masses. Thirdly, by the correctness of the political leadership exercised by this vanguard, by the correctness of its political strategy and tactics, provided that the broadest masses have been convinced through their own experience of this correctness."[43]

39 Lenin Complete Works, Chinese 2nd ed., Vol. 39, p. 378.

40 Lenin Collected Works, English ed., Vol.26, p. 201.

41 Ibid., p. 239.

42 Ibid., p. 258.

43 Lenin Complete Works, 2nd Chinese edition, Vol. 37, Beijing, People's Publishing House, 1986, p. 301.

Lenin also pointed out that one of the most serious and frightening threat for working-class political parties holding the state power would be isolation from the people. The War Communism policy undermined the interests of the people and sparked their discontent which led to the rebellion in 1921 in Kronstadt. Lenin pointed out, if the wartime polices cannot be adjusted timely, the party would be isolated from the people and the class base of the Soviet regime would be destroyed. "One of the greatest and most serious threats that can endanger the numerically small Communist Party, which, as the vanguard of the working class, is guiding a vast country in the process of transition to socialism (for the time being without the direct support of the proletariat of the more advanced countries), is isolation from the masses, the danger that the vanguard may run too far ahead and fail to "straighten out the line", fail to maintain firm contact with the whole army of labour, i.e., with the overwhelming majority of workers and peasants."[44]

We need to:

Keep in touch with the masses.

Live close to them.

Know their *moods*.

Know *everything*.

Understand the masses.

Be able to approach them.

Win their *absolute trust*.

Leaders must not become isolated from the masses they lead,

or the vanguard (Party) should not get isolated from the whole army of labor...

Do not flatter the masses and do not break away from them."[45]

Lenin also proposed to recruit and educate all the workers to participate in state administration and socialist construction. He pointed out that the idea of building communist society only by a minority of communists was very naïve. "Socialism cannot be implemented by a minority, by the Party. It can be implemented only by tens of millions when they have learnt to do it themselves."[46] It was because of Lenin's idea that a large number of outstanding people of the working masses were recruited for the various departments of state administration.

However, with the continuous advancement of socialist construction, the Soviet Communist Party gradually deviated from Lenin's idea of relying on the people and maintaining close contact with the people, gradually formed

44 Lenin's Monographs on Socialism, pp. 304.

45 Lenin Complete Works, 2nd Chinese ed., Vol. 42, pp. 525-526.

46 Lenin's Monographs on Socialism, p. 72.

a bureaucratic style and was isolated from the people, eventually leading to the end of the party and the state. When Lenin was sick and could not work, Stalin founded the official hierarchy system. By the beginning of 1924, the total number of leading cadres selected and appointed by the Central Committee was 13,163. Local leaders at all levels were organized hierarciclally and apppointed from above. For instance, the Ural State Council stipulated that the number of the state's leading cadres should be 1066. The leading cadres in relatively high positions gradually transformed into a special social group which nurtured and sought group interests, followed a group lifestyle and a group ideology. Till the 1960s and 1970s, the number of this specific group (a political class on the top of social hierarcy) reached 500,000 to 700,000. These people together with their families accounted for 1.5% of the whole population.[47] In the early days after the end of the Second World War, Stalin implemented a specific wage system for this top class. Later on, a special "bonus" system emerged in addition to their formal wages. Their privileged status was rapidly consolidated. In some of the party's organizations, some leaders have become corrupt and started to embezzle public money and steal state property. After the death of Stalin, especially in the days of Brezhnev and Gorbachev, this bureaucratic privileged class that had got out of control and grown steadily became more corrupt. During the administration period of Gorbachev, the privileged class further expanded. This new hierharcy of political classes promoted by the central authority, had greatly expanded after the death of its "chief designer" Stalin. Various political classes in the upper ranks of hierarchy included no less than 10 million people which included high-level party and government bureaucrats, upper parts of social science and natural science workers and the enterprise managers and their family members. According to an estimate estimate, the privileged class plus their family members accounted for about 3% of the total population.[48]

Lenin had repeatedly pointed out, "domestically, the most hateful enemy is the bureaucracy"[49], and proposed to "fight against bureaucratism"[50], "It is necessary to improve the state organs that are still very bad"[51] and that bureaucrats "should be severely punished"[52]. On February 22, 1922, in the letter to the People's Commissariat for Finance, Lenin said, "the biggest

47 See, Russian History in the 20th Century, pp. 570-571, Moscow, ACT, 1996., Liu Keming: On the Bureaucratic Privileges of the Soviet Communist Party published in Russian, Journal of Central Asian & East European Studies, 2003(3).

48 See article published in Social Science and Contemporary Era, 1991(3) by Aubrensky, from the Institute of State and Law attached to the Soviet Academy of Social Sciences.

49 Lenin Complete Works, 2nd Chinese ed., Vol. 43, p. 14.

50 Ibid., p. 147.

51 Ibid., p. 212.

52 Ibid., p. 651.

problem in all the work of all our economic institutions is bureaucracy. Communists have become bureaucrats. If there is anything that will ruin us, that is this."[53]

He also proposed a way to overcome the bureaucracy by maintaining close contact with people. He proposed to choose 75 to 100 central inspectors from the workers and farmers class and reduce the staff in workers and farmers' Procuratorate to 300 to 400 people. Lenin made a request to the Central Control Commission, as follows: "It will then be possible (and necessary) to institute a stricter and more responsible procedure of preparing for the meetings of the Political Bureau, which should be attended by a definite number of members of the Central Control Commission determined either from a definite period of by some organisation plan..... The reform I recommend should help to remove this defect, and the members of the Central Control and Inspection Commission, whose duty it will be to attend all meetings of the Political Bureau in a definite number, will have to form a compact group which should not allow anybody's authority without exception, neither that of the General Secretary [Stalin] nor of any other member of the Central Committee, to prevent them from putting questions, verifying documents, and, in general, from keeping themselves fully informed of all things and from exercising the strictest control over the proper conduct of affairs."[54]

However, bureaucracy could not be eliminated. As the CPSU (the Soviet Party) became more isolated from the people, personality cult and privileged class took form which ultimately ruined the party and the socialist system.

4. To improve organizational construction and system construction and improve the ability of democratic governance

Whether the Communist Party has fighting capacity, attraction for people and cohesive power is not only determined by upholding the guidance of Marxism-Leninism, but more importantly the high degree of organization and discipline under the guidance of Marxism-Leninism. With a high degree of organization and discipline, the party can unify members' thinking and action. Unity and solidarity within the party organizations is the strength of the party. Lenin attached great importance to the unity and solidarity within the party organizations. In the early days of the party, he stressed that, "We not only need formal unity, but need a very strong unity."[55] "Unity is a great

53 Lenin's Monographs on the Proletarian Party, p. 348.

54 Lenin's Monographs on Socialism, p. 364.

55 Lenin's Monographs on the Proletarian Party, p. 306.

thing and a great slogan. But what the workers' cause needs is the *unity of Marxists*, not unity between Marxists, and opponents and distorters of Marxism."[56]

Stalin also pointed out that Lenin's contribution was that he had always stressed: "If there is no iron discipline in the party, the task of suppressing the exploiters by the dictatorship of the proletariat and transforming the class society into a socialist society cannot be realized."[57] However, the CPSU (Soviet Party) had not achieved real unity. There have been many groups in the Party, among which the most famous were "democratic program group" and "Marxist program group". With the slogan of democracy, freedom and diversification, these groups were allowed to exist and grow freely, which caused an unprincipled unity within the party. This in fact weakened the party's leadership. In the reform launched by Gorbachev, "new thinking" was advocated, and the slogan of "openness", "democracy" and "diversification" was also put forward, and attack and criticism of the Soviet socialist system wrere allowed, in order to promote the further strenghtening of "Humanitarian Socialism" Gorbachev preached. The consequence was that the party organization lost its organizational leadership. Finally, with the resolution which put forward the falsified slogan and stipulation "All Powers Should Belong to Soviet Congresses", Communist Party of the Soviet Union has destroyed its leadership in socialism building.

At the beginning days of the founding of the Communist Party, Marx and Engels emphasized the basic spirit of implementing democratic principles within the party. Democracy was strictly adopted both in Communist League which was the first communist organization founded by Marx and Engels in 1847 and the First International founded in 1864. Engels wrote: Communist League, "These organizations were thoroughly democratic, with elective and always removable boards. This alone barred all hankering after conspiracy, which requires dictatorship, and the League was converted—for ordinary peace times at least—into a pure propaganda society. These new Rules were submitted to the communities for discussion—so democratic was its procedures"[58]. Lenin also pointed out: "More light, let the party know everything"[59], "it is ridiculous to talk about democracy without freedom of publicity and free and open election"[60]. When Lenin was alive, the affairs of the Soviet Communist Party were open and transparent,

56 Lenin Complete Works, 2nd Chinese edition, Vol. 25, Beijing, People's Publishing House, 1988, p. 81.

57 Stalin Selected Works, Vol 1, p. 615.

58 Marx-Engels Collected Works, Vol. 2nd ed., Vol. 4, People's Publishing House, Beijing, p. 200.

59 Lenin Complete Works, 2nd Chinese edition, Vol. 8, Beijing, People's Publishing House, 1986, p. 87.

60 Lenin ,Complete Works, 2nd Chinese edition, Vol. 6, p. 131.

and the party's democratic life was normal and very lively. Lenin laid the right principles for carrying out inner party discussions, which was to separate the free discussion of different views from political and ideological work within the party, and to separate the inner fight for the party's political program from the theoretical debates. In addition, Lenin also raised the issue of democracy to political level and considered "there is no socialism without democracy."[61]

When Stalin was in office, this normal party life and former benign party style was completely changed. Since the long-term implementation of a high degree of centralization by the CPSU there was no democracy within the party and the party's democratic nature was undermined Inner-party democracy became the democracy only for a minority of party members rather than democracy for all. In particular, in Stalin's later years, he was more arbitrary and turned the Communist Party's politics into personal politics, which fundamentally undermined the party's democratic centralism principle. The rights to know, to participate, to choose and the supervision right which can be used by all party members were violently trampled. The democratic provisions in the CPSU Constitution became useless, such as "democratic centralism being the guiding principle", "leading organs of the party at all levels being elected from bottom to top", "freely and effectively discussing the party's policy issues in the party organizations and the whole party being the inalienable rights of the party members and major principle of inner-party democracy", "ensuring that party members can freely express their views in extensive debates, especially participation in the discussion of the party's policy issues in respect to whole the Soviet Union" and "violation of inner-party democracy being intolerable within the party" became new unhealthy practices.[62]

As a socialist democratic party, all the organizational activities of the Communist Party should strictly follow the principles of democracy. In other words, it should fully promote democracy within the party, timely inform the party members all major issues within the party in order to let them discuss, listen carefully to the views of all party members, so as to collect and transmit all the wisdom of the party to the leading organs and improve the scientific leadership of the party. The natures of the party's democracy and centralism are not fundamentally opposed. Democracy emphasizes the democratic rights of party members, while centralism emphasizes the power and will of leadership. Democracy emphasizes that the party's power center is the party's national congress, while centralism emphasizes

61 Lenin Selected Works, 3rd edition, Vol. 2, Beijing, People's Publishing House, 1995, pp. 782.
62 Compilation of Soviet Communist Party Constitutions, Beijing, Qiushi Press, 1982, pp. 208-211.

the power belongs to a leader or a leading collective such as the Central Committee and party committees at all levels. It can be seen that the opposition between democracy and centralism is actually the antagonism between democracy and autocracy. The implementation of democracy ensures that the party members truly have the rights to participate in the discussion on the formulation and implementation of party's policies, to criticize any party organizations and members in the meeting, and to offer suggestions on all the work of the party. When these basic democratic rights are deprived, democratic centralism cannot be achieved, the supervision by party members, especially supervision over the party's leading cadres, cannot be implemented. A party leadership without supervision and limitation by möembers and the people will inevtably perish. Therefore, it is important for the Communist Party to maintain its ability to govern and achieve democratic governance by emphasizing and strengthening democratic centralism, reforming the party system, avoiding replacement of government functions or organs with the party functions or organs thus we should achieve division of labor between party and government.

5. To strengthen contingent of talented cadres construction and ideological construction, and play a vanguard role

In *The Communist Manifesto*, Marx discusses the advanced nature of the Communist Party. "Communists are distinguished from the other working-class parties by this only: 1. In the national struggles of the proletarians in the different countries, they point out and bring to the front the common interests of the entire world proletariat, independent of all nationalities. 2. In the various stages of development which the struggle of the working class against the bourgeoisie has to pass through, they always and everywhere should represent the interests of the movement as a whole."[63] Lenin had also repeatedly stressed that the party is the vanguard organization of the proletariat guided by advanced theory. The party is component part of the working class, but it is not an ordinary part. It is armed by Marxist theories and it is the vanguard detachment composed of the best and most enlightened and advanced members of the working class. Therefore, "confusing the party—as the advanced force of the working class—with the entire class, is absolutely unacceptable, this is obvious."[64] This comment by Lenin fundamentally negates the concept of a Communist Party as a "collective of average members of the class and a party of all class" and elaborates the major issue of maintaining the purity of this vanguard.

63 Marx-Engels Collected Works, Vol. 2, p. 44.
64 Lenin's Monographs on the Proletarian Party, p. 104.

One of the basic Marxist principles of party construction is to enhance ideological construction. After the Russian communist party became a ruling party, it was arrogant with its power and ruling status. Lenin considered arrogance as the number one enemy of the party. Therefore, it is necessary to strengthen the ruling party's own construction. In order to prevent the spread of personality cult because of the arrogance, Lenin made a scientific exposition of the relationship between the masses and the leaders. He pointed out, "The leaders of workers are not angels, not saints, not heroes, but ordinary individuals."[65] Therefore, we must constantly strengthen the party's ideological construction and cadre contingent building, to maintain the absolute unity in respect to party's ideology.

In the early days of the establishment of the Bolshevik Party, in order to defeat the ideological trend which emphasized the spontaneous nature of the workers' movement and which opposed the establishment of a unified and independent working class party and in order to change the situation of disarray in the ideological and organizational fields within the party, Lenin stressed: "In the first place, it is necessary to work for solid ideological unity which should eliminate discordance and confusion that—let us be frank!—reign among Russian Social-Democrats at the present time." "As we have said, the ideological unity among Russian Social-Democracy has still to be created, and to this end it is, in our opinion, necessary to have an open and all-embracing discussion of the fundamental questions of principle and tactics raised by the present-day "economists," Bernsteinians, and "critiquers group." Before we can unite, and in order to achieve unite, we must first of all draw firm and definite lines of demarcation."[66] Otherwise, our unity will be purely fictitious.

The central committee of the Russian Communist Party (Bolsheviks) led by Lenin attached great importance to the construction of party schools at all levels. The Party did not only set the education standards and the number of party schools at all levels, but also paid attention to summing up experience of the party school's education achievements. At the first congress of the national Soviet party schools held in 1922, Lenin personally recommended several teachers for the party school. The comrades who truly grasped the Marxist theories were recruited for the teachers' teams of the party schools. Based on party building principles of Marxism, Lenin strengthened the Marxist theoretical education of the party members. The RSDIP was united in ideology and became a strong Marxist political party which could lead and achieve the victory of the Russian revolution. Mao Zedong had repeatedly stressed: in order to develop the revolutionary movement more effectively and lead it to a speedier success, "we must in our all seriousness put things in order both ideologically and organizationally," "organizationally,

65 Ibid., p. 344.
66 Ibid., p. 49.

to put things in order requires us, firstly to focus on its ideological aspect, i.e. we should launch a proletarian ideological struggle against non-proletarian ideologies,"[67] so that the majority of party members are unified with the proletarian ideology and will join the party ideologically, so that the party's advanced nature can be maintained.

One of the most aspect of the drastic changes in Eastern Europe and the disintegration of the Soviet Union was the chaos in the guiding ideology of the Party. All these started with the campaign of "diversification of ideology" launched by Gorbachev. Firstly, Marxism was abandoned. And then the guiding ideology and Marxist theories were revised, which were followed by the change in the party's political line and nature. And ultimately the Communist Party lost its ruling position, and changed from a legitimate party into an illegal party. Yeltsin, Gorbachev and Gaidar were the representatives of the generation which denied Marxist theories and the socialist path due to their past flawed ideological and political education. They became the center of subversive activities against the socialist Soviet Union. Therefore, it is necessary to strengthen the ideological construction, strengthen the Marxist ideological education of the party members and cadres, improve their level of Marxist ideology, improve their ability in applying Marxist theory and firmly establish the Marxist scientific world view, of members, in order to maintain the ideological unity within the party.

While strengthening the ideological construction, cadre contingent building is also essential. After the transformation from a revolutionary party to the ruling party, our Party encountered not only changes in status, but also arduous tasks of socialist construction and struggles against all kinds of non-proletarian ideology. Consolidating and strengthening the vanguard role of the Communist Party members and strengthening Party's self-discipline are the fundamental ways to maintain the ideological purity of party members.

In his speech on the occasion of the victory of the October Revolution, Lenin paid particular attention to protect the stability, firmness and purity of the Bolshevik Party. He proposed to constantly enhance the capacity and role of the party members. In the practice of building a new proletarian party, in order to maintain the party's advanced nature, Lenin gave a resolute fight against the mistaken party building views, such as the Russian economism and Menshevik's loose organization idea, all of which confused the Marxist party with labor union organization and all of which undermined the party's advanced nature. During the administration period of Gorbachev, the Communist Party was no longer the vanguard of the working class. Instead, it was defined ambiguously as the "party of the working

67 Mao Zedong Selected Works, 2nd ed., Vol. 3, People's Publishing House, Beijing, 1985, p. 875.

class", "the party defending the interests of the workers", "the party serving all the people". The party defined as the party for "All the People" completely obliterated the vanguard nature of the Communist Party, leading to the huge chaos in the CPSU in ideology, politics and organization and led to the pershment of it.

In order to strictly rule the party, Lenin launched a series of major initiatives, mainly including keeping speculator elements out of the party, expelling the bad elements and corrupt officials from the party, eliminating factional clique activities within the party and strictly punishing the discipline violatitions and corrupt party members. On the education and improvement of party members, Lenin pointed out: "Only the ruling party like ours, the Party of the revolutionary working class cannot pursue for the increase in the number of party members, instead its pays attention to raise the quality of its members, and care for their purity and hinder those who enter the Party to seek benefits."

In addition to cultivating and observing the potential party members, extending the preparatory period for new party members when needed and implementing more strict member reviews, Lenin especially emphasized the principles for the introduction of the potential party members. "If the new party member violates the party discipline, the introducer member should also be subject to disciplinary measure. If they repeatedly take a careless and reckless attitude when introducing new party members, they should be dismissed from the party".[68] In this way, the bad elements and interest seekers were hindered to penetrate the party. The Marxist ruling party, which relies on a healthy and powerful advanced class, must be good at cleaning its own ranks.

Meanwhile, Lenin also paid attention to combine the two policies of "preventing" and "combating" to achieve a purified the party by "cleaning the party". In May 1919, according to the resolution of "the 8th Congress", the Russian Communist Party (Bolshevik) carried out the nationwide re-registration campaign for all party members, during which the number of members who were expelled accounted for half of the total number. In 1921, regarding capitalist elements and their increasing influence in the party, a second round of party review campaign was carried out, during which 170,000 party members were expelled, accounting for 25% of total number of party members. Thus, the party was further purified. Lenin hated and resolutely opposed the shielding of those convicted party members. These strict measures applied by Lenin and the Party reflect the importance and arduousness of maintaining the purity of the Communist Party members. The emergence and growth of privileged groups in the Party during Stalin's

68 Compilation of Resolutions in the Congresses, Representatives Conferences and Central Plenums of the CPSU, Beijing, People's Publishing House,1964, p. 55.

administration and especially Brezhnev's administration undermined the purity of party organizations and ultimately caused its degeneration from inside.

6. To properly handle all kinds of relationships and improve the ability to deal with complex problems

Whether in the period of revolution or in the period of socialist construction, whether be the revolutionary party or the party in the ruling status, the communist party cannot play its leadership role in isolation. To maintain the ruling position of the Communist Party, we must be good at dealing with various complex relationships and problems and strengthen its benign style of governance.

Lenin believed that no Communist Party should regard its views and practices as the best model of sscientific ocialism and ask other Communist Parties to blindly follow itself. Lenin asked other parties to avoid copying things that were only suitable for Russian conditions and not suitable for their countries. In the spring of 1919, hearing that the German Communist Party prepared to study the experiences of the Russian revolution and socialist construction, Lenin pointed out: "we must act in such a way as to prove to our comrades from abroad that we are strong, to enable them to see that in our revolution we are not in the least exceeding the bounds of our own Russian reality, and to provide them with material that will be absolutely irrefutable. It would be absurd to label our Russian revolution as the ideal model for all countries, to imagine that it has made a number of brilliant discoveries and has introduced a heap of socialist innovations. I have not heard anybody who made such an absurd claim and I assert that we shall not hear anybody make such a claim. We have acquired practical experience in taking the first steps towards destroying capitalism in a country where specific relations exist between the proletariat and the peasants. Nothing more. If we behave like the frog in the fable and become puffed up with conceit, we shall only make ourselves the laughing-stock of the world, we shall be mere braggarts."[69]

Obviously, on the issue of properly handling party-to party relationships, the CPSU had not followed Lenin's instructions, but instead adopted the "chauvinist big party" approach. In the War against the Nazi Germany, led by the CPSU- (Bolshevik),when the Fascist invaders were defeated was the very period when Stalin's great-power chauvinism started to demonstrate itself. During Khrushchev's administration, the Soviet Union sent troops to Poland and Hungary to intervene the domestic struggles, intensified the conflicts between the Soviet Union and Yugoslavia, and magnified the scope of the debates with Albanian and Chinese parties. From the end of

69 Lenin, Complete Works, 2nd Chinese ed., Vol. 36, pp. 163-64.

1967 to 1968, the Soviet Union criticized the "Prague Spring movement" in Czechoslavakia and then blatantly sent troops to Prague which marked the peak of "the big state and big party chauvinism". Even worse, Brezhnev provoked the Sino-Soviet border conflicts, sent troops to Mongolia, occupied Afghanistan and supported Vietnam's invasion of Cambodia. Deng Xiaoping once pointed out, "Hegemonism under the banner of socialism is the most prominent sign of the betrayal of principles of socialism by a Marxist-Leninist Party that has won political power."[70] "The Communists in any country should decide by themselves what path to take so as to achieve the victory of their revolution, because the parties of other countries cannot know the real circumstances there. If foreigners give orders to other parties, they will inevitably make mistakes." So if the Communists of a particular country want to win victory, the fundamental lesson is that they must find their own path in light of the conditions in their country.

No big or veteran party should see itself as the supreme arbiter. During the period when Stalin was in power, the Chinese Communist Party did not follow his advices in dealing with certain crucial questions, and with its independent decision making CPC led the revolution to victory. Of course, I don't mean that we need not draw on the experience of other countries. The Communists of any party will inevitably make mistakes, but when they do, they should analyse their experience and solve their problems by themselves. That is the only reliable approach.[71]

The Communist Party of the Soviet Union had also improperly handled the domestic ethnic, religious issues and also the issue of intellectuals. Due to national grievances accumulated in the era of tsarist Russia, a great centrifugal force lurked. Therefore, Lenin advocated national self-determination, ethnic equality, free association and the establishment of a unified communist party regardless of nationality, which positively solved the national issues. During the Stalin period, Russian national chauvinism began to grow. Ethnic contradictions were considered equal to class contradictions; national process was considered equal to social process; extreme emphasis was laid on the trend of national integration. Focusing on countering local nationalism and ignoring the growth of Russianism enhanced the sense of oppression among the ethnic minorities. The single product economy in the ethnic minority regions and artificially "balancing" regional disparities gave damage to the economic interests of the minorities. The will of leading officials ignored the national characteristics and the boundaries of minority regions were randomly decided.[72] These factors led to increasingly sharp

70 Deng Xiaoping Selected Works, 2nd ed., Vol. 2, p. 172.

71 Deng Xiaoping Selected Works, 1st ed., Vol. 3, p. 27.

72 Ji Zhengju, Ten Experiences and Lessons of the Success or Failure of the Soviet Communist Party, published in Contemporary World and Socialism, 2004(1).

ethnic conflicts; the national separatist movements never ceased and this later led to the disintegration of the Soviet Union. Now, the ethnic separatist movements in today's Chechnya were inherited from the Soviet Union era. Similarly, due to the increasingly centralized political and economic system of the Soviet Union, the cultural system was also greatly affected. During Stalin's administration and after Stalin's era, the ideological differences and academic debates were often raised to political struggle; academic study was forced to be in line with the party's political line, the free academic debates were not allowed; coarse cultural system and excessive political intervention caused serious damages to academic research and suppressed the intellectuals. Socialist culture became rigid, closed and conservative. The cultural diversity was replaced by cultural totalism. Culture gradually lost its spiritual links with the people and society and became a tool in the hands of those in power.

(Zhang Xu, Professor of Institute of Marxism Studies, Renmin University of China)

PART FOUR

Socialism Theories by Marxists Abroad

The history of the development of the international communist movement shows that when socialism is at a low ebb era, it is often the peak time in the theoretical studies on socialism. After the Cold War, the study on the issues of socialism by foreign Marxists showed three new features.

Firstly, there are an increasing number of academic research activities and meetings worldwide. "International Marxist Congress" in France, "International Symposium of World Socialist Scholars" in the United States and the Cuba based "Marxism Congresses" have become regular international forums and are increasingly becoming influential.

Secondly, the study of socialism is becoming more free and open. After the drastic changes in Eastern Europe and the disintegration of the Soviet Union, due to absence of a restrictive "theoretical authority" many foreign Marxist researchers began to openly express their own views, and organized their own research institutions to discuss issues of common interest and seek truth.

Thirdly, the study of socialism became more profound, and the research fields gradually expanded. Foreign Marxists' research on socialism has broken the boundaries of the disciplines and shifted from the past independent research fields to overall, interdisciplinary research mode. The foreign Marxists mentioned here include Western Marxists and scholars of the communist and socialist parties of the world, as well as scholars who believe in Marxism but are not attached to any political group. The discussion of socialism theories by foreign Marxists mainly focus on what socialism is, the transition from capitalism to socialism, and the socialist development model and socialism with Chinese characteristics. Based on the drastic changes in Eastern Europe and the disintegration of the Soviet Union, many scholars have made a thorough reflection on the history of socialism and carried out an in-depth study of the basic theory of socialism. By examining the studes of socialism by foreign Marxists, we can further understand the prospects for the development of world socialism and the future of socialism with Chinese characteristics.

Foreign Marxists' Discussion on "What Socialism Is ?"

After the end of the Cold War, foreign Marxist schools encountered further splits and became less influential. But there are more and more political activists and scholars who participate in the discussion of socialism abroad. Foreign Marxists' discussion on "what socialism is?" involves a lot of content. Only a few aspects of their research will be discussed here.

1. The value goal of socialism

Since the publication of Thomas More's *Utopia* in 1516, there has been a history of 500 years since the emergence of socialism and socialist thoughts. For centuries, the socialist ideas were put forward one after another and the socialist movements have kept flourishing. The development of socialism has repeatedly suffered heavy adverse conditions. But every time after difficult days, people always found the way out. The history of the development of socialism was repeatedly evaluated as being in "fatal crisis or ended". But after each "fatal crisis", a new climax in its development was achieved. In this regard, people cannot help but ask: What is the enduring motive force of socialist movement? Why do people demand socialism? To answer this question, first of all we need to find out what the value goal of socialism is.

Foreign Marxists and communist organizations generally believe that democracy, freedom, equality, justice and humanity and several other value elements are the embodiments of the whole value system of socialism, and the goal of socialism is to achieve these values. Humanism is the primary value goal pursued by Western Marxists or foreign communists. Western Marxists believe that socialism is a kind of value and its essential characteristic is humanism. Man is the foundation of Marx's thought in respect to socialist ideal goal construction and human liberation has always been the fundamental purpose of communism advocated by Marx. Foreign Marxists have proposed the slogan: "people are the purpose, not the means". From the aspect of humanitarianism, the supreme principle of socialism is: "human is higher than all and men are always the center of society and constitute the highest value. Therefore, all social activities should be centered on human needs. They advocate man as the blueprint of the future ideal society with man as the core valueThey argue that future humanitarian society is the one that aims the realization of human freedom and one in which people love and live in solidarity with each other. Humanitarian socialism is also an aesthetic world in which people shape and organize the world in accordance with the laws of aesthetics; life will become entertainment and labor practice will change to recreation. In short, humanitarian socialism is a world unifying truth and goodness where there is no governance, repression and alienation, but embodies happiness and freedom.

Democracy, freedom and equality are other important values pursued by Western Marxists or foreign communist and socialist parties. Most of them believe that the socialist model of the Soviet Union was rigid and deformed because it has destroyed the image of socialism, strangled democracy and freedom, and transformed itself into "state control and intervention upon the society", was indulged with bureaucracy and egalitarianism. Thus when defining socialism, several communist parties emphasize that socialism should appeal for democracy, freedom, equality, human rights and other values and consider democracy, freedom and human rights as the most basic characteristics of socialism.

In Europe and the United States, the French Communist Party believes that the future socialist society should be a democratic and autonomously managed society in which all members of society can participate in the decision-making and enjoy freedom, democracy and equality. In this society, better working and living conditions should be guaranteed. Former General Secretary of the French communist party and an advocate of "new communism" Robert Hue has argued that the term of "new communism" expresses a desire for a more humane, more upright, more just and more free society. The Spanish Communist Party has stressed that their future goal is to "establish a socialist society that eradicates exploitation and build a communist society with no class and no state". They have argued that only such a society can solve all kinds of injustices in the contemporary world and end all forms of oppression and exploitation in order to achieve justice, freedom and mutual solidarity and assistance. The Portuguese Communist Party believes that the fundamental purpose of socialist revolution is to eliminate exploitation and establish a society with the guidance of humanitarian values and without class antagonisms. The documents of 14th Congress of Portuguese Communist Party pointed out that the social development prospect still requires the ideal of realizing a better future society pursued by human (i.e., the communism), and building a society without class in which everyone is equal, free and can work with free will. In a report entitled "New Century, New Development, New Struggle" in March 2000, Sam Webb, the chairman of the Communist Party of the United States, pointed out that their socialist goal is to eliminate exploitation, insecurity and poverty, end unemployment, hunger and homelessness, eradicate racism, national oppression, all forms of discrimination and inequality in respect to women's social status, expand democratic rights, exterminate ownership, and create a humane and rational planned society in which human's creativty and abilities are given full play.

Within the Eastern European regions and in the former territories of the former Soviet Union, the Communist Party of Russian Federation is the party that insists on Marxism. This party believes that socialism is to establish a just society, build a real Soviet-style peoples' regime featuring collectivism, freedom and equality, that will defend the interests of workers, farmers, intellectuals and all the other laboring groups. Verdet the chairman of the Romanian Socialist Party of Labor, has argued that the mistakes of the socialist model of the former Soviet Union and Eastern Europe could not be equated with socialism: "totalitarianism, dictatorship, abuse of human rights and restricted democracy cannot be synonymous with socialism. Socialism is to establish a society that rejects the current capitalist society based on exploitation and inequality, it is also not the socialist society with "unrestricted collectivism" which is already proven wrong. It has to get rid of over centralization of political powers and over-centralized administrative management of the economy, and build a society in which people are enthusiastic and have their values acknowledged, a society that is truly just and men enjoying equal opportunities, but not egalitarian, a society without social and national exploitation and oppression and with real free working envitoment, and a society in which men enjoy real human dignity, freedom and democracy. The Yugoslav Communist Party has argued that socialism needs to increase the opportunities for both individual and collective choices of people and free people from poverty, hunger, illiteracy, unemployment, class differences and racial oppression.

The communist parties of developing countries also share roughly the same views with the other communist parties of the North. The Communist Party of South Africa believes that socialism has four characteristics: democracy, equality, freedom and socialization of major economic sectors, the core of which is democracy, equality and freedom. The Communist Party of Sri Lanka believes that socialism cannot be achieved without proper attention and respect for political democracy and free development of individuals. The Communist Party of Israel also believes that the socialist society should be a people-centered society that ensures a high degree of democracy in all aspects. The Brazilian Communist Party believes that socialism is based on the widest possible participation of workers, which ensures freedom to the people and respect for the law and civil rights. Cyprus's Progressive Party of Working People (AKEL) also argues that the party should commit itself to for a society which is democratic and humane socialism based on peace, freedom, justice and that respects human rights. The Communist Party of India advocates the establishment of a democratic and just socialist society. After the drastic changes in Eastern Europe and collapse of the Soviet Union, the socialist view of political parties in Latin America has also undergone great changes. They believe that both the planned economy and privatization have drawbacks, and they advocate a mixed economy, emphasize state's regulation and control over the economy, and advocate the establishment of a development model which not only includes democracy and justice but also social policies in education, health, housing and public transportation. Its goal should be to establish a free, just and sovereign state.

The reasons why foreign Marxists, socialist and communist organizations have made democracy, freedom, humanity, equality and human rights as the value goal of socialism include the following: firstly, these goals themselves are the principles and goals which are already inherent in Marxist scientific socialism; secondly, contemporary capitalist society tramples these values; thirdly, Socialism in the Soviet Union and Eastern Europe have failed to achieve these goals. Therefore, there is certain rationality and truth about their ideas in respect to the value goals of socialism. However, they have separated the inherent unity of scientific principles of Marxism and its thoughts on value system, which can lead to the abandonment of Marxist scientific principles and means laying unbalanced emphasis on value issues which may lead to utopian socialism.

2. What are the basic characteristics of socialism ?

To establish the socialist system according to socialist value goals is another important issue for foreign Marxists and the communist & socialist parties. İf we analyze their main ideas on socialist society design after the end of the Cold War, they focus on the following principles: such design should be conducive to the realization of the socialist value goals and reflect the value orientation of the needs of the whole society; secondly, it must respect the diversity of socialism paths an model and the future socialist society should be more closely accord with the characteristics of the times, i.e. science and technology, market economy and national conditions; thirdly, it should fully reflect the unity of efficiency and fairness, nationality and worldliness, and personality and generality; fourthly, it must be the unity of constant change and relative stability, autonomy and openness, and learn from all the past valuable achievments human civilization.

On the issue of socialist ownership, in the past they had generally accepted the view that socialist public ownership is the essential feature of socialism. But after the end of the Cold War, this view was questioned to varying degrees. They argue that the public ownership of the Soviet socialism model did not bring about the expected prosperity, nor ensured the superiority of socialism in its competition with capitalism. The ownership system of the Soviet model was not "public or social", but "bureaucratic", "one-party system with the ownership controlled by the privileged class" or was the "ownership of nobody", or "vacuum or absence of true ownership."Although they have questioned socialist public ownership, most of them still believe that socialism must implement the public ownership of the means of production.

Summing up the experiences of socialist construction in the Soviet Union and Eastern Europe, they believe that the socialist public ownership cannot be simply defined as state ownership and collective ownership; instead "social ownership" should be established. According to their explanation, the so-called "social ownership" should actually be "mixed ownership". In their view, a single state ownership system not only lead to low efficency or productivity in economy which is a serious impediment to the development of productive forces, but also politically lead to bureaucracy and authoritarian dictatorship. Socialist social ownership ahould be a mixed economy, in which private, cooperative, and public enterprises will compete with each other, and direct state regulation and control should be limited. Most of the European communist & socialist parties hold this view. For instance, the Portuguese Communist Party advocates that in the socialist society, the main means of production should be owned by the whole society, and self-employed, cooperative, collective, family and private economic elements should coexist together with public ownership. The Greek Communist Party believes that the essence of the "shock reform" conducted by the Soviet leadership was to change public ownership in to capitalist private ownership, which was the deliberate restoration of capitalism. In today's Russia and other CIS countries, many former communist but now left-wing parties have also proposed the theory of coexistence of multiple ownership in economy. In developing countries, there are many communist & socialist parties holding similar views. For instance, Cyprus' Progressive Party of Working People (AKEL) advocates the implementation of a policy of economic development based on modern mixed economy. The Communist Party of South Korea advocates the establishment of a socialist society based on the co-ownership, sharing and control of the main means of production by producers. In this society, all non-exploiting personal property and all other necessary private property that can effectively promote economic development and growth will be respected and protected.

Regarding the socialist distribution system, most of the communist & socialist parties of the world and foreign Marxists all agree with the Marxist classic writers' idea of "from each according to his ability, to each according to his work (contribution)." After the end of the Cold War, many of them still adhere to this view of Marxism in designing the future distribution system. For instance, the Communist Party of the USA believes that in the field of distribution, the basic socialist principle of "from each according to his ability, to each according to his work (contribution)" Socialism will provide incentives to encourage people to work harder, but will not implement egalitarianism in distribution. The Communist Party of the USA also believes that, in addition to upholding the general principles, socialism in the USA should have some specific features, including the improvement and expansion of social services and housing, the reduction of working hours, the eradication of poverty, free medical care, child and elderly protection and labor protection, thus bringing together the ideal of socialism with the practical conditions of the USA. The Portuguese Communist Party believes that in social field, laborers should be freed from all forms of exploitation and oppression, people will have the right to full employment and get paid according to their work contribution, and citizens would build social relationships based on mutual respect for individuality and human dignity. The Greek Communist Party also advocates the socialist principle of payment according to work and advocates complete change of the capitalist social relations.

Regarding the political system of socialism: when designing the future political system, foreign Marxists, communist organizations, without exception, stress the importance of democracy and advocate that the state power should be in the hands of the working people. The CPUSA believes that political power will be in the hands of working people; the government style will be based on comprehensive democracy, and it will be based on economic democracy; more and more people will participate in the management of economy. In March 2000, the National Congress of the Communist Party of the USA pointed out that the core of their socialist theory were democratic rights, promotion of democratic structures and democratic practices. It has argued that socialism in the United States should strengthen the propaganda of the socialist rights bill thus make the people feel that socialism is true democracy. The 29th congress of the Communist Party of France proposed to restore democracy, expand democracy to all spheres of the society such as business, public life, state institutions, and news media, enable people to enjoy much more rights and powers than representative democracy, thuıs give full play to the role of representative democracy, and push representative democracy to learn from direct democracy, so as to create a new era of democracy in France.The Portuguese Communist Party believes that socialism is the deepening of democracy. In Portugal's socialist political system, workers will have the powers to carry out constant supervision of the activities of state institutions, and people's participation will be constantly strengthened, democracy will be extended to all aspects of state affairs, and people's democratic rights will be protected. The content of fight for political democracy aims to strive for the establishment of a modern and democratic society in which people can control their own destiny and widely participate in state affairs.

Regarding the socialism and market economy, after the end of the Cold War, foreign Marxists and communists have begun to argue that the planned economy built on the basis of public ownership was the main reason for the failure of socialism in the Soviet Union and Eastern Europe. Therefore, they actively began to explore the relationship between the market and socialism and tmore and more favored for the combination of socialism with market. They believe that the purpose of socialism is not to achieve public ownership and planned economy, but fairness, democracy, freedom and a series of value goals. This means that public ownership and planned economy can only be used as a means of achieving socialism. Although capitalism is dependent on the market, the characteristics of capitalism are private ownership of means of production and wage labor, not the market economy. In this sense, they argued that there is no necessary connection between capitalism and market. The market economy can serve both capitalism and socialism. The market is more conducive to social development than the planned economy. In addition to the higher efficiency than the plan, the market can promote the development of freedom and democracy.

However, there are still many communists who do not advocate abandoning the planned economy. While criticizing the planned economy, they have also pointed to the limitations of market economy, such as the possibility of leading to injustice, causing environmental pollution and dstruction of natural resources, which can negatively affect the realization of social welfare undertakings, and so on. For instance, the Communist Party of USA argues that the socialist government should plan the whole economy. This kind of planning will involve all classes as much as possible. With the planned economy, the progress of science and technology and the protection of natural resources and natural environment, the production efficency of the socialist society will be much higher than that of capitalist society. The Portuguese Communist Party also advocates the important role of the market, but it stresses the need to combine economic planning and direct initiative and participation by production units and workers. The Communist Party of Greece still advocates the implementation of the socialist planned economy, emphasizing that the planned economy accords with the basic principles of socialist construction.

In terms of ideology, foreign Marxists and communist parties believe that, in realizing the socialist goals, Marxism should always be upheld. They argue that the setbacks of socialism in the Soviet Union in Eastern Europe are not the fault of Marxism but due to misinterpretation of Marxism. They stressed that Marxism still has vitality and remains our guidance for practice and action. But Marxism is not a dogma. Marx's writings should not be read as religious books. It should be enriched, developed and applied in accord with development of the times, accord with the development of human knowledge, economics and political science. For instance, the Portuguese Communist Party insists that Marxism still has a strong vitality. The documents of the 16th congress of Portuguese Communist Party pointed out: in the process of developing the workers' movement and carrying out social transformation, it is still necessary to uphold Marxism as the guiding ideology, and the communism based on the scientific theory of Marxism can be realized, even in the civilization framework created by the capitalism. The New British Communist Party, as well as the communist parties of Finland, Norway, Sweden and Denmark, also emphasize adhering to the guidance of Marxist theory and advocate the integration of Marxism with the domestic conditions. In addition, there are some communist parties, such as the French Communist Party and Italian Communist Party (Refoundation), stress the diversity in guiding ideology and assert that Marxism should only be one of the ideological sources of the party. It can be seen that foreign Marxists and communist and socialist parties still regard the socialist and communist system as the concrete form of the future society that will replace the capitalist system.

3. The subject to rely in achieving socialism

After the socialist value goals are defined and the design of the socialist society is drafted according these value goals. They have argued on whom

to rely on in order to establish such a socialist system? This has been another important issue of research among them. Classical Marxist theory considers the working class as the subject which can realize socialism and argues that with the deepening and intensifying of inherent contradictions of capitalism, the working class will stand up to undertake the historical mission of realizing socialism. This assertion has been endorsed and accepted by most schools of socialism and their theories. However, the changes in the social structure and class structure changes caused by the great changes in the contemporary capitalism began to challenge the traditional view in respect to the subject which will realize socialism. To re-understand and re-determine the subject which will realize socialism has become an important issue in the eyes of foreign Marxists.

In the developed countries of Europe, a small number of Marxists and communist parties still insist that the working class is the main subject for realizing socialism. For instance, the Communist Party of Finland, the Communist Party of Norway and the British Communist Party still insist on relying on the working class for the social revolution which will overthrow the capitalist system. In their view, the decline or even disappearance of the working class in its original sense do not mean that the decline or disappearance of the working class, the changes in contemporary capitalism do not change the basic class structure of the capitalist society, so the working class is still the main force for realizing socialism. In the 12th congress of the New British Communist Party held in October 2000, the resolution entitled as "Class, State and Control" was passed, reaffirming the historical mission of the working class. British Road to Socialism, the current program of new British Communist Party, points out that the working class and the labor movements are the leading forces of the socialist revolution. In order to win leadership, the organized working class should fight against all forms of oppression and exploitation and win all the allies possible. In the developed capitalist countries of Europe, the Fourth International, namely the Trotskyite socialists of the left wing, also insist that the working class will be leader of the socialist revolution. They argue that the changes in the social structure and class structure of the contemporary capitalist countries have not weakened the working class's dominant position among other forces of socialist transformation; instead the working class has expanded and strengthened. For instance, Ernest Mandel once the leader of the Fourth International had argued: "although dramatic changes have occured in the economic and social structure of advanced capitalism, the working class delineated by Marxism is still the only force that has the potential to defeat capitalism, the force which can save humanity and achieve higher civilization in the face of disasters that threaten humanity, it has the power which has the required potential and which can promote and boast the social power of freely associated male and female producers, to achieve the above goals. Today, there are more than one billion working people in the world, the working class is stronger than ever."..."if we evaluate the long-term historical trend of the next few decades, contrary to those pessimistic and vague views, the trend is toward the growth of the working class and its unity strengthening, rather than tending to weaken or disintegrate."[1]

There are still a few political parties who insist that the working class is the leading force in the realization of socialist change and propose to combine the working class and all the laborers as the subject of social revolution. They basically adhere to the Marxist-Leninist theory, value the importance of alliances with other classes, and try to unite with more and more progressive forces. For instance, Portuguese Communist Party believes that the main subject of the socialist revolution is the working class and all other laboring strata. It advocates the alliance of workers, staff, small and medium-sized farmers, intellectuals, technicians, small and medium-sized businessmen, who oppose the exploitation and oppression of capitalism, and who strive for democratic socialism and communism. The Greek Communist Party also holds a similar position. It argues that the anti-imperialist and anti-monopoly struggle strategy against capitalism to be carried

1 Ernest Mandel, "Socialism and the Future", see his book The Future of Socialism, Beijing, Central Compilation Press, 1994, pp. 159.

out in Greece will occur as a social change led by the working class. The regime established after the revolution will mastered by the working class and its allies, representing the interests of working class, farmers, the urban middle class and the social movements who fight for democratic rights. Please note that currently Greek Communist Party has changed the above strategy.

In contrast to above views, majority of foreign Marxists are more likely to deny the theory of working class being the main subject. They advocate the theory of multiple subjects. They argue that with the development of new technological revolution, the class structure of society has changed radically. The revolution in science and technology has promoted the automation and computerization, resulting in large-scale structural unemployment. Laboring in rhe traditional sense is disappearing; the traditional proletariat has greatly changed; scholars, engineers, technicians, managers who control the production process have gradually become the class controlling the new means of production. In the western developed countries, the traditional working class could not become the largest social group, and history hasn't allowed the proletariat to become the subject of building the new society. So majority of foreign Marxists invest their hopes for new revolutionary forces, who are not yet assimilated by the capitalist society and who hate the existing mode of production. They include elite intellectuals, young college students, blacks, ethnic minorities, the marginalized people at the bottom of the society, the unemployed, and the homeless and others. The values embodied in the ideology of these groups which reject the existing society contain certain positive factors which can enable transformation to the new society. They use their new feelings and consciousness to criticize the evils of the capitalism and they can further expose the ills of capitalism. These majority of foreign Marxists also believe that the future society will be a multi-level technological society, and the Marxists should take this assumption as a starting point to predict the new subjects of socialism. Therefore, they have completely abandoned the theory of working class being the main subject and began to assert that all the progressive forces of the society should be equal subjects of the social revolution. For instance, the theory of "new communism", advocated by the French Communist Party rejects the thought of "workers' movement being central" and assertsd that "new communism" does not require preferential treatment in respect to the interests of a certain class, but unite people from all classes who suffer from capitalism. Robert Hue has argued that, currently the Communist Party should ndeavor to establish a "Joint Convention on Progress" defending the interests of all citizens and establish an agreement between the citizens and the left-wing parties, and fight against the right-wing parties, positively absorb everything that can be absorbed from the right-wing parties, develop a people's movement, and develop dialogue with and ally with all progressive political parties and forces.

Italian Communist Party (Refoundation) and the Spanish Communist Party akso hold a similar position. They have gone beyond the framework of traditional class analysis and advocate a new strategy for the realization of socialism by allying with the progressive forces. These progressive forces concept should be broad and include all the socialist political parties, independent leftists, ecological socialists and all other forces against capitalism. Italian Communist Party (Refoundation) claimed: in order to change and surpass capitalism we cannot just rely on the working class movement, but the people's political movement. In the current new stage, the main problem is to redefine the subject of revolution. In the contemporary capitalist society, the traditional theory of the working class as the subject of revolution does not accord with the new changes in the contemporary society. But the new revolutionary subject has not emerged or taken its form. The Communist Party should stand out to represent it and its mission is to promote the transformation of the old subject into the new subject. The Spanish Communist Party emphasizes that socialism and communism are the result of voluntary action and true revolution of the majority and social revolution should include all members of the society. It aims to give priority to the common interests of the liberation movement, thereby promoting the alliance of different social liberation movements for the liberation of mankind. It can be seen that these parties have abondoned the conception of class, and shifted to be the revolutionary party of the whole people and seek to seize power through parliamentary elections.

In the developed capitalist countries, other left political forces have made a more profound theoretical explanation in respect to diverse subjects of social change. They believe that in the future capitalist society, diversity and differentiation will be dominant. The old uniformity, especially the class uniformity, will be surmounted. Various social movements, based on different identities and those who are victims of different forms of oppression, grow rapidly. Accordingly, the importance of the working class movement is markedly declining. In order to achieve the transformation of capitalist society, the left must rely on all the progressive social forces, including a variety of new social movements. Some of them even suspect the working class's "special status" and "special role" advocated by Marxism, argue that the traditional pure working class did not become the largest social class as Marx had predicted, thus "today we should rely on various left-wing forces in our fight for the realization of socialism". In this way, they expand the subject of social revolution from one or more classes to broad social movements and to multiple subjects. Also in the vast number of developing countries, many communist parties emphasize alliances with other progressive forces. For instance, the Communist Party of Sri Lanka advocates the alliance with other democratic forces. The Communist Party of South Africa participates in the coalition of all classes and groups in the society in line with the party's minumum program namely the coalition led by the African National Congress (ANC) and shares four ministers of the government.

Briefly, after reviewing the exploration of the foreign Marxists and communists on the issue of "what socialism is", we can draw the following conclusions:

Firstly, socialism is both the product of the development of world civilization and the realistic trend based on the contradictions and evils of capitalism. Current world without socialism, will be incomplete and unimaginable. The socialism thought and the whole socialist movement are also the products of the development of world civilization and these two reflect the demand of the times. Capitalism is absolutely unable to solve the problems of men as individuals and as human mankind. As long as there are exploiters and the exploited, socialist and communist thoughts will not disappear. Socialism represents the future of human society, and the socialist movement will see a surge again.

Secondly, the socialist model, established by the Soviet Union in the 20th century, is out of date and can no longer meet the requirements of the higher stage of civilization. The future development of socialism requires the abandonment of the old socialist paradigm and the search for new forms. The development of contemporary society requires re-evaluating some of the foundations of Marxist socialism ideology and seek a new form of socialist development based on the new reality.

Thirdly, it is too early to judge the historical destiny of socialism. But it can be said with certainty that the failure of the Soviet socialism model does not imply the failure of socialism, nor does it mean that socialism has completely lost its future. The socialist development paths in all countries need to be reexamined. The communists of all countries need to advance with the times, keep innovating, continue to explore and solve new problems according to the actual situation of their countries, and blaze a new socialist development path suiting their national characteristics and in line with their own national conditions.

(Qin Xuan, Professor of Institute of Marxism Studies, Renmin University of China)

A Probe into the Prospect of Socialism by Foreign Marxists

There have been several major events since the 1990s: firstly, the drastic changes in the Eastern Europe and the disintegration Soviet Union, and the end of the Cold War, which have changed the world pattern and a new world order began to shape. Second, the wave of globalization is sweeping all nations and have a profound impact on the history of mankind. In the face of these new development trends, foreign Marxists and some left-wing scholars have made in-depth discussions in respect to the future prospects of socialist development.

1. An analysis of the current situation of capitalism in the context of globalization

Since the 1990s, the process of globalization has accelerated, and the capitalist social form has changed to a certain extent. Some foreign Marxists believe that it is necessary to study the form of capitalist society stage by stage in the context of globalization and explore the new strategy of socialist development and the fate and future of human society. In "Capitalism in the Age of Globalization", Egyptian Marxist economist Samir Amin, from the core of Dependency Theory, namely "unbalanced development", divides the capitalist history into four periods. In particular, he makes special study on the "recent period" since 1990, which has laid the foundation for the discussion of globalization from the perspective of socialism.

Amin believes that the uneven development of the regions is a major feature of human history. Till the modern times, with the whole world incorporated into the capitalist system, polarization has become the internal by-product of this process. In the evolution of the capitalist mode of production, the polarization of modern capitalism presents several continuous forms. The first is the "mercantilism" (1500-1800) which was prior to industrial revolution. This commercial capital obtained a monopoly position mainly in the central Atlantic countries. Its outer region was the Americas. The formation of an outer region is in full compliance with the logic of commercial capital accumulation. The second is the so-called "classical model of polarization" (1800-1945) that originated in the industrial revolution and determined the basic form of capitalism. Peripheral countries have further developed and included Asia (excluding Japan), Africa and Latin America, which were in rural regions and in non-industrial state and could only rely on agricultural products and minerals to participate the division of labor in the world. From the industrial revolution to the end of the Second World War, the world system was characterized by this "classical form" of polarization. The third period is the "post-war period" (1945-1990), namely the industrialization of the periphery countries. This kind of industrialization was inevitably unequal and unbalanced. In Asia and Latin America, industrialization is the dominant social factor. While the national liberation movement has further accelerated the process of unequal and unbalanced industrialization, the self-centered national production system has gradually collapsed and reconstructed the organic elements of the integrated world production system. This double recession was also a sign of the deepening of globalization. The fourth period was the "recent period" (since 1990). During this period, the accumulation of the transition mentioned above led to the final collapse of the balance of the world system after the Second World War. Amin stressed: "Moreover these negative evolutions occured in an atmosphere of relative stagnation, and therefore led to growing poverty and exclusion, such as more unemployment and/or marginalization, sometimes covered many countries in a region or even of a continent, such as Africa. Such a system does not deserve to be seen as a "new world order", it is rather a new world disorder, or chaos as I chose to name in my book "the empire of Chaos" "this chaos can be seen everywhere with its all aspects as the crisis in the political, social and ideological spheres." Amin has analyzed the three major failures behind this situation as follows: "(1) it has not developed new forms of political and social organization going beyond the nation state-which is a new requirement of the globalized system of production; (2) it has not developed economic and political relationships capable of reconciling the rise of industrialization in the new peripheral zones of Asia and Latin America,and neglects the pursuit of global growth; (3) it has not developed a relationship, other than an exclusionist one, especially in respect to African periphery which is not engaged in competitive industrialization, yet."[2] In Samir Amin's view, this current chaotic situation cannot maintain and push the process of globalization, but reveals its extreme vulnerability.

Wallerstein is a famous Marxist scholar, the representative of the world system theory. As early as the 1980s, he had predicted that the globalized free market economy would go into despair, and in 2025 there would occur a "new order" which will replace capitalism. When the "9/11" incident rekindled the discussion theme of how to judge the future of the world capitalist system, he was interviewed by "Common Wealth Magazine". When talking about his view about the future of capitalism, he still argued that the free capitalist world system was moving towards disintegration. Wallerstein predicted that there will be two main reasons for the disintegration of the "world capitalist system". First, in the future capitalism, the

2 Samir Amin, Capitalism in the Age of Globalization, London & NewYork, Zed Books, 1997, p. 2.

profits will be less and less. This is an inherent constraint of the capitalism, which cannot be changed by men's will. That is to say, the development of the global system of capitalism has inherent limitations. Second, the role of politics is also declining. In other words, the role of the state is diminishing. For these two reasons, more and more people are increasingly dissatisfied with their future because of fewer gains. Now, the people of the world have lost their "hope" of changing the situation through political activities.

The companies in the world sense that it is more and more difficult to make money. Capitalists are dissatisfied and have lost their patience. Therefore, Wallerstein pointed out: "The economic plus political pressure naturally causes the crisis of the global capitalist system that I have predicted."[3]

Professor of the Department of Political Science at the University of New York and Hegelian Marxist Bertell Ollman believes that today's Western capitalism is going to collapse. He likens today's Western capitalism to an airliner flying 600 miles per hour without direction. It shows that the material wealth of Western capitalism is increasing, but such abundant material wealth cannot guarantee its spiritual and institutional self-sufficiency, so it inevitably leads to a decline. Ollman acknowledged that since the Second World War, the capitalist countries have proposed and adopted a series of measures and carried out public opinion propaganda, so that people no longer focus on the various ills of capitalist system. For example, in order to prove the rationality of their governance, the bourgeoisie mainly rely on the government to get its support as in the following: "Firstly, relying on the government to accumulate capital; secondly, relying on the government to broaden commodity information; thirdly, relying on the government to prove their own legitimacy, fourthly, relying on the government to suppress social forces against the capitalists." Although these measures have eased class contradictions to an extent, socialism cannot be established on the basis of capitalism. On the contrary, in the global context, Western capitalism is gradually losing the foundations on which it exists, and thus inevitably in a decline. He said, "Today's Western capitalism is like a chicken whose head has been cut off. Although it is running around and might hurt someone else, it will soon fall down. Because it has no head, which means the conditions of the existence of capitalism have ceased to exist."[4]

3 Wallerstein, The Collapse of Capitalist Globalization, see on KL.gz.cn.

4 Bertell Ollman, Western capitalism is now going to collapse, published in Foreign Theoretical Trends,1997(1).

2. Discussion on globalization and the new strategy for socialist development

Foreign Marxists believe that globalization is an objective historical necessity. It is progressive to a certain extent and provides us with an opportunity for designing a new socialist strategy. Amin argues, "in accord with a socialist perspective, we must fight back against the current globalization, by developing an alternative globalization with a humanistic program." "Socialism has the responsibility to propose an alternative globalization program, which will include a true global sense of globalization and an approach which is humane and cosmopolitan which should not be in the service of a global market."[5]

Amin emphasizes the urgency of an alternative globalization program, because socialism should help people in grasping why capitalist globalization is produced, multiplied and what its flaws and restrictions are. "The current globalization gradually deepens the polarization in the world society. In other words, the historical limitations of capitalism can be clearly seen in the current globalization: the bipolar world it creates becomes increasingly inhumane". Consequently, Amin believes that globalization itself heralds the idea of reshaping socialism everywhere in the world. For him it should be a new socialism, and he explains it as : Socialism is not dead, but it will not be reborn via attempts to resuscitate old national social-democratic or statist Marxist-Leninist formulas or their other versions seen in the South, all of which are superseded and proven obsolote. The new socialism should be much more internationalist, and at the same time actively contribute to the re-arrangement of regional groupings capable of supporting the internationalist struggles of peoples against capitalist groupings. These regional groupings of peoples envisaged by Samir Amin in his book are not the same as those groupings formed with the neo-imperialist logic, namely the harnessing of particular regions of the South to central rich metropoles (such as the integration of Mexico into the North American Free Trade Agreement (NAFTA), or the association of African countries subordinated to Europe, the reconstruction of an East Asian economic region dominated by Japan) On the contrary, they should bypass the constraints of the nation-state at the hearth of Europe on the one hand, and on the other hand they should reinforce the power of collective negotiation and the consolidation of the economic regions of the Third World according to their geographical organization (Arab world, Africa, Latin America, South-East Asia). If this path of resistence cannot be established, it is possible that the world will return to the past, which will feed uncontrollable conflicts among the nations and among real or virtual communities."[6]

5 Samir Amin, Capitalism in the Age of Globalization, London & NewYork: Zed Books, 1997, p. 5.

6 Ibid., p. 6.

It can be seen, that according to Amin's point of view, the "socialist" thoughts should be updated in respect to the conception of globalization. What kind of a new socialist strategy should be taken by socialists in the future? In his book "Capitalism in the Age of Globalization", Amin made a reflection on this issue. He asserted that these strategies should include: first, in the peripheral countries that have achieved industrialization such as Brasil and South Korea, where the fight is taking place in the real economic management and democracy, alliance of the new working classes (farmers exploited by the contemporary financial transactions and the neglected public workers) have been able to make their voice heard. Secondly, in the fourth world, the negligence of production changed the conflict between "people" and "power holders", thus creating a practical alternative. Thirdly, in accordance with the strategic framework of humanitarian substitution provided by Amin, racial issues are replaced by certain other issues, which can be summed up as respect for diversity and unity. He wrote: this also means that we should abandon the old power theory, because "power" usually pretends to internalize and compromises with the ideology of nation and state, and represents the narrow"national interest" (in fact it often betrays the true national interest). Fourthly, respect for diversity also means accepting social reality, especially the class reality. Fifthly, respect for diversity also means accepting the social reality of women's religious and racial organizations. Meanwhile, Amin also believes that the recognition of diversity in a society does not mean infinite division which might lead to disintegration of a country. On the contrary, diversity should be the starting point for the call of unity. This is the only way to benefit the strenghening of the people's power."

German originated Mexican scholar Heinz Dieterich also explores ways that can lead to the future socialist society. He has argued that judging from the current situation, the approach of "rejecting capital" is not an effective strategy; the conditions of the armed revolutions in the traditional sense have no future; the establishment of a new communist international organization is nothing more than an abstract desire. So how can we achieve the new blueprint? He believes that it should be strongly rooted in the masses. Under the current level of science and technology, it is possible to form a "communication and supportive electronic interconnection network that can operate in a decentralized form". The Internet is the "only means" of world communication that is economically affordable. But he argues that the main obstacle to the creation of the world's democratization movement is not technical and structural, but theoretical and programmatic. Therefore, he has proposed that in the next two to three years, through a global collective action, a programmatic document for the new blueprint should be formulated, i.e., the World Declaration on Democratic Society. The possible and necessary path of evolution should be designed which can lead us a step towards a solidarity society. In addition, Heinz Dieterich also depicts the content, tasks, stages in the course of achieving the future society of socialism. The first stage, i.e., in the current transition stage, the goal is to guarantee and deepen the qualitative leap in human civilization from the capitalist period to the historical period of human democracy, to achieve real democracy which is "the culmination of this process". The second stage: its goal is "to promote the gradual and deliberate evolution of the subjective and objective structures, so that the structure and patterns of exploitation, oppression and indifference disappear." During this period, the old things and new social factors within the capitalist global society will still coexist; and different countries and societies of the world will gradually converge. It will also be a turbulent period. The third stage, i.e., the final stage of the historical process will be a period wherein there will be no market or state and different cultures will harmoniously coexist.

Heinz Dieterich believes that the final realization of this new program involves the global society, which needs a unified and collective realization at the global level, rather than a partial, regional project, because "a non-capitalist project is impossible to sustain in the medium term within a single country." The historical experience of the recent past decades has proven that the theory of building socialism in a single country cannot be affirmed. He added: "capitalism is like cancer, the solution should be a systematic an wholistic answer, not a local one."[7] Consequently, Heinz Dieterich, advocates that the revolutionary change should be started in the national and regional level, but can only be completed in the global level.

3. Discussion on the prospects of development of socialism

Some foreign Marxists have elaborated on the future prospects of socialist development. One of the most representative figures are David Schweickart, Peter Drucker and Heinz Dieterich. In the "market socialism" school, David Schweickart is famous for proposing the "economically democratic market socialism" After the drastic changes in Eastern Europe and the disintegration of the Soviet Union, faced with the obscenities of the "death of socialist future" and the "end of communism" within the Western intellectual circles, he published the book "Against-capitalism" and proposed his unique thought of "economically democratic market socialism". This socialism, as defined by Schweickart, is a worker and community controlled variant of market socialism. As such, it is also a transitional and mixed economy with a government operating for the interests of and with the consent of a progressive majority, especially the working class. It is the first phase of a new socialist order.

7 Heinz Dieterich, The End of Global Capitalism: A New Historical Project, Beijing, People's Literature Publishing House, 2001, p. 97.

With this socialist viewpoint David Schweickart has made a new argument, comparing market socialism and capitalism from the perspectives of economy, politics and ethics. David Schweickart has emphasized that according to Marx's point of view, capitalism is only a special stage in human history. It has three characteristics: private ownership of production materials, market system and wage labor. Wage labor—labor-power as a commodity—was the last to develop and is the most important nature which forms the distinctive nature of the capitalist system. Unlike earlier economic systems, capitalism is inherently dynamic rather than conservative, in that it is provides maximal incentives, both positive and negative, for continuous technological and organizational innovation.

However, it should be noted that as the capitalist system matures, its internal contradictions are also increasing. What is particularly striking now is that capitalism has four major problems worth noting: the employment problem is very serious (intractable unemployment), the social economic instability; third, poverty in the midst of plenty and fourth the development of capitalism is irrational, i.e., capitalism's "grow or die" imperative creates the conditions for a shift: "to an economy of more rational consumption, more leisure and more meaningful work". Besides capitalism puts increasing strain on the fragile ecology of the planet. All these issues are leading to the crisis of the capitalist system, and at the same time makes it possible to replace it with a better system. David Schweickart believes that it is only the "economic and democratic market socialism" that can replace capitalism. In his article "Economic Democracy: A Worthy Socialism that Would Really Work" he wrote that "economic and democratic market socialism" is not only economically viable, but it can also overcome the basic contradictions of capitalism. Specifically, it mainly includes the following two aspects: First, the democratic management of enterprises. Democracy in the workplace is the most direct democracy. The ultimate management decision making of the enterprise should be made by all the workers of the enterprise, and they should have the right to vote with the principle of "one worker, one share, one vote". Workers should define the goals, products to be produced, wages and methods of work. Workers will elect a workers' council that appoints upper management, which is equivalent to the capitalist company's board of directors, the value of the company's assets must be kept intact, so that the depreciation fund can be maintained, to be used for equipment replacement or technological improvement. Workers can own the assets of these firms directly, as cooperative ownership, or they can lease them from government, as public ownership with workers' control. Compared with the failed Soviet system, the advantage of this system is that it allows workers to control their working conditions, enables the democratization of corporate (company) management, and workers can freely choose managers of enterprises, thus avoiding the "democracy deficit" we see in capitalism and in the Soviet system.

The second is to give the workers' collective the ability to control over the disposition of the social surplus, investments should be socially controlled and socially decided, and will not be left to market forces. If these two imperatives are institutionalized, the whole economy can continue to function as a market economy. Enterprises compete with one another to satisfy consumer demands. Workers in a given enterprise receive, not contractual wages, but contractual shares (not necessarily equal) from their enterprise's profits. (Thus their incomes are determined by how successfully their enterprise performs in a market environment.) To be sure, the market will have to be regulated, for those reasons (market failures) which are well recognized by all reputable economists: in order to block monopolistic tendencies and to compensate for externalities and various other market failures. (Economist differs as to the seriousness of various forms of market failures and the efficacy of proposed solutions, but most of them accept that an unregulated market cannot lead to an optimal allocation of resources in the real world.)

David Schweickart argues for the democratic control of new investments, which will replace the allocation of investment funds by the capitalist financial and capital markets, by using state asset funds and local public banks, which will decrease the influence of the current capital markets. In the eyes of David Schweickart "social control of investment is a general requirement that can be institutionalized in a variety of ways, that will consider specific circumstances of countries. Whatever these specific circumstances are, there must be two conceptually distinct institutional components of this socialist solution that answers the two distinct questions: How will be the investment funds generated? How will they be allocated? As to the generation of investment funds, it is essential—at least as an ideal to which a socialist society should aspire—to surmount reliance on private savings as the source of investment funds, and rely on public savings, i.e., taxation. The national investment fund should be generated by public savings, not private savings. For economic reasons, the optimal taxing way is a flat-rate tax in proportion to the amount of capital assets of each enterprise. The capital assets of enterprises should be regarded as public property, which are leased to workers' collectives. The tax is in fact the leasing fee. For historical reasons, capitalism has relied on private savings to finance investment—these private savings are concentrated in the hands of the minority capitalist class. But as governments everywhere know, it is exceedingly difficult to control the quantity of such savings. Here savers must be forced to save more or spend more, depending on economic conditions. This is not so easy to do—as Japan, has recently learned this lesson. When an economy slumps, many people feel the need to save more, so as to protect themselves from an uncertain future, whereas increased"[8]

In respect to the future of capitalism, American scholar Peter Drucker is quite pessimistic. Although he has a certain degree of positive attitude towards capitalism, he believes that the future of capitalism is slim. In his book Post-Capitalist Society, Drucker analyzes and predicts post-capitalism period from the 1940s to 2020s. Thus, in a certain sense, the future of capitalism depends on the development of post-capitalist society. Drucker believes that at present, we live in such a transformation which is creating the post-capitalist society. This is a fundamental change. Henceforth, there is no "Western" history or "Western" civilization, but the world history and world civilization. But both are "Westernized". We are still in this transformation. If history can be a guide, it will not be completed until 2010 or 2020.

Drucker pointed out that only a few decades ago, everyone "knows", and capitalist society will certainly be a socialist society. Now, this is not necessarily the case. At the same time, we at least realize that developed countries are moving out of capitalist society and entering post-capitalist society. This became very clear after the events of 1989 and 1990. Although this event does not equal the entire "end of history", it does mean the end of an era, which means the end of history, the end of an era of 250 years of domination of secular religion (what he calls "social salvation beliefs"). However, the end of this era and history has not expanded capitalism, and is gradually abandoning capitalism. Therefore, capitalism and socialism are rapidly being replaced by a completely different new society, which is a post-capitalist society. The characteristics of post-capitalist society are: First, in terms of economic system and social structure, the free market becomes the only proven economic integration mechanism, and capitalist institutions will continue to exist, but some institutions, such as banks, may play completely different roles. However, the central issues of the post-capitalist society, such as its structure, its social and economic dynamics, and its social class and other social issues, made the political parties, social groups, social value systems, and personal and political commitments realize a completely different situation in the past 250 years. Second, in terms of political structure, we have transformed from a 400-year-old sovereign nation-state into a pluralistic polity, in which the nation-state will no longer be the only unit of political integration, but a composite part in the post-capitalist polity, though still a key part. In this "post-capitalist polity", the structure of transnational, regional, and nation states is both competitive

8 David Schweickart, Ten Theses on Marxism and the Transition to Communism–Presentation to the Symposium "Modernization, Globalization and China's Path in Economic Development Hangzhou, China, 2002.

and peaceful in coexistence with local and even tribal structures. Third, in the creation of wealth, basic economic resources are no longer capital, natural resources or "labor force", but knowledge. The central activity of creating wealth is neither the use of capital for production nor "labor". Now, value is created by "productive forces" and "technical innovation," both of which apply knowledge to work. The main social group in the knowledge society will be "knowledge workers", just as capitalists know how to use capital for production, they know how to use knowledge for production. Unlike employees in the capitalist system, they have both "means of production" and "production tools".[9]

Heinz Dieterich called the vision of the future "new historical project". He believes that the capitalist society and the socialist society so far were both flawed and have suffered substantial defeats because they have not created the conditions necessary for true democracy and social justice. Therefore, the new project is different from the current capitalist society and the former socialist society, but a "new program" with true participation in democracy and non-capitalist economy. When talking about the spiritual essence of this "New Historical Project", Heinz Dieterich believes that the initiative proposed by Luxembourg in the "Spartacus League" draft program at the end of 1918 still makes sense, namely socialism. The essence of society is that the broad masses of working people are no longer the ruled group, but the group that enjoys the entire political life and economic life and leads it in a conscious, free and self-determined way. Therefore, Dieterich pointed out, "If we add these third and fourth important areas of our lives to the political and economic life of workers, the cultural and military fields, the majority of the global community not only has the democratic essence of Marx's and Engels' socialist project, but also the democratic essence of our 'New Historical Project'."[10] In this way, the "New Historical Project" essentially contains the political, economic, cultural and military content.

From the depiction of the political life of the future society, Heinz Dieterich in his book *The End of Global Capitalism: A New Historical Project*, argues that since the formation of classes, people are eager to live in a just and democratic society. For thousands of years, mankind has struggled for this goal which was never realized. Because, in the process of realizing true democracy, mankind has encountered with three structural obstacles including exploitation, governance and indifference. Heinz Dieterich has made permutation and combination of the three structural factors of exploitation, governance and indifference. Capitalism has created several key elements needed by the rule of law, namely constitution, separation of powers and formal power of decision making. Capitalism itself also opposes

9 Peter Drucker, Post-Capitalist Society, London: Harper Press, 1993.

10 Heinz Dieterich et al., The End of Global Capitalism: A New Historical Project, p. 71.

despotism and has a certain form of democracy. But capitalist democracy can only be called “formal democracy”. Formal democracy is a necessary condition, but it is obviously not enough for the future socialist society. In addition, exploitation, governance and indifference still exist in capitalist world. And “capitalist-bourgeois democracy hinders the true democracy as the devil evading water”. Therefore, it should be replaced.

If we evaluate the traditional socialist societies of the 20th Century, although they have greatly reduced the phenomenon of human exploitation, they could not reduce or surpass the governance and obedience problems. This traditional socialist society eliminated exploitation but still contained governance and indifference. Its democratic appeal was flawed and incomplete. Besides the capitalist society and the traditional socialist society, there are five combinations of social state which are also unrealistic, and therefore do not exist. They are: the society with exploitation and governance but without indifference; the society without exploitation and governance but with indifference; the society with exploitation but without governance and indifference; the society with exploitation and indifference but without governance; and society without exploitation and indifference but with governance. Heinz Dieterich argues that the true ideal future society should be one with no exploitation, governance or indifference. He argues that such a society can occur and exist. It is “a society where there is no capitalism or market, or no state as a repressive tool or where the current cold society is surmounted. It is a society in which all people share culture”.[11]

(Zheng Yiming, researcher in the Academy of Marxism, Chinese Academy of Social Sciences)

11 Ibid.

Research of Foreign Marxists on the Drastic Changes in the Soviet Union and Eastern Europe

The drastic changes in the Soviet Union and in Eastern Europe mainly include three interrelated meanings: first, from the aspects of form of union of countries and the a kind of federal state, the Soviet Union disintegrated—complete disintegration of the Soviet Union as a unified coalition of states, and the termination of Soviet Union and Eastern European Socialist camp; second, from the perspective of state power and ruling status of the Communist Party, communist parties in Eastern European countries lost their ruling status successively, socialism forces in these countries were liquidated in a short time, Soviet communist party lost power and this party was banned; third, from the perspective of socialist practice and its process of evolution, from the middle of 1980s to early 1990s, Soviet Union and Eastern European socialist countries had deviated from Marxism as the guiding ideology, doubted the socialist path, which affected many other fields including politics, economy, society, etc, and all these caused a fatal failure of socialist practice in these countries. In English literature, collapse (collapse, failure, and fall) is usually for the meaning of "drastic changes". The drastic changes in the Soviet Union and Eastern European countries have drawn widespread concern in the international academic community. Especially in the past 20-plus years. foreign Marxists have analyzed this tragedy of the century—the great historical tragedy in the world socialist movement.

1. Judgment on the nature of drastic changes of Soviet Union and Eastern European countries and the destiny of socialism

Most foreign Marxists view unprecedent radical changes in the political status in Soviet Union and Eastern Europe a significant frustration of the socialist development and setback in the international communist movement. They generally argue that the drastic changes in Soviet Union and Eastern Europe was just a failure of the Soviet mode of socialism, "people have abandoned this deformed, unqualified socialism which was mixed with many mistakes and falsifications. But this does not require us totally deny the socialist system, and cannot be a basis for terminating the cause of socialism." On the one hand, foreign Marxists have closely examined the socialist practice in the Soviet Union and Eastern European region; on the other hand, most of them seriously question the socialist development path followed by the Soviet Union and Eastern European countries. Certainly, the drastic change phenomenon was caused by several deviations in the theory and practice of the relevant communist parties.Of course, Western Marxists have offered different reasons and sources for the occurance of this phenomenon, which can give us thought provoking enlightment.

Habermas, one of the important representatives of Western Marxism, pointed out: "drawing the conclusion that socialism is bankrupt, just from drastic changes that occured in the Soviet Union and Eastern European countries is not correct.[12] American scholar Paul Paolucci also argued that drastic changes in the Soviet Union and Eastern European countries is not the failure of Marxism, because after Marx died, although Leninism-Stalinism had direct casual relation with Marxism, Leninism-Stalinism has revised Marx's thoughts, this revision has developed to its zenith in a totalitarian bureaucratic state. The creativity, humanitarianism and concern for freedom did not exist, a solid, rigid, formalized and a dogmatic system have replace them.[13]

George J Neimanis argued that, as a country which practiced Marxism, Soviet Union didn't not follow the principles of Marxism benignly. Marx's conception of "mode of production" is a comprehensive system including products and labor social production, and it ultimately determines all social relations in the society, politics and ideology. But the production modes adopted by Soviet Union—the central planning, collective farm, state ownership and production distribution centralized management—caused poverty for the majority and affluence for the few, i.e. the privileged class, then a bureaucratic system was formed. This system led to a failed economy, qualified talents could not be used and promoted, the criteria for selecting talented people were: they should be easygoing, obedient, and ideologically loyal... The growing cancer of this system has terminated the system itself.[14]

British scholar Monty Johnstone argued that equaling the statist (state) socialism of the Soviet mode to socialism is a total mistake; the two concepts have great difference. He pointed out: "the view that the failure of the Soviet mode has proved that the capitalist economy is superior to socialist economy from the foundation" at least ignores the following factors: first, due to several advantageous historical conditions, most developed capitalist powers have maintained these economic advantages to a great extent; second, before the so-called "collapse of communism", capitalist powers were forced to give in to some extent, and in that period their goal was to

12 See Lu Jun, "On the Thoughts of Habermas of the Issues of Socialism after the Drastic Changes in the Soviet Union and Eastern Europe", Journal of Marxism and Reality, 1996(3).

13 Paul Paolucci, "The Discursive Transformation of Marx's Communism into Soviet Diamat," Critical Sociology, 2004, Vol. 30, Issue 3, pp. 617, 667.

14 George J. Neimanis, The Collapse of the Soviet Empire: A View from Riga, London, Greenwood Publishing Group, Inc., 1997, pp. 4-5.

offset any political challenge from the East (socialism); third, the inherent system and environment of capitalism which exploits people; fourth, the radical fall of production and of living standards felt by the people pushed the Soviet Union to the path to capitalism In fact, socialism itself can't fail; in fact the policies adopted by the Soviet Union had deviated from true Socialism.[15]

British scholar Ralph Miliband pointed out that although capitalism maintains lasting vitality, although the "real socialisms" practiced in the Soviet Union and Eastern Europe and other counties, have several defects and shortcomings, socialism and Marxism still have vitality, because "socialism indeed represents the only reasonable and humane alternative to capitalism."[16]

French scholar Michael Löwy insisted: communism is not dead, bureaucracy which ruled in the real existing socialist societies (real socialism) has died. Although we don't have the basis for optimism in the short-term, socialist utopia still remains as a "possibility" for the future direction of social development.[17]

The famous British Marxist economist Desai has argued that "the collapse of the Soviet Union" and "the ongoing existence of capitalism for more than 80 years after the October Revolution" are the two issues that

contemporary Marxists need to solve and answer. Among all kinds of disciplines and theories, only political economy has the chance to explain these two issues, and only by return to original Marxism can we make a reasonable analysis. He has argued that the productive forces of capitalism has not yet been fully tapped. Therefore, a new and more advanced social form has not yet appeared in the womb of the old society, instead capitalism is rejuvenating its old production mode.[18]

Besides, the communist parties of different countries have studied the nature of drastic changes in Soviet Union and Eastern Europe. Australian Socialist Party has changed its name to Australian Communist Party; this signifies a new communist party in Australia after self- dissolve of the communist party by the end of 1990. New ACP's view on the practice of and drastic changes in the Soviet Union and Eastern Europe is: "socialist

15 Monty Johnstone, The Mistake of Giddens "Dead Socialism", published in: Journal Foreign Theoretical Trends, 2001(6).

16 Ralph Miliband, "Socialism in Question", Monthly Review, 42 (March 1991), pp. 16-26.

17 Michael Löwy, "Twelve Theses on the Crisis of 'Really Existing Socialism'", Monthly Review, Issue 43 (May, 1991), pp.33-40.

18 Meghnad Desai, "Rejuvenated Capitalism and No Longer Existing Socialism: A Classical Marxist Explanation," in Political Economy and the New Capitalism, Essays in Honor of Sam Aaronovitch, London: Routledge Press, 2000, pp. 4-12. Also see Zhu Zhongli, Modern Foreign Marxism Economic Theories Research, Beijing, People's Publishing House, 2004, p. 4.

countries in Soviet Union and Eastern Europe are first socialist society, they fought against unemployment and were successful, provided comprehensive social welfare, education and health facilities for all people; provided housing at a very low rent level; culture flourished; they provided generous aid to developing countries. At the same time, they faced many difficulties, and made many mistakes. Especially socialist democracy was not fully implemented, social life and economy was stagnant. However, the conclusion that 'socialism has already failed' cannot be made. The communist parties have extracted deep lessons from this experience. History is a process in which people fight for better life, freedom, safety and independence. We believe that those great targets can only be realized in a society based on socialist principles and when freed from the exploitation of huge private enterprises."[19]

The Communist Party of India (Marxist) is a typical representative party in the socialist movement of Asian developing countries. In January 1992, the Political Resolution passed on the 14th Congress this party pointed out: "the drastic changes in the Soviet Union and Eastern Europe has made world power pattern change to a direction which is advantageous for imperialism", but "this setback suffered by communism and socialism will not last long". The 15th Congress in 1995, 16th in the 1998, and 17th Congress in 2002 of this party all reaffirmed insisting on Marxism-Leninism and upholding Marxism as the guiding theory and ideology: "frustration suffered by socialism and communism will not last long, socialism still has bright future." While communist parties of various countries suffered severe negative impact of the drastic changes in the Soviet Union and Eastern Europe, they also drew experience and lessons from it, and began to independently explore socialist development path conforming to their national realities. For example, in March 1990, communist parties of Costa Rica, Salvador, Dominica and Argentina summoned a conference, and criticized themselves for the dogmatic practice of copying Soviet experience, emphasized that "clear and independent position" and we should independently formulate our own policies according to national characteristics, demands of times and historical traditions." In 1992 and 1993, over 20 communist parties held a conference on party building experiences in Quito, capital of Ecuador, analyzed problems emerging from the reality due to blindly following the CPSU's practice, many speakers emphasized independent ideological building and independent strategies towards socialism.[20]

19 Yang Chengguo, Liu Chunyuan, The Australian Communist Party's propositions and attitude towards the major political parties of Australia, published in Foreign Theoretical Trends, 2006(3).

20 Miao Guangxin, The Characteristics of the Socialist Movement in the Developing Capitalist Countries after the Upheaval of the Soviet Union, published in the Journal of Xinyang Teachers College (Philosophy and Social Sciences Edition), 2004(1).

2. Analysis and research on the reasons and lessons of drastic changes in Soviet Union and Eastern Europe

Foreign Marxist scholars generally think that reasons for drastic changes in Soviet Union and Eastern Europe is not based on a single reason, but a complex system of reasons, a result of combined effect and evolution of many factors and contradictions accumulated in a long term. But many scholars agree that the reason for Soviet Union's evolution to capitalist path is the result of implementing "Stalin mode", and that Soviet Union's highly-centralized political and economic system choked vigor and vitality of socialism, which has hindered the tapping of socialism's superiorities.

American scholar Leslie Holmes has argued that the established political system and ideology in the Soviet Union's early years was basically suitable for its transformation from an agricultural country to an industrial country. But this system and ideology could only realize basic modernization and wasn't able promote the country to the post-modern stage of development. In the period from 1960s to the last days of the Soviet Union, during its transformation from a modern country to the post-modern country (marked by the rise of the third wave of technological revolution), it couldn't make timely changes in its original political system and ideology to accord with the third wave of technological revolution, or it couldn't make substantive reforms, it became increasingly rigid and conservative, many social problems grew and could not be fundementally solved, thus these factors caused Soviet Union's disintegration.[21]

Samarskaya, senior researcher of The Philosophy Institute of Russian Academy of Sciences, argued that, not only realistic socialism, but also social democracy has fallen behind the times. She pointed out: "those countries which have achieved some ideals of socialism have established an official ideology which became rigid and couldn't understand the new changes and the new era. Both, Marxism-Leninism and western social democracy were in fact suitable forms of socialism to the age of industrialization. The emergence of the post-industry age challenged both the industrial capitalism and the industrial socialism. Post-industry is different from the past industrial age, it does not encourage monopoly and opposes centralization in economy and politics. Therefore, tyrannical socialism has inevitably disappeared; thus socialism with more liberal characteristics will replace it.[22]

Ligajov, Likiyanov, and other communist leaders from Russia have all argued that the socialist system and economic management system of the

21 Pan Guanghui, A Summary of the Study on the Causes of the Disintegration of the Soviet Union by Western Academia, published in Russian Studies, 2003(2).

22 Luo Yunli, New Views on the Failure of Soviet Union's Socialism in Foreign Countries, published in International Forum, 1999(6).

Soviet Union were incomplete; but the disintegration of the Soviet Union was not inevitable.Nina Andreyeva as one of the famous leader of All-Union Communist Party of Bolsheviks has strictly denied the problems of Soviet socialist mode. This party argued: "although the CPSU made many mistakes in Stalin era, its basic path was correct. The root cause of the disintegration of Soviet Union should be traced to the deformation of Soviet socialism after Khrushchev ascended to power in 1950s, which evolved till Gorbachev's betrayal of Leninism, October Revolution, and communist movement in 1980s.[23]

Russian scholar Vladimir Kollontai has argued that Soviet mode on one hand has brought some merits to Russia's development, e.g. made Russia a major industrial country in the world, gave residents good education, etc. On the other hand, these progresses were realized under a totalitarian rule. "For these progresses, Russia paid great price in the spheres of economy, society, humanitarianism and spirit. The price was not only shown in traumas, disabilities and endless pains of the millions, but also left many deep injuries in the society. Main reasons for the radical change can be summarized as follows: first, western publicity praising attractive aspects of the western lifestyle has triggered ideological and psychological changes in the East with deep influences, the people's past opinion that the Soviet system cannot be reformed has faded. The two pillars of the Soviet system—the party and state machine became the focus of public critique. Many former anti-socialist underground activities promptly became legal and became the most important factor which determined the future path of reforms. Second, under the new conditions of reform, pluralism and decentralization were allowed, many political organizations which existed in name only in the past, gained a free hand, began to operate unchecked and grew vigorously. As a result, the interrelationship, division of function and roles in ordinary work of the new state organs were paralyzed.This all destroyed the ideological and political monopoly of the CPSU. Third, a new entrepreneur class emerged in the economy. They assumed the mission of evading the mechanisms of the planned economy, hinder the control of central administrative organs, and became strong enough to design the economic structure and adjustment system with new characteristics. Fourthly, the growth of nationalism-separatism. CPSU leaders didn't notice this issue at the beginning, and solutions they brought later to this issue were too late."[24]

Famous dependency theorist A. Gunder Frank has argued that main determining factor for the drastic changes in the Soviet Union and Eastern Europe

23 Li Xinggeng et al., Lessons: A Review of Russian Views on the Upheaval in Soviet Union, Beijing, People's Publishing House, 2003, p. 83.

24 Wang Changjiang, Chinese and Foreign Scholars' Latest Analysis of the Causes of the Failure of the CPSU, published in Contemporary World and Socialism, 2001(2).

was real socialism's failure in the economic race with Western countries. Especially in the recent technological revolution, Soviet centralized economy couldn't catch up with the developed western capitalism. If the economic development of the Soviet Union and Eastern Europe would succeed, people's dissatisfaction towards the society, unrealistic demand for democracy and nationalist-seperatist movement would not appear.[25]

After the drastic changes in Soviet Union and Eastern Europe, Zyuganov, chairman of the Communist Party of Russian Federation asserted this view many times: fundamental reason of Soviet Union's disintegration was the collapse of the CPSU. "Disintegration of Soviet Union began with the destruction of the CPSU. When the party was destructed, the disintegration became inevitable." Zyuganov argued that there were twelve historical lessons in Soviet Union's disintegration, among them, three monopolies established by the CPSU were the main ones: monopolies of ownership, power and truth.[26]

Kosolabov pointed out: "CPSU experienced a degeneration process, and this process began with the "secret report" presented by Khrushchev in the 20th Congres of CPSU in 1956. Criticism on Stalin stroked the whole CPSU and shook all aspects of the theories and practices of Lenin and scientific communism. From then on, the word "Stalinism" became weapon of dissidents and counterrevolutionaries against the Soviet socialism."[27] He added: "since 1950s and 1960s, an utopian ideology of "universal values for all humanity" prevailed, which blurred the border between labor rule and capital rule, even anti-communist subversive activities were nurtured with this ideology. Thus,CPSU lost its firmness in implementing principles of labor, workers' supervision of production and distribution. Consequently social stratification and the social division between masses and the ruling elite became extreme, as the last step, rightist attack between 1991 to 1993 was its result."[28]

Alexander Zinoviev, famous Soviet philosopher who was once a Soviet dissident wrote: "the main reason lies in the whole CPSU, both leaders and common party members are responsible for the setback, since they allowed the entry of heretic elements and dissidents into the ranks of the CPSU.[29] Zinoviev also discussed gradual loss of leadership by the CPSU to the reform

25 Xu Chongwen, Several Hot Issues in the Study of Foreign Socialism after the Soviet Union's Upheaval, published in Marxism and Reality, 1997(2).

26 Yan Shuhan: The Development and Practice of Scientific Socialism in the 20th Century, published in Studies on Socialism With Chinese Characteristics, 2006(1).

27 Richard Kosolapov: Thawing Makes the Road Muddy – Viewing the 20th Congress of Communist Party of the Soviet Union 40 years after the Soviet Union, published in Dialogue, 1996(4).

28 Wang Changjiang, Chinese and Foreign Scholars' Latest Analysis of the Causes of the Failure of the CPSU, published in Contemporary World and Socialism, 2001(2).

29 Yan Shuhan, The Development and Practice of Scientific Socialism in the 20th Century, published in Studies on Socialism with Chinese Characteristics, 2006(1).

process and the national seperatism issues. He argued that Gorbachev were increasingly close to western concept in political system reforms after he ascended to the leadership post of the CPSU. At the same time, other leaders of the CPSU were by-passed in the decision-making except for Gorbachev and his relatives. In fact, with Gorbachev's reforms, CPSU lost the leadership and control of the state.[30]

Wadih Halabi from USA pointed out: the fundamental mistake made by CPSU was, they didn't grasp the fact that Soviet Union was just part of the integrated world economic system. Soviet leaders underestimated the huge class interest motive of capitalism which aimed to overturn the Soviet Union and all countries established by the socialist revolution. CPSU leaders created an illusion of eternal "peaceful coexistence". Also, CPSU lost its confidence to the Soviet working class and international working class, underestimated their power, and didn't respect the material interests the working classes.[31]

In his book *Communism and Its Collapse* published in 2011, British scholar Stephen White argued that explanations on the disintegration of Soviet Union from the aspect of ideology, national issues and economic problems cannot grasp the true causes of this historic event. CPSU's rule collapsed by itself and was not overturned by others. To a great extent, this was caused by the inner power struggle, especially Yeltsin and Gorbachev's short-sided power strategies. And after the disintegration, in many regions, at least in the Moscow region, over two thirds of the administrative officials were still the cadres of the CPSU.[32]

Some Marxists abroad have argued that the disintegration of the Soviet Union was related to the guiding ideology of the CPSU and the weakening of ideology. Robinson wrote: "the history of the Soviet Union has manifested in many ways that it could cope with various crises. Before the Gorbachev reforms, the ideology of the CPSU had already weakened. The ideological reforms by each Party leader was a kind of depreciation and a kind of revision of the original ideology of the party, but since there didn't occur a big heated active, the ideological differences didn't become so obvious. One of Gorbachev's mistakes was that he couldn't not adequately maintain the stability of ideology, and therefore could not establish stable and orderly social conditions like his predecessors.[33]

30 Zinoviev, "The Soviet Union 1985-1990: After Communist Rule the Deluge", Soviet Studies, 1991(3), Vol.43, p. 429.

31 Wadih Halabi, Some Views on the Disintegration of the Soviet Union, published in Foreign Theoretical Trends, Issue 2003(1).

32 Stephen White, Communism and its Collapse, London: Routledge Press, 2001.

33 Neil Robinson, Ideology and the Collapse of the Soviet System: A Critical History of Soviet Ideological Discourse, Brookfield: Edward Elgar Publishing Company,1995, p.189.

British scholar John Gooding began his analysis from changes in Lenin and Leninism's role in the Soviet politics between 1985 to 1991, argued why Marxism-Leninism were betrayed in the Soviet Union in these 6 years. He pointed out: when Gorbachev initiated the reform after taking office, in a disguised manner, he used the name and prestige of Lenin, so that working class in the Soviet Union generally felt that upholding Lenin's heritage required the supporting of the reforms not oppose them. But during the reforms, radical reformers just firmly seized the command of Lenin's party; they abandoned the beliefs, conduct and practices of Leninism, and finally openly went against Lenin, consequently they abandoned Leninism.[34]

After studying the rise and fall of Soviet Marxism-Leninism, Alfred Evans has argued: in the past, each General Secretary of the CPSU would express his unique views after taking office and attempted to explain the stage of social development of the Soviet society at that time as a step in the realization of Marx's communism. The policy adopted was to turn the highest ideological goal into reality. For them, the period between 1930-1980 was considered to be the primary stage of socialism and next the society would gradually move toward the advanced stage of socialism, that is, the communist society as explained by Marx's theory. Therefore, when Gorbachev declared that communism could no longer be realized, society lost its original spiritual support, and the Marxist-Leninist ideology was abandoned.[35]

Russian historian Roy Medvedev pointed out: the prelude to the rapid disintegration of the state system of the Soviet Union was the collapse of the ideological theories of the CPSU and the CPSU itself. After these occured, Soviet Union's existence as a new social system with its own ideological system became impossible. Dogmatic understanding of the Marxism-Leninist theories and ideology did not only hamper the healthy theoretical and ideological building in the Soviet Union, but also fostered bad habits in the ruling party and state elite class. In 1980s, many of the CPSU leaders didn't support socialism, they wanted to seize selfish opportunities from the collapse of CPSU and collapse of its ideology and theories. Dogmatic doctriniarism and corruption of the CPSU cadres made this party lose ability to resist threats. By deleting the original legal restrictions and control on news media and publications triggered a wave of rampant criticism, and this wave first attacked the established ideology of the CPSU. But CPSU wasn't prepared for it and didn't have ability to counter this attack and take responsibility. People began to doubt the legitimacy of the state system.

34 John Gooding, "Lenin in Soviet politics,1985-1991", Soviet Studies, 1992(3), Vol. 44, pp. 403-423.

35 Alfred. B. Evans, Soviet Marxism-Leninism: The Decline of an Ideology, London: Greenwood Publishing Group, Inc.1993, p. 3.

CPSU had huge resources and a bright heritage but lost the required support and authority among the masses.[36]

Also, many foreign Marxists have argued that the failure of Gorbachev reforms caused the disintegration of CPSU and even the Soviet Union. Chris Miller from the University of Washington argued that, the main reason for the disintegration was Gorbachev's reform design which by-passed the CPSU. David Kotz has argued that the disintegration of Soviet Union originated from three policy mistakes of the CPSU leaders: one, openness in ideology; two, introduction of the western market economy; three, political democratization. Democracy and openness promoted by Gorbachev paralyzed the original ideology, and greatly confused people's minds. British economist Catherine Biss argued that, democratization itself can hardly form a general consensus to foster people's support to reform, in fact it was the rampant ideological pluralism which challenged the authority and legitimacy of the Soviet state and the CPSU.

US scholars Richard Layard and John Parker have argued that as the supreme leader of the Soviet Union who led the party and politics, Gorbachev played a key role in the disintegration, since he made two critical decisions after assuming the leadership of the CPSU: first, "if the Eastern Europe wants to abandon communism, Soviet Union will not intervene"; second, "both political and economic reforms should be implemented simultaneously… These critical decisions have determined most of the events which occured from then on".[37]

Some scholars have argued that, Gorbachev has buried the cause of socialism unconsciously. Valery Boldin, the former Secretary of Secretariat of the CPSU, once director in Gorbachev's presidential office, said: evolution of Soviet Union to capitalist path was caused by Gorbachev's "abandoning" and "betrayal of the CPSU". "But there is no doubt that after Gorbachev asumed the leading post, his reform thoughts, and desire to change the society and economy were progressive; the problem was that they were unrealistic and lacked solid theoretical and organizational basis", "he ignored traditions and habits of people and attempted to change people's psychology", "jumped out of a system formed in decades with just one trial. As a result, the country couldn't bear various new theories and programs, seams began to appear, and the state finally disintegrated completely."[38]

36 Roy Medvedev, The Last Year of the Soviet Union, Beijing, Social Sciences Academic Press, 2005, pp. 284-285.

37 Richard Layard & John Parker: The Coming Russian Boom, Beijing, Central Compilation & Translation Press, 1997, p. 56.

38 Valery I. Boldin, A Decade Shocking the World, Beijing, Kunlun Press,1998, pp.287-296.

On the contrary, some people have argued that Gorbachev has consciously buried socialist Soviet Union. Ryzhkov, chairman of the Soviet Council of Ministers, and B.A. Kryuchkov, chairman of the KGB, have such opinion. Ryzhkov pointed out that: Gorbachev's reform history is "a history of betray", Soviet Union's evolution to capitalist path is "totally conscious action aimed at changing the social system" which was led by Gorbachev and Yakovlev. Kryuchkov wrote: "Gorbachev consciously guided people into a wrong path. Things which occured in the Soviet Union didn't have objective necessity. The result was caused by subjective factors, i.e. some people's behaviors caused it. The culprits are Gorbachev and Yakovlev in this destructive process."[39] "They tried to destroy the union, they had true plans to overturn current constitution and Soviet Union's national system....which were implemented openly and firmly just from the beginning."[40] Although these two differeent opinions have disagreements in whether Gorbachev "consciously" buried the socialism cause, they believe that Gorbachev was the "main reason" for Soviet Union's change and they both over-emphasize Gorbachev's role as an individual. We think although Gorbachev cannot be freed from responsibility, the key reason for the change of the Soviet Union was not his role as an individual.

The famous Russian historian Medvedev has argued that Gorbachev was not cautious enough, his thinking was confused, thus he had followed a messy politics. He overestimated his support and power and underestimated the risks and the possible hostile threats. He rarely made rational calculation on how to find ways to overcome the difficulties and risks. He did not rely on the support of the people, he hastily started to deal with and change many things, but overlooked to evaluate and analyze the complex situation determined by numerous factors and situations, consequently this tragedy was inevitable. Throughout the whole process, Gorbachev made many mistakes. Thus, he played a major role in the disintegration of the Soviet Union, but his role should not be exaggerated, as some people have been advocating.[41]

Some researchers have argued that the main reason behind Soviet Union's evolution to the capitalist path was the "peaceful evolution" strategy of the Western forces. German scholar P. Schneider said: Soviet Union disintegration was caused by the US "intervention", "the United States always puts his hands into all corners of the world, like an elephant in a department store and causes many troubles around the world." Baker, former secretary

39 Vladimir A. Kryuchkov, Personal Files, The Eastern Publishing House, Beijing, 2000, p. 232.

40 Ibid., p. 262.

41 See Roy Medvedev, "Why did the Soviet Union disintegrate?", in: Russian Central Asian Studies in Eastern Europe, 2004(1).

of state council of the USA said: “our containment policy has worked well” which promoted the evolution of Soviet Union.[42]

Zinoviev analyzed many factors causing the disintegration and specifically emphasized the western intervention factor among them: the west with its power advantages fostered and established a “fifth column” in the Soviet Union. Zinoviev reminds us the prologue of the Chinese text, i.e. “The Tragedy of Russian Communism” which said: Western powers are implementing carefully designed social and political strategies against China, because these strategies had made “so” great achievements. If China's social stability and order is unfortunately destroyed (this is just what the western conquerors are dreaming), everything which happened in the Soviet Union may happen in China. China should draw lessons from those painful lessons.[43]

Polish economist Grzegorz. W. Kolodko pointed out:“although ‘Washington Consensus’ doesn’t have any direct connection with the countries in transition, however this ‘consensus’ has greatly influenced the thinking, attitudes and acts of socialist Eastern Europe, former Soviet Union and the socialist countries of Asia”. In Kolodko’s eyes, “Washington Consensus” did never offer standard definitions and solutions; different practitioners always quote parts from its text and interprete it by themselves.[44]

Perry Anderson argued that, in the era of globalization, due to accelerated informationization and person-to-person exchanges, Neo-liberalism could easily get access into the Soviet Union and Eastern Europe by all means, and deeply influences some state leaders. Former Polish vice prime minister Leszek Balcerowicz, Russian Minister of Treasure Geidar (then acting prime minister) and Vaclav Klaus from Czechoslavakia, prime minister (later President) were faithful disciples of Friedman and Hayek. American economist J. D. Sachs frequently visited these leading officers and politicians in Prague, Budapest and Warsaw, promoted his “shock therapy” policy to the political upstarts of the Eastern European countries.[45]

David Kotz has argued that the US and the West really played a great role in the disintegration of the Soviet Union. But their effect upon politics and economy was not so strong. Especially the liberal ideology had effectively penetrated into the minds of intellectuals and party cadres. Immanuel

42 Liu Yunxian, An Analysis of the Causes of the Evolvement of the Soviet Union Concluded by Chinese and foreign scholars in the past decade, in: Journal of Henan University (Social Science), 2002(1).

43 Alexander Zinoviev, The Demise of Russian Communism, 2nd ed., Beijing, Xinhua Publishing House, 2004, p. 96.

44 Grzegorz W. Kolodko, From Shock to Therapy, Shanghai, Shanghai Far East Publishers, 2000, pp. 142-147.

45 He Wei, Understanding of Some Problems in the Process of Economic Transition in the Former Soviet Union, published in Russian, Central Asian & East European Studies, 2004(5).

Wallerstein has argued that President Carter's human rights policy was an important political factor, it made some effect in promoting the transformation of socialist countries, towards "democratization and equity".[46]

3. On the other questions in respect to drastic changes in Soviet Union and Eastern Europe

Most of researchers have argued that there were no bloody fights during the drastic changes in the Soviet Union and Eastern Europe, in politics it was a relatively peaceful transition. Except Romania, reforms in Central and Eastern Europe was a "velvet mild" revolution, it was different from any revolution since the French revolution, so it was mainly a "non-violent process".[47]

In the consequent economic reforms after the drastic changes, only few countries like Hungary adopted a gradual reform. Some scholars did comparative studies on different paths followed in the reforms. For example, Peter Murray has advocated gradual reform, criticized the prevalent "Neo-classical Walrassian" models in the economic reform discussions, and argued that dual economic structure should be maintained in the transition economies, i.e., the dual structure in which state-owned and private sectors would co-exist, contradiction between the influence of the past and new requirements of the transition should be benignly balanced.[48] (See Can Neoclassical Economics Underpin the Reform of Centrally Planned Economies?)

Yuri Polyakov, one of the Russia's most famous historians, said: "The disintegration of the Soviet Union was not a partial, temporary crisis for Russia, but a profound geopolitical crisis. It has interrupted the lifeline and potential of national development of Russia for centuries" … "the prospect of national recovery will not appear in the foreseeable future".[49]

Vladimir analyzed economic reforms and privatization process in the Russian Federation after the drastic changes in Soviet Union and Eastern Europe at the turn of century, he used macroeconomic indicators to judge development status of Russia in 1990s. He argued that economic crisis was still unsolved, privatization didn't bring enhancement in the production capacity thus the economic crisis was "the second collapse" after the "collapse of the Soviet Union".

---

46 Immanuel Wallerstein, New Anti-system Movements and Their Strategy, published in the Journal of Foreign Theoretical Trends, 2003(4).

47 Xue Jundu, Central and Eastern Europe in Transition, Beijing, People's Publishing House, 2002, p. 42.

48 Ibid., p. 115.

49 Quoted from Wu Enyuan, "A Review of Some Popular Views on the Lessons of the Disintegration of the Soviet Union", in: Marxist Studies, 2005(3).

After analyzing the situation in Kyrgyzstan, Kubat Kanimetov pointed out: regime crisis was caused by the loss of state power, regime crisis has caused social instability but not financial instability in our country, because the stability of the financial system in Kyrgyzstan was mainly supported by external forces which were interested in such stability. But in ordinary life, frustrations, deviations, changes obviously increased, since the former social adjustment system was eliminated, bureaucratic custody of incompetent high-level state officers could not completely replace these systems.[50] Ivan T. Berend, famous scholar of the Hungarian Academy of Sciences wrote a paper titled: Economy of Eastern Europe" the best situation in 2000 after economic recovery could only reach the economic level of 1988".[51]

In the studies which compared the transitions in China and the Soviet Union', the US scholar Christopher compared system reforms of China and Soviet Union in the period before Soviet Union's reverse evolution. He pointed out: in early 1980s, Soviet Union disapproved China which began economic reforms earlier; after the middle of 1980s, Soviet intellectuals gradually saw the fruits of China's reform, and regarded China as the "laboratory" of their own reform, tried to start reforms as soon as possible. The ideological trend of liberalization has influenced China and Soviet Union deeply in the late1980s. But after the political turmoil in 1989, China took cautious measures, while Soviet Union thought more democratization was needed. Their future different paths were caused by this major difference. American scholar Christopher Marsh, wrote an article titled "Learning from Your Comrade's Mistakes: The Impact of the Soviet Past on China's Future". He argued that China's current identity as the heir of the communist ideal three decades after the Soviet Union disintegration lies in their careful understanding of the "will" behind this disintegration. An important reason for China's success in avoiding system collapse was that Chinese leaders drew lessons from this disintegration, China has properly adjusted its policies, sought a feasible development path, and took proper measures to consolidate its political power.

(Zhang Xu, Professor of Institute of Marxism, Renmin University of China)

50 Kanimetov, The Paradox of the Theory and Practice of Social Transformation after the Disintegration of the Soviet Union and Its Development Prospects–A Case Study of the Kyrgyz Republic, published in International Forum, 2006(1).

51 Kan Sijing and Liu Bangyi, A Historical Reflection on the Evolution of Eastern Europe, The Contemporary World Press, Beijing, 1997, p. 15.

Research by Foreign Marxists on the Development Mode of Socialism

Foreign Marxists made valuable research on socialism development mode which they think "may possibly" replace capitalism. In Foreign Marxism at the first stage, "humanistic Marxism" prevailed, later since the end of WWII to 1960s, "Structuralism Marxism", "New Positivist Marxism" appeared, which broke the dominance of "humanistic Marxism";since 1970s, foreign Marxists have shifted their theoretical focus from philosophy to actual problems, reviewed and applied some theories of Marxism, tried to solve practical problems in the capitalist societies including the socialist countries, and proposed a development path which socialism should follow from certain aspects, consequently many new schools has appeared, such as analytical Marxism, Ecological Marxism, Deconstructivist Marxism, cultural Marxism, and feminist Marxism, etc; in 1990s, drastic changes in Soviet Union and Eastern Europe caused the collapse of the "real socialism" mode of the Soviet Union, consequently various schools of socialism have put more emphasis on the research of new modes of socialism. To solve actual problems, they have attempted to re-explained Marxism, re-interpreted socialism, and drew a new development blue print for socialism.

In 1993, the French journal Modern Marx (Vol.14) published some views of US, British, French scholars on the new modes of socialism with "socialism" as the general title. These scholars asserted: "history missions us to build a new mode of socialism, at present, ideological materials and enough experience for building this new mode is at our hand, "new mode of socialism will be a certain product of reflecting on the collapse of the Soviet 'communist' system, decline of social democracy, and the crisis of new liberal capitalism, the characteristics of the new mode should display its advantages in comparison to capitalism."[52] These scholars have focused on the nature of social change which may possibly replace capitalism, they have proposed new ideas on the basic principles of socialism, i.e. which can achieve freedom and equality in the economic and political life, however some of their propositions seem detached from reality, but some seem quite realistic.Such new mode of socialism should realize effective, harmonious development of material and cultural conditions for social life. Our article below will evaluate and introduce Market Socialism and Ecological Socialism which can render us new and valuable thoughts for our current efforts to construct a new mode of socialism.

52 Li Qiqing, Western scholars on the "New Mode of Socialism", in: Foreign Socialism Research, 1994(1).

1. Research on market socialism

Market Socialism is an academic school of socialism formed by some scholars and statesmen who study Marxism and socialism.They have studied the problems of socialist and capitalist economic practices in respect to market economy and propose to combine market and socialism. Th theoretical origins of this school can be traced back to some socialism schools in Europe that appeared in late 19th century. From then on, it has experienced three development phases and assumed three representative theoretical forms.

From 1930s to 1950s, it was the emergence and gradual formation phase of market socialism. In those days the first socialist country Soviet Union had a successful economic construction practice and great achievements were realized, which caught the attention of the West. In 1920s and 1930s, an argument on the feasibility socialist plans and planned resource allocation occured in the West. Oskar Lange, a Polish associate scholar in America, proposed a decentralized model of socialist economy in his argument with Mises and Hayek, and for the first time theoretically introduced the role of market mechanism for the socialist economy. Between 1936- 1937, Oskar Lange published the "Socialist Economic Theory", and proposed the "competitive socialist" economic mode, also known as the "Lange model". In this debate another Russian-British scholar Abba Lerner had a similar view with Lange; their views are known as the "Lange-Lerner theorem." Although Oskar Lange or Lerner didn't clearly use the concept of "Market Socialism", but "Lange Mode" and "Lange-Lerner theorem" is generally known as the initial theory of market socialism, major form of early market socialism theory. But, since Soviet Union's centralized planned economy system seemed successful generally, the "Lange Mode" mode didn't catch the attention of the socialist countries; socialist countries even gave a critical attitude. After the mid-1950s, with the development of economic practice in Eastern Europe, demerits of following Soviet planned economy model began to appear, "Lange-Lerner theorem" began to be taken seriously. Yugoslavia was the first socialist country which explored combining socialism with the market economy, Market socialism theorists represented by Edward Kardelj, Bronko Horvat and experts from Poland, Czechoslovakia, Hungary and Romania also explored this model in various degrees, more or less. Overall, the exploration by the Eastern European countries were unsuccessful, due to the influence of various factors. But this was just the preliminary practice phase of market socialism.These explorations before the drastic changes in Eastern Europe, can be seen as the second theoretical form of market socialism, which came after the "Lange model".

The appearance of "Lange model" also aroused the interest of US and British scholars. Evaluating the economic reform explorations in the Eastern European socialist countries, US scholars John Galbraith, Benjamin Ward, Abram Bergson wrote several books to introduce the experience and the theories proposed in these countries. British scholars' studies on the relation between market and socialism has a long history and has reached to a remarkable level in 1980s. In 1983, Labor Party lost its governing position in the general elections. Some famous scholars who sympathized with and supported Labor Party thought that a breakthrough in socialism theories was necessary for a Labor victory. Then guided by the "socialist philosophy" research group organized by these scholars, British theoretical circle held a heated debate on market socialism. David Miller, from the Oxford University clearly proposed the concept and issue of "market socialism". Many related books appeared: co-edited by Prof. Saul Estrin from the London School of Economics and Julian Le Grande, the book "Market Socialism" was published as the most representative work in these days, and David Miller, P. Holmes, Abel Aganbegyan, and David Winter participated in the writing of this book. It systematically and briefly explained theories and questions of market socialism and was a programmatic document for the Labor Party's market socialism theories.

After the drastic changes in the Soviet Union and Eastern Europe, scholars from US, France and Russia began a new wave of research on Market Socialism, thus a new generation of market socialism researchers appeared, and they proposed some new theories, such as "market socialism of economic democracy" by the US scholar David Schweickart, "market socialism of fair distribution" by John Roemer, "open market socialism" by the French communist Paul Boccara, and "elemental structure socialism" of Jacques Bidet, etc. These new theories which appeared since 1990s can be called as the third theoretical form of market socialism—the contemporary western market socialism theory.

Market should be combined with which kind of socialism? Market socialists have several differences on this issue. Generally, there are two trends: one argues that socialism should be based on public ownership of means of production. As an economic operation mechanism or an economic regulation mechanism, market is bound to be combined with a certain economic system. Early theories of market socialism and Eastern Europe market socialism generally agreed on the combination of market economy with the public ownership economy. O. Lange and Abba Lerner have argued that socialism can have many economic modes: "on the basis of public ownership, we can simulate competitive market under capitalist private ownership economy to reasonably allocate resources; market mechanism under socialist public ownership can be more effective than under capitalist private ownership in respect to production efficiency (economic equilibrium, especially in distribution fairness, welfare optimization); state-owned enterprises can play or simulate capitalist roles in the free market, then socialist economy can be adjusted by market". Some market socialism theories formed during the economic reforms of Eastern European socialist countries, also agreed with those views of O. Lange and Abba Lerner (Lange–Lerner theorem). The two views only had differences on the connotation of public ownership.

For example, Edward Kardelj, the party and state leader of former Yugoslavia, founder of socialist autonomy theory, argued that the nature of public ownership is the "individual ownership" of laborers themselves, and public ownership is a relation among laborers. He disagreed with the view that state ownership is equal to public ownership, "state ownership can't be seen as a high-level form of public ownership". Famous economist Paul Boccara—who developed the idea of state monopoly capitalism—and a former central committee member of the French communist party, has argued:"the ambiguous view that socialist ownership is state ownership or ownership of the whole people ahould be broken; it is clear fact that socialist ownership is mixed economy of many ownership forms." He argued: "public ownership is not just state-owned; it could be urban, regional, collective or cooperative ownership economy.

The New Palgrave: A Dictionary of Economics published in the US in 1987 gave such a definition for the market Socialism:"Market Socialism is a theoretical concept (or mode) of economic system. Under this economic system, means of production are owned by public or collective groups, resources allocation obeys the laws of the market (including commodity, labor and capital markets). Currently, in various socialist economies, this term is widely used to summarize the two economic systems: first, like the system formed in Yugoslavia after 1965 which is close to above definition in the strict sense.The second aspect mentioned in the New Palgrave was: adjusted and regulated markets, like in the "new economy mechanism" reform explored in Hungary after the upheaval of 1968,which used financial adjustments and various stimula for the aim of streamlining the implementation of the central plans."[53] The New Palgrave obviously clarifies the ownership properties of the market socialism, i.e., mainly public ownership of production means or collective (group) ownership of production means. There is another trend which avoids connection between market and public ownership.The socialism of this trend is not based on material or physical public ownership, but pursues a socialism which can achieve or realize those values like democracy, fairness, equality, etc. For

53 The New Palgrave Dictionary of Economics and the Law, Volume 3, Beijing, Economic Science Press,1994, p. 363.

example, Saul Estrin and Julian Le Grande from the Fabian community—a think-tank of Labor Party, have argued that "using market to realize socialist value goals is our market socialism concept." "Socialist goals" include eliminating exploitation, realizing substantial equality on income, welfare, status and equal rights among people, satisfying basic material and spiritual/intellectual demands of the people, etc. Although "eliminating exploitation" is proposed above, it is actually an empty word. Because even Labor Party can seize power, abolishing private ownership will be impossible in Britain. Although Labor Party theorist Saul Estrin praised the new type of cooperatives in Great Britain, and called them "socialist islands", and advocated the possibility of realizing socialism could be increased by cooperatives, this is just his own subjective wish. The US scholar John Roemer's "market socialism of fair distribution"can also be categorized in the same trend. Roemer argued that reasons for the failure of the economics in the traditional socialist countries economy have following three connected aspects: public ownership of enterprises; allocation of resources by central administrative plans instead of allocation by market; thirdly, political dictation or intervention. Socialist economic mode has three problems in realizing its goals: relation between leaders and laborers in the factories and collective farms; relation between planners and its practioners; relation between people and planners. Therefore, Roemer advocated new socialism theory: "my definition of socialism cannot tolerate the supervision of state upon enterprise management and cannot allow enterprises' profits to be squeezed by the state. I think socialism should have a prerequisite: political democracy, but I put more emphasis on economic democracy requirements." Specifically, socialism should be built on egalitarianism, but not public ownership. A considerable part of socialist movements may create another type of ownership, i.e. the enterprises owned by labor unions and people working in it; government can use loan interest rates to intervene the economy, thus can guide the level and the type of investment. People can use democratic politics to "collectively control" the use of social provident funds to some extent; profits of public and private companies can be equally distributed among adult citizens in the form of "social dividends" after taxation. Citizens can three incomes: salaries, interest from saving deposits and dividends from profits, thus income distribution will be fairer than the capitalist society. This view of socialism has great similarity with the democratic socialism of Social Democratic Party of Sweden.

Another aspect often discusses by the market socialists is the relation of market and planning. Market socialists generally believe that using market and perfecting the market economy is necessary and inevitable under socialism. The market should play a fundamental role in resource allocation. This is because market economy can make up for the flaws of the planned economy. For example, market can promote freedom as the British scholar David Miller argued:socialist market economy can guarantee freedom of private consumption choices, job selection, and freedom of speech. Market is a fair and "natural" stimulation system. British scholar Saul Estrin and David Winter have argued that market can provide simple signals compared to the complex and detailed guidance of the central planning and thus market can enable people act in a way praised by the society. Market can scatter economic decision rights and powers, thus working people will not be dominated by a manager who is difficult to be dealt with; and people will not be disturbed by disobedient workers. If people don't like the service of a certain supplier, they can find suppliers which can provide the service with better quality. Market allocation is not always unfair. Under the same conditions, market will better reward those people who work hard and are thrifty. This result is in accord with fairness or equity ideas of socialism. Certainly, market has demerits like being spontaneous or blind, when regulating the economy. If the nature of capital which has the nature of pursuing maximum profits cannot be properly controlled, then excessive use of natural resources and environmental problems will be easy to occur and the losses will be paid by the society and masses; monopoly may hinder the fairness of the market; the income distribution sphere is also prone to social polarization and full employment cannot be realized, etc.

Existence of such problems tells us why market socialism cannot completely give up planning. Yugoslavian noted economist and politician Bronko Horvat argued that two points should be obeyed in dealing with the relation of planning with market: first, market should be seen as the indicator for planning and the barometer of economic life; second, planning is the premise for the effective operation of the market. Neither planning nor market are goals they are only means, they are just means which can be used to increase social economic welfare. On this base, Horvat proposed "the theory of combining five economic mechanisms" and argued that only the coordinated combination of five economic mechanisms we can increase social and economic welfare. They are: firstly, "free and loose" market, "invisible hand"; secondly, "visible hand", i.e., regulation of economic activities by central administrative planning; thirdly, macro economic policies—"indirect hand", this is the method for economic regulaton chosen by the West after the Great Depression of 1930s, which is in between the first two mechanisms; fourthly, information sharing and information transmission among economic decision makers which can give them information about the economic situation, decrease future uncertainties; fifthly, non-market, non-state coordination, i.e. agreement, negotiation, arbitration, in the society.

How can the planned socialist economy be transformed to market economy in real conditions? Polish scholar Leon Koziminski proposed following transition modes: first, political phase: reforming the political structures and institutions, solve racial conflicts, and eliminate the roots of dissatisfaction and turmoil; second, establish an early market phase: release the prices, freely exchange foreign currencies in the country, remove legal barriers for those who tend to become private entrepreneurs, implement "small privatization"; third, the phase of restraining inflation: tightening monetary policies, enforce budget discipline by controlling subsidies and other forms of government expenditures; fourth, the phase of establishing the market system: commercialize the state-owned enterprises, design and develop a plan for privatization, identify the proper functions of the government in the transition period and restructure government accordingly, reform the banking and taxation system, establish a capital market, establish a legal framework for foreign investment, partially marketize several social service sectors; fifth, the phase of anti-recession economic policy: close those enterprises which cannot survive and cannot be improved, support and accelerate the modernization and reconstruction of the state-owned enterprises which strong survival potential, create jobs, develop and modernize infrastructure. Establish credit and financial support policies to promote small enterprises, formulate and implement proper agricultural policies, adopt temporary protective foreign trade policies, attract foreign investment, etc; sixth, the phase of growth policies: give full freedom for foreign currency exchange, formulate and implement comprehensive industrial policies to increase exports in order to stimulate economic growth.

Market socialists have argued that socialism can also use markets, develop market economy, and that market and planning means are both complementary and necesarry. These views are valuable and can help enriching socialist economic thoughts, help us in perfecting our socialist market economy, in China. Of course, market economy conception of foreign scholars is not equal to our market economy, the most fundamental difference is: our market economy is integrated to our basic socialist system. The nature of market socialism is an economic mode to realize economic development in, not a socialism mode. Although many western scholars have argued that market socialism can replace capitalism, they haven't achieved to propose a practical path and hasn't yet transcended the theoretical exploration phase, even the ideas argued by some are just utopic or fantasy.

2. Research on ecological socialism

Ecological Socialism is a social thought wave created in western Green Party movement and Ecology movement. It originated in 1970s, and gradually became a vigorous socialist thought wave and school in 1990s. Human ecological problems are becoming increasingly serious since 1950s, phonemena of ecological crisis have become abundant all over the world: natural resources like soil, forest, fresh water are decreasing; some resources are exhausting, many species are extinction or are on the verge of extinction, global population is rapidly expanding; human industrialization brings unprecedented environmental pollution, global natural disasters occur frequently. Contradiction between survival and development of human on the one side and supporting potential of natural-ecological environment is getting sharper. Ecological Marxist Reiner Grundmann has summarized global ecological problems in eight aspects: air and water pollution; underground water decrease; spread of poisonous chemicals; spread of dangerous trash; corrosion; waste materials, acid rains and new chemicals.

Deteriorating of human survival environment has promoted the development of western ecological movement. From 1960s, far-sighted people in western countries have organized spontaneously,held demonstrations, gathered signatures, demaded that the factories with heavy pollution stop production or be rehabiliated, forced the government to care for the survival of environment and take effective measures to curb the deterioration of human's ecological environment. Meanwhile, ecological organizations like "Green Action", "Friends of the Earth", "World Health" came into being, sprang up like mushrooms. In some countries, ecological organizations promptly became political and even established political parties, i.e., the "Green Party", in many western countries the attaction of the Green Party has developed rapidly, and became an important force in domestic politics. Since 1981, green party candidates entered the parliaments in Belgium, Germany, Finland, Austria and France. Thus, ecological movement became an important force in the western "New Society Movement", even regarged as "the fourth political force" after capitalism, communism, democratic socialism by some experts.

Ecological Socialism trend of thought has experienced three historical phases: emergence, integration of red and green, thirdly the Red Green Party. Ecological Socialism emerged in 1970s, and its representatives then were "Ecological Marxist"—Rudolf Bahro a leader of the Socialist Unity Party of Democratic Germany and Adam Schaff, responsible for ideological work of the Communist Party of Poland. In 1980s, Ecological Socialism supported the unity between red and green parties and unity in their policy and principles. Its representatives were Canadian scholar Wiliam Leiss and

Ben Agger. Since the end of 1980s to early 1990s, Ecological Socialism developed into the second phase: "Red Green Party" and its independent complete theoretical system was gradually shaped. Its representatives in this phase were the European scholars and Left-wing social activists such as Georges Lebica, Rainer Grundmann, Andre Gorz, David Pepper and Lawrence Wilder, and others.

Ecological Socialism begins from the fact that natural environment faces serious crisis, absorbs some ideas of Marxism, assumes certain connection between the capitalist mode of production and social system and global ecological crisis, criticizes the flaws of the contemporary capitalism while re-evaluates and discusses the basic issues of the contemporary development of socialism, puts forward some unique theories and political ideas. The Greens especially Ecocentrists represented in the mainstream Green Party often simply attribute global ecological crisis to the unchecked development of technology, the future of industrial society, selfishness and greedy nature of the capitalists, ill and improper views of consumption in the developed countries. Therefore, firstly the solution to ecological problems need us to change our ideas, way of living, set up an ecological awareness, advocate thrifty life, such as vegetarianism, decentralized and ruralized residence, being self-sufficient. Ecological socialists of 1970s and 1980s were deeply influenced by this Green view.

Since 1990s, ecological socialists have exceeded the awareness level of common Greenists. They believe that there is certain link between capitalist mode of production and social system and the occurance of ecological crisis. Looking from the purpose of production, pursuing for profit is the unique goal of capitalist production, and capitalists regard nature as an object of plunder and source of profit. When average profit rate is declining, only excessive exploitation of natural resources by the power of technology can guarantee the profits of few magnate enterprises. In the production process, the cost of restricting environmental pollution caused by the production should be included in the cost of production, capitalists are always doing everything possible to externalize this part of the cost, or pass it onto nature and society (e.g. let the polluted air go into atmosphere, let the polluted water go into rivers, and let the state and ordinary people carry the burden of maintaining environment), or pass it onto later generations, let them to pay for the cost.

Cost externalization by the capitalists does not just exist in one country, it is an international issue. With awakening and rising of environmental protection awareness among the people of the developed countries and increasing governmental constraints and limitations to polluting enterprises, "ecological imperialist" countries pass environmental problems and ecological crisis to other countries, especially to economically backward developing countries, and the deepening of economic globalization strenghten the conditions for this imperialist behavior. "Ecological imperialist" countries use two ways to export the ecological crisis: one is direct robbery, i.e. developed countries transfer some enterprises with high enviromental costs, high pollution and labor-intensive to developing countries, even build landfills in these countries so as to directly rob soil, land, natural resources, clean air and water. Another form of robbery is the indirect way, implemented by the so-called "structural violence".[54]

From one aspect, in the era of capital internationalization and globalization, strong foreign capital and domestic upper-class bourgeoisie give farmers "structural violence" by political, social, economic policies of the governments, lobby for the privatization of publicly owned land in rural areas in order to put them into the capitalist world market. Farmers are forced to excessively cultivate the remaining little land plots for their subsistence thus more and more land becomes barren even deserted. From another aspect, when the national markets are internationalized, the agriculture of the developing countries is challenged by the products of the developed countries. This situation forces developing countries to predatorily use the limited land to reduce cost of produce and this measure exacerbates depletion of natural resources and environmental damage in the developing countries.

Ecological socialists have argued that capitalist system is the main reason for contemporary global ecological crisis, so they thought only abolishing capitalist system and establishing ecological socialist society can solve ecological crisis and fundemetally save our surviving environment. Oskar Lafontaine, the vice president of German Social Democratic Party, summarized the progressive meaning of ecological socialism as a new people-centered view of value, and its opposing the exploitation of labor by capital: "another progress we should mention is ecological socialism, it is a combination of fights opposing people's exploitation by people and exploitation of nature. To realize this progress, we must abandon idea of economic growth; we must allocate social wealth fairer; we must thoroughly reform the society and enable citizens to participate in deciding social and economic affairs. In this respect, basic commonality of socialism and ecological socialism is: maintain workers' right to self-determination, to regain the autonomy of people in the laboring process."[55]

In terms of the relationship between man and nature, ecological socialists believe that in the contemporary capitalist society, the relationship between man and nature is a relationship between the "dominant" and the "dominated" (master-slave).The relationship between man and nature is a kind

54 Yu Keping, "Socialism" in the Era of Globalization, Beijing, Central Compilation & Translation Press,1998, p. 132.

55 Quoted from Zhou Suiming, "Some Situations on Ecological Socialism", in: Foreign Theoretical Trends, 1994(33).

of hostile relationship–the relationship between plunderer and plundered. The ecological socialist society of the future, will essentially form a new relationship between man and nature. The purpose of human production should first serve to meet the needs of society, and surpass the pursuit of maximum profit. Human beings must rationally and systematically use natural resources (including wind energy, tidal energy of the oceans, solar energy, etc.) in order to develop production in a rational way, thus satisfy the limited and rich and diverse needs of human beings. Man and nature need to form a "natural harmonious" relationship.

In this new socialist society, with the major changes in the relationship between man and nature, inferior aspects of human nature, such as arrogance, greed, aggressiveness, competition, barbarism and ferocity, will be replaced by humility, peace, friendliness, unity and rationality. On the economic front, ecological socialists do not pay much attention to the ownership of means of production, (but there are also some thinkers who argue for implementing some form of public ownership), instead they pay more attention to the benign management of the means of production. They advocate combination of market and planning, i.e, the "mixed" socialist economy, they pay attention to both allocation of products and reasonable use and allocation of natural resources. In respect to some specific opinions, ecological socialists of different eras have different views. In general, there are following views, as in below:

Schumacherism: in the western world, Schumacherism has been a theoretical school of the 1970s which first became known with the book Small is Beautiful. The book was published in 1973 written by British-German economist Schumacher. He revealed some problems of capital-intensive, resource-intensive industries of developed countries, pointed out that professional, large-scale production caused decrease in economic efficiency, environmental pollution, resource depletion. He has argued that our abuse of non-renewable resources like fossil fuel will menace civilization; if we destruct the surrounding nature, human being's survival will be menaced. With this reasoning, he argued big enterprises may not be good and "small is beautiful". He pointed out that the solution is to develop a new way of life, new production method and new consumption mode. In agricultural production, a mode of production which can raise productive force of soil and keep land intact in long term should be adopted. In industrial production, a "humane technology" should be developed. He called this technology "middle technology", "democratic technology". This technology can fully use modern knowledge and experience, be adaptive to the laws of ecology, serve people and does not allow people become the servant of machines. He advocated that a small-scale, decentralized economic mode should replace large-scale, centralized economy.

Most of the Ecological Socialists of 1970s and 1980s affirmed the ideas of Schumacherism."Ecological Marxist" view of "decentralized, non-bureaucratic" socialist economy was directly inspired by Schumacher's thoughts. They have argued that capitalism itself has ability to digest global ecological crisis, consequently they advocated using free market, decentralized economy, grass-root democracy to partially transform and reform capitalism in the framework of capitalist system. Their representative figures William Leiss, Ben Agger designed "a mixed technological design which can combine some highly automated production sectors with other sectors using primitive technologies,"[56] and asked people "to get enjoyment from small-scale production and crafty consumption"[57] in this way the current society can be transformed to an ecological society. Ben Agger combined small-scale, decentralization with realization of socialist reform, argued that only democratically organized and regulated production process embodying small-scale technologies can free workers from bureaucratic organizational system.

Many scholars have argued that Schumacherism is not only utopian but a "historically retrogressive" trend of thought, since small-scale and decentralized economy is unrealistic. The ever increasing socialization of productive forces makes the division of labor finer and more complex and makes labor relations among people more and closer. Economic globalization makes social division of labor and economic connection more and more international and global, the world economy is integrated as a whole, and it cannot be divided into independent, decentralized parts. So ecological socialism has abandoned Schumacherism in 1990s.

"Steady-state economy", i.e., the "zero growth" economy, was the consensus among the majority of the ecological socialists in 1970s and 1980s. Leiss, and Agger were once active supporter of this idea, and believed this would be a solution to ecological crisis. Major merit of this solution is to control the rampantly increasing economic development rate, stabilize production scales and economic development rate, and realize zero growth in the economy. Thus, social production can satisfy people's need while keep ecological system intact, establish harmonious relations between man and nature. But the predictions for a "steady-state economy" seem unrealistic. At present, rich countries and poor countries have great wealth disparity. Asking developing countries to accept the steady-state economy is to ask them for a suicide and will not work. Therefore, in 1990s, ecological socialists mostly abandoned the view of steady-state economic development and shifted to moderate economic growth model, i.e. economic goal should be satisfying people's need (not profit), and this moderate growth would not create conflicts between man and natural ecology.

56 Ben Agger, Western Marxism, China Renmin University Press, Beijing, 1991, p. 498.
57 Ibid., p. 491.

"Semi-self-sufficient"economic development mode.This is the ecological socialist economic model raised by Frank, which has similarities with the economic model raised by Andre Gorz in 1970s—"combining of self-sufficient and non-self-sufficient regions of the world". In Frank's development mode, planning and administrative roles of central and local governments, and autonomies of family and individual producers both co-exist. Affairs controlled by central planning should be three: one is administration, including taxation, currency, international trade, telecommunication, financial budget and guaranteeing minimum income, etc; two is planning, should mainly include formulating development plans and promote the planned use of natural resources, raw materials and energy; three is coordination, state-regulated industries should mainly include manufacturing, including manufacturing of machinery, heavy equipment and steel production. Areas which should not be controlled by central planning but only softly guided by central planning (allocation of capital, raw material and income) should also include three parts: first is jobs in the national system, including health, education, traffic, etc, these areas cannot be completely decided by market; second is self-organized cooperatives of workers which can serve local and regional demand, these cooperatives should be guided by both national planning and by market; third is production activities of families and individual producers, food production, handicraft production, maintenance, individual service should be regulated by market, some areas can adopt non-currency exchange, i.e, barter system.

In politics, ecological socialism has raised the idea of autonomy, which uses the concept of "biological space" (human living environment defined according to biosphere principle) to replace nation state and demands regional autonomy divided by "biological space". It is necessary to transform the current political ideology of the nation-state interest and national security into a new political thinking which upholds interests of humankind and global security. Ecological socialism is highly concerned with women issues, believing that human domination of nature in the past ages was in fact synchronized with the domination and control upon women. For a long time, women were treated similar to nature and became the object of domination. Women's equal rights with men are the basic prerequisites for establishing a non-exploitative society which can also meet the ecological requirements.

Ecological socialism holds that the proletariat is the leading force in the transformation of capitalist society and that we should pay full attention to the role of the working class and trade union organizations. Contemporary social forces against capitalism, the global "anti- system forces against capitalism" formed by the new social movements, including the anti-imperialist-ecological movement of the Third World countries, the anti-racist-ecological movement in the developed countries, women's movement, etc., are the main forces of social change. They advocated the implementation of "non-violent" green movement, through education and the establishment of "model green ecological zones" to guide the development of society, while opposing the old unequal international order and unequal North-South relations.

As a school and a political trend of thought, ecological socialism criticizes and denies capitalist system, concerns about the future and fate of mankind, evaluates the serious negative effects, consequences, root causes and solutions to ecological crisis faced by men, reveals that root of the global ecological crisis is capitalist system itself, puts forward a lot of theoretical and practical propositions worth evaluation and discussion, such as the relationships between mankind and the environment, how to achieve economically and socially sustainable development, how socialism can deal with the relationship between mankind and nature, etc. These aspects of ecological socialism are more realistic and positive if compared with other green parties. Currently, it is of great significance for the construction of socialist ecological civilization in our country, and at the same time, we should also notice that some of the economic and political ideas of ecological socialism still remain in the stage of theoretical exploration and some views of it are obviously utopic, superficial and contradicts with development trend of human civilization.

(Wang Tingyou, Associate Professor of Institute of Marxism, Renmin University of China)

Foreign Marxists' Understanding of "Socialism with Chinese Characteristics"

In late 1970s, China began to follow a new path, i.e., the great cause of Reform and Opening-up. Since then, China's face is changing, causing widespread concern from the international community, including foreign Marxists scholars.With the advancement of our reform and undertakings,we have gradually formed the theory of socialism with Chinese characteristics in practice. Foreign Marxists' understanding of socialism with Chinese characteristics is accompanied by the deepening of China's Reform and Opening-up practice. They have differences in evaluating the cause of socialism with Chinese characteristics, but in the whole, they affirm our achievements. In respect to the experience of China's Reform and Opening-up, they have profoundly analyzed it from different points of view, some unique insights they have proposed are quite inspiring for the improving the socialism with Chinese characteristics. Of course, due to the lack of comprehensive literature and information about the Chinese reality and due to interference of some other factors, some scholars' point of view does not accord with China's national conditions and reality.

1. Understanding of the achievements of socialism with Chinese characteristics

Since the Reform and Opening-up, China's socialist construction has made great achievements, it is obvious. Therefore, for the achievements of socialism with Chinese characteristics, except some biased ideas, the majority of foreign Marxists in general hold a positive attitude, in particular, the achievements in economy.Russian scholar Boris Slavin, who served as the executive director of the Central Committee of the Communist Party Russian Federation, pointed out in his book After Socialism: Metamorphoses of Russian Political Evolution at the end of the 20th Century published in 1997, says: China is showing to Russia a more dynamic economy than the West. The Chinese economy has proven its efficiency with an annual growth rate of 12%, which causes panic and dissatisfaction in the US. He further argued that socialism cannot be established at one stroke. The achievements of China's economic reform have proven the inevitability and progress of socialism.[58]

Polish left-wing scholar Hab Victor has argued that the Communist Party of China and China are the greatest hope for the development of Marxist theory in the world, Socialism with Chinese characteristics is the greatest

58 Li Xinggeng, Slavin believes that the achievements of China's economic reform have proved the inevitability and progress of socialism, in: Foreign Theoretical Trends, 1998(12).

contribution of Chinese Marxists and Communists to the development of contemporary Marxism. In the difficult situation of the Soviet Union and collapse in some other socialist countries, China has upheld the socialist political and economic system.[59]

Eike Kopf, a German scholar who has worked as an expert in the Central Translation and Compilation Bureau, attached to the Central Committee of the Communist Party of China, has enthusiastically praised China's Reform and Opening-up: "No matter how people evaluate it, in such a vast and internationally influential country, which includes one-fifth of the world's population—the communist party, with 89 million members, leads the people of this country on the difficult path to the 21st century. The path China follows is a unique and a new path which shapes the people's life in a new way! People of this country are in a difficult journey in an unknown and new continent, which is full of difficulties which is rare in the world history, if it succeeds, it will benefit the workers of other countries in the world!"[60]

Some scholars, including some left-wing groups or scholars in the West, has linked socialism with Chinese characteristics to world socialism, and fully affirm the role of socialism with Chinese characteristics in promoting world socialism and expresses high hopes. They argue that Deng Xiaoping's creation of the socialism with Chinese characteristics "has created one of the most spectacular economic miracles of the 20th century", "it shows the superiority of socialism with Chinese characteristics" and "reversed the situation of low-ebb tempo of the world socialist movement in the late 20th century" "saved the prestige of socialism in the world", saved "sinking socialist ship", "it is the creative development of Marxism", "is the most significant contribution to 20th century international communist movement". For decades, the Egyptian scholar Fozi Mansour has devoted his efforts to the studies of socialism theory. When he came to China for academic exchanges in September 1994, he argued that: since 1990s, influenced by the drastic changes in the Soviet Union and Eastern Europe, "the world socialist system has been severely damaged, and even driven back, many people lost confidence in socialism. Socialism is an inevitable trend, I firmly believe that the socialist system will be only be achieved in the global context. But it depends on the next 20 to 25 years of China's socialist development—the strong Chinese economy and the consolidation of China's socialist system is bound to play a pivotal role in the future world economic system."[61]

59 Hab Victor, Marxism in Poland, published in Foreign Theoretical Trends, 2007(4).

60 "The German Scholar Kapf spoke highly of the 15th National Congress of the Communist Party of China", Foreign Theoretical Dynamics, 1997(31).

61 Liu Ming, Egyptian Professor Fozi Mansour on the development of world socialism and socialism with Chinese characteristics, in: Foreign Socialism Research, 1994(10).

Famous French Marxist Tony Andreani wrote: "I have high hopes for China. What happened in China was unprecedented experience in human history. Generally, I have expected that Europe would be the main power to stop the development of capitalism, still today I cannot say that Europe has completely lost that role, but prospects are not so optimistic for Europe at the moment, In the current world, only China can become a force to compete with world capitalism."[62]

Why the cause of socialism with Chinese characteristics could be able to achieve great achievements and what is the main reason behind its emergence and what experience can it offer? Foreign Marxists have many views, and generally have their unique research focus. Some scholars have used comparative research methods to compare China's development model with other countries, trying to understand the successful experience of China. In his paper in an academic symposium in October 2005 in China, Hab Viktor mentioned that an important reason for China's rapid development is that it is a permanent member of the United Nations Security Council and its peaceful foreign policy, but also it has a different leadership system compared to Soviet Union. For the differences between the two parties' leadership system, he made a detailed analysis, that in the 1930s, the Soviet Union and Eastern European socialist countries established the administrative socialist economic model, this model was the only possible option at that time, but it included many flaws and mistakes, especially in the role of party. Khrushchev's policy of supporting right revisionism undermined the international communist movement and led to drastic changes in the socialist camp of Soviet Union and Eastern Europe. At the same time, in the Soviet Union and other socialist countries, a new kind of leading class emerged, which seized political and economic privileges, which is one of the important reasons why communist party was weakened and the socialist camp disintegrated. And the drastic changes occured due to Gorbachev's "semi-socialism". On the contrary, Mao Zedong became aware of Khrushchev's right revisionist mistakes and criticized it within the international communist movement. After 1978, China adopted Reform and Opening-up policy, implemented socialist market economy, socialist construction has made great achievements.

62 Xu Yang, Famous French scholars' Academic Report on "Market Socialism", in: Foreign Theoretical Trends, 1999(9).

2. Analysis of the reform experience in development of socialism with Chinese characteristics

Russian scholar and the CPRF leader Boris Slavin, after comparing the reforms of China and the Soviet Union, analyzed the successful experience of China's reform from a unique view. He argued that in the understanding of socialism, Deng Xiaoping tried to determine a clear position based on practice. His thoughts like "primary stage of socialism", "giving priority to the development of productive forces", "opening to the outside world" are easy to be quantified and grasped. In the past, when Slavin visited China, he saw that there were still some similar phenomena in China like in Soviet period, such as the bureaucratic system, ad hoc restaurants, and privileges and so on. Boris Slavin: "Chinese have done a lot of things that we have not done: the commodities in the Chinese market are abundant, and it seems that Deng Xiaoping was much cleverer than Gorbachev."[63] From the achievements of China's reform, Boris Slavin concluded that it is possible to build socialism in a single country under the siege of stronger capitalism. Although this question has no final answer, Lenin had explored it in the Russia's NEP period, and Deng Xiaoping has evaluated NEP when designing China's economic reform. Slavin argues that if socialism aims to continue to exist and prevail in a single country, it must create a high level of labor productivity, and that people should enjoy a higher standard of living and more effective democracy than in developed capitalist countries. There is no other way.

American scholar David Kotz has compared the experiences of economic transformation in China and Russia. In his view, Russia adopted new liberalism prescription from Western countries—"shock therapy", and China has adopted a gradual transition strategy. The main theme of Russia's transformation strategy has always been the rapid withdrawal of the state from the regulation of economic life. Its obvious features were: to liberalize the control of the domestic market prices; the rapid privatization of state owned enterprises; quickly remove the residual factors of government command in corporate decision-making; sharp reduction in public expenditures; tight monetary policy; quickly eliminate barriers to transnational commodity and capital flows. This transformation strategy created a chaotic situation wherein only short-term interests were focused on. Consequently, the pursuit for private interest did not lead to productive investments, but only flocked non-productive behaviors, including speculative land acquisation transactions and speculative securities transactions. Enterpreuners concealed their corporate income, indulged in various forms of fraud, misused public funds and formed triad organizations that collect protection fees.

63 Li Xinggeng, Slavin argued that the achievements of China's economic reform have proved the inevitability and progress of socialism, in: Foreign Theoretical Trends,1998(12).

But unlike Russia, China did not pay attention to neoliberal policies recommended by Western powers, but adopted a domestically-guided transformation strategy, "China's approach of transformation was to seize rather than let go." China's transitional economy included the following elements: the gradual liberalization of price controls; the long-term postponement of the privatization of state-owned enterprises; the retention of state directives in decision-making of large state-owned enterprises; the increase of government spending on state-owned enterprises and infrastructure; the expansionary monetary policy; the government continued to control the banking system, the international trade and capital flows.[64]

While affirming China's achievements in Reform and Opening-up, some scholars have also raised some doubts about China's future development which is faced with many challenges, consequently they have expressed concern about China's prospects. Wahid Halabi, a US left-wing scholar and recently a member of the Communist Party of USA, pointed out in an article published in July 2005 that, world capitalists and their governments are fighting hard against China in order to protect their previliges and profits, just as they fought against the Soviet Union and just as they fought against the workers' trade unions and workers' parties around the world. With the increase of problems faced by the Wall Street and Washington, this attack cagainst China was also strengthened. The speculative manipulations in respect to oil prices determined by monopoly capitalist groups and speculators of the Wall Street, do not only aim at looting China, but also aim to disturb China's plans, aim to spread uncertainty and cause social instability in this country. They also make some speculative deals on the other commodities which China needs, (from soybeans to nickel). Imperialism has launched a ruthless attack against North Korea, but its ultimate goal is to squeeze China. Washington has heavily armed Taiwan and established a military base in Central Asia, renewed its security treaty with Japan and working on India to establish a similar relationship, they all point their finger at China, besides the working classes and their organizations in various countries. China is increasingly facing comprehensive challenges masterminded by capitalist forces of the world. Certainly, only with the support of the working class in China and around the world, China can be capable to overcome all these challenges. With this background, it is even more important for China to build a strong, class-conscious party and trade union movement, the unity and closer relations with the leaders of the party and trade unions are vitally important, the party should strengthen its class basis and the Party's line should be determined with this class basis.[65]

64 Zhou Yanhui, Recent Studies on China's Economic Development Model by Foreign Scholars, in: Foreign Theoretical Trends, 2007(9).
65 http.//www.politicalaffairs.net / Retrieved: 2005/07/28.

3. Comments on Chinese socialist market economy

Since the market economy was established as the target model of economic reform in 1990s, Western scholars, including Marxists, paid great attention. Foreign Marxists' comments on the Chinese socialist market economy can be divided into two categories:

One tends to favor the socialist market economy, but their views are quite varied. There is a view that China's socialist market economy is seen as a transition to the advanced stage of socialism. In other words, the market economy as the means, methods and ways of developing productive forces, can help transition to the advanced forms of socialism. This is in line with Deng Xiaoping's view that the market is the means and method for developing productive forces. US scholars James Lauer, Albert Saggis, et.al, hold this view. James Lauer argued that the theoretical basis of China's socialist market economy is similar to Lenin's NEP theories put forward in 1921, that China's socialist market economy is the Chinese version of NEP. China's conditions are not yet mature for socialist construction; the socialist market economy can lay the foundation for socialist politics, economy and culture. There is also a view that the market economy is a form of socialism, market economy equals socialism, which is the view of the "market socialism" scholars. The US scholar David Schweickart, one of the representative figures of contemporary market socialism, clearly argued that socialist market economy is the eternal form of socialism. The market should be the characteristic of all socialisms, and the socialist market economy is a fully mature socialist form. Now China is not a mature socialist market economy, but in the early stages of market socialism. This view sees the importance of the market economy for the development of socialism but sees the market economy itself as the whole of socialism, and apparently does not see the multidimensional attributes that socialism as a social form should have. We think it is not appropriate to define socialism from a certain single aspect.

Of course, some scholars have expressed concerns that the market economy is likely to slide towards capitalism. After all, the advanced form of market economy is the product of capitalism. The socialist countries have never implemented it in history. And the market economy itself has limitations. Although some people have proposed that socialism can engage in market economy, but can't it lead to capitalism thus deviate from the original intention? Many scholars have put forward their own concerns. Egyptian scholar Fozi Mansour argued that it is necessary for the socialist economic system to use market mechanisms to promote economic development but we should guard against the risk of sliding into the capitalist system.[66] He

66 Liu Ming, Egyptian Professor Fozi Mansour on the Development of World Socialism and Socialism with Chinese Characteristics, published in the Journal of Foreign Socialism Research,1994(10).

argued that the following four factors should be noted; otherwise they will restrict the consolidation and development of China's socialist economic system. First of all, the role of the price mechanism is important, but in the socialist economic system it cannot be the master, i.e. the pursuit of profit cannot be the sole purpose of production, it can only serve as a means for economic development goals and to improve the level of productive forces. Second, the use of price mechanism can stimulate production and promote economic development, but because of different economic benefits pursued by enterprises, there will be income gaps, people's income levels will have great differences, social justice and social stability will be threatened, thus there can occur the risk of change of the nature of socialism. Third, in the process of socialist development, due to the use of price mechanism, a number of "new aristocracies" will be created. These upstarts will gradually demand more political power as they grow in the socio-economic life and as they expand their social influence, and these people may become new "bourgeois" strata and threaten the socialist economic system. Finally, in the foreign economic relations, the socialist economic system introduces and absorbs numerous foreign technologies from the West, absorbs funds and advanced scientific management methods from the developed capitalist countries, and opens its markets to the world, which is conductive to the development of socialist economy. But the degree of opening to the outside world and absorption of foreign investment should be clear for us, and we should always control the direction of our own economy, do not blindly pursuit economic expansion. Moreover, the developed capitalist countries and international organizations are trying to introduce capitalist market economies to developing countries. With this strong trend, even if you are unwilling subjectively, it is difficult to avoid being incorporated into the world capitalist market economy and become subordinated to the economic control of the developed countries, consequently arises the risk that socialist economy may change to a capitalist economy. The US scholar Albert Saggis has argued that, China's socialist market economy is leading to socialism. Market economy in China is a proper way to lay the foundation for socialism. Both Marx and Deng Xiaoping believe that socialism cannot be based on poverty. The question is, after five or six decades, how will China guide socialism rather than capitalism? For these reasons China wants to uphold the Four Cardinal Principles. James Laure argued that the question in this period of China is how to organize the socialist market economy, how to ensure the direction to socialism. In his view, the public sector should be expanded, and the state should be able to control the private sectors of the economy.

The second view is exactly the opposite of the first view. Such scholars are influenced by the extreme right-wing scholars of the West, who do not agree with the idea of the socialist market economy, they argue that the market economy essentially only suits the capitalist economy; China's socialist market economy is essentially equivalent to capitalism. In the USA, about 60% of left-wing scholars hold this view. They argue that socialism should be more linked to the planned economy, rather than the market. They advocate the view that the Chinese socialist market economy is transition to capitalism. The logic of the market will overthrow the power of the state laws, the more mature the market is, the harder the government control will be, the market will turn the state into a tool of its own. The market will turn everything into commodities and divide people into buyers and sellers, owners and workers, creators and exploiters of surplus value. The values of the people who benefit from the market will affect others, and the market will spread the values of individualism and egoism which will shake the socialist ideology. There is also a view that the Chinese socialist economy is already a form of capitalism, or that this is the capitalist primitive accumulation stage or in state capitalism stage. After China has implemented a market economy, it is no longer a socialist country. This is reflected in the fact that China's state-owned enterprises are being privatized, the number of unemployed people is widening, the gap between rich and poor is widening, and the gap between urban and rural areas has increased again. About 75% of the rural population in China has no medical security, and they must pay for primary education, etc. These are deviations from the basic principles of socialism. Some even argue that China's corrupt bureaucracy, capitalists and petty bourgeoisie have allied to promote capitalism. For example, Maurice Meisner wrote in his masterpiece Mao's China and After: "Chairman Mao's period from 1960 to 1976 was the zenith of Chinese socialism, but the current China has deviated from socialist direction." Trotskyists, "Maoists" and some independent scholars such as Paul Sweezy also regarded China's socialist market economy as state capitalism. They argue that "society and economy are controlled by bureaucrats, this privileged class in China is carrying out capital accumulation. They regard wealth created by the workers as their own and turn the state property into private property." Of course, some scholars oppose the view that engaging in market economy equals engaging in capitalism. Russian scholar Boris Slavin argues that the experience of China and other countries that implement market socialism suggests that the market cannot be equaled to capitalism, and lack of markets cannot be equaled to socialism. The market is necessary factor for social modernization and for stimulating production. As long as China is still in the industrial development stage, it cannot cancel the market. Only when the society transits to the post-industrial society, and transits to full automation of production and the global socialization of the world economy, market economy may lay the foundation for the demise of market relations. But this problem is the problem of the distant future. In general, the current historical stage of China does not belong to socialism, but the post-capitalist stage. Slavin also argued that the Chinese communists are successfully "walking along the blade", on the one hand they don't slide to the "left" extreme (immediate cancellation of the market and private ownership), and on the other hand don't slide to capitalism. The Chinese communists boldly implement the economic opening, implement market relations, and besides modernizing SOEs, they establish mixed ownership enterprises, and so on. At the same time, they continue to maintain the idea of social justice, firmly control economic lifeline in the hands of the country, while introduce certain selective capitalist approaches in the leading economy. What they do is actually Lenin had done during the NEP period.[67] For the view that China is more and more like a capitalist country, the US scholar David Schweickart pointed out: I do not think China is a capitalist country and that it will not necessarily be in the future. He also said that China is not open to Western capital like a leaf controlled by the wind; China has not given up control upon the economy and has not let the economy be dominated by blind market forces. He also argued that the Chinese people continue to insist on the view that they are developing a new model of socialism. They are aware that inequality is widening, and that corruption is spreading. There are different thoughts among the Chinese party and state cadres and the people, some people want to restore capitalism, but they are absolutely a small minority. Many people simply support the policy that serve their interests, which can unconsciously lead to capitalism. And some people are concerned about the growing power of capital, worried that it will get out of control. China deeply fears from the weakening of the state due to the depths of its culture. China was long bullied by the West in its history, and they have seen everything what happened in Soviet Russia. They know that they are playing a high-risk game. In China, although the bourgeoisie exists, it is much less powerful than American bourgeoisie in the United States, but its economic (not political) resistance to government authority is stronger than in the USA. I do not want to predict the future, but it is certain that the future of mankind is more dependent on China than the progress of the West in the next few decades. The results of socialism trials in Cuba and Vietnam are still uncertain, but although they are much less populated, the significance of their exploration will be beyond national borders.[68]

67 Li Xinggeng, Slavin believes that the achievements of China's economic reform have proved the inevitability and progress of socialism, in: Foreign Theoretical Trends, 1998(12).

68 Liu Yuanqi, American Leftist Scholars' Discussion on China's Socialist Market Economy, in: Foreign Theoretical Trends, 2001(7).

In addition to the important issues such as market economy, the Western Marxists are concerned about various aspects of China's reform and development, such as China's rural reform, sustainable development, economic integration into globalization, the development of democratic politics, etc. British scholar Richard Sanders has deeply studied China's rural reforms. For the fact that some people advocating full-fledged privatization of rural land in China, based on case analysis, he pointed out that in contemporary China, the state should encourage new type of cooperatives among the poor farmers and promote new collective arrangement on the basis of collective land ownership and household contract responsibility system, rather than full privatization of rural land. New cooperatives and new collective arrangements will enable sustainable agricultural development in China, since privatization will further marginalize poor farmers. US scholar David Kotz has discussed his worries about the direction of China's economic transformation. David Kotz has pointed out that if China abandons the domestically-guided transition strategy, and adopts the neoliberal path, then this will damage China's economic development and social stability. In his view, the neoliberal view has begun to influence China, and it has begun to abandon certain elements of the state-guided transition strategy. For example, some people are advocating privatization of all state-owned enterprises. In response to this situation, how can the correct strategy be maintained? David Kotz' view is that a sustainable national strategy is only possible in a social system wherein there is no wealthy and no powerful elite and only when majority people have political and economic powers. In other words, only in the framework of a democratic socialist system (which depends on public ownership and economic planning), a state-coordinated economy is likely to survive.[69] Some scholars have suggested that there are still many theoretical problems that need to be solved in Chinese socialism. Such as the question of socialist path, the dictatorship of the proletariat, the leadership system of the Communist Party, how to treat Marxism-Leninism and Mao Zedong Thought, and how the socialist market economy deals with the contradiction between the central plan and the market and the state. For many of these problems, Marx, Engels, Lenin did not leave us a ready answer, the Communist Party of China needs to continue its exploration. The "Economy" a journal published by the Communist Party of Japan, published an article entitled "How to Evaluate the Current Development of China's Economy" by Prof. Ichikun Oki who is a researcher in the Department of Economics of the Tokyo University of Social Welfare, and a left-wing scholar. The article written by him questioned several representative views on China's economic development held by the Japanese scholars. In respect to the theory that China being in the stage of "primitive

69 Zhou Yanhui, Recent Studies on China's Economic Development Model by Foreign Scholars, in: Foreign Theoretical Trends, 2007(9).

capital accumulation," he has argued that the primitive accumulation of capital is the plunder of direct producers, along this process, the land of the peasants was plundered, and the peasants were increasingly divided into the working class and the small capitalist class, and the gap between the rich and the poor widened. On the contrary, except for few phenomena in the process of importing a market economy, China has not plundered peasants and handicraftsmen, but has taken measures to protect and reward freelancers and individual operators to prevent the deterioration of unemployment and avoid polarization, and its policies strive to promote the shaping of middle class (that is, an olive-shaped society).

For the view that "China's economy lagged 40 years behind Japan", the article said that this argument underestimated the prospects of China's economic development, there are three questions: first, if taking into account China's economic development in recent years, especially situation after 2001 and its future development prospects, I think that the above view is only static evaluation. Second, China has a vast area and economy with multiple structures, when it comes to international competitiveness, it cannot be confined to its average level, but the economic strength of its advanced coastal areas (already equivalent to several countries' economic scale) should be taken into account. Third, the theoretical base of the person who holds this view is the "flying-geese-type development model" raised by Prof. Kaname Akamatsu from Department of Economics, Hitotsubashi University in the 1960s. Not to mention the flaws of this model theoretically, if only looking from the current situation it is already defective. This view advocates that Japan is the country which can be the group leader of the geese, which can really promote the economic development of the Asian continent, but it is quite outdated.

On the view thet "China's economy is capitalist", the article has argued: "the argument that "China's economy is a capitalist" does not hold water, the Chinese government has strong control on all aspects of China's economy, controls public enterprises and administrative economic organs through financial institutions, large state-owned enterprises, higher education institutions and cutting-edge fields of technology and reserch and controls huge state-owned assets including land, and strongly controls the country's economic development direction." Looking from the actual situation of China's introducing market economy, we can see that the recognition of the privatization of production methods, the privatization of state-owned enterprises is only limited within a certain extent, the public economy is still dominant in the national economy. China has introduced some elements of capitalist economy into the national economy within a certain range, and established a mixed economic system, which can achieve a rapid economic growth and establish a vibrant socialist society. The article has discussed and doubted the view that "China will always remain to be a heaven of cheap labor", and the view that "China's economy is prone to collapse", etc.[70]

(Wang Tingyou, Associate Professor of Institute of Marxism, Renmin University of China)

70 Zhang Lijun and Guo Min, Japan's Communist Party's Representative Views on China's Current Economic Development, in: Foreign Theoretical Trends, 2005(4).

PART FIVE

Capitalism and Socialism in the Development Process of the World

Since the Second World War, socialism has undergone through an interesting fluctuating development. At the same time, capitalism has also experienced great changes. After the war, the United States formed a tyrannical rule in the world. After 1990s, with the drastic changes in the Soviet Union and Eastern Europe, the world situation changed, greatly. Todat the international political multi-polarization tends to take shape, in which the United States, Europe, Japan sometimes coordinate, sometimes struggle. The relatively independent socialist economic system which was formed at the beginning of the postwar period in 1950s does not exist today. After the late 1980s and early 1990s, with the drastic changes in the Soviet Union and Eastern Europe, the COMECON the economic cooperation organization led by the Soviet Union disintegrated and relatively independent socialist economic system is bygone. The economic globalization has become an irresistible wave, the capitalist world system has developed to a higher stage under the new situation. In the process of the world, when socialism has suffered from frustration and has constantly reflected on its own development, capitalism is constantly changing itself, partly adjusting the capitalist relations of production; and there emerge some new social factors in capitalist countries. All in all, the conditions and fundaments for socialism replacing capitalism have undergone major changes.

These changes in capitalism and socialism in the process of the world fully demonstrate that the coexistence of capitalism and socialism in the present era has shifted from pure confrontation to competition fighting for advantages of comprehensive national strength, economy and technology. In this confrontation, the "peaceful competition" including both cooperation and competition has become the main way, and the competition for developing economy and science and technology has become the main content of relations, economic and technological exchanges surpassing beyond the division of two social systems have become important basis for capitalism and socialism to enhance their own strength. In this process, capitalism will continue to develop itself and can prolong its life by cooperating and exchanging with socialism and absorbing several socialist factors. But the existence, accumulation and intensification of its internal contradictions will inevitably become its own development obstacle and destructing power for its future. And on the basis of economic development and comprehensive social progress, and by developing material, spiritual, political and ecological civilization higher than capitalism, socialism will show the world that socialism is the only path that can promote the development of human history.

New Changes in Capitalism and New Factors of Socialism

60 years after the World War II, under the impact of new scientific and technological revolution, globalization, and the socialist movement, capitalist productive forces and production relations, the economic base and superstructure, i.e., all aspects of capitalism have encountered of a series of new changes. These changes did not only change the contradiction between the political forces of the East and West and the orientation of the world pattern, but also have made a profound impact on the development process of socialism. Lenin once pointed out: "The whole theory of Marx is the application of the theory of development—in its most consistent, complete, considered and pithy form—to modern capitalism. Naturally, Marx was faced with the problem of applying this theory both to the forthcoming collapse of capitalism and to the future development of future communism."[1]

Only by developing a correct and scientific analysis on the new changes of the contemporary capitalism, and examining the new social factors that have emerged, can we correctly grasp the true nature and trends of contemporary capitalism, and thus further enrich and develop Marxism theory, and adhere to socialist ideal and faith.

1. The major manifestations of the new changes in contemporary capitalism

As well known, postwar capitalism has passed through the "Golden Age" characterized by both stability and prosperity, but it has also experienced a decline in those times of crisis and depression. One main reason behind the appearance of such a phenomenon, is that including capitalism, all social forms inevitably possess the sequential historical process of emergence, development (establishment) and decline.

On the other hand, in order to avoid the economic crises and alleviate its inherent social contradictions, and further maintain itself, capitalism has made certain adjustments and improvements related to its production relations and the superstructure and thereby contemporary capitalism has gained a series of new features as the following:

First, both the level of scientific and technological development, and economic modernization of the capitalist countries have dramatically improved.

1 Lenin Collected Works, Vol. 25, see also Lenin's "Anthology on Marxism", p. 255, Beijing, People's Publishing House, 2009, p. 293.

After the second World War with the development and application of the atomic energy and electronic technology as its main symbols, a new round of technological revolution has occurred, which has promoted the birth and development of nuclear energy, semiconductors, synthetic chemicals, aerospace industry and many other new industries, all of which have promoted major changes in the industrial structure of the Western countries. Consequently, the proportion of the primary industry (agriculture) in the economic structure has declined significantly and was even reduced to less than 3% regarding its economic contribution. On the other side the proportion of secondary industry (manufacturing) after rises and falls, generally accounts a proportion between 30% and 40%. Generally, the proportion of the tertiary industry, namely the service sector has rapidly increased to more than 60%, and the proportion of the tertiary industry in the United States has even reached as high as 72%.

Later, during the 1980s, the technological revolution has seen a new upsurge, marked by the rapid development of microelectronics, information technology, biotechnology, aerospace technology, laser technology, new materials technology, advances in new energies technology, computer and network technology among which the rapid development of the information industries (IT) constitute the core element of them. Some experts have even defined the information (IT) industry as "the fourth industry".

The new technological revolution has led the economic structure of developed capitalist countries to the direction of more modernized and upgraded nature. Thus, it has greatly improved labor productivity, and opened up a new space for the development of productive forces.

Renewal and updating of the fixed assets with higher technologies have also triggered a new change, causing the softening of the cyclical fluctuations in the economic life of capitalism. Between the years 1991-2000 the US economy saw steady and prosperous growth which was closely related to the development of the new scientific and technological revolution especially due to rapid development of the information industry. The Digital Economy 2000, a publication of the Commerce Department's Bureau of the Census has released that: in the economic growth of the US economic growth since 1995, 30% was contributed by the information technology (IT) industry.

Secondly, the concentration of production and capital has intensified monopoly and further expanded and deepened the domination of financial capital.

After World War II, with the further concentration of production and capital, the domination of the social and economic life by the capitalist monopolies has greatly strengthened on the one side, and monopolistic consortiums (magnate trusts) have begun to control almost all industries on the other side, from industrial production (manufacturing), transportation, finance to utilities, catering, tourism, entertainment and many others.

In December 1996, the Boeing has merged with the McDonnell Douglas, which was announced as "the merger of the century"—a merger worth of $13.3 billion—which aimed to further strengthen the Boeing and enhance its monopolistic power. As another example, in April 1998, the Nations Bank Corporation of the United States and the San Francisco based Bank America Corporation merged to form a new magnate bank, which then possessed total assets around $570 billion, thus formed the "super bank" of the United States, as the biggest merger in the history of US banking industry.

Although there are a lot of small and medium size enterprises which still operate, their capital assets only account a small portion of the total, consequently their role in the economic life has greatly diminished. Obviously, the financial capital constitutes the core part of the monopoly capital. But, in the post-war era, with the development of the new credit system, new capital markets and services, a variety of industrial and commercial capital elements such as commercial banks, insurance companies, securities companies, asset managers, and other financial institutions have become the organic part of the contemporary financial capital which demonstrates an extremely complex structure. Its enormous business operation sphere covers the government debt financing, all kinds of bonds and fund trade and management, can easily make use of the expansion or contraction in the amount of money in circulation, thus can enhance their control and intervention capacity over the economies. In today's Western countries, including the sphere of securities trade, loans, foreign exchange trade and including the trading of the other non-material financial instruments, the virtual economy has greatly exceeded the real economy. Third, with the acceleration of economic globalization and regional integration process, the forces of international monopoly capital have been significantly enhanced.

International movement of capital is one major premise for the survival and development of capitalism. In the post-war era, the internationalization of the industrial capital as the main form of international capital movement has led to the further internationalization of commercial capital and bank capital, thus the international monopoly capital has gained an increasingly important position and role in the world economy. Besides, multinational companies, as the main carriers of internationalization and globalization of production and capital, have seen rapid expansion both in quantity and scale. According to the data released by the "World Investment Report of 2009", sponsored by UNCTAD the number of global multinationals has reached 82,000, which lead 810,000 foreign affiliates. According to the researches made by some economist experts related to the world's 100 largest transnational corporations as the most vigorous economic actors, following results were found: the %50 of the FDI flows are controlled by the top 100 transnational corporations, and while their assets account for the 1/4 of total assets of the whole productive assets of the whole world, today 15 magnate multinational companies control the global trade of almost all basic commodities.

2. Intertwined trends of globalization and regionalization

All in all, two global trends have appeared in the world, Western countries on the one hand promote economic globalization which transcends the national boundaries in order to adapt to the requirements of internationalization of production and capital, but on the other side promote the establishment of various international organizations and regional economic organizations aiming economic integration. In this respect they encourage convening of various economic conferences at different levels, in order to coordinate international trade, finance and other aspects of international economic relations.

In 1977, the European Union has established a unified monetary and financial system (the Eurozone), and the completion of the unified European market was achieved in 1993. Later in 1998 they have formed the unified European currency (Euro), which all marked the start and formation of the European Economic and Monetary Union.

In 1989 with the initiative of the United States and Canada, FTA was established and in 1994 Mexico has joined this organization, which have then co-established the NAFTA cooperation. In Asia the APEC was established in 1989, it began its first informal leadership level meeting in 1993, and established the ministerial consultation mechanism, thus its members began to enhance economic cooperation and integration.

Despite these cooperative developments above, the US-led Western countries have continued to control and effect the IMF, World Bank, World Trade Organization, in order to consolidate their dominant position both in the economic globalization and in the world financial and monetary system. As some Western scholars have mentioned: "a transnational capitalist class (hence-forth, TCC) has emerged, and that this TCC is a global ruling class. It is a ruling class because it controls the levers of an emergent trans-national state apparatus and of global decision making. This TCC is in the process of constructing a new global capitalist historic bloc: a new hegemonic bloc consisting of various economic and political forces that have become the dominant section of the ruling class throughout the world, among the developed countries of the North as well as in the countries of the South. The politics and policies of this ruling bloc are conditioned by the new global structure of accumulation and production. This new historic bloc is composed of the transnational corporations and financial institutions, the elites that manage the supranational economic planning agencies, major forces in the dominant political parties, media conglomerates, and technocratic elites and the statesmen in both North and South."[2]

Fourthly, state-monopoly capitalism has encountered significant adjustments, with the combination of monopoly capital and state power. In the period between 1950s and 1970s, Western countries have been able to maintain a stable development known as the "Golden Period". The reason is that they have begun to adopt and utilize the latest achievements of the new technological revolution. What's more, it depended on the powerful functions of regulation and support by the state monopoly capitalism, which mainly includes the following facts: the basis of giving full play to regulatory function of the market mechanism and the law of value, the western countries adjusted the total social supply and total demand through various fiscal and monetary policies. Also, certain economic development plans were put into practice, including investing directly in certain industries, especially public goods, implementing nationalization to enhance the aggregate benefit of national economy, and carrying out proper tax policies and social redistribution policies to restrict high incomes and excessive monopoly and build up social welfare and security systems.

All these measures to some extent have imposed some restrictions on the private ownership of the means of production and promoted the development of productive forces on the one side, and alleviated the class contradictions and social conflicts, which greatly promoted economic growth in the capitalist countries on the other side. However, "oil crisis" that occurred during 1973-1974 have pushed capitalism into a "stagflation" period and began to expose the serious shortcomings of the capitalist state intervention theory and policies which is generally called as Keynesianism. In order to deal with the "stagflation" phenomenon, Britain and other Western countries have abandoned Keynesianism, and shifted to neoliberal economic theories and embraced neoconservative policies, which included monetary tightening, welfare cuts, tax cuts, relaxation of economic controls on capital flows, the privatization of state-owned enterprises, suppress the union movement and the unions, limited workers' wage increases, and other measures in this direction. Though these neoliberal measures have gradually eliminated the "stagflation" phenomenon, in turn brought about the phenomena of high unemployment, expanding budget deficits year by year, increase of state debts, international trade imbalances, which have further widened the gap between rich and poor and caused other negative consequences.

2 See William I. Robinson and Jerry Harris, "Towards A Global Ruling Class? Globalization and the Transnational Capitalist Class", in: Science and Society (USA), 2000 (Spring Issue).

During the late 1990s, a new trend of "third way" has become popular among the representatives of the Social Democratic Parties of the West in a bid to repulse the strengthened right-wing bourgeois liberal political forces, which has tried to reconcile right-wing economic and left-wing social policies. They have advocated the implementation of the so-called "new economy" and "new welfare", "New politics" and the "new governance" policies. Main proponents of "the third way" have advocated that the crucial changes such as the globalization, the knowledge economy, the revolution of information technology, post-modern society (the post-traditional social order) and social reflexivity has formed a new type of citizen in contemporary societies, and asserted that these citizens constitute a new type of society termed as the "risk society" in which these changes lead people to question authority and to wish to take greater responsibility in order to meet their needs. Consequently, "the third way" calls for "no rights without responsibility" and favors the "equality of opportunity, not the equality of outcome" and tries to market the pursuit of balancing the risk and safety (of the citizens), their rights and obligations, individual responsibility and collective responsibility, thus aims to strike a new balance between economic growth and social justice. If these goals set by the advocators of the "third way" can be reached or not, will be tested by the supreme judgment of history.

Fifthly, great changes of class, hierarchical structures and ideology have occurred in the capitalist countries. Accompanied by the changes in their industrial structures, the structure and mode of employment and the structure of working class of the Western countries have undergone significant changes in the postwar era:

First, when we examine the distribution of the workers among the three major sectors (industries), we can observe that a sharp decrease in the number of workers engaged in the agricultural labor has occurred, that the workers in the manufacturing sector saw either a gradual growth or even decline. On the other side we observe significant increase in the number of workers engaged in the service industries, namely the number of workers engaged in the non-material production sectors, have greatly surpassed those who are engaged in the immediate material production.

The second fact is that there is a shift from manual labor to mental labor, the number of blue-collar workers has greatly diminished, whereas that of white-collar workers have increased. As early as 1956, the number of white-collar workers in the US has exceeded the number of the blue-collar workers. In the 1980s, the number of blue-collar workers in the United States accounted for only 34% of the total, and those in the other developed countries of were reduced to only 30% to 40%.

Third, the "knowledge workers" engaged in the collection, processing and transmission of information and knowledge have greatly increased, accompanied with the reduction of non-knowledge workers. In recent years, with the rapid development of the knowledge utilizing industries, millions of new employment opportunities were created by the knowledge-based industries, in which the knowledge workers accounted for the 90 percent of the work force. Some experts have predicted that before the turn of the 20th Century, knowledge workers will account for one-third of the labor force, thus becoming the largest section of the employees. In the Western countries the employment of those with better education and specialization was increasingly promoted, which causes the strengthening of their "middle class" tendencies.

Especially after the drastic change in the Soviet Union and the Eastern European countries, the neo-liberal, neo-conservative and other right-wing bourgeois forces have expanded rapidly which spread the ideas of trade liberalization, the privatization and liberalization of economies, "aiming economic stability by fighting against inflation and reducing fiscal deficits". These alleged ideas, which also constitute the main content of the "Washington Consensus" has become the mainstream economic ideology of the Western countries. Thus, President of the French Association Escape Marx, Mr. Patrice Cohen-Séat, has quite correctly suggested that neoliberal ideological system is the theoretical expression of the contemporary capitalist globalization.

Since the neoliberal ideology, to a certain extent adapts well to the development requirements of the new technological revolution and the economic globalization, it has not only gained and consolidated its dominance in the ideological sphere of the Western world, but also penetrated into the countries of former Soviet Union and Latin America and acquired a world-wide influence.

From movies, satellites television, Internet media to McDonald's foods, and Coca-Cola, capitalist culture of the West generates a huge effect all throughout the world, in the cultural sphere. As the American scholar James Petras put it: "cultural imperialism can be defined as the systematic penetration and domination of the cultural life of the popular classes by the ruling class of the West in order to reorder the values, behavior, institutions and identity of the oppressed peoples to conform with the interests of the imperial classes."[3]

US scholar Robert W. Mc Chesney has also pointed out: "associated initially with Reagan and Thatcher, neoliberalism has for the past two decades

3 See article of James Petras, "China and the World, Cultural Imperialism in the Late 20th Century", 2001.

been the dominant global political economic trend adopted by political parties of the center, much of the traditional left, and the right. These parties and the policies they enact represent the immediate interests of extremely wealthy investors and less than one thousand large corporations. "... Neoliberalism is the defining political economic paradigm of our time – it refers to the policies and processes whereby a relative handful of private interests are permitted to control as much as possible of social life in order to maximize their personal profit."

Sixth, international relations and the configuration of the capitalist world system has encountered major changes.

In the post-war era under the new circumstances when a heavy blow was given against imperialism and with the collapse of the old colonial system of imperialism, the Western powers no longer rely mainly on military aggression and political domination ways of the past and old type of colonial economic plunder when dealing with the developing countries; instead they rely on the neo-colonialism ways which include the means of economic exchanges and cultural infiltration, in order to maintain and advance their various interests existing in the developing countries. Thus, the center and edge division of the capitalist system was strengthened.

Relying on their monopolistic advantages of capital abundance, of various technologies, information and other aspects, and benefiting from the unequal exchange and from the uneven distribution of the surplus value across the states of the international community, the exploitation and the plunder of the developing countries was further strengthened.[4]

While the Western countries have achieved the alleviation of the "stagflation" syndrome, and have achieved to moderate the economic fluctuations, and reached certain degree of stability mainly through the advantages brought by the globalization wave, on the other side they have developed various means so as to transfer their domestic economic crisis and social conflicts to the other parts of the world. US economy has also continued to enjoy a strong growth, mainly due to its utilization of the huge amount of free capital moving to USA from all over the world. Accordingly, the former US President Bill Clinton has admitted that the economic globalization plus the "relatively more open economy" of the US has restrained the US inflation rates. The diffusion of capital to all over the world, and the agglomeration of profit to the West, demonstrates a vivid portray of the exploitation of Western countries over backward developing countries.

---

4 See the book co-edited by Jin Huiming and Luo Wendong: "Modern Capitalism" theory, p. 561, Sichuan People's Publishing House, Chengdu, 2006. First published in Monthly Review, April 1, 1999, Quoted from, Noam Chomsky: "Neo-liberalism and Global Order," Introduction Section 1, Nanjing, Jiangsu People's Publishing House, 2001.

3. New social factors emerging within contemporary capitalism

As postwar capitalism has made adjustments to the specific form of production relations and its superstructure and the state regulatory system, "elements of disintegration of the old mode of production" were prompted to grow and thus more and more "new economic institutional factors" have taken shape. Over half a century, contemporary capitalism has encountered several major changes, and there appeared numerous new social factors within the womb of capitalism. These new factors can be summarized as follows:

First, the vigorous development of the cooperative economic sector and cooperative enterprises.

The origins of cooperative socialism theory and practice can be found in the writings and activities of Robert Owen, Louis Blanc and Charles Fourier, and others. After some early experiments in the 19th-century, consumers' cooperation took a permanent form with the establishment of the Rochdale Society of Equitable Pioneers in 1844 in England. The Rockdale Society of Equitable Pioneers, was an early consumer co-operative, and one of the first to pay a patronage dividend, forming the basis for the modern co-operative movement, which has started more than 160 years of cooperative movement practice in the economic history, and gradually took root in more than 100 countries around the world. Marx in his *Capital*, Volume III has clearly stated that: "the co-operative factories run by workers themselves, within the old form, were the first examples of the emergence of a new form, even though they naturally reproduce in all cases, in their present organization, all the defects of the existing system, and must reproduce them. But the opposition between capital and labor is abolished there, even if at first only in the form that the workers in association become their own capitalists, i.e., they use the means of production to valorize their labor. These factories show how, at a certain stage of development of the material forces of production, and of the social forms of production corresponding to them, a new mode of production develops and is formed naturally out of the old [...]"[5]

Large-scale development of cooperatives and its important social impact in the postwar Western society has further confirmed the scientific conclusions arrived by Marx. Currently, the total number of economic cooperatives in the Western countries has reached up to 640,000. The United States has nearly 2,000 grain producer cooperatives which control the 60% of the domestic grain sales. France has more than 10,000 agricultural production

5 Marx-Engels Collected Works, Vol. 7, English ed., 1974, p. 512.

cooperatives, and there are 2 million members included in these cooperatives and they have a turnover which has approached to 100 billion Francs. In addition to agricultural cooperatives, those types of cooperatives which manage industrial factories have also developed rapidly. A French agricultural production cooperative originating from Auvergne in France, as the first independent world seed company, has more than 500 farmer members, and employs more than 35,000 workers and it has reached a turnover of 4 billion francs. The economic role of cooperatives in the national economy has been increasing, their part in the total GDP of Western countries is remarkable, and in Denmark the contribution of the cooperative sector to GDP accounted for 24%, in France and the Netherlands reached to more than 10 percent, and in the United States has reached about 5 percent of the GDP.[6]

Marx had made a careful positive evaluation on the role workers' collectives and their economic connotation he emphasized their significance for the development of the socialist movement. He wrote: "The value of these great social experiments cannot be overrated. By deed instead of by argument, they have shown that production on a large scale, and in accord with the behests of modern science, may be carried on without the existence of a class of masters employing a class of hands; that to bear fruit, the means of labor need not be monopolized as a means of dominion over, and of extortion against, the laboring man himself; and that, like slave labor, like serf labor, hired labor is but a transitory and inferior form, destined to disappear before associated labor plying its toil with a willing hand, a ready mind, and a joyous heart."[7]

Second, the social security systems.

We can observe new social factors, not only in terms of ownership structure, but also in terms of the distribution system. Early in the period of primitive accumulation period of capitalism, in Britain some welfare measures called as the "Poor Laws"[8] and the like were established. But before the end of the Second World War, social welfare in western countries has mainly focused on helping the poor, which included only fewer projects, narrower coverage and the allocated funds were also limited. But, only in the 1950s after the War, social welfare systems of the Western countries have seen a rapid growth, and gradually included a wide range of spheres related to social security system, including the minimum wage limit, the low-income subsidies, unemployment payments or unemployment benefits, health insurance, pension insurance, education subsidies, and so on.

---

6 See the book co-edited by Jin Huiming, Luo Wendong: "Modern Capitalism" theory, p. 561, Chengdu, Sichuan People's Publishing House, 2006. See also: http://www.thenews.coop/36622/news/global-affairs/global-300-co- operatives-generate-16-trillion-revenue.

7 Marx-Engels Collected Works, Vol. 3, English Version, 1974, p. 23.

8 British social policy was dominated by the Poor Laws, which was first passed in 1598.

The heavy progressive tax, public and free education for all children and other social measures to be implemented after the proletariat seizes the state power, which was mentioned in the "Communist Manifesto" by Marx and Engels, has already become a reality in some developed Western countries. By 1981, the average social welfare expenditures in nine countries including the United Kingdom, Denmark, Belgium, France, Ireland, Germany, Italy, Luxembourg and the Netherlands has reached 27.1% of the GDP.

In 1984, it was the British Labor government which first declared its abstaining from the "welfare state" policy with the pretext of "modernizing" them. Subsequently, from Europe to North America, from Asia to Oceania, almost all of the developed capitalist countries have made similar turns and abandoned their welfare state policies. When we observe the recent practices in the Western countries, we see that the Western countries cannot stand to undertake the social welfare expenditures, and they strive to reform their social welfare systems. But they cannot completely abandon or cancel social welfare policies, instead only try to make some partial adjustments related to their "welfare state" policies. All in all, social security systems have been generally established in the Western countries, which brought a series of changes to workers and other laborers' status and situations as follows:

First, the gradual reduction of the laborers' working hours. In the 19th century generally the eight-hour working day was the sharpest and strongest demand of the working class and it has been achieved and a weekly six-day work week system was replaced by the weekly five-day work week system, and generally the work hour per week was decreased to around 40 hours.

Second, the income forms of workers have gradually diversified. Seniority wages, job benefits, skill related qualifications allowances, special operations allowances, benefits in kind, bonus, dividends, etc., have become important parts of workers' income. Besides, the proportion of bonuses in the total income of workers is also rising. In addition, in the West, many countries have gradually started promoting a form of bonus by delivering shares (stock ownership) to the employees, with discounted share prices. Thus, the latest statistics show that, in some Western countries proportion of shareholding benefits of employees have reached even above 50%, and in some of them to minimum 25% of their total income.

Third, the living standards of the workers have improved significantly. Workers and their families, have generally gained access to such items as telephones including mobile ones, TV's, refrigerators, cars and many other consumer goods, thus material and cultural living standards of the workers have encountered substantial improvements in different degrees, and the absolute poverty is greatly reduced. Especially in Western Europe, social welfare is not only a social relief, but also regulated by civil rights law. Currently, annual working time of the German workers is reduced to 240 days of the whole year, and they can enjoy six weeks paid holiday annually. Sweden implements the motto of social welfare "from cradle to grave", besides by issuing proper tax regulations and subsidies, the wealth gap has been narrowed and social equity has been promoted. For example, in Sweden the general income tax rate for industrial workers is reduced to 35%, while the capitalist entrepreneurs should generally pay 70% income tax, the average gap of after-tax income between the common workers and capitalists has dropped to 1:5.

No wonder people comment that the Swedish model follows the "capitalist mode of production capitalism and socialist mode of distribution." And in the United States, the community or neighborhood level social services for people have greatly increased, they provide low-cost health care, education, training, cultural development, entertainment, and other aspects of social care and security for citizens and even offer non-profit free labor and free services, so it is believed that many functions of the government is undertaken by the community.

Third, participation of the employees in the enterprise management system.

After World War II, Western countries generally started to implement the "co-determination system" which allows employees to participate in the enterprise governance in order to protect the rights of workers in terms of working conditions, working life, compensations and so on. Employee representatives have the right to seats on the supervisory board of larger companies—1/3 in companies with 500 to 1,000 employees, half of the seats in those companies with more than 1,000 workers—in which all major issues of the company can be co-determined with certain consultation mechanisms.

Meanwhile, according to laws related to industrial relations, the enterprises are required to allow workers' unions to establish workers' committees within the workplace in order to safeguard the legitimate rights and interests of the workers. According to relevant labor laws enterprises cannot freely dismiss workers, thus workers are protected against being dismissed unfairly. When an enterprise feels necessary to dismiss, it is required that it should consult with the union, and pay compensation to the employee. On the other side, in France, it is illegal to ignore the council of workers' representatives' demands or requirements or overlook the decisions initiated or agreed by the workers' representatives, which are legally termed as the crime of disrupting.

In Sweden, the law stipulates that the enterprises should allow its employees to be regularly informed about the production and personnel issues, and all the major issues related to the enterprise should be consulted and negotiated with the workers' representatives. Since the beginning of 1970s, Swedish laws stipulated that all the large-size companies must build Employee funds into which a proportion of the company profits were put and used to buy shares of the companies. The funds were controlled by representatives of the Swedish trade unions or workers' representatives themselves, which enabled them to exert greater influence on the enterprise management. This so-called "fund socialism" did get a positive recognition and support from many people.

In 1980, the US government, labor unions and the employers' unions trilaterally assented on a cooperation agreement with "full understanding". Following this agreement, some large companies began to allow the workers' representatives to participate the management of the company, and afterwards more and more companies began to practice the implementation of employee participation in the management. All in all, we can say that workers 'participation in the enterprise management has been a major achievement of the workers' movement, and it is a positive element that the new socialist society lives by.

Fourth, the gradual disappearance of the three major disparities

In the postwar era, with the development of the productive forces and policy adjustments of developed capitalist countries, the disparity between the workers and peasants of these countries, disparity between the mental and physical labor and also disparity between urban and rural areas, have greatly decreased and are gradually disappearing. Namely, the one important demand—"combination of agriculture with manufacturing industries, gradual abolition of the distinction between town and country, by a more equitable distribution of population over the country"—as stated in *The Communist Manifesto* has basically become a reality in the contemporary developed capitalist countries of the West.

Today, in the developed Western countries, the highway system is well developed, and the farmhouse courtyards are parked with cars, agricultural machines. Besides in the countryside telephones, networked computers, color TVs, refrigerators, automatic fuel boiler and so on, have been quite common and owned by the most majority.

Differences in quality of life and their cultural and educational level and differences related to the other aspects of life between the workers and farmers have also greatly disappeared. Most majority of the rural population and the farmers of the United States, Canada and Western Europe, Scandinavia have got rid of ignorance, backwardness and poverty. Most of them are university graduates, having major related to agronomics, and many individuals born into farmer families possess academic titles such as master's and doctorate degrees and even professorship. Not only the mechanization of agricultural production, and the modernization of rural economy are achieved, but also urban economy is linked to the whole national industrial and to the national technological development. Thus, the various differences both between urban and rural areas, workers and peasants, and their social consciousness are eliminated in the main.

Engels in his *Anti-Dühring* has clearly stated: "Certainly, to be able to see that the revolutionary elements which will do away with the old division of labor, along with the separation of town and country, and will revolutionize the whole of production; see that these elements are already contained in embryo in the production conditions of modern large-scale industry and that their development is hindered by the existing capitalist mode of production."[9]

This incisive discussion still has important guiding significance to our understanding of the tendency of "the three disparities" in the Western countries and the development of socialism. Fifth, the breeding and development of socialist ideology and ethic. As early as 1913, Lenin in his article titled as "Critical Remarks on the National Question" had clearly pointed out: "The elements of democratic and socialist culture are present, if only in rudimentary form, in every national culture, since in every nation there are toiling and exploited masses, whose conditions of life inevitably give rise to the ideology of democracy and socialism. But every nation also possesses a bourgeois culture (and most nations a reactionary and clerical culture as well) in the form, not merely of "elements", but of the dominant culture. Therefore, the general "national culture" is the culture of the landlords, the clergy and the bourgeoisie. This is the fundamental and, for a Marxist, the elementary truth..."[10]

After World War II, in the Western countries, although still numerous forms of bourgeois ideology and culture dominate people's social consciousness and being, nevertheless the ideology and culture of the working class and other working people are also nurtured, their own ideology and culture develop and keep on being disseminated.

In Canada and North and Western European countries, altruism, benevolence, charity helpfulness, care for the young and those suffering mentally and financially, returning the money found and politeness are valued virtues generally being praised. The spirit of honesty and keeping faith, hard work and dedicating oneself voluntarily is being advocated too, and gradually becomes favorable social morals.

9 Marx-Engels Collected Works, Vol. 9, English ed., 1974, p. 422.

10 Lenin Selected Works, 3rd ed., Vol. 2, p. 336.

In Germany, good manners have become people's common behaviors. In Italy, there is a volunteer army consisting of 1,300 million participants, which includes students, workers, retired men and women who actively volunteer free labor and services both in the urban and rural areas. They do not demand any remuneration, do not engage in volunteerism for fame when working or helping the disabled, for the environmental protection, disaster relief and many other activities.

In the United States, although social security and health benefits are poor, and criminality including murder, rape, robbery incidents is rampant, nevertheless a health moral atmosphere of altruism, benevolence, charity has gradually formed. Whenever a church calls for and initiates a charity donation or a voluntary service, the calls always get a positive response and supported by a large number of donors and volunteers.

The American sociologist Robert Wuthnow's research includes the following: according to the surveys sponsored since 1987 (field work by Gallup) 80 million adult Americans (over 18) work as volunteers to help others' social welfare and for solidarity in the society. And this accounts for the 45 percent of the population. The study estimated that the average volunteer gave about five hours of his/her time a week, or more than 200 hours over a year and this workload is equivalent to $150 annually. And according to the surveys, some 75 percent of US residents to solidarity and wish to help others, for common happiness and self-realization of the value orientation of motivation and professional achievement placed equally important position.[11]

Also, Engels, in his *Anti-Dühring* wrote: "There is first Christian-feudal morality, inherited from earlier religious times". Alongside with it we find the modern-bourgeois morality and beside it also the proletarian morality of the future, so that in the most advanced European countries alone the past, present and future provide three great groups of moral theories which are in force simultaneously and alongside each other. Which, then, is the true one? Not one of them, in the sense of absolute finality; but certainly that morality contains the maximum elements promising permanence which, in the present, represents the overthrow of the present, represents the future and that is proletarian morality."[12]

The correct understanding of, and proper evaluation of the new factors of socialist culture, that is developing in the womb of the contemporary capitalist culture is both an important task of contemporary capitalism studies and also vitally important for our understanding of building socialist spiritual civilization.

11 See, the book co-edited by Jin Huiming, Luo Wendong: Contemporary Capitalism Theory, Chengdu, Sichuan People's Publishing House, 2006, p. 566.

12 Marx-Engels Collected Works, Vol. 9, pp. 98-99.

4. The correct understanding of the new changes and new social factors of contemporary capitalism

In the early 20th century, when Lenin analyzed the new characteristics of capitalist development and its historical shift to imperialism, he clearly expounded on the status of monopoly capitalism and argued: "monopoly, which grows out of capitalism, is already dying capitalism, the beginning of its transition to socialism."[13]

And he also wrote: "state-monopoly capitalism is a complete material preparation for socialism, the threshold of socialism, a rung on the ladder of history between which and the rung called socialism there are no intermediate rungs."[14] In his view, the approaching war and war preparations of the big powers had greatly accelerated the trend of monopoly capitalism shifting towards state monopoly capitalism, which in turn promoted a fast track of development towards socialism, namely human society developing into socialism, as the dialectics of history. Socialism is appearing from all the windows of contemporary capitalism, and with each important progress forward on this basis, socialism directly and actually emerges and nears us. Numerous new phenomena and new trends occurring in contemporary capitalism imply that monopoly capitalism has developed to a new and higher stage. At this new stage, we can see different forms of capitalist monopoly forms being manifested as private monopolies, state monopolies and international monopolies, and their roles and the relationships between them have undergone significant changes, we can observe that new social factors more and more emerging and developing within the capitalist society, and their role and effects are also growing dialectically. Correct examination of contemporary monopoly capitalism reveals that it has still certain ability and capacity of self-regulation and improvement, remaining within a certain range and that it can accommodate the development of productive forces, which points to the reality that socialism, inevitably replacing capitalism may encounter a long, checkered and diversified historical process.

However, contemporary capitalism still remains to be monopoly capitalism in essence, the changes and adjustments that have occurred in the post-war capitalism not only does not change the nature of imperialism, and does not shake the truth and facts reflected in the basic principles of Lenin's analysis on imperialism., instead they still contain the evil natures of imperialism, they further expose its evil results endangering world peace and the development of the human civilization, all of which continue to provide new proofs for the historical inevitability of socialism eventually replacing capitalism. When we realistically observe and examine the capitalist society of the Western world,

13 Lenin Selected Works, Vol. 2, 3rd ed., p. 706.

14 Lenin Collected Works, Vol. 22, English ed., p. 358.

it is easy to see a series of "antagonistic" strange phenomena or "antinomies" as follows: while the scientific and technological progresses are widely utilized and greatly promote economic growth, but they also increase the intensity and the degree of exploitation of wage labor, exacerbate social inequities and social polarization among people and nations.

As another phenomenon, numerous types of securities, hedge funds, foreign exchange rates related contracts, bonds, stocks, insurance and other instruments of financial capital have seen abnormal increase, and which have in turn produced a huge gap between the financial system and the real economy, which push capitalism further towards getting parasitic and speculative.

Another contradictory and antagonistic development is that, although the contemporary wave of globalization brings certain advantages, but in turn this trend is accompanied by rampant hegemonism and power politics which threaten world peace and the rapprochement of the nations, and while a few developed Western countries and a fewer people can practice excessive consumption and lead an affluent life, the others namely the overwhelming majority face more sufferings as a direct result of the havoc, natural resources are rampantly exhausted and the ecological environment faces more threats of destruction, all going along with social and moral decay spreading among people. Social welfare policies carried out by Western countries indeed has played a positive role in improving the life of working class, which has made them feel that they not only get the salary, but also gain "extra benefits" like welfare benefits and security. Although remuneration in the form of social welfare and social security benefits implies an increase the value of wage labor, they do not eliminate the exploitation and diminish the control over working class, by the capitalists. In Western countries, those who belong to the ranks of the monopoly capitalist class, while accounting less than one percent of the total population, hold the direct control and rule over economic, political, cultural spheres.

What they squeeze from the workers are the gourmet sausage and ham, while snatch them bits, which means that they cannot completely eliminate the societal poverty. Especially in the periods when the right-wing parties are in power, workers' real incomes are forced down and social welfare benefits such as pension pays, pension terms, medical and unemployment benefits as well as poverty relief projects are cut which cause harsher conditions. During the Reagan administration period, the United States has cut $38 billion related to 83 welfare projects, which resulted in 659,000 poor families which could get poverty relief support, 750,000 poor students had to drop out of schooling, 1.5 million children were excluded from education grants. In 1987 alone, 12 million children did not have access to medical security. Even in the Clinton administration period, the US population living below the poverty line was 39.3 million in 1993, while the poor population in the EU member states, during the same year accounted 52 million. By the year 2000, in the United States the relief demand by the poor and homeless people has seen a growth of 17%, and 6 million unemployed and homeless people were pushed into severe problems.

Since the global financial crisis that occurred in 2008, the unemployment rate in the US has surpassed 9%, and increased to 10.9% throughout the EU countries. According to the US government data released in April 2009 the people receiving food stamps has exceeded 32.2 million, the highest peak of needy in the American history. It turns out that today's "welfare state" has never been realized. What's more, "full employment" and "income equality" has not thoroughly eliminated poverty. There are numerous works, that is worthy to study the theme of poverty in contemporary USA. such as Michael Harrington's *The Other America: Poverty in the United States*; Appadurai's *Poverty in the Affluent Society*, Oskar Lewis's *The Culture of Poverty*, O'Hare's *Poverty in America: Trends and New Patterns*, and others. In fact, these works truly reflect and reveal the real face of the welfare policies in the Western countries. Affirming the new development of capitalism in the post-war era, in which it attains more and more new social factors which prepares the conditions of socialism, does not mean that these social factors alone can lead capitalism "peacefully and smoothly growing into" socialism. Generally speaking, although the "new social factors" emerging and developing in the capitalist society may gradually accumulate and increase in the future and although all these prepare the conditions for socialism, they cannot be fully developed and linked to socialism, because under the capitalist rule they are always under siege, suppression and destruction of capitalism. Therefore, it will be mistaken to expect that capitalism will automatically and peacefully grow into socialism, by the accumulation and development of these social factors. Lenin has warned in his article "On Cooperation" the following: why were the plans of the old cooperators, from Robert Owen onwards, fantastic? Because they dreamed of peacefully remodeling contemporary society into socialism without taking account of such fundamental questions as the class struggle, the capture of political power by the working-class, the overthrow of the rule of the exploiting class. That is why we are right in regarding as entirely fantastic this "cooperative" socialism, and as romantic, and even banal, the dream of transforming class enemies into class collaborators and class war into class peace (so-called class truce) by merely organizing the population in cooperative societies." He has argued that: "Undoubtedly we were right from the point of view of the fundamental task of the present day, for socialism cannot be established without a class struggle for the political power and a state."[15]

15 Lenin's Collected Works, Vol. 33, 2nd English ed., Progress Publishers, Moscow, 1965, p. 467-75.

Only through social revolution, which passes the cooperatives, joint-stock companies, big banks, big monopolies, state-owned enterprises and all national planning and management institutions "from the hands of capitalism" to the hands of the people, a new socialist society can be established. As to the question of, what forms social revolutions will take and in what way capitalism will be replaced by socialism, accurate answers cannot be given, the answer can only be based on the actual situation of the struggles by the working class, the future development of capitalism and on the contest of class forces.

(Luo Wendong, CASS Researcher at the Institute of Marxism)

Capitalist Economic Crisis and the Victory of Socialism

The capitalist economic crisis is a fruit and demonstration of the various contradictions of capitalism, especially its basic contradictions. The capitalist economic crisis has both cyclical crises, structural imbalances and crises, financial system disorders and financial crises, and they often coexist and intertwined at the time when a crisis erupts. Since the first outbreak of global economic crisis in 1857, nearly 20 global economic crises had happened till the end of the 20th century and the beginning of the 21st century. From the view of long-term structural disorder of capitalism, capitalism has experienced four economic long-waves since the industrial revolution; their periods are 1790-1845, 1845-1895, 1895-1939 and from 1946 to the end of the 20th century. Basically, each time in the sub-wave stage contradictions are intensified, economic crises have occured more frequently.[16]

Looking at the history of the economic crises, we can see the fact that from the 19th century to the 1930s, the capitalist economic crises repeatedly erupted in every 5 to 10 years and became more and more violent. For example, the periods of crises in the United States, was accelerated from once in 10 years to 6 year-periods. As Marx said: "The conditions of bourgeois society are too narrow to comprise the wealth created by them. And how does the bourgeoisie get over these crises? On the one hand, by enforced destruction of a mass of productive forces; on the other, by the conquest of new markets, and by the more thorough exploitation of the old ones."[17] But all the measures bourgeoisie takes will only "pave the way for a more extensive and a more destructive crisis, and by diminishing the means whereby crises are prevented."[18] Since the 1930s, the relatively rapid development of capitalism has been associated with its softening the negative effects cyclical economic crises. 1929-1933 Capitalist world economic crises broke out such violently that the capitalist economy collapsed; capitalist countries were faced with the overall plight of social development. Marked by this great crisis, the liberal capitalist market system declared a complete failure. With the outbreak of the oil crisis in the 1970s, the rise in energy prices led to the surge in the prices of production materials and living materials. From 1973 to 1975, the developed countries plunged into the worst economic crisis after the Second World War the economic development of the Golden age came to an end, it encountered a "stagflation" stage, later plunged into another crisis in 1979-1982. Between 1990-1993, the decline in production of Canada and Australia spread to the

16 Liu Chongyi, Li Dachang, Wang Xiaoqi and Chen Weihan, Contemporary Capitalist Structural Economic Crisis, Beijing, Commercial Press, 1997, pp. 64-142.

17 Marx-Engels Collected Works, Vol. 2, p. 37.

18 Ibid.

major capitalist countries such as the United States, Japan and Europe, and the strengthening of economic globalization once again brought synchronization of crises among of world countries. By the late 20th century, the major developed capitalist countries have implemented a certain degree of self-adjustment and through neoliberal economic globalization they have transferred the burden of their domestic contradictions and crises to other countries. Therefore, more and more frequent and more extensive international financial crises and economic crises have often occured in emerging capitalist developing countries. In the 1980s and 1990s, the debt crisis first happened in Latin America and Africa, in some countries of Eastern Europe, such as Poland, were also affected by the debt crisis. in the late 1980s and early 1990s, Japan's economic bubble and crisis occurred. In the mid-1990s, the crisis first happened in Mexico, and later in Southeast Asia, South Korea, and spread to Russia, Brazil, the financial crisis ended after it spread to the Pacific ocean. After entering the 21st century, the crises are still frequent. The United States subprime mortgage crisis began in the second half of 2007. It spread, and gradually evolved into a global economic crisis. The world economy has not yet got rid of its shadow and is still in a downturn. The economic crisis not only reflects the essence and future trend of the capitalist economy, but also reveals the disintegration of the capitalist mode of production and capitalist social form, which implies the ultimate victory of the new social form-the socialist society.

1. The new trend of capitalist economic crisis

The economic crisis is a comprehensive demonstration and a forced balancing of the various contradictions in the economy. As the ultimate source of the capitalist economic crisis, the evolution of the basic contradictions of capitalism in the new period has both potential and real impact on the economic crisis brewing process, manifestations and consequences and other aspects; and determine that capitalist economic crises in the late 20th century have demonstrated various new characteristics:

Firstly, during the economic crisis, the Western countries have smaller decline of industrial production, and the stages of the crisis cycle has deformed. As a result of the government's "counter-crisis" measures, the governments have strengthened intervention and regulation of the economies, stimulated investments, expanded consumption, implemented several social welfare systems, to a certain extent, prevented the decline in consumer demand, so the cycles of capitalist economic crisis and production cycles have seen obvious deformations: the severity of the crises was reduced, the stage difference and the typical practice of the reproduction cycle are weakened and changed; the reproduction cycle is longer and production decline in the deep crisis stage is smaller, the recovery is slow and weaker; in the prosperity stage, since the contradictions in the reproduction process can't be fully resolved, the enterprises still encounter under-production status, and a certain level of unemployed population exists constantly. These changes, although they cannot fundamentally eliminate the crisis, but to a certain extent, have reduces the destruction caused by crises.

Secondly, the main source of economic crisis shifts from the developed countries to developing countries. The development from the capitalist world to world capitalism extended the occurance of capitalist crises from few countries to the whole world. Before the 1980s, the world economic crisis basically originated in the then financially most developed or more developed capitalist industrial countries. In the 1990s, the devastating massive economic crisis originated in the developing countries, and mainly affected countries and regions that were in development or transitional economies and had little impact on the economically developed countries and regions. The important reasons were the immaturity of the markets in these developing countries and the fragility of their economic structures but we cannot ignore the impact of the shock coming from the fluctuation of international capital markets and the external factor of developed countries exporting the crisis to weaker countries. Theoretically, the international speculative capital chase extreme profits regardless of any country, but the victims are mainly the developing countries. Since these countries and regions have weaker economies and low level of macro and micro economic management, the speculative capital has more opportunities to operate in these countries and even attempt profiteering. Since the Second World War, Western developed countries have mainly used financial means to transfer the crisis to the developing countries, the use of violent means such as wars were rare, which is an important reason why the developed countries did not have a major economic crisis.

In the Asian financial crisis of 1996, Japan, the major economic power of Asia and the main trading partner of East Asian countries, the largest investor and the creditor country of the East Asia region, had an undeniable responsibility for the formation of the Asian financial crisis. The flaws of its "bubble economy" and its effects were exported to East Asian countries. Therefore, the Asian financial crisis was a further extension of Japan's economic and financial crisis after its "bubble economy" collapsed.[19]

The US has been the biggest beneficiary of the financial crises in the emerging industrial countries since the mid-1990s, and this is one important reason for the outstanding performance of the US economy in these years. For example, the United States has benefited from the Asian financial crisis in the following aspects: the dependence of East

19 See Jin Renshu, "The Four Contradictions in the Contemporary World Economy from the East Asian Financial Crisis", Philosophical Research, 2000(8).

Asian emerging industrial countries have increased in respect to their exports to USA and the US's financial and trade influence in the region has strenghtened; the prices of export goods delivered from Asia to the United States have fallen which diminished the inflationist pressure in the United States. Finally, the Asian financial crisis forced the foreign capital and US capital to withdraw from Asia and flow to the United States, which promoted the continued growth of the US economy.[20]

Thirdly, the simple excess of overproduction and supply has gradually changed into a double excess of overproduction and excess capital, recently the crisis of overproduction is often accompanied by the monetary and financial crisis and crises in the balance of payments. The economic crisis is essentially a crisis of overproduction, and overproduction is also an important feature of economic crises. Since the 1980s, driven by the development of market economy and science and technology, the level of global production and supply has increased rapidly, while the global consumption has lagged behind the development of production. The contradiction between purchasing power and productivon level (supply) has accumulated, which leads to serious disruption of production and consumption. Overproduction is still an important feature of the recent economic crises. Although the Latin America debt crisis of the 1980s, the financial crisis in Mexico during the 1990s and the Asian financial crisis have a great link with the economic structure of these countries, such as the development model, their immature financial systems and other aspects, in essence, these crises are still capitalist economic crises which have occured due to the blindness of the market economy, blindly barrowing with high interest rates, we lnow that these crises have caused serious damages for both the real industry departments and the monetary aspect of their economies, and also caused "economic bubbles", all of which have led to overproduction, such as undesired export and undesired domestic real estate business bubble. This kind of overproduction under the conditions of global economic integration, will inevitably lead to crises in the newly industrialized countries which lack competitive advantages, and such crises will develop from a situation wherein the chain of credit relations in economy to a situation wherein comprehensive economic crises occur. Under the conditions of overproduction, due to the internationalization of financial capital, huge international funds are invested into a variety of newly discovered financial derivatives in a speculative manner (through the international financial markets) to seek extreme profits, instead of aiming to develop any actual or real purchasing power or instead of developing the real production capacity, thus these huge international funds have become speculative excess capital that deserves the name: speculative

20 See Zuo Baiyun, "The United States is the biggest beneficiary of the financial crisis in emerging industrial countries", in: Journal of Guangdong University of Business Studies, 2000(1).

capital. The rapid development of virtual economy has increased the financial risks and vulnerability of global economy. 'The combination of overproduction and violent fluctuations in the financial markets inevitably lead the world into double edged economic crises.

Fourthly, economic liberalization and the development of globalization have accelerated the speed of transmission and volatility of the recent crises. If we analyze the world economic crisis that occured at the end of the 20th century, in addition to competition for trade and markets, the more direct reason for crises has become the large amount of unchecked short-term speculative capital flows.These speculative capital uses the international financial markets and uses modern information technology and communication tools.With its speedy transaction ability the international financial and money capital can easily be used for speculation.This flow of large amount of short-term speculative capital can easily hit new deals in a minute or even in some seconds, thus financial crises can easily spread from one country to another and can neagtively affect a country's real economy, in a very short time.Thus, the contemporary crises, which mostly use capital flows and fund transfers, spread faster than the past economic crises which have mainly originated from production fields of the economy.[21]

Fifthly, the economic crisis, energy crisis, ecological crisis, social crisis and other forms of crises have become intertwined, all of which further accumulate and deepen the contradictions of the capitalist society. Since the British industrial revolution, capitalism and even the development of the human society was mainly based on the blind exploitation of minerals and energy sources provided by the nature and by destruction of the ecological environment.The excessive exploitation and affluent lives in the few countries of the West have directly led to the depletion of natural resources, to the destruction of the ecological environment and to the loss of natural ethics.Today,the depletion of energy sources, environmental pollution, natural disasters seriously threaten the survival of mankind. Many scholars from different countries increasingly agree with the view that such a global situation is mainly caused by the capitalist mode of production. Because this system relies on the unchecked use of natural resources and destruction of the ecological environment, it promotes unlimited consumption and wealth increase, pursues maximum capital appreciation and maximum profits. If we allow it develop unchecked, it will certainly lead to destruction of humankind. According to a report published by World Conservation Foundation on October 1, 1998, between 1970-1995, in 25 years the world lost nearly one third of its natural wealth. In the 1990s, forest wood consumed by the paper industry have become twofold compared

21 Liu Changgeng, A Study on the New Characteristics of World Economic Crisis, in: Social Science Journal of Xiangtan University, 2000(5).

to 1950s. Paper consumption of the US, Japan and Europe accounts for 2/3 of the world comsumption, almost all the wood which the industry consumes is supplied by the regions located in the third world countries.[22] In short, the natural energy sources issue and the environmental crisis increasingly deepen and becomes antagonistic under the conditions of globalized capitalism, this contradiction can be defined as: contradiction between the infinite expansion of capital accumulation and the limited material resources and material circulation adjustment capacityof the natural environment upon which the survival of humankind relies.

2. The impacts of the capitalist economic crisis

The new features of the capitalist economic crisis under the influence of the new technological revolution and economic globalization are only the changes in the formal aspects of it. It does not mean that the nature of the system based on the private capitalist ownership has changed. These changes to some extent, can extend the life of capitalism, but ultimately, they continue to accumulate and deepen the basic contradiction of capitalism on a new basis. Capitalist economic crisis is the wound which capitalist system cannot heal by itself, in the future it will eventually develop to a situation wherein this contradiction cannot be reconciled and be eased in the framework of capitalism, and lead to the demise of capitalism. Currently we are in the stage wherein it is still preparing the material basis and conditions for the passage to socialism.

The capitalist economic crisis has a significant impact on the emergence of socialist factors in the capitalist countries.In order to adapt to the development requirements of socialization of production, capitalism makes several due adjustments in the form of its production relations; such as the shareholding system (19th century), macro-economic planning, social welfare state practices, participation of trade-union organizations,which provide "clues" for us to resolve the contradiction of the capitalist mode of production and also creates the material basis for the emergence of new economic institutions and the new mode of production that will abandon capitalism.

The world-wide global production network, the global financial system, the knowledge system and the management system formed during the process of economic globalization have also prepared necessary conditions for the realization of socialism and communism throughout the world. The transition from the monopoly capitalism stage to the evolution of new forms of society accords with Lenin's classic judgement that "imperialism

22 Fu You, The Negative Influence of Globalization upon the Third World, in: Foreign Theoretical Trends, 1999(6).

is the highest stage of capitalism", "state monopoly capitalism is the most sufficient material preparation for socialism". The more capitalism develops, the more social factors develop in the womb of the old system. At the same time, we should also realize that although socialist factors emerge and develop within capitalism, they are constrained by the basic system of and socio-economic relations of capitalism, thus their growth are restricted. We cannot agree with the view that capitalism and socialism are in the process of "convergence" just because some social factors appear in the capitalist society.

On the other hand, since the 1980s and 1990s, an international trend of "anti-globalization" movement has appeared in the world which oppose bourgeois governments, its rapidly surging trend has drawn the attention of scholars studying the world socialist movement. Most of the leaders and participants of the anti-globalization movement belong to the strata which are encountering diffficulties and the individuals in the movement have lost their former social status or perceive threat due to increasing global competition among the western developed countries. Disadvantaged strata and groups in the developing countries will possibly the pioneers of the anti-globalization movement in the new round of international competition. If we examine the situation in theoretical circles, we can see that Western Marxists, the New Left, the ecologists, the pacifists, are fiercely criticizing globalization led by capitalist forces from different aspects. "Anti-globalization" trends of thoughts and movement have made fruitful contributions to the critique of capitalist globalization in a certain sense and promoted the improvement of international economic adjustment mechanisms. But in general, the "Anti-globalization" movement it is still relatively immature and lacks the scientific theoretical basis and lacks unity of organization, thus its orientation does not accord with the development of socialism at present.

The capitalist economic crisis also impacts the socialist countries and give them some important signals of warning. China is a socialist country whose economy is led by public ownership economy. It has fundamentally eliminated the root causes of economic crisis. However, in the face of real threats caused by economic crises, China cannot sit back and watch the fire. Since the market economy system in our country is basically established, the general possibility of economic crises may change from possibility to reality, due to the existence of non-public economy and due to the the imperfect status of public ownership. China will continue to insist openening to the outside world, and reject the past isolated status, given this world capitalist economic crises can effect and enter China through various means, which may cause serious fluctuations even crises in the domestic economy. During the Asian economic and financial crisis in 1997, China also suffered a great impact, although China has successfully managed a balance between domestic and foreign economy and became a pivotal stabilizing force in that regional crisis, but still paid a heavy price. Therefore deeper analysis of the capitalist economic crises can enable us have a comprehensive cognition of it and prevent us from laxity.

First, we must resist the trend of domesticprivatization and resist neoliberal thoughts and stick to the socialist path. The root cause of the capitalist economic crisis lies in the antagonistic basic contradictions of capitalism. To eliminate the economic crisis, firstly, the capitalist system should be eliminated. Capitalist production is socialized large-scale production, socialization of production requires the social ownership of production means which contradicts the private capitalist ownership on the means of production and this contradiction is temporarily/partially alleviated and adjusted in the form of cyclical economic crisis. This kind of alleviation and adjustment in the period of free competition mainly occur as a spontaneous adjustment by the market economy. In the state monopoly capitalism period, the "invisible hand" works together with the "visible hand"—the government—which means that the operation of the capitalist market economy becomes more purposeful, conscious and planned, all in all, these facts also push the capitalist economy to a higher level/stage of development. However, no matter how today's capitalism develops and flourishes, the basic contradiction of capitalism remains unchanged, which is an issue that cannot be solved by any form of self-adjustment.Therefore, we should resolutely resist the wave of domesic privatization and neoliberalism in order to ultimately avoid the economic crisis from the root. Especially the painful lessons of Russia's economic recession and financial crisis in the transition period after the drastic changes in Soviet Union and Eastern Europe, should prompt us to more firmly uphold the socialist development path.

Second, we should attach more importance to the study of the possibility of economic crisis under the conditions of socialism. China's socialist system has eliminated the capitalist system and fundamentally eliminated the root causes of the economic crisis. But this doesn't mean that an economic crisis will not occur in China and that we don't need to prevent from crises. China's resolute opening to the world determines that it is also possible that China can face an economic crisis. If not prevented timely an economic crisis may become a reality. Therefore, we cannot take this threat lightly, instead we should be good at learning from the lessons of the capitalist economic crises, especially from the crises occuring in the developing capitalist countries with similar national conditions and which are in the similar development stage with China. We should study the specific conditions and the specific reasons behind the eruption of crises specific conditions, the and do a good job in defining the signals of an approaching economic crises in order to prevent their occurance.

Third, we should further explore more effective forms of public ownership, thus open a broader space for the development of productive forces. Timely reforms have helped the capitalist countries against numerous crises. The cyclical economic crisis is the inevitable result of the fundamental contradiction of capitalism and cannot be solved in the framework of the capitalist system. The process of capitalist development is a dialectical process which includes, economic reforms to overcome crises, , eruption of new crises, then overcoming the crisis by counter measures, then self-regulation and self-renewal. We agree that the potential of capitalism to develop productive forces is not exhausted yet, thus its vitality is not exhausted, one basic fact which proves this judgement is its ability to overcome crises, we shouldn't underestimate its such ability. The way capitalism adopts to overcome the crisis can be summarized in a brief sentece: when faced by a crisis make the adjustment which accords with the general development direction, i.e. "mode of production should be adjusted according to the demands of the nature of production, i.e according to the social character of production." In its development capitalism has felt the need to pay attention to social equity, ecological environment, easing social contradictions, otherwise it wouldn't have minimum requirements/conditions necesarry for its furher development, nor could it effectively overcome crises.[23]

We are aware that the reality and conditions of the current socialism is still far from its ultimate target, and the development of the socialist system is still far from being perfect, even in many aspects we are still behind the developed capitalist countries. This situation is not in line with the requirements of socialism itself, but, that does not mean that we are not progressing. The capitalist countries still seek to make some adjustments to further improve and perfect the capitalist system, so should socialism seek for perfection, even with more enthusiasm. We should constantly improve the realization forms of the socialist system, make it better adapt to the development of socialized production and the requirements of the times, we should explore objective requirements so as to to achieve the coordination between specific form of production relations and development of productive forces, pay more attention to the harmony between man and nature, care about social equity, open a broader space for the development of productive forces. Through continuous adjustment, we can improve socialism, and ultimately achieve socialism beyond capitalism, win over capitalism.

23 Dong Jianping, The Practice and Theory of Counter-crisis Measures of Capitalism, Issues of Contemporary World Socialism, 2003(3).

3. Capitalist economic crisis and capitalism and socialism

The new phenomena and new trends of contemporary capitalism demonstrate that monopoly capitalism has developed to a new stage, the power of various monopoly capitals has greatly enhanced, and the monopoly bourgeoisie's form of exploitation and domination of the proletariat and the oppressed nations has become more complete. Similarly, contemporary capitalism is more progressive than the pre-war capitalism since it has created most abundant and most advanced productive forces of mankind, pushing the advent of the new technological revolution and informationization age. This shows that monopoly capitalism has a certain ability for self-regulation and self-improvement, it can within a certain range accommodate the development of productive forces, there may be a long and tortuous historical process before it will be replaced by socialism. However, the essence of contemporary capitalism is still monopoly capitalism, the essential nature of imperialism, i.e., the parasitic, decadent and dying nature of the imperialism created by its monopolistic nature has not fundamentally changed. Facts have proved that today's "welfare state" has never achieved "full employment" and "income equity", cannot completely eliminate poverty, the gap between the rich and the poor is still growing, the polarization among the world nations is also increasing.

The self-regulation and self-improvement of contemporary capitalism does improve the ability and level of bourgeois rule and its exploitation in varying degrees, it can thus reduce the magnitude of economic fluctuations and the destruction caused by economic crises, and ease the class contradictions within the developed capitalist countries and alleviate disputes of interests among developed capitalist countries, which has helped to the stability and development of postwar capitalism. However, this self-adjustment and self-improvement is carried out within the frarmework of the capitalist system. From Keynesianism to neoliberalism or the "third way", they couldn't ultimately overcome the basic contradiction of capitalism, instead only the eruption of crises have assumed different new forms. The global economic crisis of the western countries in 1990-1993 and the recent recession of "new economy" have fully proved that the room for self-regulation and self-improvement (in the aspect of relations of production) by contemporary capitalism is narrowing. The mechanisms of self-regulation led by the capitalist state can hardly rejuvenate capitalism. And the less developed capitalist countries which lack management experience and lesser room for improvements have faced more frequent crises in the 1980s and 1990s, this further proves that capitalism cannot solve a series of inherent major contradictions and crises faced by humanity, and cannot achieve the overall progress of human society, instead it exacerbates the existing contradictions and new contradictions are created, which lead to crises.

When analyzing the historical fate of capital, Marx pointed out:

"As long as capital is weak, it still itself relies on the crutches of past modes of production... As soon as it feels strong, it throws away the crutches, and moves in accordance with its own laws. As soon as it begins to sense itself as a barrier to development, it seeks refuge in forms which, by restricting free competition, seem to make the rule of capital more perfect, but are at the same time the heralds of its dissolution and of the dissolution of the mode of production resting on it."[24]

In the 1870s, capitalist class began to realize that it has approached to its development limits, and sought refuge and passsed to the form of private monopoly, by self-adjustment. After the World War II, capitalist class became more strongly aware of its own development restrictions, it has made a further self-adjustment from state monopoly to international monopoly and to other forms to extend its life. Although these sanctuaries and self-regulations have to a degree alleviated the "incurable disease" of capitalism and even avhieved stability and develeopment for a certain period of time,ultimately it cannot reverse the historical trend that capitalism is decadent and in decline. Capitalist mode of production is bound to constantly self-adjust and self-regulate itself, and when this adjustment reaches a certain extent and when it will lose its ability to alleviate its sharpening contradictions, the capitalist mode of production will inevitably be replaced by the new mode of social production, that is, socialism.

Socialism as a new ideological system and social system in human history, it can only survive and develop itself in the process of solving all kinds of challenges. In the early 20th century, socialism achieved a leap from theory to practice, later the victory of socialism spread from a single country to other countries. In the new period, the accumulation and deepening of the contradictions of the capitalist society and the economic crisis and social problems caused by these contradictions will lead to a situation and conditions conducive to the revival of socialist movement. At the turn of the 21st century, the western society has experienced the problems of economic recession, social polarization, war threat and terrorism events. After the drastic changes in the Soviet Union and Eastern Europe, the internal and external contradictions of capitalism were once more exposed, and Russia's crisis after the drastic changes (1991-93) is educating the people; the basic contradictions of capitalism has gradually intensified and led to economic crises and social unrest which included vast number of developing countries and regions... all these create social and historical conditions

24 Marx-Engels Collected Works, Vol. 8, p. 180.

for the resurge of socialist thoughts and the revival of socialist movement. The emergence and accumulation of social elements within the capitalist countries and the development of the socialist countries are the main factors that push forward the process of world socialism in the 21st century.

Socialism, as a benign social system cretaed by the human society, has written a glorious page in the development of world history. Although it is currently suffering from setbacks, socialism is not stagnant, and has not perished. The current development of capitalism, although its social system is not perfect; lays a more solid foundation for its transition to socialism and creats more adequate premises for the advent of this transition. No matter what ways can capitalism find for its self-adjustment, it is impossible for it to fundamentally solve the basic contradictions of capitalist society. Socialism is the product of the basic contradiction of capitalist society, it can create higher level of production relations than capitalism, and these production relation can create a broader space for the development and liberation of the productive forces, this is why socialism has a brighter prospect than capitalism. The existence and intensification of the fundamental contradictions of capitalism determines the inevitability of the eruption of economic crises. When capitalism can no longer overcome the crisis within the framework of existing social system, capitalism is bound to perish, and socialism will prevail. In terms of the general development trend of history of human society socialism replacing capitalism is the decisive condition for the ultimate solution to avoid economic crisis-- in a single country or globally. Of course, this will be a long process, as Lenin pointed out: the path of transition from capitalism to socialism is by no means smooth, but unimaginably complex.

(Zhang Xu, Professor of the Institute of Marxism, Renmin University of China)

Scientific Understanding of New Changes in the Class Structure in the Developed Capitalist Countries

There have been new changes in the class structure of the contemporary developed capitalist countries. We must analyze these changes with a scientific view and scientific theory, fully grasp the new features of these changes, and profoundly analyze the political impacts of these changes.

1. The scientific view in analyzing class structure

With the radical and complex changes in the class structure of the Western capitalist society, to enrich the Marxist class analysis theory has become more important, but it is a complicated and controversial issue. In this case, upholding the Marxist class analysis position, and absorbing some rational factors elements within the contemporary class theories is the theoretical prerequisite for scientific and comprehensive understanding of social class changes in Western capitalism.

The class theory of Marxism is profound and rich. The founders of Marxism, Marx and Engels, have made numerous comments on the issues

of class. Lenin once has given classic and often cited definition of class, as follows: "Classes are large groups of people differing from each other by the place they occupy in a historically determined system of social production, by their relation (in most cases fixed and formulated by law) to the means of production, by their role in the social organization of labor, and, consequently, by the dimensions of the share of social wealth of which they dispose and the mode of acquiring it. Classes are groups of people one of which can appropriate the labour of another owing to the different places they occupy in a definite system of social economy."[25]

Factors involving class issue and the issues mentioned by Lenin above can be summarized as in the following: position of possession of the means of production; the role in the social organization of labor; the dimensions of the share of social wealth of which they dispose and the mode of acquiring it. But these criteria are not a simple list regardless of primary and secondary, in which the relationship to ownership of production means is the fundamental one. This is the basic position of Marxism. Therefore, the division of the class must firmly grasp the core issue of position to the ownership production means, avoid dispersal of our main focus, only by this way can we see the essence behind the phenomena, grasp the trunk cloaked by the details. Of course, Marxism also affirms the complexity of

25 Lenin Selected Works, 3rd edition, Vol. 4, p. 11.

class issue, in addition to the possession of the means of production, there are other relationships. Each relationship has a complex appearance and they are intertwined, thus the issue becomes more complex. These require us not to look at the class issue naively.

Contemporary theories in respect to social structure of the developed Western capitalist societies has two categories of class theory and stratification theory. Comparatively speaking, class theory is a macroscopic qualitative analysis that attempts to divide society into classes based on certain benchmarks.

Rather, the stratification theory offers the microscopic and quantitative, analysis and divides society into several strata according to a certain index system. And these above theories are originally influenced by Marx and Max Weber. We can say that, if the theory of stratification is rather influenced by Weber, then the contemporary class theory is influenced to some extent by some aspects of Marxist tradition. Some contemporary Marxists claim that they are proposing "new-Marxist" class theories. The so-called "novelty" of the class theory is an attempt to enrich or revise the framework of the classical class analysis of Marxism. The so-called amendment, that is, to add new factors to class analysis or to re-adjust the weight of different factors in the analysis. For example, structuralists try to analyze the classes with three parallel factors of economy, politics and ideology. The so-called enrichment or expansion is to explore the classical class framework, to give it a new meaning. The most typical is the capital ownership issue. The Marxist class analysis theory emphasizes the ownership of the means of production, and means of production is in fact capital. Contemporary capital has a variety of appearance forms and a variety forms of realization. When commenting on the appearance forms of capital, some scholars view capital in a broader perspective, that is, for them capital is not only physical capital and money capital, but there is also the cultural capital, human capital, intellectual capital, social capital, and so on. This broad capital concept used to analyse social structure is clearly different from the former past concept of capital which is limited to the means of production. The biggest change in the capitalist society is those people who have more more and new types of capital, such as the intellectual class. And with the new trend of dispersal of company shares to people by stock exchange, the number of people in the society who owns capital has seen a significant increase, and the state and non-profit organizations have become an important holder of such shares or capital. Changes in the distribution of capital among people pushes us to a new kind of analysis: not only should we look if people own capital, but also look how much capital and what kind of capital they own.

I think, a Marxist examination of the changes in the social structure of the contemporary developed Western capitalist societies should be based on the following two basic points:

First, uphold the class analysis method based on the ownership of means of production. Class analysis methods, stratification analysis methods and individual analysis methods are several diffrenet views for understanding the social structure. But in the capitalist society, the most basic division in the social structure is still class, class contradictions and class struggle is still the most important factor to understand political issues. Compared with other analytical methods such as stratification, the class analysis method is fundamental and strategic. We cannot use other analysis to replace, dilute or cover class analysis. We must use class analysis to reveal the important changes in the basic social classes and the basic trend of social development. In the class analysis, we should uphold the criterion of ownership of production means as the basis of analysis. The bourgeoisie essentially exploit the surplus value created by the worker relying on the ownership of production means. As far as some of today's popular broadly defined capital concept, to what extent and degree they can be used as the criteria for classifying the classes need to be re-considered. At the present stage, the ownership of the production means still remains the essence and the core of the class distinctions compared to other various forms of capital and other factors. Leaving aside the issue of ownership of means of production does not accord with the true meaning of the class concept. Some Western scholars also affirm that the property ownership dimension of the class structure in the capitalist society is still the most basic factor.[26]

Second, we must actively utilize various rational factors in the contemporary class analysis theories. In order to explain the changes in contemporary Western social structure in a more convincing way, Marxists must also pay attention to the combination of some new analytical methods. The important feature of the new changes in the structure of the contemporary society is the increase in its complexity. In order to grasp this complex structure and change, it is necessary to make an examination from multiple angles. On the one hand, we should pay attention to the role of stratification analysis theory. There are both class analysis and stratification analysis in classical Marxist theory. Class analysis and stratification analysis both have advantages in understanding the social structure and, to some extent, complement each other. The contemporary western social structure is indeed becoming more and more complex. The combination of class analysis and class analysis is conducive to the combination of macro and micro, the combination of qualitative and quantitative, and focusing on more specific issues. Deeper and meticulous class analysis is a useful and necessary supplement to the broad-line class analysis. On the other hand, we should pay attention to the influence of some new factors in class analysis. In the class analysis, in

26 Eric O. Wright, Class Counts: Comparative Studies in Class Analysis Studies, Shengyang, Liaoning Education Press, 2004, p. 243.

addition to the essential factor of ownership upon the means of production, we must also pay attention to other factors such as ideology, social status in the society and other factors besides capital ownership. The influence of these factors on the class status of people is different in different historical conditions and different for various social groups. The general trend in the contemporary era is that the impact of these factors is increasing, especially for those who are in the management and professional status. Specific and in-depth analysis of the impact of these factors can enhance the class analysis of the times, enhance its pertinence and persuasion. The famous US class analysis scholar Erik O. Wright has tried to develop the concept of Marxist analysis and predictions on the class structure of the capitalist society into a satisfactory form of operation, so as to describe some of the obvious features of the class structure in the American society.

2. New characteristics and changes in the class structure of Western developed capitalist countries

In classical Marxism, according to the different ownership forms of production means, the social class structure of the capitalist society was divided into two basic classes and a minor class, that is, class possessing production means and employing others is the bourgeoisie, class not possessing the production means and being employed is the proletariat, members of the class possessing certain degree of production means and who earn their life with self-employment belong to the petty bourgeoisie. Due to various changes in the socio-economic life, the three basic classes of the contemporary Western society have encountered new changes.

The contemporary working class presents new features. First, the ranks of the working class are still large. Some Western theories argue that the working class is shrinking and even dying. With the dispersal of capital, the number of people in Western developed countries began to own a certain number of stocks has increased dramatically, in some of the so-called the countries of "people's capitalism" this situation is more obvious. Another example is, in accordance with cultural capital theory or human capital theory, some professionals and technical experts are owners of such capital. So many people have different amounts and different types of capital, making the proportion of people who have no capital greatly reduce. Pranchez has reduced working class to those who are directly engaged in material production, who directly create surplus values, which amounts to only 19.7 percent in the society.[27]

27 Li Qingyi, The Contemporary Capitalism Theory of "Western Marxism", Chongqing Publishing House, Chongqing, 1990, p. 107.

The result of this study contradicts the classic approach of Erik. O. Wright, according to Erik. O. Wright, 40 percent of people are in the working class (in the narrow sense) in the United States during the 1990s. In general, he has affirmed that the working class does not only exist, but its ranks has greatly expanded, when examined by the Marxist standard of its relation to the production means, i.e., its members are not the owners of production means and they are wage laborers, or wage earners. Erik. O. Wright believes that even in the narrow sense of this criterion the working class is still the largest class in the developed capitalist society, even the absolute majority.[28]

Second, the internal structure of the working class has changed. One of the most prominent features is the relative reduction in the number of traditional blue-collar workers. In the process of the development of contemporary capitalism, the service industry has grown radically and became the leading industry, the first and second branches of industries are reduced, and in the past these industries employed the blue-collar workers. And in various industries, the proportion of white-collar workers have seen a substantial increase. It should be pointed out that in the process of economic globalization, the downstream industries of the Western countries were gradually transferred to developing countries, and there are quite a number of foreign workers in various difficult industries. These factors together, significantly reduce the number of traditional workers. In contrast, the proportion of workers engaged in technical work, management and service sector is rising and becoming the main growth fields of the working class.

Thirdly, the class attributes of the working class are becoming increasingly complex. Some workers have a small amount of capital; although this cannot fundamentally change their class attributes, but it has a certain degree of impact on their ideas and thinking. Some workers have multiple identities, such as managers, who have both the working-class attribute and in fact they perform some of the functions of the total capital, which to some extent affect their class identity. Some workers have weaker working-class attributes, especially those that are relatively apart from the means of production and have quite indirect relations to the means of production. There are also women, retired groups, etc., some of them are relatively largely affected by the family relation, and some relatively largely affected by the government policies.

There is also a change in the capitalist class. With the diversification of capital forms, as we have mentioned above the composition of capitalists has also become more complex. In addition to the capitalists who directly occupy the production means there are capitalists who only hold stock capital and earn divident and interest. In addition, some people with

28 Eric O. Wright, Class Counts: Comparative Studies in Class Analysis Study, p. 75.

knowledge and management skills can quickly get rich with the new economic changes, they can become new wealth giants. For example, in the newly emerged information industry, some far-sighted people have used high-tech achievements into new commodities and services and successfuly established new companies by the help of the venture capital. They are, of course, capitalists, but in some respect we should make an appropriate distinction with them and the traditional capitalists. And even some scholars call some of them as "IT capitalists". As for the proportion of capitalists in society, Wright's quantitative study is that if the bourgeoisie is defined as employing more than 10 workers, they are not more than 2% in all the developed countries and they are less than 1% in Sweden and Norway. While Pranchez's study demonstrates the percentage of all employers are 7.5%, of course, this figure also includes all small sized employers.

The middle-class (the petty bourgeoisie) has encountered even more radical changes. In the 19th Century Marx had argued that with the development of capitalism, the middle-class, i.e. the petty bourgeoisie class would disintegrate and diminish in size and the working class would expand and the capitalist society would increasingly tend to be divided into two classes: the working class and the bourgeoisie. In the contemporary Western society changes in the class structure shows great complexity. The middle class did not shrink and disappear as expected but was maintained tenaciously and had a new growth point. The middle class in the early days of capitalism mainly refers to the farmers and so on. Self-employed people in the contemporary Western societies still share a considerable proportion, but they are not mainly the original farmers of the past, but a variety of small service providers such as retailers, especially educated professionals such as doctors and lawyers. They have a certain amount of production means, such as office space and relevant work or business equipment and have appropriate professional skills. In the United States at least 1/4 of the labor force or 1/3 of men are self-employed. With the development of the information society, the physical capital required for the service industry is relatively smaller, there also occured some self-employment phenomena in the high-tech industries.

To understand and analyze the changes in the contemporary Western class structure, it is necessary to clarify the problem of the middle class in particular. The rise of the middle-class is considered to be the most important feature of the change in the social structure of the developed West. Some of today's statistics, especially in the mass media, frequently use the concept of middle class. The concept of the middle class to a certain extent impacts the understanding of Western class structure. To accurately understand the middle class, we must pay attention to two points. First, the middle class is actually a concept with hierarchical sense. In English

Typology of Class Locations in Capitalist Society

Assets in the means of production

	Owners of means of production	Non-owners [wage labourers]				
Owns sufficient capital to hire workers and not work	1 Bourgeoisie	4 Expert Managers	7 Semi Credentialled Managers	10 Uncredentialled Managers	+	
Owns sufficient capital to hire workers but must work	2 Small Employers	5 Expert Supervisors	8 Semi Credentialled Supervisors	11 Uncredentialled Supervisors	>0	*Organization assests*
Owns sufficient capital to work for self but not to hire workers	3 Petty Bourgeoisie	6 Expert non-managers	9 Semi Credentialled Workers	12 Proletarians	-	
		+	>0	-		
			Skill/credential assets			

Erik O. Wright, Classes, 1985, Verso, London, p. 88.

"class" and "strata" is the same word, but in Chinese middle class is actually the middle strata,different from the term middle class. Second, most of the middle class are the working class and the main standard for the middle class is income. And this income is not equal to "means of production" criterion used for the division of the class. Income may come from wages, or from the capital gains. While most of the middle class's income come from wages, or mainly from wages. They do not own or rely on the ownership of production means to make their living. Their "ownership" mainly includes living means, such as houses, cars, high-end durable consumer goods, rather than means of production.

To understand the changes in contemporary Western social structure, we also need to pay attention to the following two issues. First, we should have a global vision. With the rapid and deepening development of economic globalization, the social structure is expanding from a country level to the global scale. It will not be proper to examine the changes in the social structure of the developed countries on the country level, especially for the working class, because the industrial working class in the third world is expanding globally. Second, the problem of indirect class relation. In the classical class theory, the class attribution of an individual is determined by the his/her relationship with the means of production. However, an individual's class status is also affected by various factors, especially by the relationship with other family members (parents or wives) and their relationship with the state. These constitute their indirect relationships which is relative to their direct relationship with the means of production. Class attributions of some individuals in the society are wholly or mainly determined by these indirect relations, such as their relations to spouses, wives, elders. The study of such indirect relations cannot be ignored.

As one of the representative scholars of the contemporary class analysis, Erik O. Wright, based on the ownership of means of production and by taking into account the factors of using managerial power and technology, has made a more comprehensive analysis of the contemporary Western social class structure (see table above).

Wright's analysis of the different forms of the bourgeoisie is based on who own means of production and who is self-employed. The bourgeoisie proper is those among these who employ ten or more workers. Small employers are those who employ between two and ten workers, and the petty bourgeoisie are those who employ one or no workers, and who are self-employed. All others are non-owners or wage labourers, although some may have higher incomes.

This schema has some value for reference in understanding the complexity of the classes. In Erik O. Wright's view, the main form of exploitation in the capitalist society is based on property rights upon the means of production.

There are three classes on this basis: the capitalist class, the exploiters; the working class, the exploited; the members of the petty bourgeoisie who are neither exploiters nor the exploited. Managers and supervisors are involved in the practice of controlling and supervising the production process, who are the actors exercising their powers to serve the capitalists. They are in a contradictory class status, in terms of their relation to means of production they are similar to workers, as the controllers and managers of the capitalist production process they are similar to capitalists. Their level or status in the hierarchy of production organization, determines whether they are more a capitalist or a worker. The working-class ranks consists of three positions: the working class plus the adjacent skilled workers and non-technical supervisors. The bourgeois ranks consist of capitalists and managers with expertise. The others are included in the middle-class ranks.

3. Political results of class structure changes in Western capitalist countries

The new changes in the class structure of the Western society have not altered the essence of capitalism. First, the basic classes of the capitalist society still exist. Marx regards slave owners and slaves, landlords and serfs, the bourgeoisie and the proletariat as the basic classes of slave society, feudal society and capitalist society. The modern Western society is neither a classless society nor a society in which the basic classes are fundementally changed. Although there are some changes in the quantity and labor form of the working class and the capitalist class today, the two are still the basic classes that dominate and oppose each other in the society. Second, the class contradictions of capitalist society still exist. The class contradictions in the capitalist society have both violent and moderate forms of expression and are not all manifested in the form of big strikes and even in the form of revolutions. As a result of the relatively long-term peaceful development of the West and due to the fact that the ruling class makes conscious attempts to alleviate the contradictions between classes, the class struggle of the West is not always so intense. But the capitalist class always occupies the surplus value created by the workers, and the working class is always exploited by the capitalist, or the working class does not become a capitalist class. Thus, fundamentally, the opposition between the two classes does not evoparate. Of course, today's class differences and distinctions in the West, class contradictions and class struggle appear in a new form and manifest themselves in multiple forms. In short, the economic aspects are mainly reflected in the huge income inequality and this inequality is difficult to surmount; in the social aspects we see the conflict between social openness and social closure; in the political aspect we see the contradictions between the technologicism (also known as expert governance) and democratic participation. The current new social movements, the anti-globalization movement, the movement for workers' rights and interests are all manifestations of these contradictions. It should be seen that these contradictions are not only difficult to solve fundamentally but cannot be surmounted within the framework of the capitalist system, they but may also intensify as the surrounding conditions encounter certain changes.

The new changes in the Western class structure have not changed the historical mission of the working class. Marxism has given the working class a great historical mission of transforming the Western society. However, in the face of changes in Western society, some people have questioned this.

First, the theory of working class disappearing. Adam Schaff and some other scholars have argued that the main subject of socialism is "blank" or "absent", that is, socialism will find the class to rely on. In the view of Schaff, today the process of using automation and robots in the field of production and service cause the demise of the traditional proletariat.[29]

Second, the working class is not the revolutionary class anymore. Marcuse has argued that the people belonging to working class in the West are no longer revolutionary, they are no longer the main force of the revolution, but although the working-class is incapable of acting as a revolutionary force, it is by no means to be identified politically with the capitalist class. …"[30], i.e., it has become a political appendage of the capitalist class. What was once the "working class" had become a socially and professionally stratifed and also a differentiated mass, a mass integrated and pacifed through technologies of pleasure and the lures of middle-class affluence. The social revolution should count on the new proletariat, young students and the marginalized "victimized social groups"—the poor, minorities, women and the rest. The left-wing scholar Ernest Mandel has insisted that today there are more than 1 billion people belonging to the working classes in the world, they are stronger than ever. In terms of world-wide prospects and long-term development, the proletariat does not tend to weaken, but tends to grow, not tends to scatter, but strengthens its unity."[31]

According to the definition of Marxism, the working class is still the only social force in the world that has the potential to topple capitalism and save mankind and realize a higher civilization in the face of human catastrophe. To realize this great historical mission, the working class needs to build up and deploy broad forces.

29 Gorbachev et al., Future Socialism, Central Compilation & Translation Press, Beijing, 1994, p. 105.
30 Li Qingyi, The Theories on Contemporary Capitalism by "Western Marxism" Scholars, p. 132.
31 See Ernest Mandel et al., "Socialism and the Future", p. 160.

First, seek to mobilize all those within the ranks of the working class.

With the deepening of the division of labor in modern society, more and more workers are not directly involved with machinized production and do not work directly in the production field, are not directly involved with the production of material goods, but their labor is an integral part of the entire social labor process. The ranks of the contemporary working class have become more complex and include different sub-segments, due to differences in the degree of their subjective consciousness, due to the different social impacts upon them, the political and ideological attitude of each segment is naturally different. Therefore, it is necessary to approach the working class from the perspective of overall interest of the whole working class and seek to mobilize all those within the ranks of the working class with this approach.

Second, seek to mobilize the synergy of all other progressive classes in the society. The structure of contemporary Western society is complex and various classes in the society possess the potential to change the society. Without mobilizing the potential of all kinds of different forces and without joining with them it will be impossible to achieve profound changes in the society. In this sense, even the most powerful working class should not attempt to act alone, instead the working class should seek to develop social synergy with other classes, form the "Rainbow Alliance" with them as proposed by some left-wing scholars.

Some people have even gone further in their exploration, as Jose F. Tezanos from Spain has argued: the recent technological revolution has reduced the ranks of the traditional working class, consequently the working class assumes a completely different form compared to that in the past. The increasing complexity of society requires that we should seek new ideas, there cannot just be a single social subject as the motive force of social change. More precisely, we should shift our attention to different subjects as the motive force of the socialism cause.[32] The working-class parties have a special historical responsibility to fight for social change in the Western societies. Changes in the structure of Western societies raise new challenges for political parties based on the working class. As in France, after the Second World War, the social class structure has undergone major changes. In some of the newly emerged industrial sectors, there are a lot of white-collar workers who are involved with technology and management. In the old industrial sectors such as construction, transportation, metallurgy and machine manufacturing and other classic hard labor industries, France is currently using a large number of immigrant workers. This makes the French traditional working class quite hard to understand. The decline and

32 J.F. Tezanos, Modernization and Social Change in Spain, p. 23.

ascend of the Communist Party and the Socialist Party after the war in France are closely related with these changes in this social structure. It is a difficult problem that needs deeper exploration for the working class parties to adapt to these changes and maintain the traditional nature of the party, so as to lead the working class and progressive social groups in realizing the great historical mission. The working-class party must effectively integrate and unite the working class and other progressive groups, and must strive to expand its social base, represent the interests of the whole class, also uphold integrate the social demands of all other the progressive groups. The working-class parties should also design a proper struggle strategy. Aldo, the relationship between contemporary classes and political parties is becoming increasingly complex. For example, in the elections occuring in the West workers do not support the Communist Party, nor does it necessarily support left-wing parties, and some workers even vote for conservative parties. Therefore, a political party who claims to be a working class party cannot take it for granted the support of the working class. To get the greater support of the class, they should design practical policies and strategies, in particular, they need to design policies to safeguard the interests of the majority of the lower class. In this respect, there are many past lessons to be summed up and there is a lot to be explored.

(Tao Wenzhao, Professor of Institute of Marxism, Renmin University of China)

The Relation between Capitalism and Socialism in the Process of Economic Globalization

Since the 20th century, a series of major historical events have produced a broad and profound impact on the whole world pattern and on the development of human civilization, globalization is one of the typical events. At the beginning of the 20th century, "imperialism" was the focus of theoretical discussion and ideological struggle. By the end of the 20th century, "economic globalization" has become the focus of various thought schools and focus of debates among them. In the process of economic globalization, can capitalism overcome its basic contradictions and crises so as to achieve an ultimate solution? What kind of impact can the new development of capitalism make on socialism? In the process of globalization, what are the prospects for the development of socialism? These are important issues that we must correctly answer when studying contemporary capitalism and world socialism.

1. The meaning, process and essence of globalization

In today's world, although many people are using the concept of "globalization", people from different classes, different countries and different cultural backgrounds have different understanding on the globalization process. A report by the Organization for Economic Cooperation and Development (OECD) has argued that the term "globalization" was first proposed by T. Levy in 1985 to describe the great changes in the international economy over the past 20 years, that is, the global exchange of goods, services, capital and technology in the spheres of production, consumption and investment. By the 1990s, the term "globalization" has shaken the globe, many scholars have defined globalization from different perspectives. Some looking from a technical point of view see the globalization as the development of information and communication technology, so that a variety of information can spread rapidly in the world. Some looking from the economic point of view, say that globalization is the free flow of resources and production organization on a global scale, as the former chief economist of the OECD, S. Osler has argued: the increasing flow of production factors across the globe, to achieve the best configuration of allocation of resources is globalization, the International Monetary Fund (IMF) has also given a definition of globalization as follows: "the increase of cross-border trade of goods and services and surging of international capital flows in scale and form, as well as the rapid spread of technology, the result of which increase the dependency among the economies of the world."[33]

33 Jin Huiming, Luo Wendong, A New View on Contemporary Capitalism, pp. 41-42.

Western left-wing scholars who look from the social system point of view, say that globalization is mainly the global expansion of monopoly capital, it is in essence the globalization of the capitalist system. Club of Rome scholars who look from the perspective of relationship between man and the natural environment, say that globalization is the formation of global awareness and global consensus on the enviromental problem. There are also scholars who have studied the issue from the perspective of social change, they claim that globalization refers to the transition of various fields, peoples and countries which were separated from each other and lived in closed state, today they have transited to a global level of process communication which is a great social change.

In China we should uphold the Marxist view, especially views and methodologies of the Marxist historical materialism, combine our study with the actual requirements of China's socialist modernization, and scientifically explain the historical process and the essential characteristics of the globalization. As early as over 160 years ago, Marx and Engels in the "Communist Manifesto" pointed out: "The bourgeoisie has through its exploration of the world market given a cosmopolitan character to production and consumption in every country."…. "In place of the old local and national seclusion and self-sufficiency, today we have intercourse in every direction, universal inter-dependence of nations, as in material production, so also in intellectual production." "The bourgeoisie, by the rapid improvement of all instruments of production, by the immensely facilitated means of communication, draws all, even the most barbarian, nations into civilisation. The cheap prices of commodities are the heavy artillery with which it batters down all Chinese walls, with which it forces the barbarians' intensely obstinate hatred of foreigners to capitulate. It compels all nations, on pain of extinction, to spread the bourgeois mode of production; it compels them to introduce what it calls civilisation into their midst, i.e., to become bourgeois themselves. In one word, it creates a world of its own image."[34]

Marx and Engels have used three concepts of "subordination" to outline the main features of this world system caused by the development of capitalism, as follows: "The bourgeoisie has subordination the countryside to the rule of the towns. It has created enormous cities, has greatly increased the urban population as compared with the rural, and has thus rescued a considerable part of the population from the idiocy of rural life. Just as it has made the country subordinated to the towns, so it has made barbarian and semi-barbarian countries subordinated to the civilised ones, peasant nations to the bourgeois nations, the East to the West."[35]

34 Marx-Engels Collected Works, Vol. 2, pp. 35-36.

35 Ibid., p. 36.

Since the rise of the industrial revolution in the mid-18th century, the international division of labor and international exchanges have expanded rapidly. By the beginning of the 20th century, since the monopolistic trusts and the rule of financial capital was established, and export of capital had greatly developed, international monopoly capitalist associations which divide the world among themselves were formed, and the territorial division of the whole world—as colonies, semi-colonies and dependent countries—among the biggest capitalist powers was completed. Lenin, after examining the actual situation of the evolvement of capitalism into the imperialist stage, made the following assertion: "capitalism has grown into a world system of colonial oppression and of the financial strangulation of the overwhelming majority of the population of the world by a handful of 'advanced' countries"[36] "The entire economic, political and spiritual life of mankind has become more and more internationalized under the capitalist system. Socialism will fully internationalize these three aspects of life (economic, political and spiritual life)."[37]

Today's "globalization", Marx's "world-history" and Lenin's "internationalization", thoughts are not only in the same breath, but these three thoughts have inherent and inevitable links and also several common points. We can say that today's globalization has emerged from Marx's "world historical" development and Lenin's "internationalization". Although the classic Marxist writers did not directly use the term "globalization", they made a scientific prediction of the essential characteristics and development trend of globalization from the social conditions at that time. Famous US journalist John Cassidy wrote: "When Marx wasn't driving the reader to distraction, he wrote riveting passages about globalization, inequality, political corruption, monopolization, technical progress, the decline of high culture, and the enervating nature of modern existence issues that economists are now confronting anew." "Globalization" is the buzzword of the late 20th century, on the lips of important figures including Jiang Zemin or Tony Blair, but Marx predicted most of its ramifications a hundred and fifty years ago... Globalization is set to become the biggest political issue of the next century."[38]

After World War II, globalization has gradually developed from the globalization of commercial capital and bank capital to the new stage wherein the globalization of industrial capital and financial capital occured. The capitalist mode of production began to spread to most countries and regions of the world. Western monopoly capital has integrated the world's

36 Lenin's Monographs on Capitalism, p. 102.

37 Collected Works of Lenin, 2nd Chinese edition, Vol. 23, Beijing, People's Publishing House, 1990, p. 332.

38 Yu Keping: "Socialism" in the Era of Globalization, pp. 1-4.

production and exchange activities into a united system. The reason why the concept of "globalization" was widely discussed in the 1980s and 1990s was mainly due to the process of globalization, which had already been germinated, and because it has already demonstrated a series of new features: (1) informationzation–rapid development of information industry with computer and network technology as the core, consequently the contacts and communication among people have become more and more frequent and closer, restrictions of time and space for people have become increasingly marginal, all of which have laid the new material and technical foundation for globalization. (2) marketization–Western countries have relaxed economic controls over the markets, consequently the world market has further expanded, thus the markets have begun to play an increasingly important role in the economic and social life. (3) liberalization–a radical weakening of various custom tariff barriers, the liberalization of the economies of the capitalist countries, and the smooth flow of goods, services, capital and technology.

The new scientific and technological revolution with IT and network technology as the core besides both the development of state-monopoly capitalism and supra-state-monopoly capitalism have enabled the developed countries to mobilize more human, material and financial resources to push the global expansion policy. Western countries led by the United States even manipulated the IMF, the World Bank, the WTO, to ensure that they can be in the dominant position in the economic globalization process and the whole world system. When we analyze the role of western multinational companies, which are the main carriers of global production and the internationalization or globalization of capital, we see that they have widely implemented global business strategies and these companies have expanded both in quantity and scale. According to the UNCTAD "World Investment Report 2009" statistics, the number of global multinational companies have reached 82,000, and their foreign branches have reached 810,000. Some experts estimate that among the world's 100 largest enterprises multinational companies account for half; and the world's largest 100 multinational companies possess almost 1/4 of the total pruductive assets of the total globally, 15 multinational companies almost control the trade of the basic commodities of all the world trade. To a greater extent, multinational companies control the 40 to 50% of world production and control more than 50% of the whole international trade, more than 90% of international direct investment and civil technological development, consequently they occupy an increasingly strong monopoly position in international trade, finance, investment and production spheres.[39]

39 Jin Huiming and Luo Wendong, A New View on Contemporary Capitalism, p. 44.

After analyzing the new phenomena and characteristics of recent globalization wave, it is not difficult to find that the globalization so far has made a profound dual effect: on the one hand, it is an objective process pushed by the vigorous development of social productive forces and division of labor, indicating that goods, services, capital and technology and other factors of production enter into global flow and global network which also create favorable conditions for socialism to achieve a leap-forward development. On the other hand, it is a new historical process in which capitalist relations of production and social system expand to the whole globe more deeply, so that monopoly bourgeoisie can chase extreme profits all over the world and attempts to maintain the domination of capitalism, which will inevitably exacerbate the global competition between capitalism and socialism, which means that socialism will face more severe challenges.

2. New development of capitalism in globalization era is preparing more abundant and advanced material conditions for the future socialism

As the inevitable product of scientific and technological progress and the expansion and deepening of world-wide exchanges, globalization has provided a new means of self-adjustment for the external expansion of western monopoly capital and also a new means for the relaxation of domestic economic crisis, thus opened up a new space for survival and development of contemporary capitalism. At the same time, globalization has also promoted the development of science and technology and productive forces, as well as an increase in the degree of socialization of production, laying a solid material and technological foundation for the establishment of a new society,--socialism-- which is mainly manifested as in the following:

Firstly, globalization has provided favorable conditions for the rapid development of modern science and technology and conditions for its globalized promotion and globalized utilization. Capitalism in the process of its global expansion, not only widely used science and technology in the production process, but also used them for improving the organization of production in order to improve labor productivity. As early as the second half of the 18th century, the first industrial revolution marked by the invention and application of the steam engine pushed the humanity from the agricultural society to the industrial society and paved the way for the large-scale machinized production. By the second half of the 19th century, the second scientific and technological revolution marked by the invention of electric power and internal combustion engine, the rapid development of industry was promoted in Europe and the US, pushed the human society into the electrification era. After the World War II, during 1950-1960s, atomic and electronic technology as the main symbols of the new technological revolution, also promoted birth and development of nuclear, semiconductor, synthetic chemistry, aerospace and other industries, pushed the humankind into the atomic and electronic age. By the second half of the 1980s, Western countries once again set off a new upsurge of scientific and technological revolution, microelectronics technology, information technology, bio-engineering, aerospace technology, laser technology, new materials processing technology; new energy technologies have developed rapidly. The IT industry with computer and network technology as its core has also developed rapidly, became the new leading industry, and pushed the humankind into the era of informationization and globalization. Contemporary high-tech "penetration" is very strong, when applied to traditional industries, it promotes the development of the "sunset industries", and when applied to financial industry, commerce, transportation, it can improves the efficiency of these sectors of economy. In general, the research and development in science and technology, requires a lot of funds but also need a deeper division of labor, and inevitably require the coooperation of individual enterprises and even individual countries. This funding question requires wide range of international exchanges and cooperation to achieve globalization of scientific and technological research and development. In 1985, the West European governments collectively began implementing the "Eureka" research project in the face of the growing US and Japanese dominance in the fields of high technology, to achieve the goals of "Technology Europe" and "European Technological Community", in order to enhance the competitive potential of the industries and economies of European countries in the world markets, which will also aimed to promote economic growth and employment conditions in Europe. The US and Japan have also strengthened their cooperation in scientific research and development projects, to maintain their leadership in cutting-edge technologies.

The new technological revolution has greatly promoted the recent wave of globalization, it didn't only promote development of the countries around the world to varying degrees but increasingly helped the modernization and "updating" of their industrial structures. Besides, it has provided a powerful impetus for the development of social productive forces and changes in the relations of social production. According to relevant statistical data, the US economy has encountered a steady growth between 1991 to 2000, which is closely related to the new technological revolution and the development of the IT industry. Currently, the US high-tech industries contribute to the 30% of GDP, the IT industry contributes the 15% of the GDP, thus some people even define the IT industry as "the fourth industrial revolution (Industry 4.0).[40]

40 See Li Wei, New Developments in Contemporary Capitalism, Beijing, Economic Science Press, 1998, p. 52-53.

The new technological revolution and the application of its achievements to various industries not only improve the labor productivity and economic development level, but also makes people's production capacity, production methods and their status in the production, encounter a qualitative leap, which increasingly lays the material and technological basis for more advanced social production and can help the entire social planning and socio-economic regulation. As the founders of scientific socialism, Marx and Engels have put forward a series of basic characteristics and historical conditions concerning the mode of production of the future society, material conditions of which are rapidly developing with the impetus given by the new scientific and technological revolution.

Second, globalization is conducive to further expansion of the world market, prepares conditions for the unified allocation of natural resources, capital and labor across the world. Globalization promotes the expansion of commodity production and market mechanisms to expand to the whole world, making the market economy increasingly become the economic system adopted by all countries in the world. It is conducive to the development of international division of labor and enables the flow of goods, services, capital and technology and other production factors all across the world, and forms a unified, open world market. Under such conditions, the operations of enterprises are forced to transcend smaller domestic markets, but need to operate according to the demands of the global market, need to give full play to their strengths, expand their production scales and production capacity, enjoy the benefits of economies of scale. At the same time, the competition in the world market also forces enterprises to continue to utilize new science and technology, improve their management, thus reduce production costs, improve product quality and enhance the competitiveness of enterprises at home and abroad. Since the 1980s, with the growth of world production and exchange the degree of socialization of production and the improvement in resource allocation have developed; all these are the result of the positive effect of globalization. In the 1990s, for the so-called "New Economy" featured by "Four Highs" (high growth, high share price, high exchange rate, high productivity) and "Four Lows" (low inflation, low unemployment, low fiscal deficit and low interest rates) in the US, globalization can be said to be an important reason for this New Economy. Even former US. President Bill Clinton acknowledged that economic globalization and the US's "highly open economy" inhibited inflation. It is well known that the economic forms of socialism predicted by Marx was inspired by the then historical context of the western advanced capitalist countries, Marx emphasized the historical prprerequisite for socialism, i.e, the full development of capitalist commodity economy. The market economies of the contemporary western developed countries is becoming more and more perfect, the world market further expands and deepens and a global production network system, financial system, knowledge exchange system and a global governance system are being formed, which prepare the increasingly adequate material and technical foundations for a more effective resources allocation across the world and pushes humanity to the final realization of socialism and communism.

Third, globalization promotes people's world-wide activities and exchanges, creates conditions for the formation of comprehensive relations, multifaceted needs and a comprehensive system of capabilities for the mankind. Capitalism has destroyed feudal autocracy, old hierarchical privileges and personal dependence, promoted freedom, equality, fraternity, democracy and human rights, liberated mankind from feudal autocracy and religious theology, consequently independent personality based on dependence to things dependency was achieved. Today with the global expansion of market economy, man's dependence on man (personal dependence) has further perished, men are further freed from all kinds of natural kinship or blood relationships and further freed from super-economic relations of subordination, and men have begun to establish more deeper universal relations which enable them go beyond isolated geographical regions and narrow boundaries of the nation-state, as Marx wrote: "a system of general social metabolism, of universal relations, of all- round needs and universal capacities is formed for the first time "[41] ... "production founded on capital creates universal industriousness on one side – i.e. surplus labour, value-creating labour – so does it create on the other side a system of general exploitation of the natural and human qualities, a system of general utility, utilizing science itself just as much as all the physical and mental qualities..."[42]

Marx added: "the discovery, creation and satisfaction of new needs arising from society itself; the cultivation of all advanced qualities of socialized human being, in parallel emergence of men with advanced needs, since men are becoming richer in qualities and relations – emergence of such new human beings as the most total and universal possible social product, because, in order to take gratification in a many-sided way, he must be capable of multiple pleasures [Germ. genussfähig], hence humankind attains high degree of cultural development.."[43]

Only in the process of deepening of globalization, capitalism can create those individuals who can truly possess advanced qualities who can benignly regulate his relations both with other men and with nature, "Hence the great civilizing impact of capital; pushes the formation of a new stage of society much more advanced when compared to all earlier societies which

41 Marx-Engels Collected Works, Vol. 8, p. 52 (Grundrisse).

42 Ibid., p. 51 (Grundrisse).

43 Ibid., p. 53 (Grundrisse).

appear as mere *local developments* of humanity and as *nature-idolatry.*" ... In accordance with this tendency, capital spreads beyond national barriers and destroys prejudices, worshipping of nature, as well as all traditional, confined, complacent, encrusted satisfactions ways of needs and hinders the reproductions of the old ways of life. Globalized capital destructs all these, and constantly revolutionizes peoples' lives, demolishes all the barriers which hem in the development of the forces of production, the expansion of needs, the all-sided development of production, and the utilization and exchange of natural and mental forces among people."[44]

It is precisely because of this, Marx wrote: "In history up to the present it is certainly an empirical fact that separate individuals have, with the broadening of their activity into world-historical activity, have become more and more enslaved under a power alien to them.....a power which has become more and more enormous and, in the last instance, turns out to be the world market.....Only then will the isolated individuals be liberated from the various national and local barriers, be brought into practical connection with the material and intellectual production of the whole world and be put in a position to acquire the capacity to enjoy this all-sided production of the whole earth (the creations of man)."[45]

When we evaluate the current development of socialism in China, globalization provides us with new opportunities as follows: With the free flow of capital and other factors of production globally, China's further opening can attract foreign capital and advanced science and technology and speed up the pace of socialist modernization construction; China can learn from the experience of developed capitalist countries on macroeconomic regulation and control of the national economy and improve business management, combine them with its own reality, establish economic management system and modern enterprise system; give full play to its comparative advantages, utilize both the domestic and foreign resources and markets, adjust its industrial structure, in order to achieve the upgrading of industrial structure and so on. In short, globalization provides a very broad platform and convenient conditions for China to widely absorb and draw on the outstanding civilized achievements of other countries, especially learn from the developed capitalist countries, globalization can offer China a historic opportunity to engulf the gap and catch up with the developed capitalist countries, thus further display the superiority of its socialist system.

44 Ibid., pp. 90-91 (Grundrisse).

45 Marx-Engels Collected Works, Vol.1, pp. 541-542 (German Ideology).

3. The pressure and challenge brought by new development of capitalism in the era of globalization

Before the emergence of socialist countries, the world economy was under the rule of capitalism; when the socialist countries were born, the capitalist domination of the world was broken, but since the strength of the world socialism was relatively weak, with the drastic changes in the Soviet Union and Eastern Europe socialism encountered serious setbacks, ao the developed capitalist countries still dominate the world economy. The globalization dominated by developed capitalist countries, tries to expand capitalist relations of production and capitalist social system to the world, but within this spread also the brings contradictions and ills of capitalistm to the whole world, which constitute a series of severe challenges to the socialist countries.

Firstly, the Western powers tried to expand the capitalist use of science and technology and consumptive lifestyle to the world, resulting in predatory exploitation of natural resources, which damaged the ecological balance of the world, various types of environmental pollution and other serious "global problems", directly and indirectly threaten the survival and development of socialist countries and the whole humanity. According to statistics, as early as 1989, seven major countries of the OECD consumed 43% of the world's fossil fuels, most of the world's forestry products, extracted minerals and other industrial materials. OECD countries created the 68% of industrial waste, 40% of sulfur oxides released, and 54% of nitrogen oxides. More seriously, the OECD countries not only consumed a large amount of natural resources of many developing countries, including the socialist countries, to seize and squeeze the living and developing space of socialist countries, but also transferred high-polluting industries to these countries, resulting in the deterioration of the environment and ecological damage in these countries. In addition, "global problems" such as food crisis, population explosion and resource shortages also affect the development and consolidation of socialist countries.

Secondly, globalization expands the contradiction between the planning of individual enterprises and the anarchy of the whole social production to the world, and also the spontaneity, blindness and waste of the capitalist system and spreads its market economy system, and the resulted economic and social crises are also passed to socialist and other developing countries. In the era of globalization, the basic contradiction of capitalism changes into several contradictions such as between development of the world economy and the monopoly capitalist class so as to pursue their own interests; contradictions between national economic planning, management and the anarchy of global economy; the contradiction between organized and planned inner production system of multinational companies and the disorder of global production; the contradiction between the tendency of infinite expansion of global production and the limits in global consumption; etc. The intensification of these contradictions will inevitably lead to global economic imbalances, crises and social unrest. As a result of globalization, the world encounters an unprecedented status, economic fluctuations and shocks that occur in single country can immediately spread to other countries and even the whole world, thus socialist countries will inevitably face heavy pressure. The collapse of US stock prices in 1987, the collapse of Japan's "bubble economy" in 1990, the Mexican financial crisis of 1994, the collapse of monetary and financial chains in Southeast Asia in 1997, the global "financial tsunami" triggered by the US subprime mortgage crisis in 2008, and the European debt crisis since 2010, all have affected the economic security and social stability of the socialist countries in varying degrees.

Thirdly, the global expansion of monopoly capital not only exacerbates the exploitation and domination of monopoly bourgeoisie upon the proletariat and other working people at home and abroad, leads to disparity and polarization of the rich and the poor in the whole world, but also poses a serious threat to the socialist countries and the world peace and development. In the process of globalization, developed capitalist countries on the one hand use excuse of improving the international competitiveness of enterprises by wantonly reducing the wages and other benefits of workers, reduce the taxes to be paid tax payers, in order to suppress the domestic workers' movement and the development of socialist forces; on the other hand, with their strong economic and technological strength, they strengthen exploitation of the developing countries and plunder to the vast number of developing countries, implement "peaceful evolution" strategy to topple the socialist countries, in order to achieve absolute domination of capitalism in the world, therefore the drastic changes in Eastern Europe and the disintegration of the Soviet Union in the late 1980s and early 1990s can be said to be the result of the neoliberal globalization strategy by the international monopoly bourgeoisie.

The globalization dominated and led by capitalist countries is bound to increasingly expose capitalist anti-human nature of wasting various resources, undermining social justice, suppressing individual freedoms, creating full alienation of human beings to the people of the world. More and more people recognize the evils and calamity caused by capitalism to mankind. In view of the development of socialism in China, the challenges posed by globalization targeting us mainly include: in the economic aspect, western developed countries, by virtue of their monopoly position in the world economy, formulate the "rules of the game" of international economic activities and impose them on others. Against the disobedient countries, they frequently impose economic sanctions, and even brutal military strikes. And our country is still in the stage of developing the socialist market economy, a series of supporting measures offered to Chinese companies by the state when going global in the fierce international market is not perfect; our immature national industry is difficult to withstand the great impact of Western multinational companies, therefore we will be for long at a passive and disadvantaged position in the international economic and technological competition. If we look from the aspect of politics, the Western monopoly class with the help of globalization, intensifies the implementation of "Westernization" and "change" strategy against China. The content of struggle between China and Western hostile forces can be described as infiltration and counter-infiltration, subversion and counter-subversion which have become more difficult and complex for China, sometimes these struggles will even become more intense. In the cultural aspect, with the expansion and deepening of China's opening to the outside world, the bourgeois ideologies of the West, i.e., egoism, money worship and hedonism as the main weapons aims to take advantage of this opportunity, challenges our socialist ideology and brings forward many new problems to our work of building spiritual civilization.

4. The historical mission and development prospects of socialism in the era of globalization

Globalization is like a double-edged sword, it offers both advantages and disadvantages. Marx once said that the material conditions necessary for the liberation of the proletariat are created in the course of the development of capitalist production. The historical period of capitalism has the mission of creating a material basis for the new world. On the one hand, formation of a global intercourse based on interdependence of all mankind is necessary and also a means for such global intercourse and exchanges; on the other hand, highly developed productive forces is necessary, to improve material production so that men can scientifically and benignly regulate the relation between man and nature, as Marx had mentioned. Capitalist industry and international trade create these above material conditions for the new world, just as geological changes have created the surface of the earth. Marx wrote: "When a great social revolution should inherit and absorb all the best achievements of the capitalist era, the global market of the world and the most advanced powers of production and subject them to the common control of the most advanced peoples, only after these will human progress cease to resemble that hideous pagan idol who would not drink the nectar but from the skulls of the slain."[46] By fully grasping the progressive

46 Marx and Engels Collected Works, Vol.2, p.691, see also, https://www.marxists.org/history/etol/newspape/ni/vol08/no06/marx.htm.

aspects and avoiding the negative effects of globalization is conducive to our fight against the "overall Westernization" theory which blindly affirms the globalization, but also conductive to prevent against the wrong trend of thought, i.e, the historical nihilism which fully rejects globalization.

In the era of globalization, the situation faced by the socialist countries at home and abroad is more complicated. Looking from an international perspective, the drastic changes in the Soviet Union and the Eastern Europe have caused a great impact on the world socialist movement, which has pushed the world socialist movement into a low ebb development. All kinds of anti-communist, anti-socialists forces rejoice, howl that "socialism has failed", the history "ends" at the last end point of bourgoise freedom and democracy, and socialism was the "the greatest fantasy" of the 20th century, the 21st century will be free of socialism.

If we look from the domestic point of view, China's socialist construction has made remarkable achievements, but in general, China's huge population situation, weak socio-economic foundation, imbalaced development of its vast regions, and its situation of less developed productive forces are not fundamentally changed; the socialist system is not perfect yet, the buildind of the socialist market economic system is not yet mature, the socialist democracy and the legal system is not perfect yet, decadent thinking and habits of feudalism, capitalism and small production have a wide range of influence in the society. The hostile forces at home and abroad use the advantages of Western developed countries in science, technology, economy and culture, as well as use some mistakes and problems in China's revolution and socialist construction, so as to beautify capitalism, slander socialism, in attempt to lead China to capitalism. German Chancellor Gerhard Schroeder said in his book *System Resolved*: "the 21st century will be determined by capitalism. We can say that they will launch a new round of offensive, push capitalism conquer all countries of the world. The aggressive and expansionist nature of imperialism will not change, the imperialist aim of eliminating China will never fade. In this regard, we should have a clear head and maintain a high degree of vigilance."

First of all, we should realize that globalization cannot fundamentally overcome the contradictions and crises of capitalism, it also cannot change the fate of capitalist decay and demise, instead globalism further promotes the ideals and beliefs of socialism. As early as in the 19th century, Marx was insightful to say: "Thus all the progress of civilization, or in other words every increase in the *powers of social production*. Increase in the *productive power of labour itself* – such as results of science, inventions, division and combination of labour, improved means of communication, creation of the world market, machinery etc. – enriches not the worker but rather *capital*; hence it only magnifies the power dominating over labour; increases only the productive power of capital."[47] Marx added: "capitalist mode of production consists precisely in its tendency towards the absolute, unrestricted development of productive *forces*, but at the same time, inevitably causes limited, one-sided development of individuals."[48]

The scientific and technological progress, economic growth and globalization trend of the contemporary capitalism cannot fundamentally eliminate the alienation caused by capitalism and turn it to the "rational kingdom" and "the paradise within the world". In the book *The Future of Capitalism*, US scholar Lester C. Thurow said: "although the developed capitalist countries, represented by the United States, have won the cold war, they could not solve all the profound contradictions in their societies. Facts are clear that income and wealth inequalities of capitalist countries are increasing everywhere. Most people's real wages are declining, numerous undesired vagaries of productive economies are increasing, the social contract between the middle class and the whole society is broken.The main strategy of social welfare state used for treating inequalities in the 20th Century–is retreating."[49]

Lester C. Thurow also analyzed the future of capitalism: "Technology and ideology are shaking the foundations of the 21st Century capitalism. Technology is making skills and knowledge the only sources of sustainable strategic advantage... When technology and ideology start moving apart, the only question is when will the "big disaster" will occur(the earthquake that rocks the system). Paradoxically, at the very time when capitalism has no social competitors – i.e., its former competitors, socialism and communism, which have died – it will have to undergo a profound metamorphosis."[50]

Secondly, we must correctly grasp the essential characteristics and development trends of today's globalization, and correctly formulate strategies and tactics to deal with globalization in order to ensure that China can gain benefits and avoid its harms and stand forever in an invincible position in the process of actively participating in the globalization. Since globalization does not directly and automatically bring benefits to the working class and other working people, the proletariat and the working people must fight for their rights and freedoms through economic, political and cultural struggles. The only solution to enable an invincible position is to do a good job in the construction of the party and state power, and also do an effective

47 Marx-Engels Collected Works, Vol. 30, 2nd Chinese ed., Beijing, People's Publishing House, 1995, p. 267.

48 Ibid., p. 406.

49 Lester C. Thurow, The Future of Capitalism, Beijing, China Social Sciences Publishing House, 1998, p. 307.

50 Ibid., pp. 318-319.

ideological work, in handling the relationship between independence and opening to the outside world, and effectively resist against "peaceful evolution" strategy of the West in order to ensure that the socialist revolution and the cause of construction can flourish and be everlasting!

Deng Xiaoping has made the following warning when he made the South Inspection Tour: "The United States and some other Western countries are trying to push a peaceful evolution towards capitalism in socialist countries." .... "The imperialists are pushing for peaceful evolution towards capitalism in China, they are placing their hopes on the generations that will come after us." ... "So we must educate the army, persons working in the organs of dictatorship, the Communist Party members and the people, including the youth. If any problem arises in China, it will arise from inside the Communist Party. We should be glass clear on this issue. We must pay attention to training people, selecting and promoting to positions of leadership persons who have both ability and political integrity, in accordance with the principle that they should be revolutionary, young, well educated and professionally competent. This is of vital importance to ensure that the Party's basic line is followed for a hundred years and to maintain long-term peace and stability. It is crucial for the future of China."[51] We should proceed from the fundamental issues of party building, political building and army building, and carry out the struggles of "anti-infiltration", "anti-subversion" and "anti-peaceful evolution". When treating the globalization trend, we should firmly grasp that socialism and communism can achieve ultimate victory in the world only when the socialist countries can play an increasingly important role in the process of globalization and gradually assume a leading position within it.

Under the conditions of globalization, the socialist countries are faced with new historical tasks: the first is how to effectively use both domestic and international resources and markets, further liberate and develop productive forces and meet the growing material and cultural needs of the people; the second is how to establish and improve the new socialist system full of vigor and vitality, improve the international competitiveness and charm of socialist countries and be confident that socialist system can finally win in the contest with the capitalist system. We must be able to consolidate and develop socialism with Chinese characteristics promote the new round of surge of the world socialist movement in the 21st century, we should actively absorb and draw on the "positive civilized achievements" of all countries, especially of the capitalist developed countries, and consciously resist corrosion by capitalist system and its decadent ideology!

(Luo Wendong, CASS Researcher at the Institute of Marxism)

51 Deng Xiaoping Selected Works, 1st ed., Volume 3, p. 380.

PART SIX

The Future of Socialist Development

Socialism is the alternative and successor of capitalist development, which is the inevitable historical process and trend of human social development. Marx and Engels made a bright statement 160-plus years ago that capitalism was a historical and temporary form of society, and it will inevitably be replaced by a higher social form, the communist society. This statement was confirmed by the process of historical development. Socialism is the future of capitalist development. The theory of socialism replacing capitalism, which is the unity of theoretical logic and historical process and the inevitable result that any social form should inevitably adapt to the development level of development of productive forces and that the relations of production must adapt to the nature of productive forces.

Socialism replacing capitalism is a long-term natural history process, similar as capitalism replacing the feudal society was a long-term natural history process. In the contradictional movement between productive forces and relations of production, economic foundation and superstructure, historical development trajectory of human society has moved forward from primitive society to slave, feudal society, and from feudal society to capitalist society, and then from the capitalist society to the socialist society, in the long course of human history, Capitalism is not an eternal social system, but a transitional social system like the various social systems of the past. Socialism will inevitably replace capitalism and no human will can be able to divert the general trend of historical development.

In the process of economic globalization, under the conditions of two socio-economic systems coexistenin in tandem, socialism should oppose capitalist "economic war" by learning from and inheriting all the civilized achievements of capitalism, oppose "overall Westernization" and resist agains its degenerated and corrupt aspects. Socialism must stick to the socialist system when utilizing the advanced mode of operation and management technologies of capitalism, stick to the principle of independence, self-reliance; socialism must sum up its past experience by reflecting on its own development mistakes and frustration, grasp the opportunity, develop firm confidence in its future and better develop itself, in this way socialism will be able to move towards a more brilliant future!

The Movement of Fundamental Contradiction of Capitalism and Its Historical Trend

The contemporary capitalist world is an intricate world full of contradictions. This world not only creates the most advanced material civilization of human society, but also produces an unprecedented spiritual crisis; creates great material wealth and rich material conditions, but also accumulates social poverty and other chronic social evils; creates the means to promote production relations to break through their original boundaries, but also exacerbates its own various contradictions hindering the development of productive forces. How to understand the current world, how to look at the impacts of its current existence and its effects on the historical process of human society have become the urgent issues of developing socialism with Chinese characteristics and even the the urgent issues of development of world socialism movement. The analysis of the issue of historical direction of capitalism can be studied from various aspects, here we will mainly discuss the issue from the perspective of the movement of the fundamental contradiction of capitalism.

1. The mechanism of movement of the fundamental contradiction of capitalism

Since its birth, capitalism has given to the emergence of abundant contradictions involving economic, political, cultural and other aspects of social life, these contradictions are intertwined and are in constant motion, as important demonstration form of the basic contradiction of capitalism, that is, the contradiction between the socialization of production and private ownership of the production means.

The occurrence and development of the scientific and technological revolution is an important motive for the continuous evolution and movement of fundamental contradiction of capitalism. and scientific and technological revolution is an important motive for the continuous evolution and movement of fundamental contradiction of capitalism. Scientific and technological revolution promotes the rapid development of the capitalist economy and causes profound changes in the capitalist economic structure and material life, but has also brings about some severe problems such as "stagflation", social polarization, ecological crisis and so on, all of which deepen the basic contradiction of capitalism. Looking at the history of the development of capitalism, we can see the sharp, sometimes eased, and sometimes re-sharpened waves in the development of basic contradiction of capitalism. This wave of development process is achieved through continuous self-adjustment and self-change of capitalist relations of production so as to adapt to the higher degrees of development of the productive forces.

The movement of the basic contradictions of capitalism in the real economic life of capitalism is manifested in many concrete and vivid forms, and in the course of time new mechanisms are formed in the movement of the basic contradiction of capital. In *Capital*, Marx has analyzed various forms of the basic contradiction of capitalism, such as the contradiction between the production and demand of two major sectors in the reproduction of social capital, the contradiction between the production of surplus value and the realization of surplus value, the contradiction between the expansion of production and the appreciation in the value of capital (valorisation) and others. The movement of the basic contradictions of capitalism in the real economic life of capitalism is manifested in many concrete and vivid forms, but all of them occur on the basis of free competition and free operation mechanism. When the technological revolution developed in the second half of the 20th century, new hi-tech industries have developed whose core was the IT revolution, thus occured a new change in the operation mechanism of the basic contradiction of capitalism, and a new mechanism was formed.

Firstly, the first new mechanism is the coexistence of monopoly with competition (monopolistic competition). Monopolistic competition mainly occurs: a)internally, within the monopoly organization itself, b) among the monopoly organizations, and, c) between monopolies and non-monopolies. The monopoly grows up from free competition, and after monopoly occupies dominant position upon free competition, cannot totally replace, and it can impossibly eliminate the competition. On the one hand, capitalist competition is the inevitable outcome of commodity economy, and capitalist competition is the product of commodity economy based on capitalist private ownership; the monopoly does not change private capitalist ownership of the production means, and the commodity economy based on the capitalist private ownership still exists. So the competition among various commodity producers and operators still exists; at the same time, in addition to monopoly, there are still some "outside enterprises" that have not joined the monopoly organization, and there is also free competition among these "outside enterprises" in a certain scope and to a certain degree. On the other hand, on the basis of monopoly, a new kind of competition, that is, monopolistic competition emerges; Monopolistic competition mainly occurs within the monopoly organization, among the monopoly organizations, and between the monopoly organization and "outside enterprises". The internal competition within the monopoly organization is around the who will lead the enterprise (leadership), control of company shares, market share, competition in respect to sales markets and others; the competition among various monopolies is around the source of raw materials, and sales market; thirdly the competition among the monopoly enterprises and out-of-bound enterprises is around control and anti-control, and swallowing and resistance against swallowing. Marx wrote: "In practical life, we find not only competition, monopoly and the antagonism between them, but also the synthesis of the two, which is not a formula but a real movement. Monopoly produces competition, and competition produces monopoly. Monopolists are made from competition, competitors become monopolists."[1]

This mechanism was formed in the mid-20th century and has continuously assumed diverse forms with the development of capitalist economy. For example, the competition among monopoly enterprises in the same sector is manifested in the price competition and non-price competition. Price competition refers to that the largest and most powerful monopoly enterprises "secretly cutting the price of their products" by colluding with some other companies, deceive rival groups in order to expand their production, market share and sales amounts, so as to obtain more economic interests brought by expanding sales. However, once the scope of secret price cutting is expanded, further price cutting usually causes open price wars. The non–price competition is usual and universal. It is manifested as competition of sales conditions–advertising and expansion of sales networks, etc.,–after and pre-sales services and after-sales service, convenient conditions for consumers, and competition over product quality and design (improving product quality and appearance, etc.). As another example, we see the competition among monopoly enterprises operating in different sectors, here a strong and a large scale company uses mergers to expand its power in another sector. This merger can be defined as a hybrid kind of merger, between unrelated enterprises operating in different sectors, after an intense competition. This merger can be defined as a hybrid kind of merger, between unrelated enterprises operating in different sectors, after and intense competition between them, the two companies develop into a mixed joint conglomerate, thus under the leadership of the strong company their production lines are diversified and their operation scope is expanded. We see the struggle and competition between merger and counter-merger: behind this competition, there are two aspects, firstly the fight by a company which aims to expand its market share of a product or a segment of product; secondly, it is the result of a company strategy which seeks more favorable investment regions or countries, through a merger.

Again, competition between monopoly enterprises and small and medium-sized non-monopoly enterprises has attained a new situation with the scientific and technological progress and due to extensive specialization in the production process, some companies are specialized in producing a part of the end product, for example a chip of a PC computer, the small and medium-sized enterprises are not only the targets of big monopolies for

1 Marx-Engels Collected Works, Vol. 1, pp. 636-637, see also, https://www.marxists.org/archive/marx/works/1847/poverty-philosophy/ch02c.htm.

merger & acquisition but they also provide conditions for the expansion of large enterprises, and guarantee high profits for them.

Therefore, under the conditions of monopolistic competition, big monopoly enterprises not only merge and promote the establishment and development of small and medium-sized enterprises but also eliminate, exclude or utilize them for their self-interests. Such, co-existence of monopoly and competition causes many particularly sharp and violent contradictions, frictions and conflicts among the enterprises.

This mechanism wherein monopoly and competition co-exists, both monopoly enterprises and non-monopoly enterprises are forced to embrace a more fierce competition for their own survival and development, they constantly need to adopt new technologies, new type of production processes and use advanced production equipment, need to constantly strengthen the research of basic science and applied science & technology, constantly improve the way of company operation and management, improve labor productivity, thus competition becomes a powerful mechanism so as to further promote the continuous development of social productive forces. On the other hand, this mechanism wherein monopoly and competition co-exists also continuously strengthens the capitalist private ownership of means of production, making the socialized means of production and products of labor increasingly concentrated in the hands of a few largest private monopoly capital enterprises. Therefore, in the development of capitalist economy, this mechanism wherein monopoly and competition co-exists deepens the basic contradiction of capitalism and seriously wastes and destroys the development of the social productive forces.

Secondly, the second new mechanism in respect to the movement of basic contradiction of capitalism is the coexistence of state and market. Production and market are the two core contents of all contradictions of capitalism. In the contemporary capitalist economic life, this second new mechanism is reflected as the establishment of the state monopoly regulation system wherein state's influence on economy and regulation by market mechanism is combined. The coexistence of the state and the market in the contemporary capitalist economic life manifests itself as the establishment of the monopoly regulation system by led by the state, which implies the power struggles between the government and markets aiming to influence the economic sphere. The market is the basic force which influences the operation of capitalist economy; the market is also an important means to optimize the allocation of resources, but due to the existence of monopoly, the market when regulating the economic activities, will lead to improper use of resources, to inefficiency in resource utilization and to other market failures. And also due to "external" failures of the market (such as beneficial or harmful effects of economic activities to enterprises, to consumers, to other enterprises, or the enterprises cannot receive proper compensation or cannot bear the corresponding cost), the market mechanism cannot consider the social costs and benefits, which leads to market failures in the production of public goods. And also due to the spontaneous, blind natures of the market mechanism, market cannot adjust itself to the needs of society as a whole, cannot adapt to the great changes in the economic structure which occur during the economic development. Therefore, in order to solve the problems of market failures, it is particularly necessary for the government to regulate the operation of the economy, curb the shortcomings of the market, which means that the government should undertake those economic and social tasks which markets cannot solve effectively.

In the capitalist real economic life, the main means of state monopoly adjustment are: the redistribution of national income through state's financial revenues income expenditure activities in order to achieve macroeconomic goals in the economy; through the state's participation in financial activities, that is, state through the central bank's issuance of money and by determining the credit interest rates manages and regulates the economy, thus affects the process of social reproduction. State monopoly adjustment also includes the state's "economic planning" of production and circulation of the whole society on the basis of market economy, state implements a certain degree of regulation, affects the scale of economic development, growth speed and proportion among sectors, and so on.

The state's such intervention in production and the market is a "repair" made within the framework of capitalism, this intervention "restricts" "certain individual bad aspects" of the capitalist system, and "restricts" the "individual extreme issues" in the economy, which means that it partially transforms the capitalist relations of production, such intervention to a certain extent curbs the negative effects of the basic contradictions of capitalism, reduces the chaos and imbalances in social production, eases the cyclical economic crises, provides certain necessary regulations to expand employment, production and the market. However, the state intervention in the economy and the role of market, combination of the two is reaalized without touching the foundation of private capitalist ownership. Therefore, no matter in what ways the state intervenes in the economy, or to which degree and extent state intervenes in economy, economic operation of capitalism is always based on private ownership, state intervention not only impossibly overcome the basic contradictions of capitalism fundamentally, but also cannot overcome the inherent contradictions in the capitalist reproduction process, instead state intervention within the state monopoly adjustment mechanism further deepens this contradiction, which is always pregnant with new malpractices and crises.

2. The profoundness of capitalist fundamental contradiction movement

Under the two major mechanisms, i.e., the coexistence of monopoly and competition, the coexistence of the state and the market, the movement of the basic contradictions of capitalism is increasingly deepening. This is not just a general description but a real fact, as Marx explained: "capital posits every such limit as a barrier and hence gets ideally beyond it, it does not by any means follow that it has really overcome it, and since every such barrier contradicts its character, its production moves in contradictions which are constantly resolved but just as constantly posited."[2] It is more important to use today's facts to demonstrate that capital's exploitation of wage labor, income distribution between capital and labor, the relationship between man and nature, appreciation of capital, naked means of capitalist exploitation are increasingly becoming hidden, although polarization between capital and labor is increasing, the contradiction between man and nature is intensifying.

The more subtle forms of exploitation of wage labor by capital are mainly manifested in the class status of laborers, the ways of capital management and the ways of exploitation. If we examine the class status of the laborers, the form of bourgoise democratization obscures the exploitation exploition and socially enslaved position of the laborer. The practice of "employees-owning-stocks" programs in the capitalist countries has increased the number of workers who own stocks. In essence, this is only a kind of investment for the purpose of saving money, since the wages of the laborers are limited, and the dividends they get by their stocks can be compared—more or less—to bank deposit interest rates, and their divident incomes are unlikely to be reproduced as capital inputs; they do not hold the corresponding means of production according to the amount of stocks they hold in their hands. They cannot become capitalists by this way. The implementation of the "employees-owning- stocks" program does not aim the real transfer of capital power, but only changes the way of capital control. Looking from the aspect of capital management, this form of corporate management hides the increase in the labor intensity of workers.

The widespread use of high and new technology in production has led to the use of automatic control of production and office automation, this system of production organization has not only become the new method for capital to obtain more surplus value, but also becomes the most effective method to manage labor, equipment, materials in an automated operation. The result is: the workers are forced to realize a constant labor process with the least number of employers possible, forced to work under greatest labor

2 Marx-Engels Collected Works, Vol. 8, p. 91, see also the English version (Marx 1973: 409-10).

intensity. In this case, the practice and concept of producing workers has expanded, as Marx had defined: "In order to work productively, it is no longer necessary for you to do manual work yourself; that will be enough, if you are an organ of the collective labourer, and perform one of its subordinate functions."[3]

Although the operation of the machines is not directly managed by these kind of workers, although people are no longer seeing the fact that the workers are "whipped" as in the past, the workers are still wage earners and still create surplus value for the capitalists. With the adoption of high technology, although the total number of employees is relatively and absolutely reduced, the degree of exploitation is not reduced but has become even more higher. As argued by David Schweickart: This is the typical nature of the current management form of capitalism, "jobs usually are in short supply, therefore workers can be induced by capitalists, by an *appropriate combination of* technical *speedup*, tight *monitoring*, and job losing threat, the workers are induced to do more than whichwas bargained for in the work contract." "this causes a real opposition between capitalists and the employed wage laborer." "Capitalism alienates workers from their work. The trend of labor alienation, although it will be to a certain degree diminished by some productivity-enhancing welfare programs and workplace management participation programs—which will benefit workers—aleniation will continue to develop further. Under capitalism, it is impossible for the capitalists to allow workers have more leisure time, and it is impossible for the workers to work mmeaningfully, this is the inherent structure of capitalism."[4]

The exploitation of employed labor by capital is no longer "once originally practiced naked super-exploitation", but "a cleverer, more civilized and more effective and brutal exploitation." In terms of capital exploitation, the form of "equal exchange" (between capitalist and worker) obscures the essence of the exploitation of laborers. In the capitalist commodity economy, the "equal exchange" principle in labor commodity transactions is universal in the labor market. However, in the production process, the combination of laborer and the production means produce a much greater value than this "equivalent exchange". Equivalent exchange form masks the exploitative essence of unequal exchange.

In the process of surplus value production by contemporary state-owned monopoly capital, this hiding gains new features. Since the owner of the state-owned monopoly capital is the state, the state represents the whole society in form (formally), also it places the whole workers in equal status in form (formally), so it gives the fake impression that all laborers are

3 Marx-Engels Collected Works, vol. 5, p. 582.

4 See David Schweickart, Against Capitalism, Beijing, Renmin University of China Press, 2000, pp. 227-232.

ownthose production means and produced commodities as state property. The formal equality here hides the reality of separation between the wage laborers and the production means and the state-owned monopoly capital becomes the legitimite owner of the surplus value created by the wage laborers.

Moreover, state-owned monopoly capital is also integrated with private monopoly capital to strengthen the exploitation of wage laborer. In the movement of the state-owned monopoly capital into the social capital, the surplus value exploited by state-owned monopoly capital does not directly appear as its own capital proliferation, but through a variety of ways it is transferred to private monopoly capital and participate in the profit segmentation of the private monopoly capital through fiscal and taxation mechanisms, in this way ultimately/finally the proliferation the state-owned monopoly capital is realized.

The concealment of capital's exploitation of employed labor does not eliminate or weaken the antagonism of the basic contradictions of capitalism. In line with this, there is an increasingly serious polarization between the rich and the poor in the distribution sphere. On the one hand, while the total value of surplus capital available for capital allocation is growing, capital income by various functional capitalists is expanding; but labor income growth is declining. If we exclude inflation, rising prices, the real wage of workers is declining. On the other hand, the gaps in incomes will inevitably lead to differences in living styles. The real living conditions and the consumption structure of the laborers have made significant changes due to the improvement of the level of productive forces, the improvement of economic conditions and due to the regulation of re-distribution of the national income by the governments. We have no longer see the work-day of 14 to 18 hours per day, we no longer see workers without proper clothing and food, the leisure time of workers has also increased. But, compared with the leisure time by capitalists or compared with the level of general social development, the degree of social satisfaction that laborers get is reduced. The income gap between the rich and the poor in capitalism has not only diminished, but expanded, and the polarization between the capitalists and the workers has not only diminished but increased. At present, the richest 1% housholds of the US owns 40% of the whole wealth; 1% housholds own more than 90% of the Americans' wealth. In the UK, wealth possessed by the richest 20% of the population is 10 times the wealth of the poorest 20% people. The polarization of the rich and the poor in the capitalist society illustrates the intensification of the contradiction between capitalist production and consumption. Although the income of the laborers has increased to some extent, it is impossible for the monopoly capital to allocate all the surplus products which they own to laborers, but this part of the surplus products cannot be all consumed by the capitalists, so this fact further exacerbates the contradiction between production and consumption. On the one hand there is a large amopunt of excess consumer goods; on the other hand, the majority of workers live in poverty. Of course, the survival of capitalism lies in continuously relieving this contradiction, as Marx said: "bourgeoisie cannot exist without constantly revolutionising the instruments of production, and thereby the relations of production, and with them the whole relations of society."[5]

The contradiction between man and nature also tends to intensify with the development of capitalism. With the development of moderm capitalist industry, most of the creatures in the life circle of the earth were destroyed. A serious decline in arable land, land desertification became serious, the forests wre destroyed, and rare creatures are randomly hunted, These facts not only damage a large part of arable land andforests, but also poses a great damage to natural respiratory organs of men, damage their own survival basis. The rapid development of economy is accompanied by a blind, unrestrained exhausting of natural resources that pushes natural resources at risk of depletion. Economic development is accompanied by the high production, high consumption and higher waste of resources, environmental pollution, resulting in ecological imbalance. While developed capitalist countries are rich, developing countries are forced to an ecological crisis. The intensification of contradictions between man and nature not only from the aspect of damaging the natural environment, but also from the aspect of waste or exhaustion of natural resources, shake the economic basis of the entire capitalism, leading to the decline of the whole human society. It can be seen that the intensification of the contradiction between man and nature manifests the inherent limitations of the nature of capitalism, as Marx said in Capital Volume I: "The universality towards which it irresistibly strives encounters barriers in its own nature, which will, at a certain stage of its development, allow it to be recognized as being itself the greatest barrier to this tendency, and hence will drive towards its own suspension."[6] These limitations arise when capital develops to a certain stage,

Obviously, there is a dangerous trend in capitalist society which splits the existence of people, pollute the environment, undermine the nature; puts man and nature in a sharp conflict. However, the existence of this dangerous trend, the intensification of such a contradiction between man and nature is inseparable from the deepening of the basic contradictions of capitalism. The profit-driven production inevitably leads to an increasingly large scale use of technology and enormous production growth. However, people's

5 Marx-Engels Collected Works, vol. 2, p. 34 also, https://www.marxists.org/archive/marx/works/1848/communist-manifesto/ch01.htm.

6 Marx-Engels Collected Works, Vol. 8, p. 91.

consumption needs are suppresed, especially consumption demand of the vast majority of working people is suppressed. If this contradiction cannot be resolved, it will be difficult to fundementally solve the contradiction between man and nature. If the dangerous trend of capitalism which splits the existence of human beings, pollution of the environment and devastation of nature develops further, the intensification of the contradiction between man and nature may destroy capitalism itself.

The above three aspects reflect the profoundness of the basic contradictions of capitalism. It is through these ways that the capitalist countries ease the basic contradictions of capitalism and suppress the possible occurances that lead to social explosions. Therefore, the ups and downs of the basic contradictions of capitalism are in fact the result of the self-adjustments by the capitalism in order to maintain the economic interests of capitalists. These self-adjustments to a considerable extent have injected a new vitality to the capitalist economy, extends the life of capitalism. However, the implementation of these methods is pregnant with deeper impetus and factors which will intensify contradictions, and these impetus and factors will hinder the development of capitalism and to promote its destiny to perishment.

3. The intensification of fundamental contradictions of capitalism in the world

The intensification of the basic contradictions of capitalism is closely related to the rapid development of economic globalization. Current economic globalization is an inevitable process of economic development. This process develops under the guidance of contemporary developed capitalism, it is the result of economic progress pushed by capitalism, such as the rapid acceleration of information exchange brought about by the innovation of IT technology and with the rapid development of international economic exchanges, as well as the increased role of state intervention in economic life, etc., which provide the economic inevitability of this process, and also provide realistic possibility of this process. In the process of economic globalization, the production factors flow at an unprecedented level across the world to find the proper location for the best allocation of resources; the scope of trade liberalization, the process of financial internationalization is developing rapidly; a global production network system has gradually formed, the phenomenon of foreign direct investment is increasingly prominent. Economic globalization inevitably leads to a true global capitalism, and globalized capitalism has become the main feature of contemporary capitalism. The economic globalization dominated by contemporary capitalism extends the basic contradictions of capitalism to a global scale and has become one of the most profound changes in the history of capitalism.

The movement of basic contradictions of capitalism in the course of economic globalization is manifested in the contradiction between the infinite development of productive forces and limitation of national borders. Current spread and expansion of science and technology and rapid development of productive forces are facts which ignore the borders and nationalities. Their influences have become increasingly global. The internationalization of economy has reached an unprecedent level and has become an irreversible historical trend, and has brought a new vitality into the capitalist economic development. However, the historical, cultural and social conditions of many regions and nations of the capitalist world are different. Some countries have high level of developed productive forces and enjoy a dominant status in the world economy, their economic development cannot be tapped in their national territories, so they need to find development opportunities in other countries and leads to competition to capture world markets, to bullying of backward countries. In order to adapt to the high degree of development of productive forces around the world, lesser developed nations are bound to join together to form regional economic partnership organizations to enhance their economic strengths in order to counter against the exploitation and control of developed countries. The contradiction between the infinite development of productive forces and the limitations of national borders is manifested as the contradictions between developed and developing countries. When the developed countries want to surpass the limitations of national boundaries, use their monopoly power in the world market, and try to develop into the developing countries, on the other hand lesser developed countries are trying the method regional economic cooperation to enhance their economic strength, improve their position in the international division of labor. However, on the one hand this cooperation method brings technology, information, capital resources and other vitalities to economic development of lesser developing countries, on the other hand brings some difficult problems, such as economic dependence, natural&ecological imbalances, and may even cause the deterioration of economic conditions, the intensification of contradictions between the North and South. Therefore, in essence, the contradiction between developed and developing countries is the manifetation of the fundamental contradiction of capitalism in the world.

In the process of economic globalization, the movement of the fundamental contradiction of capitalism manifests itself in multiple ways. First, the deepening of contradictions and failures of market economy. Market economy can realize the role of optimizing the allocation of resources and bring higher efficiency, but also it has the negative aspects of blindness, spontaneity and hysteresis. In the current world these features of the market economy are extended to the global level, which increasingly intensifies the basic contradictions of capitalism, bring about the inherent cyclical fluctuations of capitalism and the outbreak of the globalized economic crises. Second, the motives and purposes behind the expansion of capital. The essence of capital is the the pursuit for profit, so it demands infinite appreciation and pushes forward the fetish of commodity and fetish of money, the "relations between men are mediated through things", such fetishes and such thing-ified relations becomes a social force.

As the French scholar Lucien Sève analyzed: the capitalist mode of production is universal. This kind of "universality" has two dimensions of both extension and connotation. The extension aspect of "universality" indicates that capital needs to break through any border and establish deeper intercourses within the world market and among the nations. The connotation aspect of the "universality" indicates that capital pursues for the maxiumum profit rate, infinitely promotes the development of productive forces and promotes all kind of human activities to realize profit maximization. The unity and opposition in the development process of the basic contradictions of capitalism are fully demonstrated in the process of economic globalization.

Another issue is the deterioration of the imbalanced development of the capitalist economy and politics. The process of economic globalization is in fact the process of realization of economic hegemonism, technological hegemonism and financial hegemonism. In this process, the coexistence of traditional and modern, advanced and backward which is existent in the capitalist countries expands to the whole world, so the real threat of economic hegemonism targeting the less developed countries is formed, which undermines the normal status of sovereignty and economic development of these countries.

Finally, the polarization occuring in the development of capitalism in a single country expands to the global level. Although we see social wealth increase in the world economic development, the gap between rich and poor is constantly expanding, some countries and some people are moving towards poverty and exclusion. The Global Wealth Report published in 2011 has pointed: "nearly 40% of the world's wealth is concentrated in the hands of 1% of the rich, and this 1% of the rich has a strong influence on the economy and society, resulting in the other 99% suffering from unfair distribution of social wealth, unequal income distribution. There is a trend of growing gap between the rich and the poor. As Samir Amin said, "The consequences of capitalist globalization are polarization, inequality on a global scale, which are the consequences of the inherent logic of capital relations."[7] Economic globalization contributes to the extension of the movement of fundamental contradiction of capitalism to the global level.

7 The Third World in the Context of Globalization–An Interview with Samir Amin, published in World Economy and Politics, 2001(2).

Current economic globalization reflects the expansion of the fundamental contradictions of capitalism and demonstrates its drawbacks on a global scale, reflects the extension of capitalism to the global scale, manifests the domination of the capitalist economic system in the world, and mainifests that capital is completing its historical mission. Therefore, economic globalization gives certain time and space for the development of contemporary capitalism, so that capitalism gains certain degree of vitality. On the other hand, economic globalization also gives time and space for the further development of the movement of the basic contradictions of capitalism, in this way capitalism has accumulates various factors which hinder its development. The dissertation made by Marx is as follows: "No social order ever disappears before all the productive forces for which there is room in it have been developed; and new, higher relations of production never appear before the material conditions of their existence have matured in the womb of the old society itself."[8] This statement is extremely significant for understanding the current direction of capitalism from the view of movement of basic contradictions of capitalism. Capitalism, as a kind of production mode and social system, possesses antagonistic contradictions which cannot be overcome by itself, with its maladies of profit maximization pursuit, cyclical fluctuations, expansion of polarization in the global scale, it is destined to have no future.

(Zhang Leisheng, Professor of Institute of Marxism, Renmin University of China)

8 Marx-Engels Collected Works, Vol. 2, p. 592.

"The Third Way" Thought and the Development of Human Society

In the process of exploring the path of human social development, since the mid-1990s, a new "Third Way" thought quietly rose in the Western European countries. It was first proposed by the Democratic Party of the US in the early 1990s, then the British Labor Party vigorously advocated the "Third Way", followed by the German Social Democratic Party, the Dutch Labor Party, and the Italian left-wing Democrats. With the British, German, French and other Labor, Socialist and the Social Democratic Parties ascending to power one after the other and those "the third way" thoughts promoted by the scholars have made a greater impact, and in the Western European political circles a powerful group formed around the "third way" thought.

1. The emergence of "The Third Way" thought

"The third way" is not a new term, in history it has had different forms of expression, such as "middle way", "middle position", "third power", "third force", "third way" and so on. This trend has experienced a hundred years from its budding, formation, development till now.

"The third way" means neither socialism nor capitalism, but between capitalism and socialism. It is reasonable to say that this idea could not emerge before the birth of the socialist system—the opposite of the capitalist system. However, in the struggle between capitalist ideology and socialist thought, this idea has begun to sprout. As early as the end of the 19th century, the European bourgeois thinkers had proposed the "middle way" from the perspective of economics, against the laissez-faire capitalist economy and the planned economy idea proposed by utopian socialism school, which was recognized and further demonstrated by Marxism. They have advocated implementing public ownership of the means of production in some sectors of the economy to a certain extent, while maintaining the private ownership of the means of production as the main pillar together with the dominance of market economy in the whole socio-economy. In the 19th century, Louis Blanc in 1841 conceived the role of government in running the "social workshops" which would replace private firms operating in a free market, workshops established by the loans given by the government in the key sectors of the national industry. All workers with high moral qualities would be allowed to work in *social workshops*, until enough initial capital is gathered to purchase tools of work. The Fabian socialists in Britain have advocated the expansion of public utilities sector owned by local governments, which they called "municipal socialism". Also a part of German "Prussian socialists" have advocated "state socialism", wherein the state would operate a number of public utilities to promote the social economy and limit the magnitude of the private economy. In short, their basic arguments aimed to prove that a "middle way" would be possible, between the private ownership of the means of production, i.e., capitalism and public ownership of the means of production, i.e., socialism, and between plan and market.[9]

Although their so-called "middle way" was quite different from the "third way" we will discuss here in this article, their thoughts have an important influence on the "third way" thought that had later evolved and developed. At the end of the 19th century and the beginning of the 20th century, Western capitalism, through the development of the relative "peaceful" development period, entered the stage of monopoly capitalism and the strategy of the bourgeoisie also changed. The international workers' movement was internally divided, as well as the struggle within the Marxism, and the revisionism of Bernstein and Kautsky appeared. They opposed violent revolution and the dictatorship of the proletariat, advocated the legal struggle and reformist path for achieving capitalism "peacefully" transiting to socialism, advocated "middle way" between Marxist socialism and realistic capitalism. Due to the proliferation of revisionism, the right-wing Social-Democrats degenerated into social chauvinists when the World War I broke out, consequently the initial attempts for the "middle way" has thus failed.

2. The formation and practices of "The Third Way" thought

After the victory of socialist October revolution in Russia, the world's first socialist country was established. In the background of intensifying struggles between capitalism and socialism, the "third way" became a kind of major ideological trend. It is noteworthy that the "third way" since its debut as a trend of thought, has attained different forms in different regions:

Firstly, within the international communist movement, the "third way" began to proliferate with various propositions. After the victory of the socialist October revolution in Russia, the famous representative of the second international revisionism, Hilferding, put forward the idea of "organized capitalism". According to him, by drawing on the organizational and planning advantages of socialism and relying on the organizational achievements of the capitalist monopolies, and utilizing the parliamentary democracy system, the socialist movement can move along development road of reforming capitalism, instead of following the path of October Revolution.

9 See Thomas Meyer, et al.: On Democratic Socialism, People's Publishing House, Beijing, 1987 and C.C. Sarechev (former Soviet Union): "Seeking the Third Way"–History of the Development of Contemporary Social Democratic Thought, People's Publishing House, Beijing, 1991.

Secondly, in Western Europe, in the 1920s and 1930s, the Social Democratic Party began to put forward the "third way" theory. In 1929 an unprecedented economic crisis has erupted in the capitalist world. The economic crisis began in the most developed areas of capitalism–the United States, which not only hit the United States, but also hit other "powerful" capitalist countries of the world, giving the capitalist system a significant impact. Contrary to capitalism, in this crisis, the Soviet socialist economy, which was just newly established, was not greatly affected, but also managed to overcome the difficulties in economic construction. The comprehensive national strength has become stronger and the socialism has initially shown its superiority. The economic crisis led to the comparison of the two different economic systems of socialism and capitalism, which caused the emergence of the pioneers of Keynesianism in Western countries who "sanctioned" the self-regulating, defusing and self-healing ability of liberal market economy. In the face of the increasingly troubled capitalism and the vigorous development of socialism, the Western European Socialist Party had to change its former approach against Soviet socialism and embraced the idea of "organized capitalism", once again raised the banner of "middle way", advocating the establishment of the democratic socialism in Europe which would be different from the type of capitalism, United States as its representative, and also different from socialism with the Soviet Union as its representative. There were two important reasons for Western European Socialist Party raise the banner of "middle way": First, in the face of the unprecedented economic crisis of capitalism, they could not openly express their support for capitalism, because capitalism as a result of launching the World War I and the deep economic crisis has lost its charm among the people; second, they could not openly oppose to the successfuly growing socialism, since opposing socialism would make them lose the trust of the part of the masses. By following the so-called "middle way" on the one hand they could please the bourgeoisie, because they didn't advocate the overthrow of capitalism, instead just reform it and allow it repair itself; on the other hand they could be able to confuse the proletariat, by advocating to borrow from some strong aspects of socialism, besides avoiding some shortcomings of socialism, thus promoted their democratic socialism.

Thirdly, in Nordic European countries, in 1932, the Swedish Social Democratic Party gained voters' support and ascended to power, by propagating a "third way" program which was different from Soviet socialism and the US capitalism and initiated the practice of "third way". In 1936, a US based journalist Charles Maguire wrote a book titled "Sweden: the Middle Way", based on the ruling experience of the Swedish Social Democratic Party, which made a detailed account of the Swedish social, economic, political situation, and praised the practice of "middle way". In 1938, Harold

Macmillan, the famous British economist and former Prime Minister of the Labor Party cabinet, published the book "The Middle Way: A Study of the Problem of Economic and Social Progress in a Free and Democratic Society". In this book, Macmillan comprehensively discusses the need and feasibility of taking the "middle way" and has argued that the "middle way" aimed to regulate capitalism. This regulated type of capitalism would not only promote the economic development but would also provide people certain social benefits. The "Third Way" had become a fashionable term in Europe at the time and in the days before the World War II, fascist ideologues from all over the world were propagating "the Third Way". They claimed: "Fascism offers a third way between the capitalist anarchy and communist dictatorship."[10]

Fourthly, in Latin America, in the 1920s and 1940s, a "third way" idea also emerged. In the 1920s, the founder of the Apura Party in Peru, Victor R. H. Torre, proposed the theory of social democracy with Latin American characteristics and advocated the "restructuring" of Marxism to "adapt" to Latin America, and advocated neither traditional capitalism nor communism, but to achieve "statist capitalism" and state control of industry. Torre advocated the overthrow of the land-owning oligarchies that had ruled Peru since colonial days, replacing them with an idealistic socialist elite for building a kind of "socialism" in the future".[11]

In the 1940s, President of Argentine, Juan Peron also raised a program similar to "third way" and created the "third position" (Justicialismo) doctrine which had a great impact in Latin America. This doctrine argues that "both capitalism and communism are obsolete systems. Capitalism exploits people by capital, and communism exploits people through state, both harm people through different systems", "choosing any kind of system cannot bring our people twelfare, so we decided to create a third position, that is neither capitalism nor communism."[12]

Fifthly, in the period of China's new-democratic revolution, a number of intermediate forces also held the banner of the "Third way". In 1927 the Great Revolution failed, the first Kuomintang-Communist cooperation broke down and their ways parted. Under these conditions some people who left the CPC after the failure of the Great Revolution established the "Chinese Peasants' and Workers' Democratic Party" together with some people who belonged to

10 Tony Just, "The 'Third Way' Is No Route to Paradise", in: The New York Times, 1998/09/27.

11 Xiao Nan, et al., Political Trends in the Contemporary Latin America, China Eastern Press, Beijing, 1988, pp. 195-210.

12 Xiao Nan et al.: Political Trends in the Contemporary Latin America, China Eastern Press, Beijing, 1988, pp. 238-256.

left-wing of the KMT to explore a "Third way".[13] "Third way" idea has continued its influence in the next decades, too. At the beginning of the victory of the War of Resistance against Japanese Aggression, democratic parties (including the Democratic League Party), which represented the *middle*-of-the-*roaders*, were neither satisfied with the Fascist one-party dictatorship rule of the Kuomintang, nor with the armed struggle of the CPC and its full fledged new democratic revolution program. They planned to follow the "third way" apart from the KMT and the CPC. They launched wide political campaigns and extensive publicity. Zhou Enlai pointed out: "Since the War of Resistance has developed towards victory especially due to the contributions by the CPPCC, objectively led it to assume a third party status, and made many of his leaders express the ideas of the "*middle*-of-the-*roaders*", in an attempt to seek a third way program apart from the sharp confrontation between the KMT and the Communist Party."[14] Mao Zedong also commented on this fact: "In the early stage of the People's War of Liberation some democratic personages fancied that they could find a so-called third way, apart from the Kuomintang dictatorship of big landlords and big bourgeoisie and apart from the people's democratic dictatorship led by the Communist Party of China. This third way was in fact the road of a dictatorship of the bourgeoisie with British and U.S. model.[15] But with the all-encompassing launching of the War of Liberation in China, the propositions for "the Third way" had soon fainted.

3. The development of "The Third Way" thought during the Cold War era

After the end of the World War II and with the formation of the Cold War pattern, the Western European Social Democratic Party once again held the banner of the "third way". After the establishment of the Socialist International in 1951, the Socialist Parties of Western Europe always adopted the position of both criticizing capitalism and opposing communism, trying to appear as a "middle power" or "third force", taking a "third way" of neither capitalism nor communism. The reason why the socialists who believed in democratic socialism were led to take the "third way" was that "for them capitalism, had developed great productive forces, but this was at the expense of expelling the vast majority of citizens' influence on production… ,thus this had sharpened the struggle between classes." "The history of capitalist development proves that it cannot run without disastrous crises and large-scale unemployment, resulting in social instability and wealth

13 Li Bei, Comment on the Middle Route in the period of New Democratic Revolution, published in Journal of Shanghai University (Social Sciences Edition), 1990(2).

14 Zhou Enlai Selected Works, Vol I, Beijing, People's Publishing House, Beijing, 1980, pp. 283-284.

15 Mao Zedong Selected Works, 2nd Edition, Vol. 4, p. 1262.

differences." While "communism is a kind of rigid theology that does not match the critical spirit of the Marxism."[16]

Therefore, the Socialist International argued that these two roads have their own shortcomings, and only the "third way could surpass the flaws of the two" In order to promote the "third way", the Socialist International also used its international branches across the world to strengthen the "third way" publicity, which have produced a large number of "Third way" believers and political parties in the third world and Eastern European countries, consequently the "third way" changed from the ideology/ program of Socialist International to a global influential thought and movement.

Besides around 1968, the European youth movement, student movement, and various social movements which proposed the initial demands of grass-root democracy also propogated the thoughts of "third way" beyond capitalism and real socialism.

In 1960s and 1970s, the theory of "the third way" was further developed, and there were more and more political parties and scholars who advocated taking the "third way". In addition to Western European left-wing political parties who continued to advocate the "third way" ideas, over 20 European, Asian, Oceania, Latin American communist parties, among them most representative ones were the communist parties of Italy, France, Spain advocated the strategy of "European communism". They chose a middle path between "peaceful" path towards socialism, i.e., the path of social democratic parties and the "violent" revolutionary path and the proletariat dictatorship practiced in the Soviet Union and other socialist countries. Consequently, they advocated a path that would be different from democratic socialism and Soviet model of socialism. European communism argued that "the path taken by the Social-Democrats has improved the living conditions of the laborers in this or that country, but it does not show that it can really overcome capitalism. On the other hand, the model adopted by Eastern European socialist countries does not meet the special conditions of Western countries and the demands of the broad workers and masses." Therefore, we must adopt a solution that combines national characteristics and contemporary conditions which should also be in line with common features and basic requirements of developed countries including the democratic parliamentary system strongly established in current Western Europe.[17] European communism argued that transformation of the capitalist system and breaking away from capitalist system cannot be the same as before, it isn't necessary to follow a violent and painful path. Instead such

16 Documentation of Socialist International, Heilongjiang People's Publishing House, Harbin, 1989, pp. 1-3.
17 Selected Works of Contemporary World Socialism, China Renmin University Press, Beijing, 1990, pp. 433-435.

transformation can be achieved by a path wherein various property and economic forms can be combined, and plurality of lifestyles will be allowed. Thus, the new, contemporary path to socialism can follow democratic path without restricting freedom, consequently the concept of "dictatorship of the proletariat" does not fit the actual situation of the European countries.

In Eastern Europe, some economists of the Eastern European socialist countries such as the Czech Republic, Hungary, and Poland have also publicly proposed the "Third way"; the Czech Economist Ota Sik in his books The Third Way: Marxist-Leninist Theory & Modern Industrial Society (1972) "For a Humane Economic Democracy" (1979) "A Feasible Economic System", "The Argument about the Third way" has made a unique discussion on the "Third way", which aimed to find a new model to replace the Soviet mode of socialism.[18]

In the vast third world countries, with the twists and turns of the national liberation movement and the third world countries' exploration for a path of national development after winning independence, there have emerged a variety of "third way" ideas. In Asia, Indian Prime Minister Nehru in 1956 proposed to "establish a new type of socialism–an intermediate path between the orthodox practice of communism and capitalist countries"[19]; in Africa, Mali President A. Massamba-Debat also held the banner of "the middle way", advocated "opening a new path in the valley formed by the slopes of the capitalist system and socialism."[20] Gaddafi the leader of Libya put forward the unique "Third Universal Theory", hoping to take the "third way" in order to establish a system beyond the capitalism and socialism, guided by the teachings of Islam, based on Arabic traditions, a just and equitable society.[21]

In addition, during this period, the Western European Socialist parties' proposal for the establishment of democratic socialism spread widely in the third world, and some political parties in the third world also followed the Western European Socialist Parties and proposed similar claims of the "third way", such as Panama President O. B. Herrera proposed "the Panamanian road which is neither the traditional capitalist road nor the communist road", the Movement Toward Socialism (later merged into Chavez led United Socialist Party of Venezuela) proposed to establish a "Venezuelan-style socialist society" which would be both different from capitalism and real socialism.[22]

18 Ota Sik, The Third way, Beijing, People's Publishing House, 1982.

19 Nehru, Our Socialist Economy, published in Economic Review (Party Organ of the Indian National Congress Party), 1956/12/01.

20 Massamba-Débat's Talk with reporter from the newspaper L'Humanité of France, March 1964.

21 Gaddafi, Green Book, World Affairs Press, Beijing, 1985.

22 Xiao Nan, et al., Political Trends in the Contemporary Latin America, China Eastern Press, Beijing, 1988, pp. 110-129.

It is noteworthy that during this period, some of the Western Marxist scholars also proposed to take the "third way", such as H. Marcuse. He proposed that in a country we can implement a policy of establishing socialism and achieve a peaceful coexistence with capitalism. He argued that the shortcoming of Marxism-Leninism is that it only sees the evil and ills of capitalism, only stand on the opposite of capitalism and fights it, and "never admits that there is a real third choice outside of socialism and capitalism."[23] H. Marcuse argued that capitalism and socialism can be perfectly combined through his "cultural revolution" theory, so as to establish a new society.[24]

When history entered into the 1980s, in Eastern European socialist countries, "the third way" saw a certain degree of development. After, the Soviet leader Gorbachev promoted "humane and democratic socialism", and relaxed the Soviet control upon the Eastern European countries, "ideological pluralism" rampantly grew in the Eastern European real socialist countries, consequently democratic socialism relatively lost its charm in these countries and a kind of "third way" trend began to grow. Contrary to the situation in the post-World War II era, wherein democratic socialism trend had faded, in 1980s this trend saw a resurge. In 1980s the ruling parties of the socialist Eastern European countries changed their names to Socialist Party or the Social Democratic Party, and claimed to "fight for the realization of the basic values of democratic socialism."

In 1989, the leader of the Polish Solidarity Union, Lech Walesa, publicly argued that he proposed the "third way" which was different from real socialism and contemporary capitalism. After the drastic changes in the Soviet Union, after the social turmoil and economic downturn, in most of the Eastern European countries, the left-wing parties, mainly Social Democratic Party, came to power in elections. In summing up the results of the 1993 parliamentary elections, former Polish Prime Minister Bielecki said: "The winner of the election is the supporter of the third way." The Eastern European Social Democratic Parties represented by the Polish Social Democratic Party argued: "a set of practices adopted by the real socialism should be abandoned, but also "predatory capitalism" of the 19th century should be rejected in East Europe, instead a "third way" should be adopted. Specifically, it is necessary to abandon the dictatorship of the proletariat, and implement multi-party system, the parliamentary democracy, replace the planned economy with market economy, do not oppose privatization and establish a mixed economy according to their actual conditions, and implement "capitalism with humanitarian spirit."

23 H. Marcuse: Soviet Marxism, Neuwied Press, 1964, p. 167.

24 Li Zhongshang, The Third Way–A Study of Marcuse's and Habermas' Social Critical Theory, Beijing, The Academy Press, 1994.

4. The rejuvenation of the "Third Way" after the Cold War

In the 1990s, with the drastic changes in the Soviet Union and Eastern Europe and with the end of the Cold War, Western European politics also changed greatly. "The Third Way" as a new political philosophy or theory, rose in Western European countries. After the end of the Cold War, in the face of new changes in the international and domestic situation, Western European left-wing political parties had to reflect on their past theoretical propositions, and adjust their theoretical thinking, began to carry out a theoretical reconstruction. Western European left-wing parties include Labor Party, Workers' Socialist Party, Social Party, etc. They belong to the social democratic ideological system. This political school after a long silence in 1970s and 1980s became active in Western Europe in the mid-1990s. In the United Kingdom, in 1994, Anthony Giddens, president of the London School of Economics, published the book "Surpassing Left and Right". In this book, Giddens criticized the socialism represented by Soviet socialism, and the social democrats of the left-wing parties in Western Europe and analyzed and criticized conservatism and neoliberalism in an attempt to get rid of the traditional opposition of "left" and "right", to construct a unique ideology that contains both "left" and "right". His thought became the theoretical basis of the later prevalent "third way" thought, and also marked that the British Labor Party's theory encountered an overall transformation.

Since 1995, Chairman of the British Labor Party, Blair has frequently used the "third way" in public to describe his political philosophy, saying that the Labor Party must transcend neoliberalism and social democracy and develop new ideas. In 1997 elections, Blair defeated the leader of the Conservative Party, the British Prime Minister, John Major, with a big margin. Thus, the Labor Party established the new government after being in the opposition for 18 years and the "Third way" became the slogan of the new British government. In order to elaborate the connotation of the "third way", in May 1998, Giddens published his book "The Third way: The Renaissance of Social Democracy", which further improved and clarified the theoretical basis of the new ideas of the Labor Party in Britain. Giddens has argued that the "Third Way" he advocates refers to a framework of thinking or a policy-making framework. He added: the term 'Third Way', since it had different histories in different countries. For me, you could just substitute 'modernising social democracy'. At its most basic, the Third Way is described as the path between the old left and old right. Sounds simple, really–which is part of the problem. The turbulent few decades provides the structural backdrop to the debate over the Third Way. "The significance of this

'Third way' is: "it aims to transcend the old-school of social democracy and neo-liberalism."[25]

In September 1998, Blair published the "Third Way: New Politics in the New Century", which elaborated the Labor Party's ruling ideology. In the same year on September 27, Blair published the article "The Third Way is the Best Way" in the Washington Post. Blair pointe out : "The third way is the path to the restoration and success of modern social democracy, and it is not just a compromise between the left and right, it seeks to adopt the basic values of the middle and the middle-left way and make it applicable to fundamental social and economic changes around the world, and not to be bound by outdated ideology." Blair argued that what he calls "the basic values of the middle and the middle-left" refers to "the traditional values of unity, social justice, responsibility and opportunity", and what he calls outdated ideology refers to "the concept dominated by the left idea which focuses on state control, high taxation and defencing the interests of the producers" and "the new right-wing laissez-faire theory that advocates narrow individualism and free market economy is not able to solve any problem." Blair argued that his "third way" theory transcends the "state interventionism" theory of the "old left" represented by the Western European Social Democratic Party and goes beyond the "laissez-faire new right" theory proposed by representatives such as Reagan-Thatcher, which is a new political philosophy or theory which is proposed to solve the problems of the present era of globalization."

Almost simultaneously with Blair's "Third Way: New Politics in the New Century"' was published, German Social Democratic candidate La Fontane defeated Helmut Kohl, the Prime Minister of the Christian Democratic Union which ruled Germany for 16 years in the 14th Federal Parliament Election. But, La Fontane as the party leader proposed Schröder for the prime minister post. In order to change the image of the Social Democratic Party and vitalitise it as soon as possible, Schröder also raised the banner of "new middle policy", joined the then popular "third way" chorus in European and the US political stage. Blair congratulated German Social democrats on the election victory and declared that British and German governments will follow the same view. Shortly thereafter, during Schroeder's visit to the United Kingdom, the two countries also set up a special Britain-Germany committee of trade and industry ministers, which would be responsible to promote "Blairism" and "new middle policy". So, Schroeder was known as the "German Blair", the German chief architect of the "third way".

With the acceleration of the EU integration process, on November 22, 1998, 11 countries ruled by the Social Democratic Parties in the Eurozone

25 Anthony Giddens, "The Third Way: The Renewal of Social Democracy", Beijing, Peking University Press, Life, Reading, Xinzhi Sanlian Bookstore, 2000, p. 27.

signed a document named "New Road in Europe"; its content reflects a clear Blair-advocated "third way" color. The signing of this document can be said to be a more extensive and important and significant cognition and recognition of the "third way" in Europe. Or, the "third way" has begun to transform from a virtual theory, political initiative to a political program that can make a substantial impact on the European politics and economy. In order to spread the "third way" thought in a broader context and discuss the problems in the development of the "third way", in November 1999, the "Scholars for European Socialism" organized an international meeting to discuss the issues of "third way" in Berlin. The theme of the conference was "A Variety of Third Ways: Convergence and Differentiation". The conference fully and enthusiastically discussed time characteristics, the basic content and different manifestations of the "third way" in different countries. The "third way" was evalutaed as the new policy liberalization of the Social-Democrats which would adapt to the current background: the globalization era, would seek a new round of unity between social democracy and liberalism. Such "third way" meetings were also held before the Berlin meeting, for example in October 1997, the theme of the meeting was "European Social Democracy in Transformation", which extensively discussed the social and historical background of European social democratic revival and the real problems it faced, such as the European integration and the future of nation-state, the welfare state, etc. Another meeting was held in November 1998, the theme of this forum was "European Parliamentary Elections and Government Practices", which focused on the German and Swedish elections and the political practice European social democracy, and "the third way" theory was also an important topic in this conference.

At the end of the 20th century, European political stage was almost conquered by the left-wing parties. Among the 15 EU-member states, except Spain and Ireland, the remaining 13 countries were in the hands of left-wing parties alone or in coalition with other political parties. Under the influence of Blair, other leaders of the Western Social Democratic Parties or the ruling Socialist Parties have also put forward claims similar to the "third way", such as the French Prime Minister L. Jospin's proposal of establishing the "democratic socialism" between "communism and extreme liberalism". In addition, the former Italian Prime Minister R. Prodi, Persson from Sweden, Denmark's Rasmussen, Portuguese Prime Minister Antonio Guterres, France's minister of economy-finance-industry Strauss Kahn, have become enthusiastic supporters of the "Third way". This trend showed that in Western Europe's political arena, the role of the left-wing parties was strong and enjoyed a great advantage and dominance in Western Europe's political arena. Since the representatives of the "third way" in Western Europe had assumed the real ruling power, "the third way" thought trend had become the mainstream trend among the various ideological trends in Western Europe. In the current world, the debate on the "third way" is also very prominent. Although at the beginning of the new century, some left-wing parties once again lost their ruling positions, the influence of the "third way" thought still exists, and some left-wing parties who did not lose their ruling status still declared to hold the banner of "the third way".

5. Conclusions

We can at least draw the following conclusions from the above analysis:

Firstly, the "third way" is not a new concept, nor was it just the political "slogan" of the 1990s. Although the earliest emergence of the concept has been unable to trace, its formation and development since the late 19th century has experienced a course of more than a century. In history, the Western European Social Democrat Party with strong left wing tradition is the main advocator and practitioner of the "third way", its advocates and leaders have played an important role in the formation and development of the West European "third way" theory, and in the development of the "third way" theory in the rest of the world. The "third way" in history is quite different from the "third way" we are talking about today in Western European countries, but the "third way" we have seen in history has a great impact on the prevailing "third way" in Western Europe today. Looking into the development history of the "third way" thought, we can say that the current prevalent "third way" thought since the 1990s has inherited and developed the theories of reformist socialist schools of the world socialist movement since the late 19th century. It can also be said that the "third way" advocated by contemporary Social Democrats of the Western European countries is the revision or theoretical innovation of the "third way" in history. However, the "third way" we have seen in history has never been so attractive as today.

Second, the "third way" is not a concept with clear connotations. In history it has had different forms of manifestations. As a theory of social development, it mainly refers to the "middle way" which is different from both capitalism and socialism, both the absorbing of strengths of capitalism and socialism and aims avoiding the shortcomings of the two. As an economic system, it mainly aims a middle way between laissez-faire capitalist economy and the centrally planned socialist economy; as the path for a socialist change, it mainly refers to the path which is different from "peacefully entering socialism" proposed by democratic socialism, and the Soviet Union and other socialist states assuming power violently and practicing proletarian dictatorship; As a foreign policy, it mainly aims to follow diplomatic neutrality between the capitalist camp led by the United States and the socialist camp led by the Soviet Union, the implementation of independent foreign policy which neither supports Washington nor Moscow. Today what we call the "third way" is a reformist political thought which aims the "revival of social-democracy", and has formed dualistic way of thinking which pursues the binary integration, which aims to go beyond the dual opposition of "left" and "right", which was proposed by Blair, Schröeder and others in the exploration of solving practical problems faced by Britain, Germany and other Western European capitalist countries in the context of globalization.

Thirdly, the existence of the "third way" thought has its objective basis of historical inevitability. "The third way" trend of thought has developed for more than a century, and its impact is growing, mainly because its emergence and development has certain historical inevitability. Because the emergence and existence of intermediate forces is an objective occurance between two opposing forces. Marxism believes that wherever there is interaction between the two sides, there must be an intermediary. Intermediary is also the transitional form of this and that. Its existence is a common phenomenon which has certain objective realistic conditions in the world. As Engels wrote: all differences become merged in intermediate steps, and all opposites pass into one another through intermediate links", we can also quote from Lenin: Everything is vermittelt = mediated, bound into One, connected by transitions."[26]

If we examine the development trend of the "third way", we can say that it is mainly a theoretical manifestation of the forces representing the middle-of-the-roaders or the intermediate forces. Such intermediate force may be within a country, or it may be international. It tries to replace two opposing ideas or systems. This thought arises from the antagonism and struggle between socialist ideology and the capitalist ideology, which is formed in the initial contest of the two systems of socialism and capitalism and develops in the process of fierce struggle between the socialist camp and the capitalist camp. The revival of the "third way" since the mid-1990s has only been a political need for the left-wing parties in Western Europe to seek power by getting support of the middle class and striving for more voters.

Fourth, the so-called "third way" belongs to the capitalist path. Although the "third way" has different forms of expression, in essence, "the third way" advocates the capitalist path. The "third way" proposed by the democratic socialism is essentially the path of reforming capitalism. The "third way" proposed by the developing countries is essentially the path of state capitalism. If we examine their later practice after the radical changes in the Eastern Europe "third way" proposed by the Eastern European socialist scholars or political figures, clearly proves to be a capitalist development path.

26 Lenin Complete Works, Chinese 2nd edition, Vol. 55, Beijing, People's Publishing House, 1990, p. 85.

And current popular "third way" in Western Europe is rather a path to promote the further development of capitalism under the conditions of the economic globalization. Lenin, when criticizing the "third way" proposed by the Social Democratic Party, pointed out: "Such socialists are theoretically myopic, captive of bourgeois prejudice and politically betray the proletariat, mainly because they do not understand that in the capitalist society, when the class struggle as the foundation of this society becomes slightly more intensified, there can be no intermediate path apart from the dictatorship of the bourgeoisie or the dictatorship of the proletariat. The third way seems a sheer fantasy, but it reflects the reactionary grievances of the petty bourgeoise."[27] As the practice has proved, in reality the "Third Way" does not exist. As Mao Zedong pointed out in his "On People's Democratic Dictatorship": "Sitting on the fence will not work, nor is there a third way."[28]

(Qin Xuan, Professor of Institute of Marxism,
Renmin University of China)

27 Lenin Complete Works, Chinese 2nd edition, vol. 35, Beijing, People's Publishing House, 1985, p. 491.
28 Mao Zedong Selected Works, 2nd edition, Vol. 4, p. 1473.

The Structure of World System and the Historical Trend of Human Social Development

The operation and development of the capitalist system in the contemporary world is not homogeneous, instead it is characterized by the coexistence of "center" (developed capitalist countries) and "periphery" (developing countries) consequently shows two different statuses of "developed" and "underdeveloped" capitalist countries. With the development of world capitalist economic system, and increasing globalization of the production and economy, the development of the world capitalist system structure is bound to significantly affect the historical trend of human social development.

1. Reasons for the formation of world capitalist system structure

The world capitalist architecture consists of the two parts as “developed” and “underdeveloped”, which is a consensus of scholars at home and abroad. However, there are divergent views on the reasons for the formation of “developed” and “underdeveloped” parts of the world capitalist system structure. The standpoint of Western modernists which assumes the position of safeguarding the interests of monopoly capitalism, ignore history and reality, and treat the “developed” and “underdeveloped” structures of the world capitalist system as a spontaneous development process, believing that their own systems, structures and cultural traditions haven't contributed to this structure. The reason why developing countries have been “underdeveloped” both historically and realistically lies in the existence of inherent inborn cultural factors that impede their “development”. While the Dependency school advocates the position of safeguarding the national interests of the developing countries and firmly oppose the "spontaneity" reasoning of the Western modernists’ explanation of the “developed” and “underdeveloped” structures of the world capitalist system. The formation of the structure of the world capitalist system of “developed” and “underdeveloped” has its historical reasons and also has its profound practical reasons. The explanation of the “underdevelopment” of the developing countries can only be grasped from the developed capitalist countries’ control of developing countries and the dependence of developing countries on developed countries. These two different interpretations of the reasons for the formation of the world capitalist structure basically represent two different views in the international context.

The history of the “developed” and “underdeveloped” structures of the world capitalist system was not formed as spontaneous process as the Western modernists have claimed. As long as the people have a little historical knowledge, they know that "developed" and "underdeveloped" is neither inborn nor fate, it is the result of Western colonial expansion and aggression. Developed countries were not inborn to be "developed"; developing countries were not inborn to become "underdeveloped". The Western colonists conquered the Asian, African, Latin American countries with the means of plunder and wars, squeezed their wealth, built plantations and gold and silver mines by the sale of slaves, colonial exploitation in other people's land was carried out by the cruel colonial rule. It was this plunder beginning from that colonial era which greatly shoook the traditional economic order and structure of Europe, so that Europe went out of backward state and rapidly ascended; it was also the plunder which began with that era which greatly destroyed the Asian, African, Latin American countries' prosperous economy and colorful culture, thus began their decline. Marx has made a concise summary of the history of capitalist development: "The discovery of gold and silver in America, the extirpation, enslavement and entombment in mines of the aborgin population, the beginning of the conquest and looting of the East Indies, the turning of Africa into a warren for the commercial hunting of black-skins, signalised the rosy dawn of the era of capitalist production."[29] Western colonial rule brought a lot of wealth accumulation for the West, but at the same time brought great disaster to Asian, African, Latin American countries, consequently the world was divided into the a world of rich and the poor parts and the world capitalist system split into developed and underdeveloped countries. The history of Western colonization tells us that "developed" and "underdeveloped" are a symbiotic historical process in which capitalism, while creating "developed", has created the "underdeveloped". "Underdevelopment" was caused by the "developed", the formation of the "developed" and "underdeveloped" structures of the world capitalist system is the result of Western colonial rule, which is the fact that no one can deny.

Is the continuation of the "developed" and "underdeveloped" structures of the world capitalist system in today's world, indeed only caused by the internal factors as the Western modernists have claimed? Of course not! We recognize that the continuation of "developed" and "underdeveloped" in today's world capitalist architecture is related with internal factors, but as long as we have a little knowledge about the relations between "developed" and "underdeveloped", we can recognize that the developed countries using unequal international division of labor and neocolonialism to control and exploit developing countries is an important reason for the continuation of this structure. They grab various privileges from the developing countries in exchange for "development aid", "gift" and "loan", and interfere in the internal affairs of developing countries in various ways, manipulate the

29 Marx-Engels Collected Works, Vol..5, pp. 860-861.

armed forces of developing countries and open the way for the expansion of monopoly capital, and also coach and push the economic development of developing countries towards the track of the international monopoly capital track; they increase foreign direct investment in developing countries through various forms of international monopoly organizations, with mergers and acquisations expand the local investments of western multinationals and swallow local companies, plunder the economic resources and markets of the developing countries, seize excess monopoly profits, control the economic lifeline of developing countries, continue to keep their former colonies under their sphere of influence. And through the method "price scissors" between the import and export prices and the unequal trade deals due to the difference between the international values and domestic values, the developed countries have acquired large sums of surplus value from the developing countries, all of which demonstrate the outward expansion of capital into developing countries.

Are all these not enough to explain the "polarization" in the world capitalist system, are all these not enough to reject that the"developed" countries are the root cause of the continuation of the "underdeveloped"structures? Keith Griffin in his famous article titled as "Underdevelopment in An Historical Context" emphasized the following: "The history of the underdeveloped countries, in the last five centuries is, in large part, the history of the consequences of European expansion." "The automatic functioning of the international economy which Europe dominated first created underdevelopment and then has hindered the efforts to escape from it."[30] Griffin's analysis on the formation and continuation of the relationships pattern between the "developed" and "underdeveloped" countries of the world's capitalist system has proposed remarkably innovative ideas.

2. The nature of structural imbalance within the world capitalist system

There is no doubt that the "developed" and "underdeveloped" structures of the world capitalist system are the continuation of the past historical structures. This continuation of the said structure is not only manifested in form, but more importantly reflected in its essence. The past "political merger" of the colonies and their plunder under brutal power politics by the developed capitalist countries were transformed into "economic mergers" and into formally "equal economic exchanges", conditions of which were determined by the developing countries. This change has not only failed

30 Quoted from Charles K. Wilbur, The Political Economy of Development and Underdevelopment, China Social Sciences Press, 1984, pp. 114-110.

to eliminate the inequality in the world capitalist structure, but on the contrary, this inequality was concealed by "equality" or equivalent "exchange coat", the developed capitalist countries has retreated to the "formally legitim" way for their exploitation, plunder and control upon the developing countries.

In the world capitalist structure, the relations between the "developed" and "underdeveloped" countries are becoming more and more interdependent with the development of economic globalization and under the situation of highly-developed productive forces. The economic exchanges between the developed capitalist countries and the developing countries, from the field of production to the circulation, from raw materials trade, from technology to capital export/import are manifested as the realations of interdependence, we must admit this news facts. However, since the new form of capitalism created by the high-level development of productive forces determines the conditions of international expansion and accumulation of capital, this kind of interdependence fully embody the unequal relationship between the exploiter and the exploited, between the dominant and dominated between the developed capitalist countries and developing countries. In their study of the relationship between the "developed" and "underdeveloped" structures of the world capitalist system, some scholars have over-emphasized the study of the "interdependence" relationship but dilute the study of the relationship of "inequality". It can be quite easy to explain the error of this research method by the analysis of trade relations, investment relations and technological relations and other aspects of the relations between the "developed" and "underdevelopment".

If we examine the trade relations between "developed" and "underdeveloped", in order to protect their dominance over developing countries in international trade, the developed capitalist countries, on the one hand, use unequal exchange by their monopoly over the factors of prouction, use the defiencies of the developing countries such as their weak situation in high-tech based manufacturing, high-precision electronic, high-precision mechanical equipment and advanced chemical products. The developed capitalist countries strive to increase their prices of such advanced industrial products which are sold to developing countries, force them to buy these industrial products at high monopoly prices.They strongly depress the prices of primary resources and products primary products which they buy from the developing countries. These primary products have low demand elasticity, short storage time, easy to find substitutes. On the other hand, they use unequal exchange, that is, they use their advantages in the international division of labor and labor productivity due to their dominant status in the international capitalist structure, in this way they grab a huge amount of excess profits. The essence of this unequal exchange in the trade realtion between the developed and developing countries also embodies surplus value transfer from developing countries to developed capitalist countries.

If we look from the investment relations between "developed" and "underdeveloped", capital export and FDI are the means by which the developed capitalist countries maintain their domination. The heavy debt burden of the developing countries is the manifestation of this relationship. In the real economic life, the developing countries have to make up for the huge deficit of foreign exchange income caused by the unequal trade with the developed capitalist countries. In order to develop their economies which lack the needed capital accumaulation, they need to attract capital input from the developed capitalist countries. Looking into the post-war capital export of developed countries, although the amount of capital flow to developing countries accounted for only one quarter of the total, the absolute amount of capital flow to them has demonstrated a clear trend of increase. There is no doubt that the large amount of capital flow to developing countries since the 1970s has, to a certain extent, compensated the lack of industrialization funds in developing countries, the capital inflow was used for the introduction of advanced technologies and for the establishment of new industrial sectors. But this capital inflow has caused the debt trap, deepened their dependence in economic development dependence to the developed capitalist countries. Developed capitalist countries when exporting capital or lending funds also exploit a part of the wealth created by the workers of the developing countries, in this way they inject a new vitality to their advanced economies, thus maintain their advantageous economic status in the world. Consequently, the investment and fund lending relations between the "developed" and "underdeveloped" countries lead to debt accumulation in the developing countries, which can be evaluated as brutal exploitation and plundering which increrase their economic and financial dependence, this is the re-establishment of the "colonial economic relations" in which developed capitalist countries monopolize the world markets, plus they use their cheaper labor.

When we analyze the technological relationships between "developed" and "underdeveloped" countries, the developed countries possess the technological monopoly in the world capitalist system. On the one hand, they transfer the production of technologically less complex products to developing countries; on the other hand, they also transfer those enterprises using old technologies and production facilities which are harmful tfro ecological environment to developing countries.In this way, they can reduce the costs, occupy the market of developing countries, but in this way they can also focus their educated manpower and capital resources for high-level technological industries, invest in R&D thus maintain their leading position in the new-technology driven industries.Thus the developing countries, remain in the lower ladder of the production chain and remain in a technologically inferior status,only crawl behind the pace of developed capitalist countries, technological know-how they need for technological improvements must also rely on transfer from developed capitalist countries, but this transfer of know-how and technology is sold to them at high prices or most often this know-how and technology is not the latest version.The capitalist states issue regulations which restrict the transfer of high technologies to developing countries.Thus the developing countries face huge economic losses, and also lose initiative in developing their economies and industries. In the current world capitalist structue the facts we see in trade, investment and technology exchanges between the "developed" and "underdeveloped" are unequal relations of interdependence, i.e. domination of "developed" upon the "underdeveloped" and subordinate status of the "underdeveloped" to "developed".

3. Wallerstein's analysis of the world system

Immanuel Wallerstein is a renown US sociologist who has made remarkable studies on the contemporary world capitalist system. Since the 1970s, he has systematically studied the patterns of the world capitalist system. His relevant works include: *The Modern World-System* (Vol. I published in 1974, Vol. II published in 1980, Vol. III published in 1989), *World Inequality* (1975), *The Capitalist World-Economy* (1979), *World-Systems Analysis: Theory and Methodology* (Immanuel Wallerstein with Terence K. Hopkins et al., 1982), and *Historical Capitalism* (1983). Looking from the perspective of the overall development and change of the world capitalist system, Wallerstein, has used the analysis method of the system theory and combines the various disciplines of economics, politics, history and sociology in his study, thus examined the world capitalist system starting from its overall development process, and he has re-analyzed the relationships between the "developed" and "developing" countries. Wallerstein's analysis of the world system and his creative discussion on the former theories in respect to relations between the "developed" and "underdeveloped". His study has greatly inspired the Western scholars and the scholars of the developing countries to seek for a new theoretical research realm, which affirms the innovative character of his theoretical research vision, research content and research methods.

Firstly, Wallerstein taking the "world system" as his analysis basis, has formed a new theoretical research vision. The "world system" he has developed is an original concept of his world system theory, which is a social system composed of various different "elements" such as demarcation lines, structures, groups, and legal structures. These elements in the system are sometimes integrated by mutual attraction, but sometimes they collide and split due to internal competition. The world system of Wallerstein is a social system that can self-regulate itself and its develeopment can be promoted by various interrelated and interacting "elements".[31] This "world system" is a holistic economic unit, has its law of overall development and change, this law can dominate and restrict development and change in the various countries and regions. Therefore, Wallerstein has argued that both "developed" and "underdeveloped" are only concrete manifestations of the overall development and change of the world in its each component part. The study approach of the world system structure analysis emphasizes applying the research method of starting from the whole to parts, and studies the constraints and impacts of the overall law of the world system upon the "developed" and "underdeveloped". Wallerstein fundamentally opposes the paradigm of Western economic development theory which focuses on internal causes of the "underdevelopment" and also opposes the dependency theory which focuses on the external causes of the "underdevelopment".

Development theory of the Western economics safeguards the interests of monopoly capital and takes the experience of early stage of development in western developed countries as its basis, and uses the economic theories prevalent in the Western developed capitalist countries to study the socio-economic development issues in the developing countries from the aspects of capital accumulation, development programs, economic growth. This theory focuses on exploring the internal causes of underdevelopment in the developing countries and uses early development experiences of developed countries as a model to change the realities of the underdeveloped countries.

Dependency theory represents the national interests of developing countries, resolutely opposes Western centralism, and opposes to equate the current situation of the developing countries with the past situation in developed countries, advocates seeking the reasons of underdevelopment in the practices of the developed countries: their domination upon and exploitation of developing countries and their dependence on developed countries. They have also meticilously explored the socio-economic development issues of the developing countries. Although these two theories have fundamental differences of stand point, they have two similarities in terms of their analytical methods: (1) They take the "nation" as basic unit of analysis, emphasis on the study of the development of capitalism in a nation, discuss and compare the relationships between the development in different countries, but ignore the overall development and change in the entire capitalist world; (2) they divide the world into developed countries (core countries) and underdeveloped countries (periphery) according to social and economic development of all countries within the world capitalist system. Wallerstein's analysis from the new perspective of the "world

31 See, Wallerstein, The Modern World-System, Vol. 1, Academic Press, New York, 1974, p. 347.

system" fundamentally breaks this analysis model of Western economic development theory and the dependence theory.

Based on this new research perspective, Wallerstein has further examined the characteristics of the world capitalist system within its wholistic development and change. He has argued that in the development history of the world capitalist system, there have been two completely different social systems, the "world empire" and the "world economies". The "world-empire" (examples, the Roman Empire, Han China) are big bureaucratic structures with a single political center and with an axial division of labor, but contain multiple cultures. On the other hand, the world-economy is a large axial division of labor with multiple political centers and also contain multiple cultures, but this system lacks a central authority. In English, the word hyphen is essential conception to indicate these concepts. "World system" without a hyphen suggests that there has been only one world-system in the world history. The "world empire" relies on a common political system and political rule, the economic surplus is plundered from direct producers in the form of "tribute" (from the "periphery" to the "core"), but World-empire systems were basically had re-distributive structures in their economic forms; on the other side the world-economy system uses the unequal exchange (trade) mechanism to exploit the economic surplus from the "periphery" to the "core".

Since this single division of labor, multiple cultural systems, and the transfer of economic surplus are determined by capitalism in the current "World system" it can be defined as the world capitalist system. According to Wallerstein, such a world economy----which was promoted by capitalism from the 16th century to the present is the only long-lasting historical instance. It is based upon a geographically differentiated division of labor, featuring three main zones of ---core, semi-periphery, and periphery- linked together by trade of bulk commodities in the world market that are necessities of everyday consumption. Wallerstein evaluates the "world economy" and capitalism as the obverse sides of the same coin, but one side does not determine or cause the other. He defines the same indivisible phenomenon by different characteristics, thus he calls the "world system" as the "capital world economy". Since the formation of the "capital world economy" in the 16th century, it has undergone a process of successful expansion using various means including military, political, economic and other means.

Wallerstein has argued that this long process has the three main characteristics:

(1) In the form of constant development of capital accumulation, and with the economic expansion as the means, there occurred the gradual inclusion of Asia, Africa and Latin America in its own sphere.

(2) The unequal relationship is the basis for the formation of the "core" and the "periphery" countries and this unequal economic relationship is the root cause for the backward development of the capitalist economies in Asia, Africa and Latin America, such division is also the important means of capital accumulation in the contemporary world.

(3) It contains many forced cultural changes, such as the forced introduction of Christianity to several regions of the world, the imposing of European languages and certain European technologies, compulsory education of legal norms, etc. And, these compulsory cultural changes have deeply affected the behaviors of Asian, African and Latin American peoples."[32]

Secondly, Wallerstein has adopted a new approach of theoretical research from the perspective of "core—semi-periphery—periphery" divisions in the world system. Wallerstein has argued that the world capitalist system is unbalanced, in which there are core countries with developed industries, rational industrial distribution and a powerful bourgeoise class, and there are "periphery" countries that mainly produce raw materials, lack such a strong bourgeoisie class and have single cultural and social structures. Wallerstein has defined the last category as the "semi-periphery" zone countries and argued that such countries are those which are controlled by the core states and are partially able to control the periphery countries. They include some economically stronger countries in Latin America and some countries in Europe. In Wallerstein's view, "semi-periphery", as the "third category", has a very important political significance.

Firstly, in the world trade, the trade goals of the "semi-periphery" countries are two-sided. They do not only export the products of the periphery countries to the core countries, but also export the products of the core countries to periphery, thus the economy of world system tends to be roughly balanced.

Secondly, in the world system, the existence of the "semi-periphery" zone plays a role as a kind of "buffer zone" which alleviates the contradictions between the "core" and "periphery". If there was no "semi-periphery" the world system would be polarized, confrontations between the "core" and the "periphery" would intensify, thus the "semi-periphery" plays the role of a "safety valve" in the world system.

Thirdly, in the world system, the position of "semi-periphery" countries still continue to change. With the emergence and adaptation of revolutionary changes in science and technology and the detoriation of the ecological environment within the world system, some semi-periphery countries can have

32 See Wallerstein, The Politics of the World Economy, London, Cambridge University Press, 1984, p. 169.

the possibility to join the "core" zone, but some of them may decline and fall to the ranks of the periphery countries.[33] However, even if the "semi-periphery" changes its position and aims to join the "core" zone in the world system this will not be sufficient enough to change the world system itself.

It can be seen that the analysis of the structure of the "core/semi-periphery/periphery" of the world capitalist system has made an important supplement and enrichment to the "core-periphery" structure proposed by the Western economic development theories and the Dependency theories, which has been proven by changes in the world pattern after the mid-1970s. After the mid-1970s, the absolute superiority of the United States in the post-War period, from the aspects of economy, politics, military and others in the in the world capitalist system has gradually declined and its sole hegemony began to shake.

Western Europe and Japan have surmounted the Post-war economic difficulties and achieved the economic take-off using the new technological revolution. They have nearly caught-up the United States in respect to GDP and other major economic indicators. The post-war world capitalist system with the United States as the sole "core" power has changed. A situation of tripartite confrontation among the United States, Western Europe and Japan has formed. Meanwhile, after nearly 30 years of exploration, socio-economic structure of the developing countries has developed to a certain extent. Some developing countries began to enter the ranks of the world's advanced countries in terms of per capita income, GDP and other major economic indicators. Some developing countries have also joined their forces to form regional economic cooperation organizations to oppose the hegemonic status of developed countries and began to resist exploitation and control of international monopoly capital. There are some profound changes in the underdeveloped countries of the world capitalist system.

These changes are mainly manifested as in the following:

The bipolar pattern of developed and developing countries formed after the World War II, has gradually transformed into one in which the United States, Western Europe, Japan and other developed countries saw similar economic growth rates, on the other hand newly emerging industrial countries of developing countries became prominent and continued to grow fast, especially oil exporting developing countries saw enrichment and fast growths, but on the other hand the number of least developed countries at the bottom has greatly increased. This new pattern of multi-polarization-reflects the multidimensional nature of the world's capitalist system, also

33 See Wallerstein, "World-Systems Analysis: Problems of Theory and Interpretation", in: Hopkins, Wallerstein, etc., "World-Systems Analysis: Theory and Methodology", Sage Publishing, 1982, p. 93.

reflects the diversity and complexity of the world's power structure, its plurality and a criss-cross pattern.

Thirdly, Wallerstein has developed new horizons of theoretical research by utilizing the view of "world system". In the past, the theoretical research on the relationship between "developed" and "underdeveloped" was generally confined to capitalism analysis. Besides, the research on the relationship between "developed" and "underdeveloped" did not involve the socialist mode of production and the world socialist system. Wallerstein's analysis of the world system not only explores the world capitalist system, but also explores the world socialist system and the relationship between the world's capitalist system and the world socialist system, which means research vision is innovative.

Wallerstein has argued that capitalism is a complete global system. Since the birth of capitalism, the world only included a single system. Other forms of systems were no more than an integral part of the capitalist system. In the world market, the socialist countries still have to follow the laws of the capitalist world economy. It is impossible for them to get rid of the world capitalist system and form an independent system. However, in the future the practice of socialist countries could accelerate the demise of the world capitalist system.

In Wallerstein's view, there are two paths available for the periphery countries:One is the revolutionary path that completely denies the world capitalist system, which are based on social and national (including state level) movements, i.e. "the anti-system movements".

The second is the path which aims to ascend from the "periphery" to the "core" within the framework of world capitalist system, which is, the "catch-up" path. Wallerstein regards the "catch-up" (developmentalist) path as a way of following the footsteps of the Western modernization. He believes that this path "tends to reinforce rather than weaken the current existing world-system", "we should not promote the developmentalist" path taken by the newly emerging states, instead we should strive to change this system as a whole, and recognize that our own state is both the motive force and an obstacle to this transformation." Only the path followed by "anti-system movements" is the best option for the periphery countries to benignly develop themselves. The goal of the "anti-system movements" is to transform the capitalist world-system into a socialist world-system that can focus on overcoming the shortcomings of the existing capitalist world-system.

Seizing the state power can be both an "element" of advantage or disadvantage for the "anti-system movements". When the nationalist anti-system movements win imminent success, i.e., effective participation of some kind of government power, they face an opportunistic influx, which is quite hard to overcome. This is a bandwagon effect. Were all this not enough, the seizure of state power (partial or even totally) within a given state-machinery only brings a partial increase in real power. On the other hand, in some respects it brings a decrease in real power "Nonetheless, the collective momentum of these anti-system socialist and national movements over time has been anti-systemic when we evaluate their effects, despite some of them have "reformist" or revisionist" natures, if analyzed individually."35

Wallerstein has also examined the world socialist system. He pointed out: "some people think that when a country has achieved the nationalization of industries and declares loyalty to socialism, it can be out of the capitalist world system due to implementing such nationalization measures", which is a mistaken view.[34]

In fact, the characteristics of the socialist mode of production (the socialist-world-government) should be based on the production of use values, fair distribution and a collectively agreed-upon exchange (trade) of use-values, namely based on a "planning" at the world level. Only this "planning" can eradicate the unequal exchange in the current world trade and achieve the production for use values. The replacement of world capitalist system can only be possible in the framework of a holistic world structure based on such a socialist mode of production, namely the socialist world system or the "socialist world-government". Wallerstein believes that, although this "socialist world government" is still far away from us, it will eventually be achieved. The geographical expansion of the world capitalist system has reached its limits. With the recurrence of the capitalist crises, the socialist countries will become more and more powerful. The world capitalist system will be unable to contend them and will tend to collapse. Consequently, in the difficult process of realizing the global transformation from capitalism to socialism, it is vital to design certain effective strategies.

In Wallerstein's analysis of the prospects of the world system, his idea of incorporating contemporary socialism into the world capitalist system is undoubtedly wrong. This approach to a certain extent, denies Lenin's idea of initiating the building of socialism in a single country and denies the fact that socialism as a thought, a movement and as a system is still existing and growing in the contemporary world. It is an undeniable fact that socialism still has a strong vitality and appeal. In the analysis of the characteristics of the socialist mode of production, Wallerstein has neglected the analysis of the basis of the establishment of the socialist mode of production, and ignored the analysis of the state ownership of the means of production for the realization of the socialist mode of production, which makes the analysis on the prospects of socialism within the world system theory becomes out of touch with the current world situation.

34 Wallerstein, Historical Capitalism, Beijing, Social Sciences Academic Press, 1999, p. 6.

Fourthly, Wallerstein's analysis of the world's system has great implications for our study and discussion on the relationships between contemporary "developed" and "underdeveloped" countries.The analysis and research of the "world system theory" not only offers a separate study of the developed capitalism and underdeveloped capitalism, but also offers the study of relations between "developed" and "underdeveloped" in the context of world system. Besides, Wallerstein's analysis offers the study of the development of capitalist production mode and its historical trend. His multidisciplinary research on the relationship between "developed" and "underdevelopment" in the world system is a new breakthrough in the history of the theoretical research on the relationship between "developed" and "underdevelopment".

It applies the dynamic sociological analysis and structural analysis method, also studies the historical development of the world system, integrates sociology, political science, economics, history and other disciplines, deepens history and sociology with economics and political science and provides a benign model for our comprehensive study of relations between the "developed" and "underdeveloped".

Marx has attached great importance to the study of the relationship between "developed" and "underdeveloped" regions of the world and took the "world history" level as the starting point in his the study of this relation. Marx argued that the basic characteristic of the modern capitalist society is the fact that the narrow regional national histories are being transformed into a world history. For Marx, the root cause of this transformation was the expansion of the world trade and the initial formation of the world markets. "The further the separate spheres, which interact on one another, extend in the course of this development, the more the original isolation of the separate nationalities is destroyed by the developed mode of production and intercourse and the division of labour between various nations naturally brought forth by these, the more history becomes the world history."[35]

The formation of world history meant the formation of the world system, consequently regions and countries has merely become the "knots" within the "network" of the world system, and their development would be inevitably determined whole by this "network". Only from the perspective of "world history", can we correctly understand and grasp the historical status, development direction and the future path of a country in the world system. Wallerstein's analysis of the world system absorbs and applies Marx's historical theory and methods, takes the world history as the starting point for the study of the relationship between the "developed" and "underdeveloped", and also takes the "countries" and "nations" as the elements

35 Marx-Engels Collected Works, Vol. 1, p. 540-541.

of “world system”. He emphasizes the importance of studying the whole world system. In this regard, it is an elucidation of the application of Marx’s theory of world history. Its profound study of production relations, the socio-economic and political structure, the unequal exchange mechanism and the development of world system are the results of this view.

One of the most striking features of Wallerstein’s analysis of the world system is its critique of the Western-centrism. Western-centrism emphasizes that the world system is centered around the Western countries, other countries or regions in the world system is insignificant and such westernization equals modernization. Although Wallerstein used the concepts of periphery and semi-periphery to classify the developing countries, he was more objective and impartial when analyzing the status quo of developing countries, recognized their status in the world system, and analyzed their rise in the world system. Meanwhile, he also incorporated the analysis of economic and political diversity and differences among the countries into the comprehensive analysis and macro research of the world system.

In terms of critizing the “Western-centrism”, if the dependency theory established after the mid-1960s can be said to be the first step, and the world system analysis rising in the late 1970s and early 1980s has benn the second step. Dependence theory is against the western development path and rejects copying of the western model. The analysis of the "world system theory" suggests that the developing countries should only actively seek their own development path but should regard the relationship between the “developed” and “underdeveloped” as an important issue that affects the current situation and future prospects of the whole world economy. Today, with the rapid development of science and technology, the degree of interdependence in the fields of production and collaboration among countries is becoming deeper and deeper. The relationships in the world economy, politics and culture are increasingly becoming closer, thus all peoples and nations of the world have become involved in the broad river of world history. In this case, it is even more necessary to make comprehensive research on the relationship between the “developed” and “underdeveloped” in the world capitalist system.

4. The way to equality in the world capitalist system

The domination of “developed” over the “less-developed” and the dependence of the latter on the “developed” countries reveal the profoundness and sharp antagonism of the internal contradictions of the world capitalist system. Developed capitalist countries are the monopolists, rulers, predators and oppressors. Developing countries are the dominated, exploited and the oppressed non-monopolies. Although both sides follow the capitalist path, they have a sharp conflict of interest. One party want to use the existing unequal international economic relations, aim to maintain the privileges left by history, in order to firmly control the developing countries, and push the developing countries to the abyss of poverty and backwardness. The other party wants to fight for an independent sovereignty, aims to realize a rapid economic development, and free itself from the control and constraints of developed capitalist countries by forming coalition among the developing countries, so that the world economic system and existing operational mechanisms will be adapted to the newly formed political configuration of world system. With the inevitable future solution of this sharp contradiction the developing countries will be in an equal footing with the developed capitalist countries in the world capitalist system.

The fundemental way to change the current world capitalist structure towards such an equality is to establish a new international economic order. The old international economic order formed in the past which favors the developed countries is the main obstacle for developing countries which seek national economic development. In the world capitalist system, in order to free themselves from the exploitation and domination of the developed capitalist countries and their dependence, the developing countries should participate in international division of labor on equal footing, participate in the decision-making of global economic affairs, they should be able to effectively control their own resources and their products should enter the world market without restrictions. In order to independently develop their national economies, they need to have a benign international environment, which means a new international economic order should be established.

Since the 1960s, developing countries have made numerous efforts to pave the way for a new international economic order. They have criticized the old international economic order publicly airing their views in various international conferences such as the Non-Aligned Countries Summit meetings, the United Nations Conference of Trade and Development, the Conferences of International Economic Cooperation and others. They have established regional, semi-regional economic organizations, developed cooperation among themselves in the field of trade, capital and technology and have struggled against the old international economic order with practical measures and actions. However, the solution of some substantive issues directly harm the interests of developed capitalist countries, so the establishment of a new international economic order is rather difficult. The main reasons of difficulties for the developing countries to establish a new international economic order are: On the one hand, currently it is the national bourgeoisie classses with different degrees of comprador character which leads the developing countries this gives a reformist character to the fight for a new international economic order; on the other hand, more importantly the overall economic strength of the developing countries is relatively weak. In the antagonistic conflict with the developed capitalist countries, they have no power to intensify the contradiction. Even if the contradictions are likely to be intensified, they can't take strong preventive measures. Therefore, developing countries must continue to accumulate their own strength, actively create the conditions and timing for the establishment of a new international economic order.

The path to equality in the world capitalist system will not stop at the establishment of a new international economic order. The establishment of a new international economic order is only about the issue that in what way the capitalist countries will participate in international division of labor, it will change the re-distribution of interests. It can be said that its establishment will prepare for the replacement of world capitalist system structure with world socialist system. As a social system, capitalism will eventually advance to socialism. Marx said, "No social order ever disappears before all the productive forces for which there is room in it have been developed,"[36] this is both true in the case of capitalism of a single country and for the world capitalism. And, "new, higher relations of production never appear before the material conditions of their existence have matured in the womb of the old society itself," this is both true in the case of emergence of socialism in a single country and also that of emergence of world socialism as well. Finalization of the development of world capitalism is that all the productive forces it can accommodate are given full play. Then the starting point of world socialism is that the material conditions that capitalism has prepared for socialism are mature. Therefore, it can be argued that the fundamental way to move the world capitalist system toward equality is to establish a world socialist system. It should be said that the world capitalist system completed its historical mission in the sharpening of contradiction between the "development" and "underdevelopment". However, because the world capitalism is a huge system, the contradictions between the "developed" and "underdeveloped" in this system are complicated and tortuous. Developed capitalist countries might self-adjust the contradictions with the developing countries at any time. Therefore, the transition from world capitalist system to world socialist system is a long historical process.

It should be said that the world capitalist system finalizes its course while the socialist forces are keeping growing. However, as a young social system, socialism must go through a process from emergence to consolidating and later to perfecting. In this process, there will be contradictions and conflicts with the capitalist system, so there will be attacks and retreats, and victories and failures as well. Because of the complexity and difficulty of this process, the growth of the world socialism forces will inevitably be a long-term process. Especially today, the world socialist movement is suffering major setbacks, and socialism is facing the test of whether it could

36 Marx-Engels Collected Works, Vol. 2, p. 592.

charm, attract and influence the peoples of the world. Therefore, the process of replacing the world capitalist system by the world socialist system is more complex, tortuous and a long course.

We must see that for a social and economic system to be established or perishing, will inevitably go through a long historical process, this is the same for the world socialist system to replace the world capitalist system. We must also see that there is nothing completely equal within the world capitalist system. The only way for all nations and countries to seek true equality in the world is to involve in the world socialist system. We must establish a firm belief that the victory of socialism in the world is inevitable, and this is a law of the development of human history which cannot be changed by human will or anything else.

(Zhang Leisheng, Professor of Institute of Marxism Studies, Renmin University of China)

"Two Inevitabilities" and "Two Nevers"

"Two Inevitabilities" is Marx and Engels' judgement on the trend of the emergence of the socialist society. "Two Nevers" is Marx and Engels' theoretical exposition on contradictory movement of productive forces and relations of production in the development of human society and its evolution. "Two Inevitabilities" and "Two Nevers" are the most important part of Marxist theory. They together reveal the law of the development of human society, a theory with a high degree of inherent unity. In term of the development trend of capitalist society, "Two Nevers" judgement is relative and expresses the internal requirements of "Two Inevitabilities"; "Two Inevitabilities" judgement contains the judgement of "Two Nevers" and expresses the final result of "Two Inevitabilities".

1. "Two Inevitabilities" as the final result of the movement of the "Two Nevers"

"Two Inevitabilities" and "Two Nevers" together in unity are the embodiment of the basic law of movement of societies. "Two Nevers" is the embodiment of the general law of contradictory development movement of contradictions in the society and the "Two Inevitabilities" is the final result of this former law which we can clearly observe in the capitalist society.

In "Preface to The Critique of Political Economy" (Referred to as "Preface"), when summing up the "overall results" of his economics studies, Marx for the first time clearly revealed the dialectical development process of human society with his classical words and put forward the judgement of "Two Nevers". Marx pointed out that the production relations that are compatible with the developmental stages of material productive forces are the real basis of society, and "the *mode* of *production* of *material life* determines the *social*, political and intellectual *life* process in general"."At a certain stage of their development, the material productive forces of society come into conflict with the existing relations of production, or—what is but a legal expression for the same thing—with the property relations within which they have been at work hitherto. From forms of development of the productive forces these relations turn into their fetters. Then begins the epoch of social revolution." "We cannot judge an epoch of transformation by its own consciousness; on the contrary, instead this consciousness must be explained from the contradictions of material life, from the existing conflict between the social productive forces and the relations of production." "No social order ever disappears before all the productive forces for which there is room in it have been developed, and "new, higher relations of production never appear before the material conditions of their existence have matured in the womb of the old society itself (the "Two Nevers")."[37]

There is no doubt that the idea of "Two Nevers" discusses the conditions of social revolution and reform and expression Marx's idea on the general form of basic social contradictions in a society. It tells us that in terms of the general form of the human social movement, any socio-economic form will exist as long as the productive forces it can accommodate can still continue to develop. When the material conditions on which the higher production relations rely on, develop and become more mature in the old social form, the higher economic and social form will emerge. So, Marx put forward the "two nevers" judgement as a dialectical form for the analysis of human social development and change. It is the inherent content of the general law of human social development, and objective criteria for judging the era of social change.

The idea of "Two Nevers" is the consistent thinking of Marx and Engels. In their works such as "A Contribution to the Critique of Hegel's Philosophy of Right-Introduction Part", the German Ideology, The Poverty of Philosophy and The Communist Manifesto, when explaining the contradictory movement of productive forces and production relations, Marx and Engels made gradually richer and more profound elaborations on the idea of "Two Nevers".

In Contribution to the Critique of Hegel's Philosophy of Right-Introduction", Marx answered the following question: can Germany attain a practice à la hauteur des principles – i.e., a revolution which will raise it not only to the *official level* of modern nations, but to the *height of humanity* which will be the near future of those nations? … "Meanwhile, a major difficulty seems to stand in the way of a *radical* German revolution. Because, revolutions require a passive element, a material basis. Theory is fulfilled in a people only insofar as it is the fulfilment of the needs of that people." He also added: "Will the theoretical needs be direct immediate practical needs? It is not enough for thought to strive for realization, but reality must itself strive towards thought."[38]

By analyzing the specific conditions of the "material basis" i.e. the German productive forces and production relations at the time, Marx argued that the conditions of social revolution in Grrmany were immature. In practice, it had no social conditions for establishing new productive relations. Marx added: "Only a revolution of radical needs can be a radical revolution and it seems that precisely the preconditions and ground for such

37 Marx-Engels Collected Works, Vol. 2, p. 592.

38 Marx-Engels Collected Works, Vol. 1, pp. 11-13.

needs are lacking (in Germany)."[39] This text has been the first analysis of social revolution in Marx's view to change the world, which has initially utilized the dialectical form of social movement analysis and which also contained his first initial thought of "Two Nevers".

In The German Ideology, Marx and Engels explicitly put forward the concept of "material factors for comprehensive change", elaborated the connection between the revolutionary mobilization tasks, with the situation of productive forces and relations, and the dialectical relationship between material conditions for social change and the forms of social change.

They argued: "This sum of productive forces, capital funds and social forms of intercourse (later this term changed to production relations), which every individual and every generation finds in existence as something given, is the real basis...." "These conditions of life, which different generations find at their hands, determine also whether or not the revolutionary convulsion periodically recurring in history will be strong enough to overthrow the basis of everything that exists. And if these material elements of a complete revolution are not present—namely, on the one hand the existing productive forces, on the other the formation of a revolutionary mass, which revolts not only against separate conditions of the existing society, but against the existing "production of life" itself, the "total activity" on which it was based—then it is absolutely immaterial for practical development whether the idea of this revolution has been expressed a hundred times already, as the history of communism proves."[40] This text marks that Marx and Engels' though of "Two Nevers" had initially taken form.

In the Poverty of Philosophy which "for the first time scientifically" explained "the decisive argument", when analyzing the contradictory movement of capitalist society, Marx said: "The bourgeoisie took possession of the productive forces it had developed under feudalism. All the old economic forms, the corresponding civil relations, the old political state which was the official expression of the old civil society, were smashed."[41] Before the proletariat has not developed enough to be established as a class, struggle between the proletariat and the bourgeoisie cannot become political,yet.

In reviewing the historical conditions of utopian socialism, he also put forward the idea of "Two Befores", namely "(Before) So long as the proletariat is not sufficiently developed to constitute itself as a class, so long as, in consequence, the struggle between the proletariat and the bourgeoisie has not acquired a political character, and (before) the productive forces are not yet sufficiently developed in the bosom of capitalism itself to enable

39 Marx-Engels Collected Works, Vol. 1, p. 13.

40 Ibid., p. 545.

41 Ibid., p. 613.

us to catch a glimpse of the material conditions necessary for the emancipation of the proletariat and for the formation of a new society, these theoreticians are merely utopians..." (*The Poverty of Philosophy*)"[42]. The ideas of "bourgeoisie taking the possession of the productive forces having grown up under the feudal rule" and "Two Befores" are Marx's scientific judgment on the material conditions of capitalist development, which in fact is the "Two Nevers". In the same year, in The Communists and Karl Heinzen, when criticising Karl Heinzen Engels expressed the same idea: "Mr. Heinz is extremely ignorant about the conditions for the abolition of private property"[43]. Engels added: Herr Heinzen forcibly and ubjectively separates the abolition of private property, which is of course the condition for the liberation of the proletariat, from the conditions which are attached to it, when he considers it quite out of all connection with the real world simply as an ivory-tower fantasy, it becomes a pure cliché about which he can only talk latitudinous nonsense." "As long as (before) large-scale industry is not so far advanced that it frees itself completely from the fetters of private property, thus long does it permit no other distribution of its products than that at present occurring, Thus, the new product distribution mode will never appear."[44]

The text "Principles of Communism" marked that the Marxist theory of "Two Inevitabilities" and "Two Nevers" had become basically mature. In this programmatic document drafted for the Communist League, with a through scientific analysis of the productive forces, the mode of production and the development of ownership relations in the early stages of capitalist society and the pre-capitalist society, Engels has further elucidated the social conditions for the abolition of private ownership, the development trend of capitalist private ownership and other important ideas. These ideas include: first, the change in ownership relations is the inevitable result of the fact that the old form of ownership is no longer compatible with the new productive forces. Under the condition of this new "social order in which so much is produced that every member of society will be in a position to exercise and develop all his powers and faculties in complete freedom." "So long as (before) it is not possible to produce so much that there is enough for all, with more left over for expanding the social capital and extending the forces of production... there must always be a ruling class directing the use of society's productive forces, and a poor, oppressed class."[45] which means that before such an abundant production, that social system will never perish.

42 Ibid., p. 616.
43 Ibid., p. 672.
44 Ibid., p. 673.
45 Ibid., p. 684.

Secondly, the material conditions for the abolition of private ownership has gradually formed with the development of capitalism after the "initial stage of development of the large-scale industry." The development of large scale industries itself embodies the material conditions of the abolition of private ownership. Creating the basis and conditions for the abolition of private ownership are the qualitative provisions for the new society. Although at the "initial stage of handicraft workshops and large-scale industry development", there was no possibility for the existence of any other ownership or a social system except for private ownership and private ownership based social systems.The industrial revolution, large-scale industries and the possibility of infinite expansion of production allow people to establish such a new social system, wherein "so much is produced that every member of society will be in a position to exercise and develop all his powers and faculties in complete freedom."[46]

Thirdly, modern large-scale industries and industrial revolutions have created social conditions for the abolition of private ownership. "The repetitive economic crises" and the "extreme poverty" of workers indicate that this social system cannot adapt to the requirements of current industrial development. The contradiction between social productive forces and production relations caused by the development of large-scale industries "which produce misery and crises are those which, in a different form of society, will abolish this misery and these catastrophic depressions" completely proves that "the abolition of private ownership" is not only possible, even completely necessary."[47]

Fourthly, Engels emphasized the establishment of proletarian political domination and the abolition of private ownership shall be gradually implemented with the conditions determined by "existing productive forces". Engels argued that the social revolution in any place and at any time is the inevitable result of a variety of situations that are completely free from the will and leadership of a single political party or a whole mass of class. Engels discussed: "Will it be possible for private property to be abolished at one stroke? No, no more than existing forces of production can at one stroke be multiplied to the extent necessary for the creation of a communal society. In all probability, the proletarian revolution will transform existing society gradually and will be able to abolish private property only when the means of production are available in sufficient quantity." While the proletarian revolution "above all, will establish a democratic constitution, and through this constitution, thereby the direct or indirect dominance of the proletariat." This democracy will "be used as a means for putting through measures directed against private property and ensuring the livelihood of

46 Ibid., p. 683.
47 Marx-Engels Collected Works, Vol. 1, p. 684.

the proletariat." "It is impossible, of course, to carry out all these measures at once. But one will always bring others in its wake."[48]

In the *Principles of Communism*, as a programmatic document prepared directly as a draft text for the famous next text *The Communist Manifesto*, Engels clearly explained that the private ownership of the capitalist society, the highest form of private ownership in the history of human society, can only be eradicated when all the productive forces it accommodated are given full play and the material conditions for the new and higher productive relations become mature, otherwise it will never perish.

In *The Communist Manifesto*, "the complete party program of the proletariat with theoretical and practical significance." Marx and Engels applied the approach of thier new materialism and the cognitive methods of "Two Nevers", profoundly analyzed the development of capitalist economic and social relations, and capitalist social productive forces and relations and their contradictory movement, and made the historic conclusion that "the demise of the bourgeoisie and the victory of the proletariat are both inevitable" (namely the "Two Inevitabilities").

If we can say that before the 1848 European revolution, the theory of "Two Inevitabilities" and "Two Nevers" were the conclusions of Marx and Engels based on the analysis of the laws of human society development and the logic of the contradictions of capitalist society, then we can say that the 1848 European revolution has been a test for this theory. After the failure of the European revolution, Marx's first attempt to explain a piece of contemporary history by means of his new materialist conception, was the work, i.e., *The Class Struggles in France*, 1848 to 1850. In other words, he used his new materialism to "explain a piece of contemporary history by means of his materialist conception, on the basis of the prevalent economic situation."[49] In this work, through the analysis of European economic, political situation and its prospects, Marx argued that the social contradictions that caused the European revolution in 1848 were not resolved and predicted that the class struggle would never stop, "as long as there is any new proletarian uprising in France, it is bound to cause a world war."[50]. But, because in capitalist society, especially in the United Kingdom and the United States, the new industrial boom was clearly demonstrated and reached a very high level. Marx analyzed: "Given this general prosperity, wherein the productive forces of bourgeois society are developing as luxuriantly as it is possible for them to do within bourgeois relationships, a real revolution is out of the question. The foundation of bourgeois social relations are being consolidated at the moment." "Under these conditions, all the reactionary attempts to

48 Ibid., p. 686.

49 Marx-Engels Collected Works, Vol. 4, p. 532.

50 Marx-Engels Collected Works, Vol. 2, p. 105.

hold back bourgeois development will rebound." "A new revolution is only a consequence of a new crisis. The one, however, is as sure to come as the other." On the one hand, Marx firmly believed that the new crisis will come again when the contradictions between modern productive forces and capitalist mode of production will reach a new stage, but on the other hand, he acknowledged: "the productive forces of bourgeois society are developing as luxuriantly as it is possible for them to do within the framework of bourgeois relationships"[51], therefore social revolution that eliminates the new crisis is never going to happen. This is another important exposition of Marx's idea of "Two Inevitabilities" and "Two Nevers".

More than 40 years later, in 1895, in the *Preface* he wrote for Karl Marx's work *Class Struggles in France 1848-1850*, Engels fully affirmed Marx's theoretical summary of the 1848 European revolution. Engels pointed out: Marx "demonstrated the inner causal connection in the course of a development which extended over some years, a development as critical, for the whole of Europe, as it was typical. The level of this explanation has been unprecedented."[52] "A new revolution is possible only in consequence of a new crisis. It is, however, just as certain as this (author added: new) crisis"[53] Engels added: "But that was the only major change which had to be made in Marx's work. There was absolutely nothing to alter in the interpretation of events given in the earlier chapters, or in the causal connections established in that chapter, as proved by the continuation of the narrative from March 10 up to the autumn of 1850 in the said review. I have, therefore, included this continuation as the fourth article in the present new edition of the book."[54]

It is precisely because Marx's and Engels' rigorous theoretical analysis of the basic contradictions of human society before 1850 and due to proof of the theories of historical materialism in the European Revolution in 1848 and Marx's careful study of new phenomena regarding the capitalist society which had entered into a new development stage after 1850 that the later work of Marx, i.e., the *Critique of Political Economy* could be finished. In the preface to this new work, Marx finally expressed the idea of "Two Nevers" with his classical words and once again reaffirmed the idea of "Two Inevitabilities". He wrote: "The bourgeois mode of production is the last antagonistic form of the social process of production". "The productive forces developing within bourgeois society create also the material conditions for a solution of this antagonism. The prehistory of human society accordingly finalizes with this social formation."[55]

51 Ibid., p. 176.
52 Marx-Engels Collected Works, Vol. 4, p. 535.
53 Ibid., p. 535.
54 Ibid., p. 536.
55 Marx-Engels Collected Works, Vol. 2, p. 592.

The development trend of the capitalist society is the objective requirement of the dialectical movement of "Two Inevitabilities" and is based on the "Two Nevers". The above literature shows that: (1) the ideas of "Two Inevitabilities" and "Two Nevers" were the consistent basic idea of Marx and Engels in their whole life and we can never say that the latter can be amended or ignored and latter can be supplementary to the former. (2) The ideas of "Two Inevitabilities" and "Two Nevers" are mutually contradictory, interrelated and complementary and are in unity. (3) "Two Inevitabilities" can be said that it is more deeper or fundamental judgement of Marx and Engels, because they have confirmed that: For a practical materialist, that is for a communist, the *thing* is to *revolutionize* the *existing world*—that is, practically turn against *things* as he finds them, and *change* them."[56]

2. The idea of "Two Inevitabilities" contains the idea of "Two Nevers"

The idea of "Two Nevers" discusses the conditions of social revolution and change. In other words, a social form is inevitably going to perish after all the productive forces it accommodates are given full play; and the new and higher production relations will inevitably emerge when their material conditions (including the new productive forces and classes that represent

new productive forces developing and becoming mature in the womb of the old society. This is the logic of *The Communist Manifesto* in demonstrating the theory of "Two Inevitabilities". When making the conclusion that "the demise of the bourgeoisie and the victory of the proletariat are both inevitable", *The Communist Manifesto* demonstrates the conditions for the demise of the bourgeoisie and the victory of the proletariat. It means that the highly developed productive forces lead to economic crisis that is increasingly endangering the survival of the entire bourgeois society; workers become poorer, poverty is growing faster than population and wealth, and the working class cannot maintain its slave-like living conditions.

The task of *The Communist Manifesto* was to declare that modern bourgeois ownership must perish. In the *Preface to the English Version in 1888*, Engels' brilliant summarized the "core ideas"[57] of *The Communist Manifesto* was in fact a summary of the logic of argumentation and basic theory of *The Communist Manifesto*. In *The Communist Manifesto*, Marx and Engels made rigorous theoretical arguments for "Two Inevitabilities", among which said: "The bourgeoisie has played a most revolutionary part in history."[58], "the history of these class struggles forms a series of evolu-

56 Marx-Engels Collected Works, Vol. 1, p. 527.
57 Marx-Engels Collected Works, Vol. 2, p. 535.
58 Marx-Engels Collected Works, Vol. 2, p. 33.

tions in which, nowadays, a stage has been reached where— the proletariat — cannot attain its emancipation….without, at the same time, and once and for all, emancipating society at large from all exploitation, oppression, class distinction, and class struggles."[59] These sentences obviously contain the idea of "Two Nevers". This argument fully estimates the development trend of capitalist social productive forces and relations, and proves that "Two Inevitabilities" is the ultimate result of the movement of capitalist mode of production and the inevitable result of the full development of the material condition (the contradictions between productive forces and production relations, and between proletariat and the bourgeoisie) for the existence of capitalism with irrefutable facts and logic. *The Communist Manifesto* made use of the historical materialist view founded by Marx and Engels, with deep insight discovered the core issues of "modern society", started from the evolution of the productive forces in the "bourgeois era", and revealed the contradictory movement of capitalist productive forces and productive relations. With the discovery of America, the rounding of the Cape, opened up fresh ground for the rising bourgeoisie, and promoted the productive forces of capitalist society. "The East-Indian and Chinese markets, the colonisation of America, trade with the colonies, the increase in the means of exchange and in commodities generally, gave to commerce, to navigation, to industry, an impulse never before known, and thereby, to the revolutionary element in the tottering feudal society, a rapid development." The rapid development of the revolutionary forces within the feudal society prompted handicraft workshops to replace the feudal and organizational way of industrial management. The expansion of the market, the increase in demand, especially the revolution in the industrial production caused by the steam and machinery, made a great change: "The place of manufacture was taken by the giant, Modern Industry."[60] The establishment of the world market promoted by the modern large industry has promoted great developments to commerce, to navigation, to communication by land, all of which in turn further promoted the industrial expansion. The bourgeoisie has continually promoted the revolution of production tools. From the simple tools to accumulation of tools and to the synthesis of tools, from the synthesis of tools worked by manpower to the tools worked by the use of natural powers, from the machine to "a single machine with an engine" and to "the system of machines working automatically"[61], and with the application of machinery and steam, the division of labor had further deepened, "the bourgeoisie has through its exploitation of the world market given a cosmopolitan character to production and consumption in every country…. it has drawn from under the feet of industry the national ground on which it

59 Ibid., p. 14.

60 Ibid., p. 32.

61 Marx-Engels Collected Works, Vol. 2, p. 626.

stood. All old-fashioned national industries are destroyed or are daily being destroyed."[62] Through a series of changes in the mode of production and exchange (trade), "the bourgeoisie, during its rule of scarce one hundred years, has created more massive and more colossal productive forces than have all preceding generations together."[63] However, the great development of capitalist productive forces has led to an increasingly sharp contradiction between the development requirements of socialization of productive forces and the private ownership of the means of production. Marx analyzed the revolutionary role of the modern productive forces as follows: the history of industry and commerce is but the history of the revolt of modern productive forces against modern conditions of production, against the property relations that are the conditions for the existence of the bourgeois and of its rule."[64] "The conditions of bourgeois society are too narrow to comprise the wealth created by them." The bourgeoisie can only rely "on the one hand by enforced destruction of a mass of productive forces; on the other, it relies on the conquest of new markets, and by the more thorough exploitation of the old ones. That is to say, by paving the way for more extensive and more destructive crises, and by diminishing the means whereby crises are prevented." "The weapons with which the bourgeoisie knocked down feudalism to the ground are now turned against the bourgeoisie itself"[65].

Based on the analysis of contradiction movement of productive forces and production relations in modern society and full demonstration the degree of contradiction between productive forces and production relations, Marx and Engels put forward the great and scientific thought of "Two Inevitabilities".

The theoretical conclusions of the Communists are only: "express, in general terms, actual relations springing from an existing class struggle, from a historical movement going on under our very eyes."[66] When demonstrating the theory of "Two Inevitabilities" in the Communist Manifesto, Marx and Engels expounded on the true relationships within the history of the modern bourgeois society, they have fully explained the complexity and long-term nature of the contradictory movement between the capitalist productive forces and relations and affirmed conscious and unconscious adjustment on production relations and social relations to adapt to the development of productive forces, which contains the idea of "Two Nevers". What is the difference between the bourgeois era and all other times of the past: "Constant revolutionising of production, uninterrupted disturbance of all social conditions,

62 Ibid., p. 627.

63 Marx-Engels Collected Works, Vol. 2, p. 36.

64 Ibid., p. 33.

65 Marx-Engels Collected Works, Vol. 2, p. 37.

66 Ibid., p. 45.

everlasting uncertainty and agitation distinguish the bourgeois epoch from all earlier ones."

All previous historical movements were movements of minorities, or in the interest of minorities. The proletarian movement is the self-conscious, independent movement of the immense majority, in the interest of the immense majority. The proletariat, the lowest stratum of our present society, cannot stir, cannot raise itself up, without the whole superincumbent strata of official society being sprung into the air. According to Marx and Engels: "The bourgeoisie cannot exist without constantly revolutionising the instruments of production, and thereby the relations of production, and with them the whole relations of society."[67]

This means that the constant transformation of production tools and production relations is the basis of the existence of the bourgeoisie. As long as the production tools, production relations and social relations in the capitalist mode of production could be changed, and as long as the relationship between them still allows for the transformation of production tools, the bourgeoisie will be able to survive. In other words, the capitalist society "will never perish until all the productive forces it can take are given full play". In fact, in its development process, the bourgeoisie constantly, consciously or unconsciously adjusts the social relations, and changes the means of production and the form of social relations. They run around the world, "settle down, develop and establish contact everywhere". They make the production and consumption of all nations cosmopolitan. The local and national self-sufficiency and closed status are replaced with communications and interdependence among all nations. They force all nations to take the bourgeois mode of production. They make countryside succumbs to the rule of the city. Uncivilized and semicivilized are subordinate to civilized countries. The farmers' nations are subject to the bourgeois nations. The East is subject to the West. They destroy the scattered state of production, property and population, so that the population is concentrated, the means of production are centralized in the hands of the few and the wealth also in the hands of a few people. The bourgeoisie's self-adjustment of social relations will reached such a stage, that if the capitalist relations of production are not completely changed, social productive forces would not be further developed. The material conditions for the demise of capitalism and the development of contradictions between productive forces and relations are now fully mature. The era of social change is coming. Marx and Engels' full demonstration of the development trend of capitalist social productive forces and relations contains a concrete description of "Two Nevers" thought.

67 Marx-Engels Collected Works, Vol. 2, p. 34.

The material conditions for the inevitable demise of capitalism also exist in the social relation it has created, namely the contradictions and struggles between the proletariat and the bourgeoisie. The modern bourgeois society that emerged from the demise of feudal society could not eliminate the class antagonism. It merely replaces the old ones with the new class, the new oppressive conditions and the new forms of struggle and makes the whole society increasingly be divided into two directly opposing classes, namely the bourgeoisie and the proletariat. In proportion as the bourgeoisie, i.e., capital, is developed, in the same proportion as the proletariat... so long as their labour increases capital. "Not only are they slaves of the bourgeois class, and of the bourgeois State; they are daily and hourly enslaved by the machines, by the overlooker, and, above all, by the individual bourgeois manufacturer himself."[68] The proletariat is a true revolutionary class, and its struggle with the bourgeoisie begins with its existence. In the struggle, the proletariat kept being tested, their consciousness continued to improve, and their unions continued to expand. Their party organizations "became more powerful and stronger, than ever"[69]. The proletariat goes through various stages of development. With its birth begins its struggle against the bourgeoisie. At first the contest is carried on by individual labourers, then by the workers of a factory, then in one locality, against the individual bourgeois who directly exploits them. Later they establish trade unions against the bourgeoisie and next organize their political party, with the improved means of communication "the workers from different localities get into contact with one another. It was just this contact that was needed to centralise the numerous local struggles, all of the same character, into one nation-wide struggle between classes."[70] This political struggle has now developed to such a stage: if the oppressed proletariat cannot liberate the whole society once and for al from all exploitation, oppression, class differences and class struggles, it will not be able to emancipate itself from enslavement of the ruling and exploiting bourgeoisie. "The proletariat, the lowest stratum of our present society, cannot stir, cannot raise itself up, without the whole superincumbent strata of official society being sprung into the air."[71]

The class struggle based on the capitalist economic relations will surely destroy the bourgeoisie and its political domination and replace it with the political rule of the proletariat. The material conditions of the victory of the proletariat are already there and the higher production relations that will replace the old private ownership have matured in the capitalist society. This is the inevitable result of the development of human society, the ultimate result of the development of capitalism, and the ultimate outcome

68 Marx-Engels Collected Works, Vol. 2, p. 38.
69 Ibid., pp. 40-41.
70 Ibid., p. 40.
71 Ibid., p. 42.

of the proletariat's fight against bourgeoisie. The bourgeoisie's self-adjustment efforts of production relations and social relations has never ceased. In order to adapt to the requirements of socialization of production, contemporary capitalism is still constantly self-adjusting its own production relations and class relations. This self-adjustment is, to some extent, even more comprehensive than the era of Marx and Engels, with a wider scope and greater impacts. Within the contemporary capitalist system, as the production becomes more and more socialized, the forms of capital is becoming more and more socialized, from the original sole proprietorship to the partnership, then to the joint-stock enterprise form, then to the private monopoly capital, to the state monopoly capital, and finally to multinational corporations and international monopoly capital. All these changes indicate that capitalism is a "society which is not solid crystal, but an organism capable of change, and is constantly changing"[72].

However, even if a society has discovered the laws its own movement, it can not skip or issue a decree to abolish the natural-historical developmental stages but can only shorten and alleviate the pain of birth. There is a limit to the self-improvement or self-adjustment of capitalism. This limit is the basic economic law of capitalist society created by its basic contradictions (namely the law of surplus value). In capitalist society, the development of productive forces is subject to the limitation of value proliferation of capital. This limitation will restrict the infinite development of productive forces. Capital is always trying to break through these restrictions in the process of developing productive forces and thus need to constantly change its production relations. The problem is that every time this "creative destruction" occurs, it will lead capital falling into a greater crisis, because "the *real* barrier of *capitalist production* is *capital itself*."[73]

Whether the capitalist society takes laissez-faire measures or planned state intervention into the economy, its foundation is the private enterprise system and its economic purpose is to enable the private enterprise to operate normally in the whole society and assure capital accumulation. If capitalism does not change its greed for surplus value, it is impossible to eliminate the capitalist private ownership of means of production and eliminate its own limitation upon the infinite development of productive forces, thus cannot change the historical trends of "Two Inevitabilities". Similarly, the historical trend of "Two Inevitabilities" does not affect the bourgeoisie's self-adjustment of production relations and social relations at all. The basic contradiction of contemporary capitalism can be softened, but it will still exist. This contradiction works in the long river of history with its inevitability, and will inevitably push capitalism to perishment, regardless of its specific process.

72 Marx-Engels Collected Works, Vol. 2, pp. 10-13.

73 Marx-Engels Collected Works, Vol. 7, p. 278.

3. We should evaluate the "Two Nevers" as relative

Among the studies on the "Two Inevitabilities" and "Two Nevers" and their relations, there is a kind of opinion that the "Two Inevitabilities" can only be achieved when the contradiction between the productive forces and production relations become fully mature. Since productive forces are the ultimate motive force of social development, the inevitability of socialism replacing the capitalism is determined by the level of development of productive forces. Only when the productive forces reach such a height that it cannot be accommodated by the capitalist production relations, the replacement of capitalism with socialism can eventually become a reality.

This view is only general illustration of the law of human social development and points to the general trend of social development, so it is true only in principle. The problem is that, it will be too simple to use this monstic-line general approach to illustrate the complex process of human social development, because the decisive factor in the historical process is the production and reproduction of real life. But the historical development process is the result of the interaction of multiple factors. Especially for a country and nation, the various elements of the superstructure and the extensive international communications also influence the process of its historical fate in many cases, and can determine the forms of struggle. In the whole process of world historical development, due to social contradictions and their complexity, the development of human society has both the universal law of social and historical development and also its particular law. The universal law of the development of world history does not exclude the particularity of individual nations, does not exclude countries and regions which can have different development form and development order; on the contrary, the universal law of the development of world history is the general prerequisite. The specific historical development law here refers to the following two cases: firstly, when a number of social forms at different stages of development coexist and interact with each other, the social form at the lower stage is likely to skip some of the stages that used to be inevitable to go through and can connect with a higher stage that used to be unconnected due to the guiding effect of the higher society, thus leads to a situation that its development goes beyond a stage.[74]

Secondly, two or more different social forms usually coexist in a single country in a certain historical period.[75] The profound social causes of the specific historical laws lie in this complexity of the social structure: the

74 Li Yanming, The Principle of Exceeding the Stage, published in the Journal of Studies on Marxism, 1995(2).

75 Mei Rongzheng, On the Scientific Basis of the Conception of "One Country, Two Systems", in: Wuhan University Journal (Philosophy & Social Sciences version), 1997(4).

unsynchronized development of productive forces within various countries, the imbalances in the international exchanges and the relative independence of social consciousness from the economic base.

According to the new materialist view of history, the social structure can be divided into five levels: productive forces, production mode, productive relations, exchange relations and ideological relations. Productive forces are the subject's capacity for action; on the other hand the production mode, production relations, exchange relations and ideological relations are the forms of subject's activities. The various levels of social structure interact with each other and have their own relatively independent development stages. Production mode, productive relations and exchange relations change with the changes in the productive forces. It takes a certain amount of time for this change to pass from the lower level to a higher level. The changes that occur in higher levels are usually hysteretic. So, the speed of change in the whole process will gradually slow down; thus the time period of stable development within the higher level will correspondingly increase. Since the capacity and forms of the activities of the subject are relatively independent at all levels, in the whole world historical development process, the time-period of a social development stage at a certain level in different places which live in the same time-period is some times shorter or sometimes longer.Therefore, under the effect of specific historical conditions, the correspondence between the social developments stages at all levels will be dislocated. This dislocation will manifest itself in the socio-economic age measured by the development of production tools. In other words, in the same socio-economic era there might be different social and economic forms (social forms). If there is no external influence, there will be difference in development speed in the isolated development of different nations. This difference may lead to the coexistence of human societies which are at different development stages in the same age. Thus, in the overall process of world history development, the development of a social form which is motivated by the internal specific special contradictions in a certain nation will be non-synchronized (time).This non-synchronicity is manifested as the diversity of social forms in different regions.

If human societies at the different development stages exchange with each other, logical clues (namely the order of social development stages) will be changed. In general, the productive forces and social forms created within a higher stage of society are more suitable for the general requirements for the survival and development of human beings. In the interaction with each other, it is often the case that the social form at a lower development stage will be influenced by the social form at a higher development stage and the former tries to approach towards the higher social form, in all aspects which are contained within the higher social form. Various forms of interactions can enable the productive forces, production mode, productive relations, exchange relations and ideological relations of a society to be exported or integrated into another society and cause changes in it.

The coexistence of countries at different stages of development and their interaction and mutual influence generate multiple choices for the social development of a certain nation or country. One possibility is that a nation in the absence of strong external forces, will continue to evolve to the next stage according to its inherent order under isolated conditions. Another possibility is that under the traction of various social factors in the higher development stage, the social form of the lower development stage absorbs the productive forces in the higher development stage, and can use the production mode, production relations and exchange relation which are compatible with this kind of productive forces, to advance faster into the next stage or to a social form that is higher than the next stage. This situation can be called as the "post-development effect" or "beyond-stage development" that can occur in certain nations (leapfrog development). The "post-development effect" or beyond-stage development has it own conditions, which are: (1) Two or more social forms at different stages of development are coexisting; (2) the different coexisting social forms interact with each other; (3) the two social forms at different stages of development are generation-skipping societies. When two or more social forms are separated by one or more development stages, the social form at a lower stage, with the traction of a higher society, can achieve a "beyond-stage development", such as an African primitive society can transit to capitalism.[76]

Marxism regards productive forces as the ultimate determining factor, "but it does not regard the absolute level of productive forces as the mark or criterion for a revolution."[77] As capitalism for the first time created a world history, the establishment of new industries has become a vital issue possbile for all nations. Nations or countries are involved into the universal international exchanges without any exception, so that the social revolution in a nation or country does not have to wait until the sharpening of contradictions between the productive forces and the production relations, in this specific country. Famous philosopher Chen Xianda wrote: "Due to extensive international interrelationships and national contacts and competitions with countries possessing more advanced industries, similar contradictions can intensify in those countries wherein industry is less developed."[78] The conditions of a nation or state's social change are caused by a specific

76 See Li Yanming, The Principle of Exceeding the Stage, published in the Journal of Studies on Marxism,1995(2).

77 See Chen Xianda's comments on the "Two Necessities", "Collected Works of Chen Xianda", Beijing, Contemporary China Press, 1995, pp. 420-421.

78 Marx-Engels Collected Works, Vol. 1, p. 568.

concrete contradiction in an era, so it is not necessary to wait until productive forces of that nation or society will reach to an overall level or the highest level at that time. To judge the conditions of a nation or country's social change, we must fully consider the traction of the social productive forces of a higher society and the traction of social contradictions caused by extensive international exchanges. The task of social revolution we are talking about is always born from "the task itself arises only when the material conditions necessary for its solution already exist or are at least in the process of formation", and mankind "always sets itself *only* such *tasks* as it *can solve*"[79], based on the actual situation of social contradictions, which includes these above traction factors. When we study the idea of "Two Nevers", we should never ignore this point.

The general law and the specific law of the development of social history show that the development of human society is the unity of both necessity and contingency, there is also the unity between the uniformity as the main form development and the diverse forms in development of social forms as the secondary form of development. The process of social development is generally progressive or gradual, however leapfrog type of development is quite rare. "Two Inevitabilities" imply the general inevitable trend of the world historical process and the "Two Nevers" imply the specific way of social development within this general trend. Whether the social development of a nation will follow the basic regular and progressive way or the derivative (secondary), or the unconventional leap-frog way, the key factor for this difference is the development of social productive forces and social interaction. We can call this phenomenon as the concreteness and relativity of social evolution in a country, which lead to the relativity of the specific conditions (namely "Two Nevers") for social change in a country. The relativity of "Two Nevers" imply that the realization of "Two Inevitabilities" is a long process. The realization process of the "Two Inevitabilities" is full of twists and turns, during which there will be leapfrog development or substantial retrogressions. As Lenin pointed out: "This is unprobable. But it is *not* impossible, because to picture world history as advancing smoothly and steadily without sometimes taking gigantic strides backward is undialectical, unscientific and theoretically wrong." (The Junius Pamphlet).[80]

(Co-authored by Mei Rongzheng, profesor of Institute of Political Science and Public Administration, Wuhan University and Zhang Qianyuan, associate professor of Institute of Political Science and Public Administration, Wuhan University)

79 Marx-Engels Collected Works, Vol. 3, p. 592.

80 Lenin's Monographs on Dialectical Materialism and Historical Materialism, p. 263.

Afterword

This book is entitled as *Theory and Practice of Socialism in Development*, which means that socialist theory and practice is a major issue in development and our studies on it are also under development. Moreover, the outline and content of this book are arranged in accordance with the developmental process of socialist theory and practice.

The co-authors of this book are from various universities and research departments of China who are engaged in extensive disciplines and fields, and have made in-depth studies regarding their writing topics. They are Zhang Leisheng (Professor of School of Marxism Studies, Renmin University of China), Gu Hailiang (Professor of School of Marxism, Wuhan University), Mei Rongzheng (professor of School of Political Science and Public Administration, Wuhan University), Gu Yumin (Professor of School of Marxism, Fudan University), Luo Wendong (researcher of Academy of Marxism, Chinese Academy of Social Sciences), Zheng Yiming(researcher of Academy of Marxism, Chinese Academy of Social Sciences), Dong Zhengping (Professor of College of Political Science and Law, Capital Normal University), Qin Xuan (Professor of School of Marxism Studies, Renmin University of China), Tao Wenzhao (Professor of School of Marxism Studies, Renmin University of China), Zhang Xu (Professor of School of Marxism Studies, Renmin University of China), Zheng Jiwei (Professor of School of Marxism Studies, Renmin University of China), Li Yufeng (Associate Professor of School of Marxism Studies, Renmin University of China), Wang Tingyou (Associate Professor of School of Marxism Studies, Renmin University of China), and Wu Jingmin (Associate editor and copy editor of Journal of Renmin University of China).

Under the auspices of Prof. Zhang Leisheng and through much discussion and joint work, the framework and the main research topics were decided and the writing tasks were divided among the contributing scholars. Editor Wu Jingmin have offered valuable comments and suggestions on the framework structure and main research topics of this book, and has been responsible for compiling and editing of all manuscripts. As the last stage, this book was finalized by Prof. Zhang Leisheng.

The studies in this book are entirely a staged achievement in the development of socialist theory and practice.The inadequacies are inevitable.We are eager to hear criticism and correction from the readers. And I would like to express my deep gratitude for the great support and help of China Renmin University Press for the publication of this book!

Zhang Leisheng

December 30, 2014

www.ingramcontent.com/pod-product-compliance
Lightning Source LLC
LaVergne TN
LVHW042300190726
843491LV00015BA/1194
* 9 7 8 6 0 5 7 6 9 3 2 4 2 *